European City Breaks

Contents

Introduction

It's only 65 years since the end of the Second World War but the transformation of Europe in that time is nothing short of staggering. The continent that tore itself apart, then built a physical and ideological barrier through its heart before knocking it all down, may not yet be ready to embrace Churchill's vision of a 'United States of Europe' but 25 of its nations are now members of a single trading market and 12 have so far signed up to a single currency. Such startling political developments have, inevitably, had a major impact on European travel. Passport and customs checks are a thing of the past at most borders, there's no need to change currency every time you leave home and air fares have been dropping faster than the temperature on a winter's night in Reykjavík. It is now possible to fly from London to Naples for less than the cost of a pizza, see the best of the city and fly back in time for Sunday dinner. You can gaze in awe at Picasso's Guernica in Madrid one weekend and climb to the top of Norman Foster's Reichstag in Berlin the next; spend a night at the opera in Verona one week, and a night on the tiles in Tallinn the next. Rome or Brussels? Valencia or Venice? Each has its own appeal, whether it's museums and galleries stuffed with priceless treasures, delicious food, cheap booze or stunning architecture. There's so much choice it's hard to make one. So read on...

About the book

Footprint's European City Breaks is the perfect thing for those who want to get away but don't know where to let off steam, propose to their lover, hide, or simply wallow indulgently in a bit of luxury. The 30 cities listed in this book are all worth at least a weekend of anyone's time and we have taken the strain out of choosing where to sleep, where to eat and what to see by selecting the very top hotels and restaruants, divided into three price categories – expensive, mid-range and cheap – the best bars and clubs and the pick of the sights. From the Acropolis in Athens to Bilbao's Guggenheim Museum, we've highlighted the best of Europe's heritage, old and new, artistic and technological. In the guide you'll also find handy star ratings in the introduction to each city which give an immediate idea of the city's stong and weak points (see also page 6). But wherever you end up going, European City Breaks is there to point you in the right direction. Go on – give yourself a break.

Sleeping price codes
€€€ Expensive, over €200
€€ Mid-range, €100-200
€ Cheap, under €100

Prices are for a double room in high season.

Eating & drinking price codes
€€€ Expensive, over €200
€€ Mid-range, €20-40
€ Cheap, under €20

Prices are for a 2-course meal without drinks or service.

LEGEND

Tourist Info	Train Station
Point of Interest	Ferry Boat
Museum	Tram Line
Post Office	Parking
Theatre	Taxi
Concert Hall	Cable Car
Monument	One Way Streets
Landmark	Walking path
Shopping	Library
Market	Viewpoint
Church/ Synagogue	Beach
	Historic Gate

Map scales are approximate

Picture credits

Julius Honnor:
pages 1, 6, 7, 8, 12, 13, 15, 16, 17, 28, 32, 33, 34, 39, 40, 44, 46, 47, 78, 80, 82, 83, 84, 86, 87, 88, 92, 93, 116, 119, 120, 121, 122, 124, 125, 136, 140, 141, 142, 143, 144, 146, 148, 151, 154, 155, 166, 168, 169, 180, 182, 184, 185, 186, 187, 202, 203, 204, 209, 228, 230, 232, 233, 234, 235, 237, 238, 239, 240, 242, 244, 245, 256, 258, 260, 262, 264, 266, 268, 269, 270, 272.

Shutterstock
Kevin George: 6; Ljupco Smokovski: 7; J van der Wolf: 7; Chris Mole: 18; Dimitrios: 20; Dhoxax: 22; Lelde J-R: 23; Krechet: 24, 25; Cristina Ciochina: 26; Paul Cowan: 27; Lubomir Pištek: 44; Tobias Machhaus: 44; Tom Tomczyk; IH-Images: 46; Nhtg: 50; Camilo Torres: 52; Tim Tran: 52; Jarno Gonzalez Zarraonandia: 54, 55; Toni Sanchez Poy: 55; Ruth Berkowitz: 56; Rob van Esch: 57; Jakez: 58; E.Pals: 60; Petersvetphoto: 62; Nrg123: 63; Rostislav Ageev: 63; 50u15pec7a70r: 63, 174; Alexander Gatsenko: 68; Horia Bogdan: 70; Tupungato: 72, 160, 252; Anthony Shaw Photography: 73; Jorisvo: 74; Veniamin Kraskov: 75; Monkey Business Images: 76; Alison Cornford-Matheson: 77; Mika Heittola: 90; Paolo Airenti: 92; Marco Cannizzaro: 93; Jose Antonio Sanchez: 93; M Reel: 96; Javier Soto Vazquez: 98; Zbynek Burival: 101; Eireann: 102; RixPix: 103; EML: 104; PSD Photography: 106; Brendan Howard: 108; Bzzuspajk: 110; Heartland: 111; Bill McKelvie: 112; PerseoMedusa: 113; StockCube: 114; Curioso: 156; Raj Krish: 158; Amra Pasic: 159; Stefano Ember: 160; Maridav: 161; FedericoPhotos: 163; Kevin George: 164; Nickolay Vinokurov: 172; Rodion: 176; Mirenska Olga: 176; Juergen2008: 176; Mammut Vision: 177; PHB.cz (Richard Semik): 210; Kajano: 212; S.Borisov: 214; alehnia: 215; Aron Brand: 216; l i g h t p o e t: 219; Jules_Kitano: 220; Kesu: 222; Vacclav: 224; Dalish: 225; Tony740607: 248; Mr.D: 250; Willem Tims: 251; Svand: 253; L. akhundova: 254; Steve Heap: 274; David Ionut: 276; Chameleons: 278; Goran Bogicevic: 279; Khirman Vladimir: 279; Perov Stanislav: 280; Giancarlo Liguori: 282; Alexander Cyliax: 284; Fritz16: 285; TP Gronlund: 287.

Tomasetti-Rutherford:
pages 7, 126, 130, 131, 132, 135, 188, 190, 192, 193, 194, 195, 198, 204.

Front cover Glen Allison/Getty Images
Inside front cover Julius Honnor
Back cover Julius Honnor; Pepi Bluck
Inside back cover Pepi Bluck

Star cities

We've given every city in the book scores out of 5 (1 = lowest, 5 = highest) in 8 categories: Arts and culture, Eating, Nightlife, Outdoors, Romance, Shopping, Sightseeing and Value for money so you can see their weak and their strong points. These scores are shown in the introduction to each city and should help you choose the right destination for your city break. The highest scoring cities in each category are listed below.

★ Arts and culture

Berlin p40; Budapest p78; Florence p116; London p144.

Cities that have an outstanding reputation for all-round cultural excellence, with vibrant art, literature, theatre and music scenes.

★ Eating

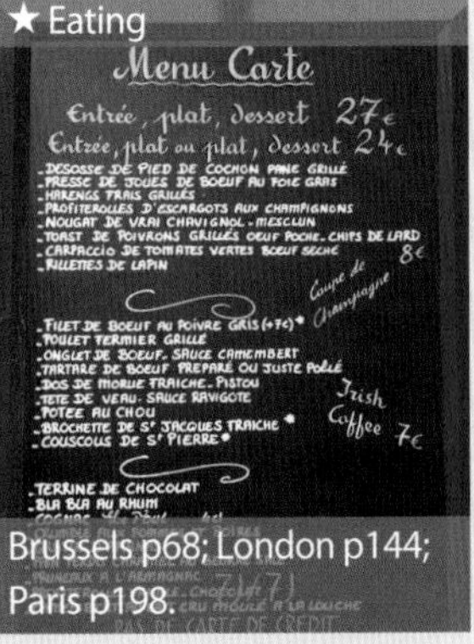

Brussels p68; London p144; Paris p198.

Cities that have a thriving culinary scene and a number of world-class restaurants.

★ Nightlife

Athens p18; Barcelona p28; Berlin p40; Lisbon p136; London p144; Madrid p156; Valencia p256.

The ultimate places to party after dark.

★ Romance

Florence p116; Istanbul p116; Paris p198; Prague p210; Venice p264.

The best places to propose or to enjoy a spontaneous romantic weekend.

★ Sightseeing

Florence p116; Istanbul p126; London p144; Paris p198; Rome p228; Venice p264.

The places to go for world famous sights: museums, monuments, castles, towers, Ferris wheels, etc.

★ Outdoors

Bilbao p50; Edinburgh p106; Reykjavik p220.

Cities that incorporate plenty of green space or provide easy access to nearby wilderness areas.

★ Shopping

Barcelona p28; Istanbul p126; London p144; Milan p166; Paris p198.

Cities with outstanding and varied retail therapy opportunities.

★ Value for money

Lisbon p136; Naples p180.

The best places to go if you are on a tight budget.

Ratings

Art and culture ☆☆☆☆☆
Eating ☆☆☆☆
Nightlife ☆☆☆☆
Romance ☆☆☆
Shopping ☆☆☆
Sightseeing ☆☆☆☆
Value-for-money ☆☆☆
Overall city rating ☆☆☆

Amsterdam

Amsterdam shouldn't really exist. The city was dragged out of marshy bogs, dried and carved into the place we know today. It was an unconventional start and one which seems to have set the tone for things to come. Today, despite something of a conservative Dutch backlash Amsterdam remains Europe's most nonconformist city. Locals shun the car and choose instead to career around on bicycles. Prostitution is both legal and public, and this is the only city in the world where you can peruse a cannabis menu and smoke a joint in a coffeeshop. The Netherlands was also the first country to legalise marriage between gay couples.Alongside these progressive ways are, conversely, some of Europe's greatest traditional attractions. The Rijksmuseum and Van Gogh Museum hold two of the finest art collections in the world, while smaller museums, such as the Anne Frank House or Rembrandthuis, provide a real insight into the city's past.The city's future direction seems less certain. Its 'anything goes' attitude is under threat from the government's new hard line on soft drugs, which has seen a fall in the number of coffeeshops, while both main political parties are distancing themselves from the tradition of multiculturalism. Is Amsterdam becoming less tolerant, more like the rest of Europe? It somehow seems unlikely in this engaging liberal oddball of a city.

City-cycling.

At a glance

Amsterdam's old centre is hemmed in by the Ij River and Centraal Station to the north, and spreads south in a web of medieval streets and canals. The main arteries are Damrak and Rokin, busy thoroughfares which split the centre into the **Nieuwe Zijde** (New Side), to the west of Dam Square, and the **Oude Zijde** (Old Side) to the east.

The **red-light district** lies on the Old Side and is a predictably seedy grid of streets, though not without its charm. Beyond here are the **Nieuwmarkt** and **Plantage** districts, home to Amsterdam's biggest flea market and Rembrandt's house. To the north are the **Eastern Islands**, extensively renovated docklands holding some impressively adventurous architecture.

West of Damrak, Nieuwe Zijde is Amsterdam's main shopping area and leads to the **Grachtengordel**, the four major canals that ring the old centre. South of the Grachtengordel is the **Museum Quarter**, full of grand old buildings, including – most famously – the enormous, neo-Gothic Rijksmuseum, overlooking the grassy Museumplein.

24 hours in the city

Sip a coffee at **Café Luxembourg** before heading south to the Museumsplein. Pop into the **Rijksmuseum** and ogle Rembrandt's Nightwatch, one of the highlights still on view while the museum undergoes renovation. A few steps along Museumplein brings you to the **Van Gogh Museum**, which warrants a good few hours. After a perk up at **Het Blauwe Theehuis**, a popular tea house near Vondelpark, wander north along the canals of the Grachtengordel to **Anne Frank's House.** Lunch at one of the pavement cafés on Nieuwmarkt and then either head south for a snoop around the **flea market** on Waterlooplein, or east to gawp at the painted ladies of the **red-light district**. (Don't miss the attic chapel in the Museum Amstelkring while you're there.) Have an early evening drink in **Café Sluyswacht**, on Jodenbreestraat, and then cross town for contemporary Dutch cuisine in the history-soaked interior of **d'Vijff Vlieghen**. Finish off in the **Sugar Factory**, a 'multi-disciplanary night theatre' where nightclub and performance mix.

Dam Square

Tram 4, 9, 14, 16, 24 or 25. Map C2.

Known simply as the 'Dam', this broad, tourist- and pigeon-filled square lies at the core of Amsterdam's medieval centre. It was the location of the original dam across the Amstel which gave the city its name. The **Koninklijk Paleis (Royal Palace)**, originally the town hall, was built between 1648 and 1665 in an imposing Dutch Classicist style. It became a royal residence when Louis Bonaparte kicked out the mayor in 1808, during the French occupation, and it is now used for state functions. Nearby is the Nieuwe Kerk, dating from 1408, while, in the centre of the square, is the city's war memorial, a rather stark obelisk and a popular meeting place.

De Wallen red-light district

Tram 4, 9, 14, 16, 24 or 25. Map D2.

Amsterdam's infamous red-light district covers the area to the east of Damrak and is as seedy as you'd expect. Prostitutes pose in windows, groups of beery lads barter with pimps, and touts try to entice passers-by with promises of live sex shows. But the area is also such a tourist attraction that it rarely feels threatening (at least not during the day). You'll be sharing the pavement with giggling couples and family groups wandering nonchalantly past the brothel windows. The area also has some of the city's most attractive old houses. Stroll along **Warmoesstraat** to take in the elegant façades, interspersed with sex shops and red-lit windows, and along any of the little streets branching off between **Oudezijds Voorburgwal** and **Ousezijds Achterburgwal** canals.

Two important sights in the area are, ironically, religious. Just east of Warmoesstraat is **De Oude Kerk**, *Oudekerksplein 23, map D2, Mon-Sat 1100-1700, Sun 1300-1700*, Amsterdam's oldest church, an attractive Gothic structure with a beautiful tower, dating from the 14th century. A few steps north is **Ons' Lieve Heer op Solder (Our Lord in The Attic)**, *Oudezijds Voorburgwal 40, T020*

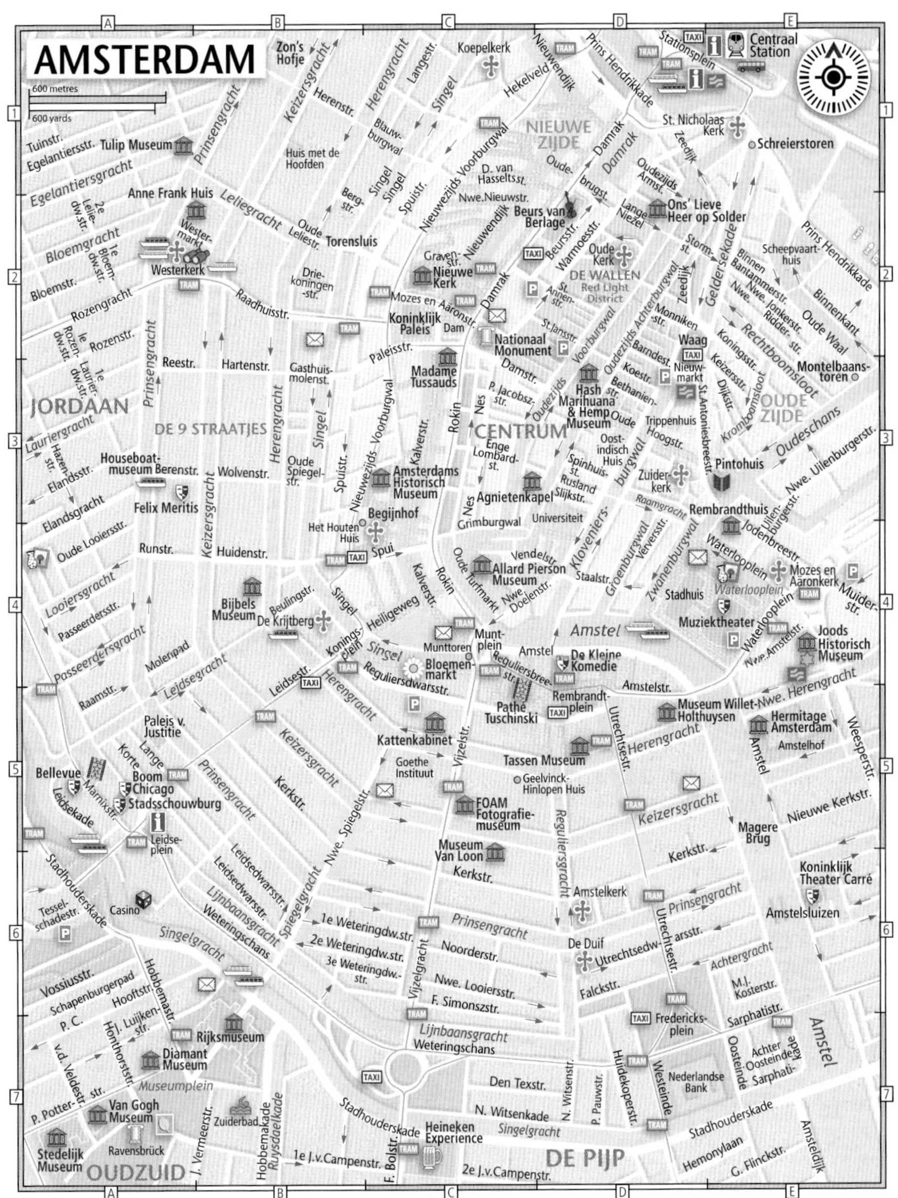
AMSTERDAM
600 metres
600 yards
A
B
C
D
E
1
2
3
4
5
6
7
Centraal Station
Stationsplein
Prins Hendrikkade
Zon's Hofje
Koepelkerk
Nieuwendijk
Hekelveld
Keizersgracht
Herengracht
Langestr.
Singel
Herenstr.
Blauwburgwal
Prinsengracht
Tuinstr.
Egelantiersstr.
Tulip Museum
Egelantiersgracht
Huis met de Hoofden
NIEUWE ZIJDE
St. Nicholaas Kerk
Schreierstoren
Zeedijk
Damrak
Oudebrugst.
D. van Hasseltsst.
Nieuwezijds Voorburgwal
Nwe.Nieuwstr.
Spuistr.
Berg-str.
Anne Frank Huis
Leliegracht
Oude Leliestr.
Torensluis
Beurs van Berlage
Oudezijds Armst.
Ons' Lieve Heer op Solder
Lange Niezel
Bloemgracht
Westermarkt
Westerkerk
Bloemstr.
Rozengracht
Raadhuisstr.
Drie-koningen-str.
Gravenstr.
Nieuwe Kerk
Beursstr.
Warmoesstr.
Oude Kerk
DE WALLEN
Red Light District
St. Annenstr.
Storm-st.
Geldersekade
Binnen Bantammerstr.
Nwe. Jonkerstr.
Nwe. Ridderstr.
Scheepvaarthuis
Binnenkant
Oude Waal
Rechtboomssloot
Mozes en Aäronstr.
Koninklijk Paleis
Dam
National Monument
St.Jansstr.
Oudezijds Voorburgwal
Oudezijds Achterburgwal
Monniken-str.
Waag
Nieuwmarkt
Koningsstr.
Keizersstr.
Dijkstr.
Montelbaanstoren
Rozenstr.
Reestr.
Hartenstr.
Gasthuis-molenst.
Paleisstr.
Madame Tussauds
Damstr.
P. Jacobsz-str.
Barndest.
Koestr.
Bethanien-
Hash Marihuana & Hemp Museum
St.Antoniesbreestr.
Kromboomssloot
OUDE ZIJDE
JORDAAN
Lauriergracht
DE 9 STRAATJES
Rokin
Nes
Kalverstr.
CENTRUM
Enge Lombard-st.
Oude Hoogstr.
Trippenhuis
Oost-indisch Huis
Oudeschans
Nwe. Uilenburgerstr.
Pintohuis
Houseboat-museum
Berenstr.
Wolvenstr.
Oude Spiegel-str.
Amsterdams Historisch Museum
Spinhuis-st.
Rusland
Slijkstr.
Zuiderkerk
Elandsstr.
Felix Meritis
Elandsgracht
Agnietenkapel
Grimburgwal
Universiteit
Raamgracht
Rembrandthuis
Jodenbreestr.
Begijnhof
Het Houten Huis
Spui
Oude Looiersstr.
Runstr.
Huidenstr.
Vendelstr.
Allard Pierson Museum
Oude Turfmarkt
Kloveniersburgwal
Groenburgwal
Verversstr.
Staalstr.
Zwanenburgwal
Waterlooplein
Mozes en Aäronkerk
Muiderstr.
Stadhuis
Looiersgracht
Bijbels Museum
Beulingstr.
De Krijtberg
Heiligeweg
Nwe. Doelenstr.
Amstel
Muziektheater
Joods Historisch Museum
Nwe.Amstelstr.
Passeerdersstr.
Passeerdersgracht
Munttoren
Muntplein
Koningsplein
Bloemenmarkt
Reguliersbree.str.
De Kleine Komedie
Amstelstr.
Molenpad
Leidsegracht
Leidsestr.
Reguliersdwarsstr.
Pathe Tuschinski
Rembrandtplein
Museum Willet-Holthuysen
Nwe. Herengracht
Hermitage Amsterdam
Amstelhof
Weesperstr.
Raamstr.
Paleis v. Justitie
Kattenkabinet
Vijzelstr.
Tassen Museum
Utrechtsestr.
Lange
Korte
Boom Chicago
Bellevue
Marnixstr.
Stadsschouwburg
Leidsekade
Goethe Instituut
Geelvinck-Hinlopen Huis
Nwe. Spiegelstr.
Kerkstr.
FOAM Fotografie-museum
Reguliersgracht
Nieuwe Kerkstr.
Leidseplein
Stadhouderskade
Leidsedwarsstr.
Lijnbaansgracht
Museum Van Loon
Magere Brug
Koninklijk Theater Carré
Tesselschadestr.
Casino
Weteringschans
Spiegelgracht
1e Weteringdw.str.
2e Weteringdw.str.
3e Weteringdw.-str.
Amstelkerk
Amstelsluizen
Singelgracht
Noorderstr.
De Duif
Utrechtsedwarsstr.
Achtergracht
Vossiusstr.
Schapenburgerpad
Hobbemastr.
Hooftstr.
P. C.
Nwe. Looiersstr.
F. Simonszstr.
Falckstr.
M.J. Kosterstr.
J. Luijkenstr.
Rijksmuseum
Vijzelgracht
Fredericksplein
Sarphatistr.
v.d. Veldestr.
Honthorststr.
Diamant Museum
Museumplein
Huidekoperstr.
Westeinde
Nederlandse Bank
Oosteinde
Achter Oosteinde
Sarphatikade
Den Texstr.
N. Witsenstr.
P. Pauwstr.
P. Potter-str.
Van Gogh Museum
Zuiderbad
J. Vermeerstr.
Ruysdaelkade
Hobbemakade
N. Witsenkade
Heineken Experience
Singelgracht
Stadhouderskade
Stedelijk Museum
Ravensbrück
OUDZUID
1e J.v.Campenstr.
F. Bolstr.
2e J.v.Campenstr.
DE PIJP
Hemonylaan
G. Flinckstr.
Amsteldijk

624 6604, www.opsolder.nl, map D2, Mon-Sat 1000-1700, Sun 1300-1700, €7, an ordinary townhouse with an extraordinary attic, containing the city's only surviving clandestine church. It dates from the Reformation, when public Catholic worship was outlawed.

Nieuwmarkt

Metro Nieuwmarkt. Map D3.

Once a major market for inhabitants from the nearby Jewish quarter – all but wiped out during the Nazi occupation – this broad square is today flanked by cafés and shops, leading to the city's Chinatown in Zeedijk, just to the north. The square is towered over by **De Waag**, a 15th-century fortress-like structure, once a city gate. During the week there's a small fruit and vegetable market and, in summer, an antique market is held every Sunday.

Waterlooplein

Tram 4, 9 or 14. Metro Waterlooplein. Map E4.

Amsterdam's oldest **flea market**, *Mon-Sat 0900-1700,* is a labyrinthine sprawl of stalls, stuffed with second-hand clothes, old vinyl records and leather jackets. The square is lorded over by the 1986 Stadhuis and Muziektheater, designed by Willem Holzbauer and known locally as the **Stopera** (a combination of 'Stad' and 'Opera'). Although the complex was hugely controversial when it was built, the theatre now has an excellent reputation. Free concerts are held here at least once a week.

Rembrandthuis

Jodenbreestraat 4, T020 520 0400, www.rembrandthuis.nl.
Daily 1000-1700. €9. Metro to Nieuwmarkt, Hoogstraat exit. Tram 9 or 14. Map E4.

This graceful house was Rembrandt's home from 1639 to 1658. He lived in the elegant rooms on the ground floor and worked in the large studio upstairs during his most successful period. Today the rooms are stocked with original fittings and period furniture. Also on display is a superb collection of his etchings – over 260 pieces.

Nieuwe Zijde

Tram 1, 2, 13 or 17. Map D1.

The New Side of the medieval centre was actually settled earlier than the Oude Zijde and today covers the area west of the Dam. It's a mixed area of uninspiring shopping and pretty side streets, leading to the Grachtengordel. Worth a look is the **Amsterdam Historisch Museum**, *Kalverstraat 92, T020 523 1822, www.ahm.nl, Mon-Fri 1000-1700, Sat, Sun and public holidays 1100-1700, €7,* located in the old city orphanage. As well as housing some interesting paintings, the building itself, with its two courtyards and winding corridors, is fascinating.

Above: Houses in the city centre.
Below: Antiques shop.
Opposite page: Rijksmuseum entrance.

Anne Frank House

Prinsengracht 263, T020 556 7100, www.annefrank.org.
Mid-Mar to mid-Sep 0900-2100; mid-Sep to mid-Mar 0900-1900, closed Yom Kippur. €8.50. Tram 13 or 17. Bus 21, 170, 171 or 172 to Westermarkt. Map B2.

The gripping, heartbreaking story of Anne Frank is one of the most enduring accounts of life in hiding during the Second World War. The unassuming house, where the Frank family hid with friends for two years during the Nazi occupation, provides a harrowing glimpse of the claustrophobic lives led behind blacked-out windows. The diary itself, sitting alone in a glass case, is startlingly poignant. The only survivor of the Frank family was Anne's father Otto, who returned to the house, published the diary and helped to open the museum in 1960. The entrance is now in a modern building next door.

Rijksmuseum

Jan Luijkenstraat 1, T020 674 7000, www.rijksmuseum.nl.
Sat-Thu 0900-1800, Fri 0900-2200. €12.50. Tram 2 or 5 to Hobbemastraat, 12 to Concertgebouw, or 6, 7 or 10 to Spiegelgracht. Map B7.

Amsterdam's enormous flagship museum displays masterpieces of Dutch art as well temporary exhibitions. The building itself, designed by Pierre Cuypers, is a striking neo-Gothic riot of towers, turrets and stained glass windows and dominates the Museum Quarter. Inside, the collection is split into various sections, most famous of which is the extraordinary Dutch Golden Age collection of paintings. Other sections include sculpture, decorative arts, prints and photographs. The museum's prize piece, Rembrandt's *Nightwatch*, is still on show and it's worth a visit for this alone. The painting was originally called *The Militia Company of Captain Frans Banning Cocq* but became known as the Nightwatch as the picture darkened with grime over the years; it has since been cleaned to reveal its true daytime setting.

Van Gogh Museum

Paulus Potterstraat 7, T020 570 5200, www.vangoghmuseum.nl.
Sat-Thu 1000-1800, Fri 1000- 2200. €14. Tram 2, 3, 5 or 12 to between Paulus Potterstraat and Van Baerlestraat. Map A7.

One of Amsterdam's finest museums holds the world's largest Vincent Van Gogh collection: over

Up in smoke

Thank heavens for Bob Marley. Without Bob and the Rastafarian flag – green, gold and red stripes – tourists would have a tough time spotting a coffeeshop in Amsterdam. That's coffeeshop, not coffeehouse. The difference, of course, is that the former is permitted to sell cannabis, although it's illegal to advertise this fact. Hence all the Rasta paraphernalia, a sure-fire way to tell tourists that they've come to the right (or wrong) place, depending on their views. Amsterdam remains the only city in the world with such a liberal view on soft drugs, attracting a fare percentage of drug tourists, much to the annoyance of many locals and politicians. The law is very clear on what it will tolerate: an individual can possess 30 g and can buy up to 5 g of cannabis at a time from a licensed purveyor – any use of hard drugs (heroin, cocaine and ecstasy) is strictly illegal. Coffeeshops aren't permitted to sell alcohol and there's an age limit of 18. Recent rumblings about limiting tourists' access to coffeeshops have proved unfounded, and for now it seems this unique side of Amsterdam is here to stay.

Travel essentials

Getting there

Schiphol Airport (www.schiphol.nl) lies 15km southwest of the city centre. Trains run from beneath the main concourse to Centraal Station every 15 mins 0445-2400 and every hour thereafter, taking 15 mins (€3.80 single). Buses also run to the centre, including the 370 which stops in the Museum Quarter. A taxi to the centre takes around 20 mins and costs about €45. **Schiphol Travel Taxi**, T0900 8876, is a good-value shared minibus.

Centraal Station, T0900-9296, www.ns.nl, Amsterdam's main station, is right in the centre of town at the end of Damrak. There are regular international connections, including a high-speed link with Brussels Midi for connections to the Eurostar. Another high-speed service, the Dutch Flyer, links Centraal Station with the Hook of Holland for ferries to and from Harwich.

Getting around

Most of the city's main sights are within easy walking distance of each other. The public transport system is excellent; trams are the most useful but there are also buses and a small metro (best for outlying districts). All public transport is run by the GVB, www.gvb.nl, which has an information and ticket office opposite Centraal Station. Its website is also a great source of travel information. Tickets can also be bought at tram stops, newsagents and on board trams and buses. A new smart-card ticketing system, OV-chipkaart, has been introduced, but the €7.50 fee for the card itself means that it probably isn't worth buying for short visits to the city. Alternatively, travel passes, valid on the whole network, cost €7, €11.50 or €15.50 for 24, 48 and 72hrs. Taxis have ranks around the city but are pricey.

Tourist information

The main office is opposite Centraal Station, T0900 400 4040, www.amsterdamtourist.nl, daily 0900-1700. There's another inside the station, Mon-Thu and Sat 0800-2000, Fri 0800-2100, Sun 0900-1700; and another on the corner of Leidseplein and Leidsestraat, daily 0900-1700. The IAmsterdam Card, www.iamsterdam.com, offers unlimited travel on public transport, a free canal boat trip, and free entrance to most of the city's museums. Tickets cost €38, €48 or €58 for 1, 2, or 3 days and are available from the tourist and GVB information offices. Among the canal tours, the most useful is Lovers Museumboat, T020 530 1090, www.lovers.nl, a hop-on/hop-off service stopping at all major museums. Tickets cost €12.50 and include reduced entry to museums.

200 pieces bequeathed by his art-collector brother, Theo. The modern building is split into five periods, starting with Van Gogh's dark Dutch works and evolving, via Paris and Arles in the south of France, into the extraordinarily lively and colourful palette for which he is known. Strikingly, Van Gogh's career lasted little longer than a decade but this marvellous collection does much to highlight how rich and productive those ten years were. Highlights include The *Potato Eaters*, *Bedroom in Arles* and *Wheatfield with Crows*. Also in the museum are the artist's sketches, as well as works by his contemporaries, including close friend Paul Gauguin; Van Gogh famously cut off part of his ear lobe after an argument with his artist friend.

Joods Historisch Museum

Nieuwe Amstelstraat 1, T020 531 0310, www.jhm.nl.

Daily 1100-1700, Thu until 2100, closed Yom Kippur. €9. Metro Waterlooplein. Tram 9 or 14. Map E4.

The Jewish History Museum is housed in a beautiful series of four synagogues dating from the 17th century, lined by walkways. First opened in 1930, the museum was closed and ransacked during the Second World War and it was not until the 1980s that it was restored and re-opened. It now houses a thorough collection depicting the history of Jewish life in the Netherlands, highlighting the enormous contribution Jews made to the development of Amsterdam.

Sleeping

Amsterdam's status as a hip city break destination means its vast number of beds don't often come cheap; moreover, most places get booked up, particularly in late spring (tulip season) and summer, so it's always essential to book ahead. Avoid the hotel touts, who hang around Centraal Station.

Amstel InterContinental €€€
Professor Tulpplein 1, T020 622 6060, www.amsterdam.intercontinental.com.
The city's grande dame towers on the bank of the Amstel and attracts an impressive list of rock stars and royalty. It's a classically large, elegant hotel, with posh rooms complete with Dutch wallpaper and huge beds. The Michelin-starred La Rive restaurant is highly acclaimed.

The Dylan €€€
Keizersgracht 384, T020 530 2010, www.dylanamsterdam.com.
Style guru Anouchka Hempel designed this small hotel (formerly Blakes). Rooms are individually themed, all centred on a courtyard, and there is an excellent fusion restaurant downstairs.

Hotel 717 €€€
Prinsengracht 717, T020 427 0717, www.717hotel.nl.
This hotel feels like a mix between a glossy magazine shoot and the home of a rich art-collector friend. Each of the eight rooms is impeccably designed, crammed with artwork, beautiful fabrics and an eclectic mix of antiques. Good canal-side location.

Ambassade €€€-€€
Herengracht 341, T020 555 0222, www.ambassade-hotel.nl.
Ten 17th-century canal-side houses make up this hotel in a lovely spot on Herengracht. This is one for bibliophiles: John Le Carré, Umberto Eco and Salman Rushdie have all stayed here (check out the signed copies in the library). Rooms are traditional and plush; those in the eaves are the most appealing.

Seven Bridges €€€-€€
Reguliersgracht 31, T020 623 1329, www.sevenbridgeshotel.nl.
Set in a 300-year-old house, this hotel is quiet, with rooms overlooking either the canal and the famous Seven Bridges or a small garden. Breakfast is served in your room. Book months in advance.

Canal House €€
Keizersgracht 148, T020 622 5182, www.canalhouse.nl.
Reopened in 2011 after an impeccable modern refurbishment, Canal House is styled with sleek contemporary greys and purples and fabrics and a touch of humour in the contemporary art. The location on the Keizersgracht Canal is peaceful.

Amistad Hotel €
Kerkstraat 42, T020 624 8074, www.amistad.nl.
Run by husband-and-husband team, Johan and Joost, the Amistad is one of the most popular gay hotels in town. Simple, colourful rooms come with or without en suite bathrooms and have wooden floors and bright artwork. There's an internet lounge in the reception area.

Eating

Traditional Dutch fare isn't the lightest of cuisines – expect hearty meat-and-potato dishes, thick pancakes oozing all sorts of fillings, and hefty *broodjes* (sandwiches) stacked with meat, cheeses or fish. Having said that, chefs across the city are also wallowing in an orgy of fusion cuisine, which often puts French or Asian slants on Dutch dishes. Holland's colonial heritage also means lots of Indonesian flavours, and the city's multicultural population ensures plenty of Chinese, Thai, Italian and Japanese restaurants to choose from.

Breakfast

De Bakkerswinkel €
Warmoesstraat 69, T020 489 8000.
Breakfast, lunch and tea only. Closed Mon. Bustling, airy deli/café serving excellent brunches, sandwiches and fat slices of quiche.

Winkel €
Noordermarkt 43, T020 623 0223.
Big breakfasts and legendary apple cake at this lively café. Be prepared to queue on Mon and Sat (market days).

Lunch

Haesje Claes €€
Spuistraat 273-275, T020 624 9998.
Old-style Dutch comfort eating in this popular wood-panelled restaurant. Stampot – a filling stew of potatoes mashed with cabbage and served with sausage – is a speciality and perfect fare on a rainy afternoon. There are also good fish dishes, if you fancy something lighter.

Café Luxembourg €
Spui 24, T020 620 6264.
Elegant café with a long marble bar and equally long menu, including favourites like split pea soup, salmon burgers and kroketten (croquettes). Newspapers and a slow pace in the morning, more frenetic at lunch and dinner.

Pannekoekhuis Upstairs €
Grimburgwal 2, T020 626 5603.
Students flock to this tiny pancake house dolling out good-value servings of filled sweet and savoury pancakes. Service can be slow.

Dinner

Blauw aan de Wal €€€
Achterburgwal 99, T020 330 2257.
This is a real find, hidden away down an alley in the heart of the red-light district. Chic Mediterranean cuisine is the order of the day, with old wood floors, bare brick walls and a pretty courtyard making it all rather romantic.

Christophe €€€
Leliegracht 46, T020 625 0807, www.restaurantchristophe.nl.
Tue-Sat dinner.
Classic restaurant in a quiet canal-side location. The atmosphere is discreet and elegant (jackets are required) and the food is a sumptuous feast of French-inspired contemporary cooking. Reservations are essential.

Brasserie Harkema €€
Nes 67, T020 428 2222, www.brasserieharkema.nl.
Lunch and dinner daily. This weird fusion of traditional French-style brasserie and ultra-modern industrial styling is popular with locals, and the food is fast and good.

Nightlife

d'Vijff Vlieghen €€
Spuistraat 294- 302, T020 530 4060, www.thefiveflies.com.
Dinner only.
You won't have this place to yourself, but it's worth braving the tour groups for the food. The menu is top-notch Dutch, served in a lovely string of 17th-century houses filled with antiques and Delft tiles. Look out for the Rembrandt etchings on the walls.

Kantjil en de Tijger €€
Spuistraat 291-293, T020 620 0994, www.kantjil.nl.
Refreshingly free of the usual oriental decor, this large, chic space serves rijsttafel (rice table): an array of up to 20 Indonesian dishes. Arrive with an appetite. The spicy coconut prawns are good, too.

Café Bern €
Nieuwmarkt 9, T020 6220034.
Dinner only.
Typically laid-back brown café (see below), specializing in cheese fondues, which is an unofficial national dish hijacked from Switzerland. Punters wash this down with a shot of strong stuff.

The tourist office website, www.iamsterdam.com has a wealth of information on what's going on around the city, covering everything from live music and events to exhibitions and museums. Amsterdam has a huge gay and lesbian scene – many call it the gay capital of Europe – with countless gay-friendly hotels, bars and clubs. These are mostly focused on the area around Reguliersdwarsstraat.

Bars and coffeeshops

Don't be put off by the term *bruine cafés* (brown cafés) – these ubiquitous café-bars are the cosy mainstay of Amsterdam's nightlife. They're actually called that because smoke has stained the walls with nicotine over the years. Lovely. Nevertheless, these friendly pubs, found all over the old centre and along the canals, are a great place to meet locals and try Dutch beer. Note that you are not allowed to smoke (anything) in these and other bars. For legal cannabis, head to a coffeeshop, again found throughout the centre and identified by the leaf motif or Rasta flag in the window (see page nine). These generally have menus selling various types of cannabis. Take it easy, especially with hash cakes and cookies, which can pack a powerful punch.

For a chilled-out bar scene, often with DJs and dancing late into the night, try out some of the newer lounge bars around Nieuwezijds Voorburgwal, as well as the more traditional nightlife spots around Rembrandtplein and Leidseplein.

Clubs and live music

The club scene isn't as cutting edge as you might hope, although there are some good places in the centre. The **Nachttheater Sugar Factory**, *Lijnbaansgracht 238*, combines a wide range of late-night performance with a leftfield club. **Melkweg**, *Lijnbaansgracht 234a, T020 531 8181, www.melkweg.nl*, is a long-running favourite, functioning as a full-on arts centre, and therefore a good place to catch live music.

Ratings

Art and culture ☆☆☆☆☆
Eating ☆☆☆☆
Nightlife ☆☆
Romance ☆☆☆
Shopping ☆☆☆
Sightseeing ☆☆☆☆☆
Value-for-money ☆☆☆
Overall city rating ☆☆☆☆

Athens

In preparation for the 2004 Olympics, Athens was spruced up, refined and beautified, bringing it into the 21st century with gusto. Ancient monuments were restored, neoclassical façades repainted, billboards and neon lighting torn down, the metro extended, tramlines added, pedestrian zones paved and trees planted. But in a city where countless layers of history sit concrete-upon-brick-upon-stone, you'll still find a curious juxtaposition of Western European, Balkan and Middle Eastern cultures, all of which are reflected in the food, the music and the architecture. Now under serious pressure to "westernise", having accepted a $147 billion bailout from the European Union and the International Monetary Fund in May 2010 to avoid total bankrupcy, Athenians have been subjected to severe austerity measures. Hence the highly-publicised demonstrations and street riots. Nonetheless, this is also the city that, back in its ancient heyday, invented hedonism and despite the current economic hardship, you'll not be disappointed on that score – Athens nightlife is still beautiful, extravagant and inexhaustible.

Hadrian Arch at sunset.

At a glance

Take the **Acropolis** as your main point of reference. If you are on a short stay, you'll probably be based in **Plaka**, Athens' oldest residential neighbourhood, skirting the Acropolis' northern and eastern slopes. The northern limit of Plaka is marked by **Ermou** (the main shopping street), which runs east–west from **Syntagma** (home to the Greek Parliament) to **Monastiraki**, best known for its Sunday morning flea market and its metro station, then proceeds to smart residential **Thissio** and **Gazi**. On the far side of Ermou lies Psirri and, northeast of Syntagma, the rocky mound of **Mount Lycabettus** (Lycabettus Hill) rises above the well-to-do area of **Kolonaki**. **Gazi** and **Psirri** deserve a special mention: both former industrial zones, they have recently been transformed into night-time districts filled with happening bars, restaurants, clubs and art galleries.

Another welcome addition to Athens is the new **Archaeological Promenade**, a 4-km paved, lamp-lit walkway that now links the city's ancient sites. Starting from the new Akropolis metro station, Dionissiou Areopagitou curves around the south side of the Acropolis to join Apostolou Pavlou, which then runs alongside the Ancient Agora to bring you to Thissio. From here Adrianou runs east to Plaka, while Ermou runs west past **Kerameikos** (ancient Athens' cemetery) towards Gazi.

Acropolis

Acropolis Hill, Plaka, T210 321 0219, odysseus.culture.gr.
Summer daily 0800-2000; winter daily 0830-1500. €12 (this ticket also gives free entry to the Ancient Agora, Roman Forum, Theatre of Dionysus, Kerameikos and the Temple of Olympian Zeus and is valid for 4 days).
Metro Akropolis or Monastiraki. Map B5.

Most stunning at night, when it rises above the modern city bathed in golden floodlights, the Acropolis is a rocky mound crowned by three ancient temples, symbolizing the birth of Athens and indeed of Western civilization. Today it receives some three million visitors per year and is also the biggest selling point for hotel rooms and restaurant terraces claiming to glimpse its magic.

The largest and most revered temple is the fifth-century BC **Parthenon**, built entirely from marble. Supported by 46 Doric columns, it was originally intended as a sanctuary for Athena and housed a giant gold and ivory statue of the goddess. The controversial Elgin Marbles (Greeks prefer to call them the Parthenon Marbles), are a series of bas-reliefs that once formed the internal frieze. In 1816 Lord Elgin, British Ambassador to Athens, which was under Ottoman occupation at the time, sold them to the British Museum in London, where they remain to this day.

New Acropolis Museum

Dionysiou Areopagitou 15, Plaka, T210 900 0900, www.newacropolismuseum.gr.
Tue-Sun 0800-2000. €5. Map B5.

This long-awaited museum finally opened in June 2009. Designed by Swiss architect Bernard Tschumi, it combines glass, steel and concrete, creating light and airy spaces for the display of archaic and classical statues and other finds from the Acropolis site. The top floor is devoted to the marble frieze that once ran around the Parthenon – around half of what you see are the original bas-reliefs, while the rest, made up of crude white plaster copies, mark

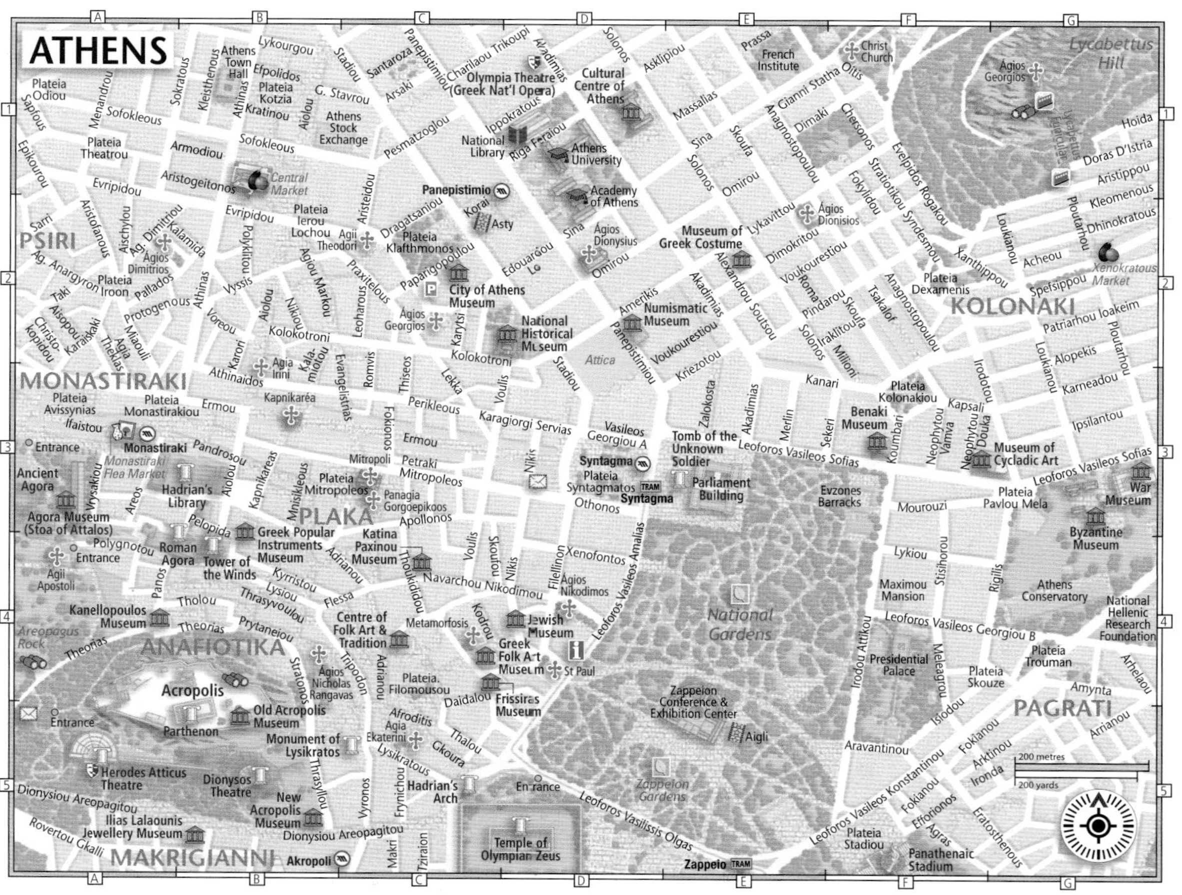
ATHENS
PSIRI
MONASTIRAKI
PLAKA
ANAFIOTIKA
MAKRIGIANNI
KOLONAKI
PAGRATI
Lycabettus Hill
Lycabettus Funicular
Agios Georgios
Xenokratous Market
Christ Church
French Institute
Plateia Dexamenis
Agios Dionisios
Museum of Greek Costume
Cultural Centre of Athens
Athens University
Academy of Athens
Agios Dionysius
Olympia Theatre (Greek Nat'l Opera)
National Library
Panepistimio
Asty
Numismatic Museum
Attica
National Historical Museum
City of Athens Museum
Plateia Klafthmonos
Agios Georgios
Agii Theodori
Athens Stock Exchange
Plateia Kotzia
Athens Town Hall
Central Market
Agioi Dimitrios
Agia Irini
Agia Theklas
Plateia Monastirakiou
Monastiraki
Monastiraki Flea Market
Hadrian's Library
Roman Agora
Tower of the Winds
Ancient Agora
Agora Museum (Stoa of Attalos)
Agii Apostoli
Entrance
Kanellopoulos Museum
Areopagus Rock
Greek Popular Instruments Museum
Panagia Gorgoepikoos
Plateia Mitropoleos
Mitropoli
Katina Paxinou Museum
Centre of Folk Art & Tradition
Agios Nicholas Rangavas
Old Acropolis Museum
Acropolis
Parthenon
Dionysos Theatre
Herodes Atticus Theatre
Ilias Lalaounis Jewellery Museum
New Acropolis Museum
Akropoli
Monument of Lysikratos
Agia Ekaterini
Plateia Filomousou
Hadrian's Arch
Frissiras Museum
Greek Folk Art Museum
Jewish Museum
St Paul
Agios Nikodimos
Temple of Olympian Zeus
Syntagma
Plateia Syntagmatos
Tomb of the Unknown Soldier
Parliament Building
National Gardens
Zappeion Conference & Exhibition Center
Zappeion Gardens
Zappeio
Aigli
Evzones Barracks
Benaki Museum
Plateia Kolonakiou
Museum of Cycladic Art
Plateia Pavlou Mela
Byzantine Museum
War Museum
Athens Conservatory
National Hellenic Research Foundation
Plateia Trouman
Plateia Skouze
Maximou Mansion
Presidential Palace
Panathenaic Stadium
Plateia Stadiou
Leoforos Vasileos Sofias
Leoforos Vasileos Konstantinou
Leoforos Vasilissis Amalias
Leoforos Vasilissis Olgas
Leoforos Vasileos Georgiou B
Irodou Attikou
Panepistimiou
Stadiou
Akadimias
Ermou
Mitropoleos
Athinas
Eolou
Dionysiou Areopagitou
200 metres
200 yards

the pieces stolen by Lord Elgin, now on display in the British Museum. This poignant presentation is intended as a message to London, that it is time the marbles returned to their homeland.

Plaka

Metro Acropolis or Monastiraki. Map A3.

Built into the hillside below the Acropolis, Plaka is Athens' oldest residential quarter. Touristy but undeniably charming, it's made up of cobbled alleys lined with pastel- coloured neoclassical mansions dating from the late 19th century. (During this period Greece was trying to re-establish its cultural identity after liberation from the Ottoman Turks.) The only really old buildings remaining here are Byzantine churches. Particularly notable is the 12th-century **Little Mitropolis,** *daily 0700-1300,* standing next to the far less attractive 19th-century cathedral and the residential area of **Anafiotika**, a cluster of whitewashed Cycladic-style houses built by settlers from the island of Anafi. Besides the countless souvenir shops and tavernas, look out for the museums of **Greek Popular Musical Instruments**, *Diogenous 1-3, www.instruments-museum.gr, Tue and Thu-Sun 1000-1400, Wed 1200-1800, free*, and **Greek Folk Art**, *Kidathineon 17, www.melt.gr, Tue-Sun 0900-1430.*

Ancient Agora

Andrianou 24, Monastiraki, T210 321 0185, odysseus.culture.gr.
Summer daily 0800-1900; winter daily 0800-1500. €4. Metro Monastiraki. Map A3.

Today, Agora is a romantic wilderness of coarse grazing land and olive trees, strewn with fallen columns and crowned by an ancient temple. During the Golden Age, however, this was Athens' main marketplace, as well as the city's political, administrative and cultural heart. It was here that Socrates and St Paul made their public speeches and where democracy was born, although now you'll need some imagination to interpret it as such.

The buildings that remain recognisably intact are the remarkably well-preserved fifth-century BC **Temple of Haephaistos** and the **Stoa of Attalos**, a two-storey structure from the second century BC, which originally functioned as a trading centre but today houses the **Agora Museum**, displaying ancient finds from the site.

Central Market

Sofokleous and Evripidou.
Mon-Sat 0900-1500. Metro Monastiraki or Omonia. Map B1.

Modern-day Athenians shop within the halls of the vast covered market, an iron and glass structure erected in 1870. A veritable feast for the eyes, it is here that you will find stalls trading in seasonal Mediterranean fruit and vegetables, dried figs, nuts, olives and spices. In the seafood section are glittering silver-scaled fish and copious quantities of octopus and squid displayed upon mounds of freshly ground ice, while the meat section (definitely not for the squeamish) is populated by blood-splattered butchers hacking at carcasses on tree trunks that improvise as chopping boards.

National Archaeological Museum

Patission 44, Omonia, T210 821 7717, www.namuseum.gr.
Summer daily 0800- 1900; winter Mon 1300-2000, Tue-Sun 0830-1500. €7. Metro Victoria. Off Map.

Holding one of the world's finest collections of ancient Greek art, this museum is a must-see. Re-opened in 2004 after renovation, the light and airy marble-floored exhibition spaces now show off elegant classical sculpture to maximum effect. It's vast so don't try to see everything but be sure to catch the subtly coloured 16th-century BC **Thira Frescoes**, found buried below lava following a volcanic explosion on the island of Santorini, and the **Mycenaen Collection**, a hoard of gold jewellery and weaponry dating from between the 16th and 11th centuries BC.

Benaki Museum

Vassilissis Sofias and Koumbari 1, Kolonaki, T210 367 1000, www.benaki.gr.
Mon, Wed, Fri, Sat 0900-1700, Thu 0900- 2400, Sun 0900-1500. €6 (free Thu). Metro Syntagma. Map F3.

Born in Alexandria, Egypt, in 1873, Antonios Benakis was an avid art collector who gave this neoclassical house and his entire art collection to the Greek state before his death in 1954. A journey through the history of Greek art from 3000 BC up to the 20th century, exhibits include sculpture, ceramics, jewellery, paintings, furniture and costumes, laid out in chronological order. Top attractions include a hoard of second-century BC golden filigree jewellery inlaid with precious stones, known as the **Thessaly Treasure**, two early paintings by **El Greco**, and the reconstruction of two wooden-panelled living rooms from an Ottoman-inspired house in northern Greece from the 1750s.

Byzantine Museum

Vassilissis Sofias 22, Kolonaki, T213 213 9572, www.byzantinemuseum.gr.
Summer Tue-Sun 0800-2000, Mon 1330-2000, winter Tue-Sun 0830-1500. €4.
Metro Evangelismos. Map G3.

Hidden below the courtyard of an Italianate villa, this open-plan, split-level, underground exhibition space opened in 2004. Pieces are displayed in chronological order, following the development of the Byzantine Empire from the advent of Christianity (when many pagan symbols were absorbed by the creed) up to the fall

Festivals

Each summer, from June to the end of September, the **Athens & Epidaurus Festival** stages open-air theatre, opera, classical music and dance at the ancient Odeon of Herodes Atticus, plus rock concerts at the hilltop Lycabettus Theatre. A stunning venue, the second-century Odeon is carved into the rocks of the southern slope of the Acropolis. The building was commissioned by the Roman consul, Herodes Atticus, in memory of his wife Regilla. The 28-m high façade serves as a backdrop to the stage, and the semicircular theatre space, with a radius of 38 m, can seat an audience of 5000. The modern festival dates back to 1955; legendary figures that have graced its stage include Maria Callas, Margot Fonteyn and Rudolph Nureyev. More recently, summer 2010 saw performances by, among others, Greece's Demis Roussos, the Royal Concertgebou Orchestra from Amsterdam, and the Rimini Protokoll theatre group. Performances begin at 2100 (June to August) and 2030 (September). Advance booking begins three weeks prior to each performance (see www.greekfestival.gr for the latest programme).

Tickets are available from: Hellenic Festival Box Office, 39 Panepistimiou (in the arcade), Mon-Fri 0830-1600 and Sat 0900-1430; **Odeon of Herodes Atticus**, Dionysiou Areopagitou, daily 0900-1400 and 1700-2000; or by telephone, credit card payment only, T210 327 2000, daily 0900-2100.

of Constantinople in 1453. The exhibition starts with stone carvings, sculpture and mosaics taken from early basilicas. It then continues with icons depicting sultry-eyed saints against golden backgrounds, frescoes illustrating biblical events and minutely-detailed silver and gold jewellery and ecclesiastical artefacts.

Mount Lycabettus (Lycabettus Hill)

Metro Evangelismos. Map G1.

Athens' highest vantage point at 295 m, Lycabettus affords panoramic views of the city, the mountains and the sea. A network of footpaths leads up through pinewoods and lush vegetation to the summit – if the hike is too steep, take a taxi or catch the funicular from *Ploutarchou St in Kolonaki, 4, every 30 mins daily 0900-0300*, for a two-minute whizz through a cliff-side tunnel. The peak is capped by the tiny white Church of St George and a series of terraces hosting the Orizontes restaurant (page 22) and a café. Carved into the rocks on the north-facing slope, the open-air Lycabettus Theatre stages summer concerts. Recent performers have included Placebo and Rufus Wainwright.

Technopolis

Pireos 100, Gazi, T210 346 1589.
Hours vary depending on exhibitions. Free. Metro Thissio. Off map.

Technopolis (Art City) occupies the former City Gasworks. A multi-purpose arts complex, the disused gas tanks and brick outbuildings have been converted to provide a series of spaces for exhibitions, concerts (Florence and the Machine, Friendly Fires and Shantel have played here) and theatre, while the towering brick chimneys are lit red at night and remain the symbol of new art in an urban environment.

Sleeping

Syntagma is where you'll find grand expensive hotels, the Greek Parliament and lots of traffic. For romance and easy sightseeing, opt for Plaka. For nightlife and a gritty downtown ambience, try Monastiraki and Psirri. Avoid Syngrou: it's functional and impersonal and aimed primarily at business travellers. Omonia is seedy and not very pretty.

Electra Palace €€€
Nikodimou 18, Plaka, T210 337 0000, www.electra hotels.gr.
The EP's yellow-and-white neoclassical façade, complete with wrought-iron balconies, was added during renovation for the Olympics. It's now Plaka's most stylish hotel. Some rooms have an Acropolis view. There's a small spa, plus an outdoor infinity pool and summer restaurant on the roof.

Fresh €€€
Sophocleous 26 and Klisthenous, Psirri, T210 524 8511, www.freshhotel.gr.
This hotel opened in 2004 and immediately featured in *Wallpaper* magazine. Close to the gritty Central Market, the look is minimalist, with fresh flowers, lounge music, and vivid orange, green and pink details adding to the fun. There's a summer rooftop bar with a pool and sundeck, and nouvelle Greek cuisine served in the ground floor restaurant.

Ochre & Brown €€€
Leokoriou 7, Psirri, T210 331 2940, www.oandbhotel.com.
This small boutique hotel has just 22 rooms and suites with stylish minimalist décor. Lying midway between the Acropolis and the Gazi nightlife district, both within walking distance, it serves an excellent cooked-to-order breakfast , and is noted for its young friendly staff and personalised service.

Hotel Plaka €€
Kapnikareas 7, Plaka, T210 322 2096, www.plakahotel.gr.
Renovated in early 2010, this smart and discreet hotel lies in a side street between Monastiraki and Syntagma metro stations. The 67 rooms have pine floors, minimalist furniture and primary-coloured fabrics. There's a roof garden with a bar on summer evenings, so you can watch the sun set over the Acropolis.

Athens Center Square €€
15 Aristogitonos Street & Athinas, Monastiraki, T210 322 2706, www.athenscentersquarehotel.gr.
This three-star hotel stands on a pedestrian-only square, overlooking the Central Market, just a couple of minutes from Monastiraki metro station. It opened in summer 2009 and the 54 rooms have wooden floors, flat-screen TV and free Wi-Fi and each storey is colour-themed.

Marble House €
An Zinni 35, Koukaki, T210 922 8294, www.marblehouse.gr.
This small friendly family-run hotel lies in a peaceful residential area, just a 10-min walk from Plaka and the Acropolis. The 16 rooms are each decorated in a different colour and have beds with wrought-iron bedsteads, mini-bars and ceiling fans.

Athens Backpackers €
Makri 12, Makrigianni, T201 9224044, www.athensbackpackers.gr.
Offering both dorms and self-contained apartments, this Australian-owned hostel is clean, friendly and well-managed. It lies on the edge of Plaka, close to the New Acropolis Museum, and has a summer rooftop bar with Acropolis views.

Eating

Plaka is fine for lunch but to really tap into Athenian nightlife dine in Psirri or Gazi, where funky new eateries breathe life into standard Greek taverna fare and stay open well beyond midnight.

Breakfast

Gallery Café
Adrianou 33, Monastiraki, T210 324 9080.
Overlooking the Ancient Agora, this café has a lounge atmosphere with exposed stonework, sofas and coffee tables, cool music and modern art on the walls.

Tristato
Dedalou 34 and Geronda, Plaka, T210 324 4472.
In a pedestrian side street just off Platia Filomousou, this old-fashioned café is a great place for morning coffee or an afternoon pot of herbal tea.

Lunch

O Platanos €
Diogenous 4, Plaka, T210 322 0666.
One of the oldest and most hidden tavernas in Plaka, O Platanos dates back to 1932. Homely meat-and-vegetable casseroles – such as lamb with aubergine and veal with spinach – are served at tables on a bougainvillea-covered terrace, in the shade of an old plane tree, after which the restaurant is named.

To Kouti €€
Adrianou 23, Monastiraki, T210 321 3229.
Playful salads, meat and seafood dishes, seasoned with spices and aromatic herbs, are guaranteed to make your tastebuds sing. Great for dinner with an Acropolis view, or lunch after a trip to Monastiraki's Sun flea market.

Dinner

Orizontes €€€
Mt Lycabettus, Kolonaki, T210 722 7065.
The high point of Athens, 295m above sea level, is the place to eat if you have only one night in town, plus the money to foot the bill. Perched atop Mt Lycabettus, Orizontes offers stunning views across the city and a menu of refined fusion cuisine. Reservations are recommended.

Café Avissinia €€
Platia Avissinia, Monastiraki, T201 321 7047, www.avissinia.gr.
On a small square where antiques shops restore wooden furniture, this old-fashioned bistro serves Greek dishes with flavours from Anatolia. There's regular live music, plus a romantic roof terrace with stunning views onto the floodlit Acropolis.

Skoufias €
Vasilaiou tou Megalou 50, Gazi, T210 341 2252.
Excellent value for money and a great starting point for a night in Gazi, this boho-chic eatery serves Cretan-inspired modern taverna fare. Both inside and out, you get mismatched wooden tables and chairs, coloured ceramics and a handwritten menu that changes daily.

Nightlife

Ask Athenians what they think their city does better than any other European capital and they will probably tell you about the nightlife. All year round Psirri and Gazi are rocking. In Psirri, Psirra, *Miaouli 19*, pulls the grungy intellectual crowd, who drink rakomelo (hot raki with honey and cinnamon) at streetside tables. Nearby, in Monastiraki, TAF, *Normanou 5, www.theartfoundation.gr*, is a bar-gallery, with semi-derelict outbuildings hosting art and photography exhibitions and installations, and a lovely courtyard garden with mellow lighting and chill-out music for drinks.

Up the road, between Monastiraki and Syntagma, arty **Booze**, *Kolokotroni 57, www.boozecooperativa.com*, occupies three levels in a restored neoclassical building. On the ground floor there are two bars staging occasional contemporary exhibitions, while up top there's alternative music, another bar and plenty of space to dance.

In gay-friendly Gazi, **Hoxton**, *42 Voutadon*, is another hip bar with exposed concrete walls, sofas and electronic music in a former warehouse. Nearby, chi-chi **Villa Mercedes**, *Andronikou & Tzaferi 11, www.mercedes-club.gr*, has a restaurant serving creative Mediterranean cuisine in a courtyard garden, plus a dance floor with guest DJs – French house producer David Guetta has played here.

In summer, many of the big clubs in the centre are closed as they move out to the coastal strip from Kalamaki to Varkiza. They have surprise new beach locations each year, but names to look out for include **Envy** and **Akrotiri**. Some, such as **Balux**, double as swanky bathing establishments during the day, with waterside music and cocktails around sunset; the party mood sets in after midnight.

Travel essentials

Getting there

Athens International Airport (Eleftherios Venizelos), T210 353 0000, www.aia.gr, is 33 km northeast of the city. Express bus services to the city include the X95 to Syntagma (€3.20). Metro line 3 (blue) runs to Monastiraki (every 30 mins, €6) via Syntagma (25-30 mins). Alternatively, take the train to the main Larissis Station (every 15 mins 0550-2250, €6). A taxi will cost you about €30.

Getting around

Most of the main attractions lie within walking distance of one another in the city centre, parts of which are paved and pedestrian only. **Buses** are cheap and frequent but often crowded (ticket €1 valid for 1 hr 30 min travel on all forms of public transport, including bus, metro and tram). There are three **metro** lines (www.ametro.gr, ticket €1), the main nodal points being Monastiraki, Syntagma and Omonia. The green line is especially useful for reaching the port at Piraeus. Two **tramlines** (ticket €1) connect Syntagma in the city centre to the coast; ideal for reaching beaches in the Glyfada area. For further information contact OASA (Athens Public Transport Organization), T185, www.oasa.gr. Athens' taxis are among the cheapest in Europe, and Athenian taxi drivers among the most erratic. Taxis are no luxury – everyone takes them and it is quite normal to share a ride with other passengers going in a similar direction.

Tourist information

Greek National Tourism Organisation (GNTO), Tsocha 7, Ambelokipi, T210 870 7000, www.visitgreece.gr, has a walk-in visitors' centre at Amalias 26 (close to Syntagma), T210 331 0716, Mon-Fri 0900-1900, Sat and Sun 1000-1600; also at the airport, T210 353 0448, Mon-Fri 0900-1900, Sat and Sun 1000-1600. You might also check out the city of Athens's official visitors' website, www.breathtakingathens.com.

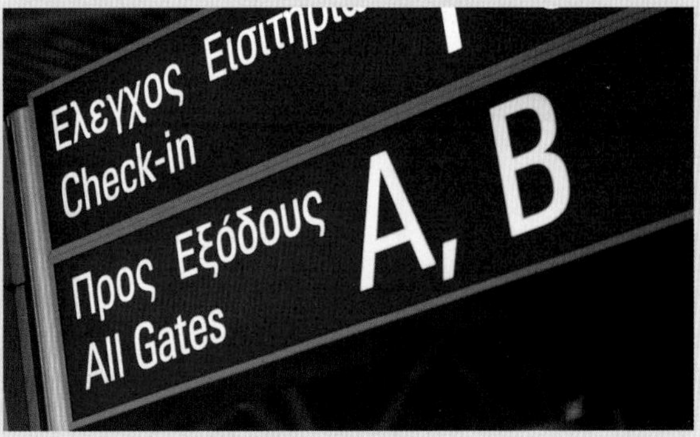

Ratings

Art and culture ☆☆☆☆
Eating ☆☆☆☆
Nightlife ☆☆☆☆☆
Outdoors ☆☆☆
Romance ☆☆☆
Shopping ☆☆☆☆☆
Sightseeing ☆☆☆☆
Value-for-money ☆☆
Overall city rating ☆☆☆☆☆

Barcelona

Barcelona dips its toes in the Mediterranean, and basks in year-round sunshine. Its skyline is indelibly marked by the visionary architect Antoni Gaudí, whose delirious buildings – resembling dragons, cliffs or gingerbread houses – seem to have magically erupted across the city. At its heart lie the ancient passages, gargoyles and ghostly spires of the old Gothic city, apparently untouched by modernity. Forget flamenco, sangría and other stock Spanish clichés, Barcelona is the proud capital of the ancient kingdom of Catalunya, with a distinct language and its own customs and traditions. These are staunchly preserved and exuberantly celebrated, with fire-spitting dragons, demons and giants.

Barcelona put itself on the map with the 1992 Olympics, which was the focus of a massive city-wide transformation. Its extraordinary collection of Modernista monuments were restored, and the seafront was entirely remodelled to become a glossy playground packed with beaches, marinas, and slick new hotels and apartment complexes. The transformation has continued apace, with a slew of celebrity starchitects from Richard Rogers to Jean Nouvel creating eye-catching new buildings which keep the city firmly in the spotlight. Add the fantastic and varied nightlife, discerning cuisine, a nose for the latest and best in fashion and design, and a population bent on having a good time and it's not surprising that Barcelona has become one of the most visited cities in Europe.

Catedral de la Seu.

Around the city

Les Rambles

Metro Plaça de Catalunya/Liceu, E3/D5.

The best introduction to Barcelona is a stroll down Les Rambles, the mile-long promenade that meanders down from Plaça de Catalunya to the port. It may look like one street but it is made up of five separate rambles, each with its own name and characteristics. Together they present an oddly appealing mixture of the picturesque and the tacky: street entertainers, fast-food outlets, crumbling theatres, whimsical Modernista mansions and pretty turn-of-the-century kiosks overflowing with flowers and songbirds. It's at its best early in the morning and on Sunday afternoons.

At a glance

Finding your way around the Catalan capital isn't difficult. The Old City (Ciutat Vella) is at its heart, divided by **Les Rambles** (Las Ramblas in Castilian), the city's famous tree-lined promenade, which meanders from Plaça de Catalunya down to the port. To the east of the Rambles is the shadowy, medieval maze of the **Barri Gòtic** – the Gothic Quarter – with the flamboyant cathedral at its centre. This has been the heart of the city since Roman times and still buzzes day and night. East of the Barri Gòtic is **El Born**, another medieval district, which has become the coolest neighbourhood in a city famed for its addiction to fashion. Packed with über-chic boutiques, designer stores and the trendiest restaurants, bars and clubs, it rubs shoulders with **Sant Pere**, still charmingly old-fashioned but rapidly rising in the style stakes. West of the Rambles, **El Raval** spreads south to the raffish old theatre district of Parallel. Once a notorious red-light district, the Raval was given a massive clean-up and the glossy Museum of Contemporary Art in the 1990s and now has hip galleries, clothes stores and bohemian bars.

When the city burst out of its medieval walls in the 19th century, the rich commissioned new mansions in the airy grid of the **Eixample** (meaning extension in Catalan). Gaudí and his Modernista colleagues had a ball, leaving a spectacular legacy which now comprises one of the greatest concentrations of art nouveau architecture in the world. Beyond Eixample is **Gràcia**, once independent from the city and still with a relaxed vibe of its own. On the outskirts is **Park Güell**, Gaudí's fairytale extravaganza with magical views over the city.

To the west of the centre, overlooking the sea, is **Montjuïc Hill**, from where you can enjoy panoramic views of the city. The Olympics left their mark here with a string of excellent sporting facilities. Close by is the Fundació Miró, dedicated to the Catalan master and, at the bottom of the hill, is MNAC.

The regenerated waterfront stretches northeast from the Columbus monument at the foot of the Rambles. **Port Vell**'s warehouses hold restaurants, museums and an entertainment complex, while the **Port Olímpic** is hugely popular, crammed with bars and seafood restaurants and flanked by sandy beaches. Beyond it lies Diagonal Mar, a new neighbourhood of towering hotels, office buildings and apartment blocks, with a shopping centre, a couple of parks, a marina and two new beaches. In contrast, the traditional dock-workers' neighbourhood of **Barceloneta** is more atmospheric, with tiny tapas bars tucked away in its depths. The city's outskirts are home to parks, funfairs and museums: the best views are from **Tibidabo**, Barcelona's funfair mountain and highest peak, reached by a rickety tram and funicular.

24 hours in the city

Get a feel for the city by strolling down the **Rambles**, with a stop at **La Boquería** market on the way to take in the sights, sounds and smells. Alternatively, have a coffee at **Café de l'Òpera** and watch the world go by. Then dive into the chaotic maze of the **Barri Gòtic**, where you'll find the Gothic cathedral (take the lift to the roof for fantastic views) and plenty of great shops, bars and restaurants. If you prefer something a bit edgier, head across the Rambles to **El Raval**, home to the excellent Museum of Contemporary Art (**MACBA**), and lots of vintage clothes stores and galleries. Have lunch on the terrace at **Plaça dels Àngels** and afterwards explore the elegant **Passeig de Gràcia**, home to the city's most emblematic Modernista buildings, including Gaudí's **Casa Batlló** and **La Pedrera**. An alternative would be to visit the extraordinary **Sagrada Família**. In the late afternoon head to the seafront for a stroll and a dip. In the evening, check out the fashionable bars and clubs of **El Born**, or take in a game at the legendary **Camp Nou** stadium – if you can get tickets.

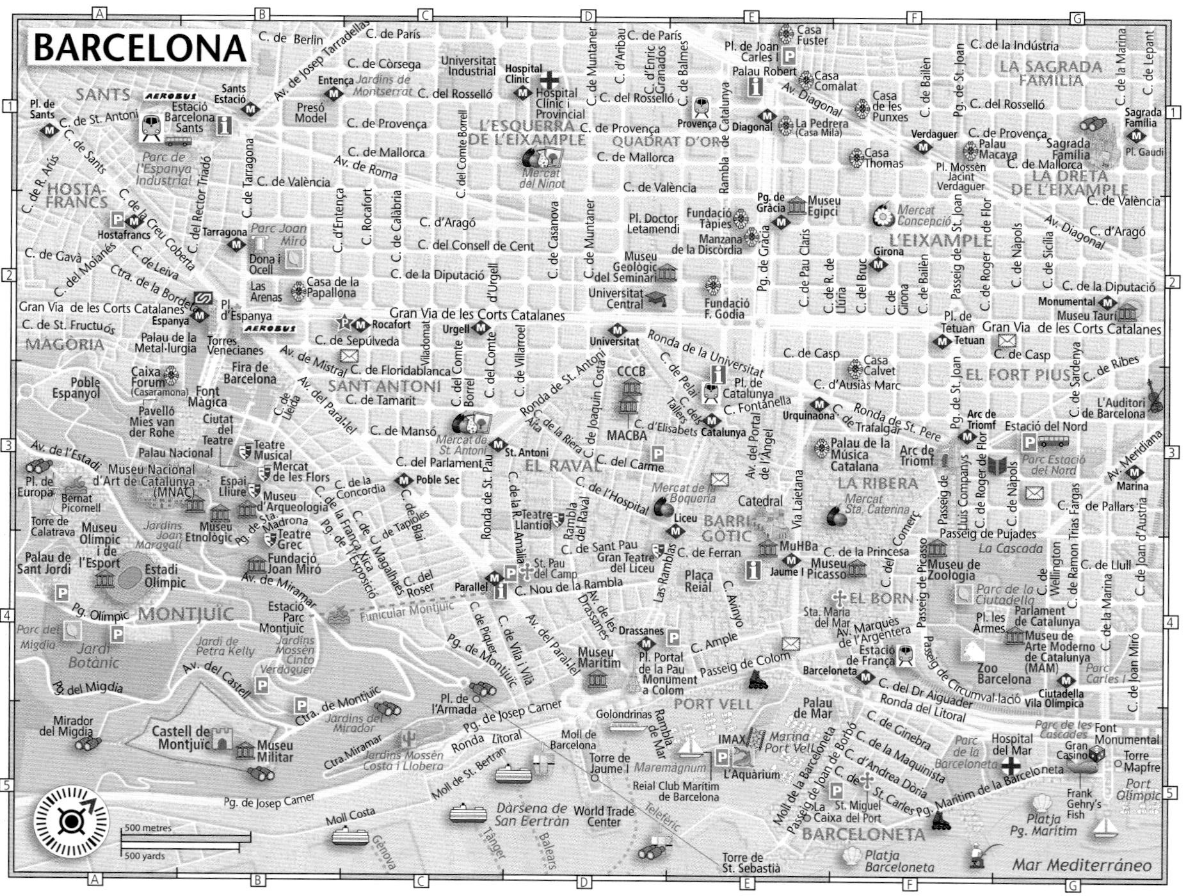
BARCELONA
SANTS
HOSTA-FRANCS
MAGÒRIA
SANT ANTONI
L'ESQUERRA DE L'EIXAMPLE
QUADRAT D'OR
L'EIXAMPLE
LA DRETA DE L'EIXAMPLE
LA SAGRADA FAMILIA
EL FORT PIUS
EL RAVAL
BARRI GÒTIC
LA RIBERA
EL BORN
BARCELONETA
PORT VELL
MONTJUÏC
Mar Mediterráneo
Dàrsena de San Bertràn
Estació Barcelona Sants
Parc de l'Espanya Industrial
Parc Joan Miró
Las Arenas
Fira de Barcelona
Font Màgica
Poble Espanyol
Museu Nacional d'Art de Catalunya (MNAC)
Estadi Olímpic
Jardí Botànic
Castell de Montjuïc
Fundació Joan Miró
Museu Militar
Mirador del Migdia
Universitat Central
MACBA
CCCB
Mercat de la Boqueria
Palau de la Música Catalana
Catedral
Plaça Reial
Monument a Colom
Museu Marítim
World Trade Center
Maremagnum
L'Aquàrium
IMAX
Palau de Mar
Parc de la Ciutadella
Zoo Barcelona
Arc de Triomf
Estació del Nord
Parc Estació del Nord
L'Auditori de Barcelona
Sagrada Família
Hospital Clínic i Provincial
La Pedrera (Casa Milà)
Fundació Tàpies
Manzana de la Discòrdia
Casa Fuster
Casa Comalat
Casa de les Punxes
Casa Thomas
Casa Calvet
Estació de França
Hospital del Mar
Torre Mapfre
Frank Gehry's Fish
Platja Barceloneta
Platja Pg. Marítim
Moll de Barcelona
Moll Costa
Torre de St. Sebastià
Torre de Jaume I
500 metres
500 yards

Halfway down is **La Boquería**, the city's irresistible market, with its wrought-iron roof and Modernista sign. Inside are piles of gleaming fruit, vegetables, fish and other local specialities, plus a liberal sprinkling of tiny bars for coffee or cava. Nearer the port is the city's 19th-century opera house, the **Gran Teatre del Liceu**.

Barri Gòtic

Metro Liceu, E3.

The Barri Gòtic has been the hub of the city for more than 2000 years. It's one of the best-preserved Gothic quarters in Europe, a dizzy maze of palaces, squares and churches piled on top of an original Roman settlement. The area is grubby, noisy, chaotic and packed with shops, bars and clubs. The streets are just as crowded at midnight as they are at midday.

Exploring the narrow alleyways, it's impossible to miss the **Catedral de la Seu** (Plaça Nova) with its dramatic spires and neo-Gothic façade. The cathedral dates back to the 13th century and the magnificent interior is suitably dim and hushed. A lift behind the altar swoops to the top for a bird's-eye view of huddled rooftops.

Close by, the imposing medieval façades of the **Generalitat** (Catalan Parliament) and the **Ajuntament** (City Council) face each other across the Plaça Sant Jaume. From here, shadowy passages, scattered with Roman ruins and ancient churches, lead to lovely squares such as Plaça Sant Just, Plaça Felip Neri and Plaça del Pi.

Above: Catedral de la Seu.
Opposite page: MACBA.

Museu d'Història de Barcelona (MuHBa)

Plaça del Rei s/n, T93 256 2100, www.museuhistoria.bcn.es.
Oct-May Tue-Sat 1000-1400 and 1600-1900, Sun 1000-2000; Jun-Sep Tue-Sat 1000-2000, Sun 1000-2000. €7 (includes entry to all seats of the museum, including the Museu-Monestir de Pedralbes, Museu-Casa Verdaguer and the Interpretation Centre for the Park Güell); free 1st Sat of month and Sun from 1500-2000. Metro Jaume I. Map E4.

This fascinating museum reveals the history of the city layer by layer. A glass lift glides down to the subterranean excavations of Roman Barcino, revealing 2000-year-old watchtowers, baths, temples, homes and businesses, discovered less than a century ago. Towards the site of the cathedral, the Roman ruins become interspersed with the remnants of fifth-century Visigothic churches. Stairs lead up to the medieval Royal Palace and the Golden Age of the city's history. The echoing Saló de Tinell, built in 1359, is a masterpiece of Catalan Gothic.

MACBA

Plaça dels Àngels, El Raval, T93 412 0810, www.macba.cat.
25 Sep-24 Jun Mon, Wed-Fri 1100-1930, Sat 1000-2000, Sun 1000-1500; 25 Jun-24 Sep Mon, Wed-Fri 1000-2000; Jul-Aug Thu until 2400, Sun 1000-1500. €7.50 for permanent collection; temporary exhibitions €6; €10 for one-year pass to permanent and temporary collections. Metro Universitat. Map D3.

Richard Meiers' huge, glassy home for MACBA was built in 1995 as a symbol of the city's urban renewal. The collection is loosely structured around three periods; the 1940s and 1950s are represented by members of the Dau al Set, a loose collection of writers and artists influenced by the Surrealists and Joan Miró. Work from the 1960s and 1970s shows the impact of popular and consumer culture on art, while the 1980s and early 1990s are marked by a return to painting and traditional forms, plus good

photographic pieces. Excellent temporary exhibitions focus on the latest digital and multimedia works. MACBA has a great bookshop and a café-bar in the spacious square that it shares with the **CCCB** (Centre of Contemporary Culture).

Passeig de Gràcia

Metro Passeig de Gràcia, E1/E2/E3.

At the heart of the Eixample is this glossy boulevard of chic boutiques, neoclassical office buildings and Modernista mansions. The most famous stretch is the **Mansana de la Discòrdia** ('block of discord') between Carrer Consell de Cent and Carrer d'Aragó, where three Modernista masterpieces nudge up against each other: **Casa Lleó i Morera**, transformed by Domènech i Montaner in 1902; **Casa Amatller** (info on guided visits at www.amatller.org), designed by Puig i Cadafalch as a polychrome fairytale castle; and **Casa Batlló**, *T93 216 03 06, www.casabatllo.es, daily 0900-2000, €17.80*, by Antoni Gaudí. Covered with shimmering trencadis (broken tiles) and culminating in a scaly roof, it gleams like an undersea dragon. The interior is soft and undulating, like whipped ice cream.

La Pedrera

C Provença 261-265, T90 240 0973, www.caixacatalunya.es.
Daily Nov-Feb 0900–1830, last admission 1800; Mar-Oct 0900-2000, last admission 1930; €11, temporary exhibitions usually free, audioguides €4. Metro Diagonal. Map E1.

Best of the rest

Santa María del Mar
Pl de Santa María del Mar, El Born, D. Metro Jaume I.
This lovely 14th-century church is one of the purest examples of Catalan Gothic.

Museu Picasso
C Montcada 15-23, El Born, www.museupicasso.bcn.es, E. Closed Mon. €9, including temporary exhibitions, or €5.80 just for temporary exhibitions. Free first Sun of month, and every Sun from 1500–2000. Metro Jaume I.
Very popular collection, which is dominated by early works created in Barcelona.

Zoo de Barcelona
Parc de la Ciutadella, El Born, www.zoobarcelona.com. Open daily. Metro Barceloneta. Adults €16.15, kids €9.65, free under 3.
The city zoo is fantastic for kids, with everything from elephants to tigers to dolphin shows, plus a petting zoo for the littlest kids. The cramped spaces inhabited by the big cats may cause some pangs, but remodelling is underway.

CCCB
C Montalegre 5, El Raval, www.cccb.org, W. Closed Mon. Admission €4.50, free first Wed of month, Thu from 2000–2200, and Sun from 1500–2000. Metro Universitat.
Hosts eclectic exhibitions on contemporary culture not covered by MACBA.

Drassanes Reials
Av Drassanes s/n, www.mmb.cat, S. Daily. €6. Metro Drassanes.
Currently under refurbishment, can only see the temporary exhibitions and the restored 1920s clipper, the Santa Eulalia, moored nearby at the Port Vell.

Museu FC Barcelona
Camp Nou, www.fcbarcelona.cat. €19 including tour, €15.50 for children 6-13. Metro Collblanc.
Football paraphernalia plus a guided tour of the stadium.

Tibidabo
Mar-Sep only. FGC to Av Tibidabo, then tram Blau, then funicular.
The mountain has a great old-fashioned funfair at its summit and breathtaking views across the city.

Casa Milà, better known as La Pedrera (the Stone Quarry), rises like a cream cliff draped with wrought-iron balconies. There's a recreation of a 1911 apartment on the first floor, with many original fittings. The attic houses **L'Espai Gaudí**, a museum of the architect's life and work in the city, but the climax of a visit is the sinuous rooftop terrace, studded with chimneys, air vents and stairwells disguised as extraordinary bulbous crosses and plump *trencadí*-covered towers. Enjoy a drink and live music on the rooftop on summer weekends.

La Sagrada Família

C Mallorca 401, Eixample, T93 080 414, www.sagradafamilia.cat.
Oct-Mar daily 0900-1800; Apr-Sep daily 0900-2000. €12, €16 with audioguide. Guided visits also available in Spanish, Catalan and English €4. Metro Sagrada Família. Map G1.

Gaudí's unfinished masterpiece, the Expiatory Temple of the Holy Family, is the most emblematic and controversial monument in Barcelona. The towers measure almost 100 m and the central spire, when finished, will soar 180 m into the sky. The temple is set for completion in 2026, the anniversary of Gaudí's death. In November 2010, the temple was consecrated by Pope Benedict XVI in the presence of the Spanish King and Queen. Although construction is a long way from complete, the nave has now been covered, an organ installed, and mass is said daily.

Gaudí designed three façades for the temple but only the Nativity façade was completed by the time of his death in 1926. The Passion façade on the other side of the church is grim and lifeless in comparison. Inside, work has begun on the construction of four huge columns to support the enormous domed roof.

There's a lift up the towers (€2.50); brave visitors can climb even higher, before descending via the vertiginous spiral staircase. Underneath, the crypt contains Gaudí's tomb and an interactive museum.

La Sagrada Família

MNAC

Palau Nacional, Montjuïc , T93 622 0360, www.mnac.cat.
Tue-Sat 1000-1900, Sun 1000-1430. €8.50, temporary exhibitions prices vary, free first Sun of the month. Metro Espanya. Map A3.

Housed in the dour Palau Nacional on Montjuïc is a magnificent collection of the best of Catalan art. The highlight is the array of spellbinding Romanesque murals gathered from Catalan churches and displayed on reconstructed church interiors. The Gothic collection reflects Catalunya's glory years from the 13th to the 15th centuries, with rooms devoted to the three outstanding painters of the time: Bernat Martorell, Lluís Dalmau and Jaume Huguet. The Thyssen bequest, with roughly a hundred masterpieces including works by Fra Angelico, Raphael, Zurbarán and others, has been housed here since 2004. There is also an extensive collection of 19th-century art and sculpture, including wonderful Modernista furniture and objets d'art.

Below MNAC, at the top of Avenida María Cristina, is the **Font Màgica**, *Pl de Carles Buïgas, May-Sep Thu-Sun 2000-2330, Oct and Nov Fri and Sat 1900-2100, free*, a fountain from 1929 that puts on a fabulous sound and light show; it's gloriously tacky, yet undeniably magical.

Fundació Miró

Parc de Montjuïc s/n, T93 443 9470, www.bcn.fjmiro.es.
Oct-Jun Tue-Sat 1000-1900 (Thu until 2130), Sun 1000-1430; Jul-Aug Tue-Sat 1000-2000 (Thu until 2130). €8.50, temporary exhibitions €4. Metro Espanya , then bus 50 or 55, or funicular from Parallel. Map B4.

The fabulous Fundació Miró is set in a white, light-drenched building by Josep Lluís Sert on Montjuïc. It contains the most important and comprehensive gathering of Miró's works in the world, from his early experiments with Cubism and Fauvism through to his later paintings, which are increasingly gestural and impulsive. There are spectacular sculptures from the 1960s and 1970s; some are displayed on the rooftop sculpture terrace.

Modernisme

The great rediscovery and celebration of Catalunya's cultural identity, known as the Renaixença (Renaissance), began in the 1850s. Architecture, literature, painting, sculpture, furniture, craft and design were galvanized by the new spirit of cultural and political optimism. This arts movement came to be known as *Modernisme* and was partly influenced by the international art nouveau and Jugenstil movements. When the medieval city walls were torn down in 1854, Ildefons Cerdà's airy grid-shaped extension (Eixample in Catalan) was constructed, giving the most influential architects of the day the chance to display their originality and virtuosity. Three names stand out: Antoni Gaudí i Cornet, Lluis Domènech i Montaner and Josep Puig i Cadafalch. You can choose your favourite in the Mansana de la Discòrdia (see page 29). The list of Modernista monuments in Barcelona is breathtakingly long; highlights include Gaudí's Casa Batlló, La Pedrera, Park Güell and the Sagrada Família; Montaner's Palau de la Música Catalana; and Puig i Cadafalch's Casa Amatller.

Park Güell

C Olot 7, T93 130 488.
Nov-Feb daily 1000-1800; Mar and Oct daily 1000-1900; Apr and Sep daily 1000-2000; May-Aug daily 1000-2100. Free. Metro Lesseps, then a (signposted) 10-min walk, or bus 24. Off map.

The Park Güell is perhaps the most delightful of Gaudí's visionary creations. Two fairytale pavilions guard the entrance (one houses an exhibition, *T93 285 6899, Mon-Fri 1100-1500, €2*), from where stairs sweep up past the famous multi- coloured salamander, which has become one of Barcelona's best-known and best-loved symbols. The steps culminate in the **Sala Hipóstila**, also known as the Hall of a Hundred Columns because of the thick Doric columns which support its undulating roof. Gaudí's talented collaborator, the architect and mosaicist Josep Maria Jujol, was given free reign to colour the vaulted ceiling with elaborate whimsy; look carefully and you'll see the designs are made of smashed china, ceramic dolls' heads, wine glasses and old bottles. Above the hall is the main square with its snaking bench, thickly encrusted with *trencadís*, like the scales of a monstrous dragon. Surrounding it are porticoes and viaducts, made from unworked stone, which hug the slopes of the hillside for more than 3 km. The **Centre d'Interpretació del Park Güell**, in one of the pavilions, is open daily 1100–1500 and is free. Info at www.muhba.cat.

Just off the main esplanade is the **Casa Museu Gaudí** (*T93 219 3811, €5.50, combined admission ticket with Sagrada Família available, info at www.sagradafamilia.cat*), housed in the small Torre Rosa, Gaudí's home for the last years of his life.

Seafront

Metro Barceloneta/Ciutadella-Vila Olímpica. Map E4/G5.

Barcelona's seafront was the main focus of Olympic redevelopment in the early 1990s. A boardwalk runs from the foot of the Rambles to the glittering **Port Vell** (Old Port) development which includes a marina, restaurants, shopping centre, IMAX and the impressive **Aquàrium** (€15). To the northeast is the old fishermen's neighbourhood of **Barceloneta**, a district of narrow streets and traditional seafood bars. From here the **Telèferic** (€9) begins its vertiginous journey over the harbour to Montjuïc. Beyond is the **Port Olímpic**, marked by Frank Gehry's shimmering copper fish.

Travel essentials

Getting there

Barcelona International Airport is 12 km south of the city (flights T93 298 3838, www.aena.es). International airlines use the new Terminal 1 and Terminal 2 (formerly terminals A and B, now called T2A and T2B). The **airport train** (€2.35) runs from outside Terminal 2 to Estació de Sants and Passeig de Gràcia every 30 mins, 0542-2338. The **Aerobús** (take the A1 for Terminal 1, runs every 5–10mins; A2 for Terminal 2, runs 10–20mins; €5.05 single, €8.75 return, under 4s free, www.aerobusbcn.com) runs from Plaça de Catalunya, via the Plaça d'Espanya 0530-2330. Taxis cost up to €25 to the centre, or more after 2200 and at weekends (supplements for luggage). **Estació de Sants** (metro Sants) is the main train station, although sleeper trains to/from Paris use Estació de França (metro Barceloneta). Many trains also stop at **Passeig de Gràcia**. For timetables and prices: T902 320 320, www.renfe.es.

Getting around

The Old City and Eixample, north of Plaça de Catalunya, are easy to walk around. The Sagrada Família and Park Güell need a short bus or metro ride; Montjuïc and Tibidabo are reached by cable car or funicular. Public transport is cheap and efficient; the main hub is Plaça de Catalunya. Eight **metro** lines run Mon-Thu 0500-2400, Fri 0500-0200, Sat 24 hours, Sun 0500-2300. **Buses** run Mon-Sat 0600-2230 (less frequently Sun), and nightbuses (N) 2230-0400. Gràcia and Tibidabo are served by **FGC** train (T93 205 1515, www.fgc.net). A single bus or metro ticket costs €1.40; a T-Dia (€6) allows unlimited journeys for 1 day; a T-10 (€7.95), which is the most useful for visitors, allows 10 trips and can be shared. For maps and information, visit the **TMB** office under Plaça Universitat (T93-318 7074, www.tmb.net). There's a taxi stand on Plaça de Catalunya, opposite the main tourist office, or call **Barnataxi**, T93 322 2222, or **Fono-Taxi**, T93 300 1100.

Tourist information

The main office is at Plaça de Catalunya, T93 385 3834 (call centre, Mon-Fri 0800–2000), daily 0900-2100. It books hotel rooms and tours and sells discount cards and maps. It also offers themed walking tours (€12.50-€19, 10% discount if bought online). There are branches at Plaça Sant Jaume, Estació de Sants and the airport. See www.barcelonaturisme.com and www.bcn.es. The **Barcelona Card** (€27/€33/€37.50/€44 for 2–5 days, www.barcelonacard.com) gives unlimited travel by public transport plus discounts at shops, restaurants and major museums. The hop-on/hop-off **Bus Turístic** (1 day €22, 2 days €29, www.barcelonabusturistic.cat) tours the sights every 20 mins.

Sleeping

Barcelona is one of the most popular weekend destinations in Europe and, although the number of beds has increased dramatically, you should always book as early as possible and never just turn up and hope to find somewhere to stay. Book through an agent or check out online deals at www.barcelonahotels.com and www.barcelona-online.com.

Most of the cheaper places are in the Old City (Barri Gòtic, El Born and El Raval); these are also the noisiest places to stay. The smartest (and quietest) places are generally concentrated in the Eixample. Hotels are ranked with one to five stars; pensiones have fewer facilities and are ranked with one to three stars. Note that a modest hotel may be known as a 'hostal'; this is not the same as a 'hostel', which will have dormitory accommodation.

Arts Barcelona €€€
C Marina 19-21, Vila Olímpica, T93 221 1000, www.hotelartsbarcelona.com. Metro Ciutadella-Vila Olímpica.
One of the city's most glamorous hotels, the Arts occupies one of the enormous glassy towers at the entrance to the Port Olímpic. It was inaugurated in 1992 and offers 33 floors of unbridled luxury, including indoor and outdoor pools, a fine restaurant, a piano bar overlooking the hotel gardens and the sea, a sauna, a gym and a beauty centre.

Hotel W €€€-€€
Plaça de la Rosa dels Vents 1, T93 295 2800, www.w-barcelona.com. Metro Barceloneta. Rooms €295-495.
The newest addition to the seafront, this huge sail-shaped hotel was designed by Ricardo Bofill and is a favourite with international fashionistas. Restaurants and bars include the panoramic Eclipse bar on the 26th floor, and other amenities include an infinity pool overlooking the beach and a Bliss spa.

Actual €€
C Rosselló 238, Eixample, T93 552 0550, www.hotelactual.com. Metro Diagonal.
On the same block as La Pedrera, Actual is decorated in the slickest minimalist style, with plenty of white marble and dark wood. The rooms are small but impeccably furnished with crisp white fabrics and ultra-modern bathrooms. It also offers triple rooms, perfect for families. There are often special offers on its website.

Banys Orientals €€
C Argentería 37, El Born, T93 269 8490, www.hotelbanysorientals.com. Metro Jaume I.
A chic boutique-style hotel close to the Museu Picasso. Rooms are a little small, but are furnished with sleek modern fabrics. A nearby annexe offers larger suites for slightly more.

Bonic Guesthouse €€-€
C/Josep Anselm Clavé 9, Barri Gòtic, T62 605 3434, www.bonic-barcelona.com. Rooms €90-95.
Perfectly located just off the Rambla, with just six stylishly decorated rooms, this sweet little guesthouse is run by charming hosts. Thoughtful extras include free tea and coffee, dressing gowns in each room, and free Wi-Fi. The rooms share three spotless bathrooms.

Gat Raval €
C Joaquín Costa 44, El Raval, T93 481 6670, www.gataccommodation.com. Metro Universitat.
A hip *hostal* painted in black, white and lime green on one of the Raval's funkiest streets. The bright, modern rooms are clean and well equipped. It also runs the slightly more upmarket Gat Xino.

Peninsular €
C de Sant Pau 34-36, El Raval, T93 302 3138. Metro Liceu.
One of the best-value options is set in an old convent. There's a charming interior patio crammed with trailing plants and Modernista detailing. The rooms are plain and basic but perfectly comfortable.

Eating

Catalan dishes are simple and rely on fresh local ingredients. Meat and fish are often grilled or cooked slowly in the oven (*al forn*). There are some delicious vegetable dishes, like *escalivada*, a salad of roasted aubergine, peppers and onions. Rice dishes are also popular. Wash it all down with Catalan wine, sparkling cava or local Estrella beer. Breakfast is usually a milky coffee (*café amb llet/café con leche*) and a pastry. Lunch is taken seriously and eaten around 1400, when many restaurants offer a fixed-price two-course menu including a drink. Tapas are not as much of a tradition here as in other parts of Spain, but there are plenty of old-fashioned bars near the harbour that offer fresh seafood versions. Dinner is rarely eaten before 2100 and tends to be lighter than the midday meal.

Breakfast

El Café de l'Òpera €

Les Rambles 74. Metro Liceu.

Opposite the Liceu Opera House, this is the perfect café for people-watching. Original Modernista fittings and an old-world ambience.

La Pallaresa €

C Petritxol 11, Barri Gòtic. Metro Liceu.

This is where to get your *chocolate con churros* (thick hot chocolate with fried dough strips) in the morning – locals swear it's the best *xocolatería* in the city.

Lunch

Cinc Sentits €€€

C/Aribau 58, T93 323 9490, www.cincsentits.com, Eixample. Metro Passeig de Gràcia or Universitat.

Canadian-Catalan chef Jordi Artal has been recognised with a Michelin star, but the set menus (including a €30 set lunch) at his elegant restaurant make it affordable for a splurge. Imaginative Catalan cuisine prepared with superb locally sourced produce is the key to his success. Book well in advance.

Kaiku €€

Plaça del Mar 1, T93 221 9082. Metro Barceloneta.

It's easy to pass this unassuming restaurant without giving it a second glance, but that would be a mistake: not only does it make the best rice dishes in town (try the *arròs del xef*, made with smoked rice), but daily specials might include such exotic delights as sea anemones in a light tempura. Note that it's only open at lunchtimes.

Bar Pinotxo €

Mercat de la Boquería 66-67, Les Rambles. Closed Sun. Metro Liceu.

The market's best-loved counter bar, serving excellent, freshly prepared food; try the tortilla with artichokes.

Pla dels Àngels €

C Ferlandina 23, El Raval, T93 329 4047. Metro Universitat.

This large, popular restaurant opposite MACBA has bright, modern decor and a summer terrace. It serves extremely well-priced salads, meats and pastas, plus excellent wine.

Dinner

Omm €€€

C/Rosselló 265, T93 445 4000, www.hotelomm.es, Eixample. Metro Diagonal.

A very fashionable restaurant in the über-chic Hotel Omm, this is overseen by the much lauded Roca brothers and as such substance triumphs over style. Expect extraordinary contemporary cuisine accompanied by one of the finest wine lists in the city.

Cal Pep €€

Plaça Olles 8, El Born, T93 310 7961. Metro Barceloneta.

A classic: there's a smart brick-lined dining area at the back but it's more entertaining to perch at the bar, as Pepe dishes up tempting treats and holds court at the same time. Reservations essential.

Arc Café €

C/d'en Carabassa 19, Barri Gòtic, T93 302 5204, www.arccafe.com. Metro Drassanes or Jaume I.

A delightful little stone-walled café hidden down a narrow Gothic street, this serves delicious international food from houmous to carpaccios and from tartiflette to curry. Great home-made desserts, too.

Nightlife

To find out what's on, check the listings guide *Guía del Ocio*, *B-Guided* magazine or look out for flyers. Up-to-date information is also provided at www.bcn.es.

Bars and clubs

Barcelona is a popular stop on the international DJ circuit, with cutting- edge clubs (*discotecas*) playing the very latest tunes. Some of the best clubs can be found on **Carrer Nou de Francesc** in the Barri Gòtic and along the painfully hip **Passeig del Born** in El Born. There are also several excellent bars in the Ciutat Vella, where you can enjoy a mellow copa on a candlelit terrace. **El Raval** has a concentration of funky bohemian clubs as well as louche bars where you can sip absinthe in timeless surroundings. Bigger clubs, catering for the frenetic summer party crowd, can be found on **Montjuïc** and around the **Port Olímpic**, while gay clubs are clustered in the so-called **Gaixample**, east of Passeig del Gràcia.

Contemporary music

There are plenty of live music venues. Popular clubs like **Jamboree** (Plaça Reial 17, Barri Gòtic) and **Luz de Gas** (Muntaner 246, Gràcia) offer a mixed bag of musical styles. Visit **Harlem Jazz Club** (Comtessa de Sobradiel 8, Barri Gòtic) for the city's jazz scene. Latin and African music are also popular.

For lovers of electronica, the **Sónar** (www.sonar.es) summer festival of multimedia music and art is fantastic. The **BAM** festival in Sep is another great time to catch alternative sounds.

Classical music and theatre

Enjoy opera at the beautiful **Gran Teatre de Liceu**, *La Rambla 51-59, T93 485 9900, www.liceubarcelona.cat*, or a rousing performance by Orfeó Català in the stunning Modernista surroundings of the **Palau de la Música**, *C Sant Francesc de Paula 2, Sant Pere, T93 295 7200, www.palaumusica.org*. **Ciutat del Teatre** complex, *Plaça Margarida Xirgu, Montjuïc*, holds a dramatic arts museum and several performance spaces, including the celebrated **Teatre Lliure**, *T93 228 9747, www.teatrelliure.com*. In Jun and Jul, see the renowned **Festival de Barcelona Grec**, *www.barcelonafestival.com*.

Shop till you drop

The designer shop **Galleries Vinçon** on the Passeig de Gràcia used to have the slogan 'I shop therefore I am' emblazoned across its packaging and this seems to be the attitude of many of the city's residents, for Barcelona has more shops per capita than anywhere else in Europe. Best buys are leather, cutting-edge fashion, homewares and local wines and food. Head to **Barri Gòtic** for quirky one-off shops, **Carrer Portaferrissa** for fashion chains, **El Raval** for vintage clothes and music and **El Born** for unusual fashion and interior design shops (on and around Passeig del Born). For international fashion, designer furnishings and art galleries head to **Passeig de Gràcia** and **Diagonal**, in Eixample.

Ratings

Art and culture ☆☆☆
Eating ☆☆☆☆
Nightlife ☆☆☆
Outdoors ☆☆☆
Romance ☆
Shopping ☆
Sightseeing ☆☆
Value-for-money ☆☆☆
Overall city rating ☆☆☆

Berlin

The capital of Germany since 1999, Berlin is a city reborn – a phoenix risen from the flames of Second World War destruction and Cold War division. Arguably the hippest European capital, it attracts some of the most progressive fashionistas, artists and musicians from all over the world. The city may have needed a long period in rehab but it is now confident enough to woo British architects, Italian designers and Polish restorers to its burgeoning multinational community. These days Babylonian mosaics, French bakeries and Norman Foster creations are comfortably integrated into the buildings of Schinkel and the operas of Wagner. Anything goes in Berlin, from illegal parties held in derelict warehouses to city beaches and an open-air swimming pool on the river Spree.

Berlin street.

At a glance

Mitte, former bohemian hub of East Berlin, is now the heart of the reunified capital and, along with its more conservative West Berlin neighbour, Tiergarten, is the focus of most visitors' attention. Here, the Brandenburg Gate and the Reichstag stand amid a rash of new government buildings and sprawling acres of woodland, grass and lakes, making it clear that Berlin is, once again, the capital of Germany. Friedrichstrasse is the main artery dividing the eastern and western halves of the city. About 15 minutes' walk east lies Museum Island, where you will find the city's most important museums, while Potsdamer Platz, south of the Brandenburg Gate, shows off Berlin's ultra-modern colours. Northeast of Mitte, Prenzlauerberg has become the hip place to live and play since the Wall came down. Friedrichshain, east of Mitte, is less attractive but still on the up. Kreuzberg, south of Mitte, in former West Berlin, has a large Turkish population and, like its more chichi neighbour Schöneberg, remains a centre for the gay community. West of Tiergarten, Charlottenburg, once a showcase of capitalism, now competes with Mitte and Prenzlauerberg.

24 hours in the city

Visit the Reichstag first thing (open 0800-2400) and climb up to the cupola for the views. Then head to the Adlon Hotel for coffee, pausing to reflect at the Brandenburg Gate. Afterwards, head east along Unter den Linden as far as Bebelplatz (where the 1933 book burnings took place) and cross the road to spend an hour or two in the newly restored Deutsches Historisches Museum. Cross the river onto Museum Island and visit the outstanding Pergamon Museum, before having a late lunch. (Try the tasty snacks from the riverside sausage stands.) Walk through the Lustgarten, across the Schlossplatz and then cross the river again, continuing west to the Gendarmenmarkt, where there may be an afternoon concert in one of the cathedrals. On nearby Friedrichstrasse, with its stylish shops, is the museum commemorating Checkpoint Charlie. From here, following the fragment of the Wall west, it is possible to reach the futuristic-looking Potsdamer Platz for a spot of dinner. Later, take a tour of the über-chic bars and cafés around Mitte.

Brandenburg Gate

S-Bahn Unter den Linden. Map C2.

Built in 1791, Berlin's most famous icon has witnessed the highs and lows of German history. Left isolated by the construction of the Berlin Wall in 1961, the gate became the emblematic backdrop to that epoch-altering event on 9 November 1989 when the border was opened and young people from both sides of the city rushed forward to scale the defining symbol of the Cold War.

On the east side of the gate, Pariser Platz has been transformed from a concrete wilderness into an elegant diplomatic and financial centre and regained its pre-war status as one of the city's most prestigious addresses. The French embassy has been rebuilt on the north side, while opposite is the newly reopened **Academy of Arts**, *Pariser Platz 4, www.adk.de*. This Günther Behnisch building houses the private archives of cultural greats such as Bertolt Brecht and Günter Grass, as well as promoting German arts through exhibitions and performances. Next to the Academy is the unmissable DZ ank building, designed by Frank Gehry. Inside is an enormous sculpture whose twists and turns provide a startling contrast with the bank's façade.

South of Pariser Platz, 150m from the Brandenburg Gate, is the **Memorial to the murdered Jews**, *Wilhelmstr 22-23, information centre Tue-Sun 1000-2000 (last entrance 1915)*. Completed in May 2005, this 'forest of stelae', represents the gravestones of Jews murdered under the Nazi regime. It initially provoked much controversy due to its bleak design and the exclusion of graves for non-Jewish victims. However, the memorial, designed by Peter Eisenman, now elicits a positive response from most Berliners.

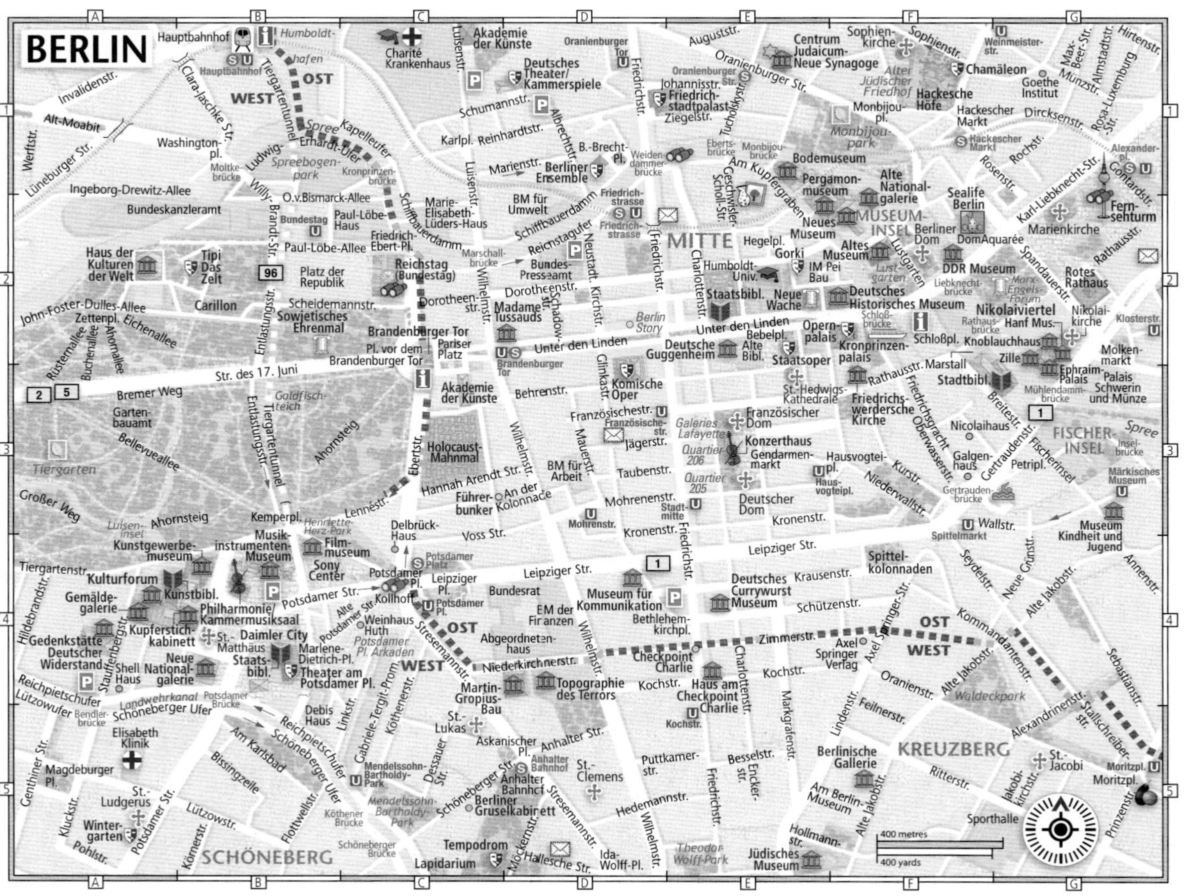

BERLIN
MITTE
MUSEUMS-INSEL
FISCHER-INSEL
KREUZBERG
SCHÖNEBERG
OST
WEST
Tiergarten
Hauptbahnhof
Charité Krankenhaus
Akademie der Künste
Deutsches Theater/ Kammerspiele
Berliner Ensemble
BM für Umwelt
Reichstag (Bundestag)
Brandenburger Tor
Pariser Platz
Holocaust-Mahnmal
Madame Tussauds
Bundes-Presseamt
Komische Oper
Deutsche Guggenheim
Staatsbibl.
Humboldt-Univ.
Neue Wache
Gorki
IM Pei Bau
Altes Museum
Neues Museum
Pergamon-museum
Bodemuseum
Alte National-galerie
Berliner Dom
Lustgarten
Deutsches Historisches Museum
Opern-palais
Kronprinzen-palais
Staatsoper
St.-Hedwigs-Kathedrale
Friedrichs-werdersche Kirche
Französischer Dom
Konzerthaus
Gendarmen-markt
Deutscher Dom
Centrum Judaicum-Neue Synagoge
Sophien-kirche
Hackesche Höfe
Hackescher Markt
Sealife Berlin
DomAquarée
DDR Museum
Nikolaiviertel
Rotes Rathaus
Marienkirche
Fern-sehturm
Alexander-pl.
Ephraim-Palais
Palais Schwerin und Münze
Märkisches Museum
Museum Kindheit und Jugend
Spittel-kolonnaden
Deutsches Currywurst Museum
Museum für Kommunikation
Checkpoint Charlie
Haus am Checkpoint Charlie
Axel Springer Verlag
Berlinische Galerie
Jüdisches Museum
Topographie des Terrors
Martin-Gropius-Bau
Abgeordneten-haus
Bundesrat
Anhalter Bahnhof
Tempodrom
Berliner Gruselkabinett
Potsdamer Pl.
Leipziger Pl.
Sony Center
Filmmuseum
Musikinstrumenten-Museum
Philharmonie/ Kammermusiksaal
Kulturforum
Kunstbibl.
Kupferstich-kabinett
Gemälde-galerie
Neue National-galerie
Staats-bibl.
St.-Matthäus
Daimler City
Gedenkstätte Deutscher Widerstand
Shell Haus
Haus der Kulturen der Welt
Tipi Das Zelt
Carillon
Sowjetisches Ehrenmal
Platz der Republik
Paul-Löbe-Haus
Bundeskanzleramt
Str. des 17. Juni
Unter den Linden
Friedrichstr.
Leipziger Str.
Wilhelmstr.
Tiergartentunnel
Spree
400 metres
400 yards

Reichstag

Ebertstr.
Daily 0800-2100 (last entry 2200). Free.
S-Bahn Unter den Linden. Map C2.

The imposing late-ninth-century Reichstag building has been restored to its former glory and is once again at the heart of German political life and is open to the public. The undoubted highlight is Norman Foster's outlandish glass dome. The views from the top are not to be missed, though the long queues certainly are (get there early or visit at night to avoid them).

The Reichstag is one of many government buildings along the Spree and backs onto Tiergarten Park. This area has seen more redevelopment than most but, despite pressure from developers, the park's wide open spaces, lakes and woods have not been compromised. North of Tiergarten is Hamburger Bahnhof, *Invalidenstr 50, www.hamburgerbahnhof.de, Tue-Fri 1000-1800, Sat 1100-2000, Sun 1100-1800, €12, S-Bahn Lehrter Bahnhof.* Trains stopped running here in the 19th century, replaced in the late 1980s by challenging artworks, including pieces by Joseph Beuys.

Potsdamer Platz

S-Bahn Potsdamer Platzk. Map C4.

Once as desolate as Pariser Platz due to its proximity to the Wall, Potsdamer Platz, at the southeastern corner of Tiergarten park, is now almost a town in its own right; a new Manhattan of skyscrapers, cinemas, embassies and museums, including the Museum für Film und Fernsehen, *Potsdamer Str 2, T030-300 9030, www.filmmuseum-berlin.de, A. Tue-Sun 1000-1800, Thu 1000-2000, €6.* Just to the west lies the Kulturforum, which encompasses not only the Berlin Philharmonie but also one of the world's most prestigious art collections at the Gemäldegallerie, *www.smb.spk-berlin.de. Tue, Wed, Fri-Sun 1000-1800, Thu 1000-2200*, €8, and international and German paintings from the 20th century at the Neue Nationalgalerie, *www.smb.spk-berlin.de. Tue, Wed, Fri 1000-1800, Thu 1000-2200, Sat, Sun 1100-1800, €8.*

Pride

Berlin has welcomed the gay scene since the 'roaring twenties' when Marlene Dietrich and Christopher Isherwood lived and entertained around Nollendorfplatz in Schöneberg. Hitler's rise to power in 1933 and his deportation of gay people to the camps put a stop to this (outside Nollendorfplatz U-bahn station there is a plaque to commemorate the victims). But now, with an openly gay mayor, the city's gay and lesbian scene is more vibrant than ever. Some areas are more gay than others, but around the centre it's all quite mixed, with lots of bars and clubs catering to a gay and straight crowd. Kreuzberg has a very liberal feel to it, whereas Nollendorfplatz is more hardcore. Friedrichshain and Prenzlauerberg are the new kids on the block and, as a result, have quite an experimental feel to them. Christopher Street Day, www.csd-berlin.de, which takes place every summer, is Berlin's most flamboyant festival. Loud and outrageous, this gay and lesbian parade was named after the New York Stonewall riots of 1969 and is not one for the faint-hearted.

Unter den Linden

S-Bahn Unter den Linden. Map D3/E2.

Unter den Linden ('Beneath the Lime Trees') runs east from the Brandenburg Gate and Pariser Platz, the trees in the centre now making a congenial pedestrian precinct between the two wide traffic lanes on either side. On the south side stands the Russian Embassy, an excellent example of social realism but now incongruous in a Berlin eager to forget its links with the former USSR. At the eastern end of Unter den Linden is the revamped **Deutsches Historisches Museum**, *www.dhm.de, daily 1000-1800, €2, U-Bahn Französischestr*, whose permanent exhibition covers 2000 years of German history through authentic objects and multimedia displays. Temporary exhibitions are staged in a new wing designed by I M Pei.

Gendarmenmarkt

U-Bahn Stadtmitte. Map E3.

If there is still a tendency to judge Germany by the worst periods of its history, a stop in Gendarmenmarkt will show the country at its most liberal. It became the centre of a French community around 1700 when Prussia gave refuge to 6000 Huguenots. On the north side, the Französischer Dom (French Cathedral), now home to the **Huguenot Museum**, *Tue-Sat 1200- 1700, Sun 1100-1700, €2*, dates from this time, as does the similarly proportioned **Deutscher Dom**, *May-Sep Tue-Sun 1000-1900, Oct-Apr Tue-Sun 1000-1800*, on the south side. The Konzerthaus, or Schauspielhaus, in the centre of the square, was one of the earliest buildings designed by the prolific architect, Karl Friedrich Schinkel (1781-1841).

Museum Island

T030 2090 5577, www.smb.museum.
Fri-Wed 1000-1800, Thu 1000-2200; Alte Nationalgalerie closed Mon. One museum €8; Museuminsel €12; free first Sun in the month. S-Bahn Hackescher Markt. Map F2.

Museum Island is an extraordinary collection of first-rate galleries in the middle of the Spree. Recognized by UNESCO as a World Cultural Heritage Site, the complex is currently undergoing a major restoration and redevelopment project that will unite all five buildings and their disparate collections by 2015.

The **Altes Museum**, *Lustgarten*, designed by Karl Friedrich Schinkel and considered his finest work, exhibits Greek, Roman and Etruscan antiquities.

The **Pergamon Museum**, *Am Kupfergraben 5*, houses one of the world's great archaeological collections, with entire complexes on display that are dramatically lit at night. The second-century BC Pergamon Altar and the Babylonian Street are the stars of the show. Some parts of the museum will close for restoration in 2008.

The **Alte Nationalgalerie**, *Bodestrasse 1-3*, exhibits 19th-century sculptures and paintings, while the reopened **Bode Museum**, *Monbijoubrücke*, houses the coin collection, sculpture collection and Byzantine art, together with Old Master paintings from the Gemäldegalerie.

After 70 years closure, the **Neues Museum** finally reopened in 2009 and now houses the Ancient Egyptian collection that was previously in the Altes Museum.

Right: Museum Island gallery.
Opposite page top: Potsdamer Platz architecture.
Opposite page bottom: The old and new iat the Reichstag.

Best of the rest

The Story of Berlin
Kurfürsten-damm 207, www.story-of-berlin.de. Daily 1000-2000, last entry 1800. €10. U -bahn Uhland strasse, S-bahn Savignyplatz.
This brings the city's eventful past to life. Don't miss the tour of the nuclear shelter, a sealed-off underground town.

East Side Gallery
Running along Mühlenstr to Warschauerstr, www.eastsidegallery.com. U-Bahn Warschauer Str.
One of the last remaining stretches of the Wall is decorated with street art.

Sans Souci
Tue-Sun 0900-1700. €10. S-Bahn Potsdamer Hauptbahnhof, then bus 695.
Frederick the Great's summer pleasure palace.

Alexanderplatz

S/U-Bahn Alexanderplatz. Map G1.

East of the museums, 'Alex' has, in an architectural sense, stood still for over 30 years, a time-warped legacy of old East Berlin. In the early 1970s, the best that the town could offer was here on a vast pedestrian precinct. The 365m-high **Television Tower**, *www.tv-turm.de, Mar-Oct daily 0900-2400; Nov-Feb daily 1000-2400, €10.50*, completed the image of a modern town centre. The Weltzeituhr (World Clock) has always been a convenient meeting point, although when it was built in 1969, it was seen by some East Berliners as a cruel reminder of all the places they could not visit.

Charlottenberg

S/U-Bahn Zoologischer Garten, U-Bahn Richard-Wagner or Sophie-Charlotte Platz, off map.

Charlottenburg has lost much of its cachet since reunification but still boasts many of the institutions that made West Berlin famous. First among these is the iconic **Gedächtniskirche (Memorial Church)**, *Breitscheidplatz, daily 0900-1900 for the church, Mon-Sat 1000-1800, Sun 1200-1800 for the exhibition*, built shortly after the death of Kaiser Wilhelm in 1888 and largely destroyed by an air raid in 1943.

Lavish **Schloss Charlottenburg (Charlottenburg Palace)**, *T030 320 911, www.schlosscharlottenburg.de, Tue-Fri 0900-1700, Sat and Sun 1000-1700, €7*, is a one-stop shop for two centuries of German architecture, from 1700 to 1900. It was built as a summer residence for Queen Charlotte (1669-1705) by her husband Friedrich I (1657-1713) and was expanded into its present baroque and rococo form in 1701 when Friedrich crowned himself King of Prussia.

A few kilometres northwest is Olympiastadion, which underwent a multi-million renovation for the 2006 World Cup.

Kreuzberg

U-Bahn Hallesches Tor, Koch Str, Kottbusser Tor. Map F5.

Once a haven of alternative living – before everyone moved to Prenzlauerberg – Kreuzberg is now home

Travel essentials

Getting there

Berlin-Brandenburg International Airport is currently under construction and will become the area's new gateway when it opens in June 2012. **Tegel (Berlin International)** is due to close in 2012 but until then, visitors arriving to **Tegal Airport** are only 8 km northwest of the centre. Buses X9 (20 mins to Zoo) and 109 (30 mins to Zoo) run to the centre, via most of the hotels. Bus 128 is better for destinations to the north or east. The **TXL express** bus goes to Mitte (single €2.10). **Taxis** are plentiful and cost about €20 to Zoo Station or €30 to Mitte. A tip of 5-10% is normal. **Schönefeld (Berlin-Brandenburg) Airport** is 20 km from the city centre. The **Airport Express** train runs to Berlin Hauptbahnhof every 30 mins (journey time 28 mins). Buses link the airport with southern and eastern Berlin, including No 171 to Rudow for U-Bahn line 7. There are night buses and S-Bahn services on this route. A taxi to Friedrichstrasse costs €40. Opened in time for the 2006 World Cup, **Berlin Hauptbahnhof**, Europaplatz 1, www.hbf-berlin.de, is the state-of-the-art hub of Berlin's upgraded rail network, linking national and international services (including sleeper trains from Brussels) with the city's urban transport system. Almost all long-distance trains also stop at **Ostbahnhof**, Straße der Pariser Kommune 5 in Friedrichshain. There are 3 other long-distance stations (Gesundbrunnen, Südkreuz and Spandau), as well as regional stations. For details, see www.bahn.de.

Getting around

The extensive and speedy urban rail system consists of **U-Bahn** (underground) and **S-Bahn** (overground) trains. Both operate at night. Rail services are supplemented by the '**MetroNetz**' of tram and bus routes. The city is divided into 3 travel zones: A, B and C. You are only likely to visit zone C if you're going to Potsdam. A ticket for any number of journeys up to 2 hrs costs €2.10. Day passes for zones A and B cost €6.10. Tickets and passes are available at the Tegel Airport office, at the BVG centre at Zoo Station (T030 19449, www.bvg.de) and from machines on all platforms. The WelcomeCard (€16.90 for 48 hrs, €22.90 for 72 hrs), available from Berlin Infostores, offers free transport in all zones and a 25% reduction on many sights. Taxis are plentiful, with ranks at most U-Bahn and S-Bahn stations in the suburbs; they can be hailed in the city centre. Fares start at around €2, then cost €1 per km.

Tourist information

Visit Berlin, T030 250 025, www.visitberlin.de, are located at the Hauptbahnhof, daily 0800-2200; at Neues Kranzler Eck Passage, Kurfürstendamm 21, Mon-Sat 1000-2000, Sun 1000-1800; at the Brandenburg Gate, daily 1000-1800; and in the Berlin Pavilion at the Reichstag, Apr-Oct daily 0830-2000, Nov-Mar daily 1000-1800. **New Berlin Tours**, www.newberlintours.com, offer excellent free tours of the city.

to a large Turkish community, and some of Berlin's most disturbing sights. Nazi crimes are detailed at the open-air **Topographie des Terrors**, *Niederkirchnerstr, www.topographie.de, daily 1000-2000, free*, while the **Haus am Checkpoint Charlie**, *Friedrichstr 43-45, www.mauermuseum.de, daily 0900-2200, €12.50*, documents East Berliners' desperate efforts to cross the border. The powerful, innovative **Jüdisches Museum**, *Lindenstr 9-14, www.juedisches-museum-berlin.de, Mon 1000-2200, Tue-Sun 1000-2000, €5*, shows 2000 years of German-Jewish history, with a harrowing section on the Holocaust.

Left: Alexanderplatz station.
Opposite page top: Street art.
Opposite page bottom: The TV Tower, Akexanderplatz.

Sleeping

Berlin has a good selection of accommodation. Its more upmarket hotels are often large, modern affairs at the forefront of contemporary design. There are also many traditional pensions, particularly on and around the Kurfürstendamm in Tiergarten and Charlottenburg. Mitte and Prenzlauerberg have some first-rate arty and individual hotels.

Adlon €€€
Unter den Linden 77, T030 22610, www.kempinski.com.
Beside the Brandenburg Gate, the Adlon is not discreet but that doesn't seem to deter a regular turnover of celebrities. They follow in hallowed footsteps: Albert Einstein, Charlie Chaplin and Theodore Roosevelt all stayed here. The current building is a replica of the original – opulent and showy but also impressively stylish.

Hotel de Rome €€€
Behrenstrasse 37, T030 4606 090, www.hotelderome.com.
U-Bahn Stadtmitte.
Once headquarters of the Dresden Bank, this majestic building now houses the five-star spa hotel, Hotel de Rome, opened in 2006. Architecturally splendid with a contemporary twist. High ceilings and original features provide guests with an insight into the regal grandeur of Old Berlin while sumptuous furnishings and the latest spa experience provide every comfort.

Hotel Art Nouveau €€
Leibnizstr 59, Charlottenburg, T030 327 7440, www.hotelartnouveau.de.
U-Bahn Adenauerplatz.
A friendly and helpful fourth-floor hotel in a restored art nouveau building with contemporary touches. There's a buffet breakfast and an honesty bar.

Ku'Damm 101 €€
Kurfürstendamm 101, Charlottenburg, T030 520 0550, www.kudamm101.com.
U-Bahn Adenauerplatz.
This bold hotel opened in 2003 and makes a good out-of-centre base. Its minimalist take on vaguely '50s and '70s themes involves curves: lots of them. Even the buffet breakfast (on the 7th floor with spectacular views) is visually striking.

Circus Hostels €
Rosa-Luxemburg-Str 39-41 and Weinbergsweg 1a, T030 2839 1433, www.circus-berlin.de.
U-Bahn Rosa-Luxemburg-Platz and Rosenthaler Platz.
Very popular and for good reason. Much smarter and cleaner than most backpacker hostels and both in perfect locations.

Pension Funk €
Fasanenstrasse 69, T030 8827 193, www.hotel-pensionfunk.de.
U-bahn Spichernstrasse or Uhlandstrasse.
A beautiful house in a central location, dating back to 1895. It was once home to Silent Movie star, Asta Nielsen, in the 1930s and is full of charm and original features. A very affordable option in a great spot.

Eating

In no other German city can you eat as well, or as internationally, as in Berlin. There are now many great restaurants and, though often pricey, they are on the whole very good value for money. As well as international cuisine, there are lots of traditional German restaurants serving generous portions of heavy but extremely tasty food.

Breakfast

Anna Blume €
Kollwitzstr 83, corner of Sredzkistr, T030 4404 8749, www.cafe-anna-blume.de.
Daily 1000-2400.
U-Bahn Senefelderplatz.
A restaurant/café/florist that smells divine. Try the three-tier breakfast (€12 for two).

Lunch

Borchardt €€€
Französische Str 47, T030 2038 7110, www.borchardt-catering.de.
Daily 1130-0100, kitchen closes at 2400. U-Bahn Französische Str.
Restaurant serving international cuisine and favoured by politicians and journalists.

The interior is 18th century and the mosaics and period-style floors make this Gerndarmenmarkt institution well worth a visit. The food is also first rate.

Restauration 1900 €€
Husemannstr 1, T030 442 2494, www.restauration-1900.de.
Daily from 0930 (summer) 1100-2400 (winter). U-Bahn Eberswalder Str, Senefelder Platz.
A local hang-out on Kollwitz Platz. Dishes include traditional German cuisine, such as pork knuckle and braised oxtail, but generally it has a global feel. At weekends a delicious and quite substantial brunch is served.

Konnopke Imbiss €
Schonhauser Allee 44a, www.konnopke-imbiss.de.
U-Bahn Eberswalder Strasse. Mon-Sat 1200-2400, Sun 1400-0200. U-Bahn Rosa Luxemburg Platz.
Serving *Currywurst* to the locals for over 80 years. A hidden gem, off the tourist trail, tucked away under the U-bahn station. A must for an authentic Berlin fast food experience.

Dinner

Nocti Vagus €€€
Saarbrucker Strasse 36, T030 7474 9123, www.nocyivagus.com.
U-Bahn Senefelderplatz.
German cuisine with a twist. At Nocti Vagus specially trained blind and visually impaired waiters and waitresses will serve you, in complete darkness. The idea is to truly awaken your taste buds and heighten your senses. There's also a "dark" performance element to the evening. A truly unique experience.

Yosoy €€
Rosenthaler Str 37, T030 2839 1213, www.yosoy.de.
S-Bahn Hackescher Markt, U-Bahn Weinmeisterstr. Daily from 1100.
The feeling that you're in a North African souk is all pervasive when visiting this late-night haunt, where delicious tapas are served on tiled counters. A pleasant alternative to the super-smart Mitte bars.

Schulter Junge €
Corner Lychener Str and Danziger Str.
U-Bahn Eberswalder Str.
This restaurant is more like a real German kneipe or pub. The food is typically German, delicious and plentiful. Try schnitzel and *eierpfann-kuchen* (pancakes) with apple sauce.

Nightlife

Berlin offers some of the best nightlife in Europe: laid-back, accessible and cutting edge at the same time. The further east you go the more shabby-chic the bars tend to be; the further west the smarter and more elegant they become. You'll never be pushed for somewhere to go. Mitte has more than its fair share of suitable watering holes, with the area around Oranienburger Str being particularly popular with tourists. For something a bit more authentically Berlin, Prenzlauerberg is the place to go. From U-Bahn Rosenthaler Platz, head up Weinbergsweg into Kastanienallee where you'll find many hip bars and restaurants. Bars usually open at 2200 and then close when the last guest leaves.

The club scene attracts top performers, be it a plethora of International DJs at the incredibly hip Weekend Club, or Kings of Leon at O2 World. Berlin also plays host to secret Geheimtip parties, part of the eastside nightlife. If you are lucky you might discover the location for favourites, such as the Mittwochclub, every Wed. Berlin's classical music scene is world renowned. The **Berlin Philharmonic Orchestra** is based at the Berliner Philharmonie, *Herbert-von-Karajan-Str 1, T030 2548 8132, www.berliner-philharmoniker.de, daily 0900-1800.* Equally prestigious is the exquisitely restored **Staatsoper**, *Unter den Linden7, T030 2035 4555, www.staatsoper-berlin.org*, where opera and ballet are performed. Unsold tickets are available for €10 before a performance.

Ratings

Art and culture ☆☆☆
Eating ☆☆☆☆
Nightlife ☆☆☆
Outdoors ☆☆☆
Romance ☆
Shopping ☆
Sightseeing ☆☆
Value-for-money ☆☆☆
Overall city rating ☆☆☆

Bilbao

In an amazingly short time, and without losing sight of its roots, the dirty industrial city of Bilbao – a name that once conjured images of rusted pig-iron – has transformed itself with huge success into an exciting, buzzy, cultural hub. The Guggenheim Museum is the undoubted flagship of this triumphant progress. A sinuous fantasy of a building, it inspires not only because of what it is, but also because the city had the vision to put it there. While the museum has led the turnaround, much of what is enjoyable about Bilbao already existed. Bustling bar life, harmonious architecture, a superb eating culture and a sense of pride in being a working city. The exciting new developments, with constant improvement and beautification being carried out, have only added to those qualities.

Calatrava Bridge.

Casco Viejo (Old Town)

Tram Ribera/Arriaga. Metro Casco Viejo. Map F/G2.

Tucked into a bend in the river, Bilbao's Casco Viejo (Old Town) has something of the medina about it and evokes a cramped medieval past. Designer clothes shops occupy the ground floors where families once huddled behind the city walls, and an array of memorable bars serve up fine wine and elaborate bartop snacks, from delicious tortilla from a generations-old family recipe, to gourmet postmodern creations that wouldn't look out of place in the Guggenheim. Most Bilbaínos live and work elsewhere in the city and the true soul of the Casco emerges from early evening, when people descend on it like bees returning to the hive, strolling the streets, listening to buskers, debating the quality of the *pintxos* (snacks) in the bars, and sipping drinks in the setting sun.

The parallel **Siete Calles** (Seven Streets) form the oldest part of town (**Somera** is particularly interesting), with the slender spire of the graceful Gothic **Catedral de Santiago** rising from the tightly packed maze. On the waterfront here is the **Mercado de la Ribera**, a lovely art deco market building with over 400 stalls of fruit, vegetables, meat and fish on three floors. **Plaza Nueva** will appeal to lovers of symmetry: its courtly, neoclassical arches conceal an excellent selection of restaurants and bars, serving some of the best pintxos in town. On Plaza Miguel de Unamuno is **Museo Vasco**, *T944 155423, 3, Tue-Sat 1100-1700, Sun 1100-1400, €3 (free on Thu)*, housing an interesting, if higgledy-piggledy, series of Basque artefacts. Across the square, the new **Museo Arqueológico**, *Calzadas de Mallona 2, T944 040 990, Tue-Sat 1000-1400, 1600-1930, Sun 1030-1400, €3*, has a well-presented overview of Vizcaya's prehistory and history through material finds, including prehistoric artefacts found in caves around the province.

Atop a steep hill above the Casco Viejo is Bilbao's most important church, the **Basilica de Begoña**, *lift from C Esperanza (25c); bear right, then turn right up C Virgen de Begoña*, home of Vizcaya's patron, the Virgin of Begoña. Take the steps back down to the old town; a charming descent.

Below left: Catedral de Santiago.
Below right: Modern Bilba.

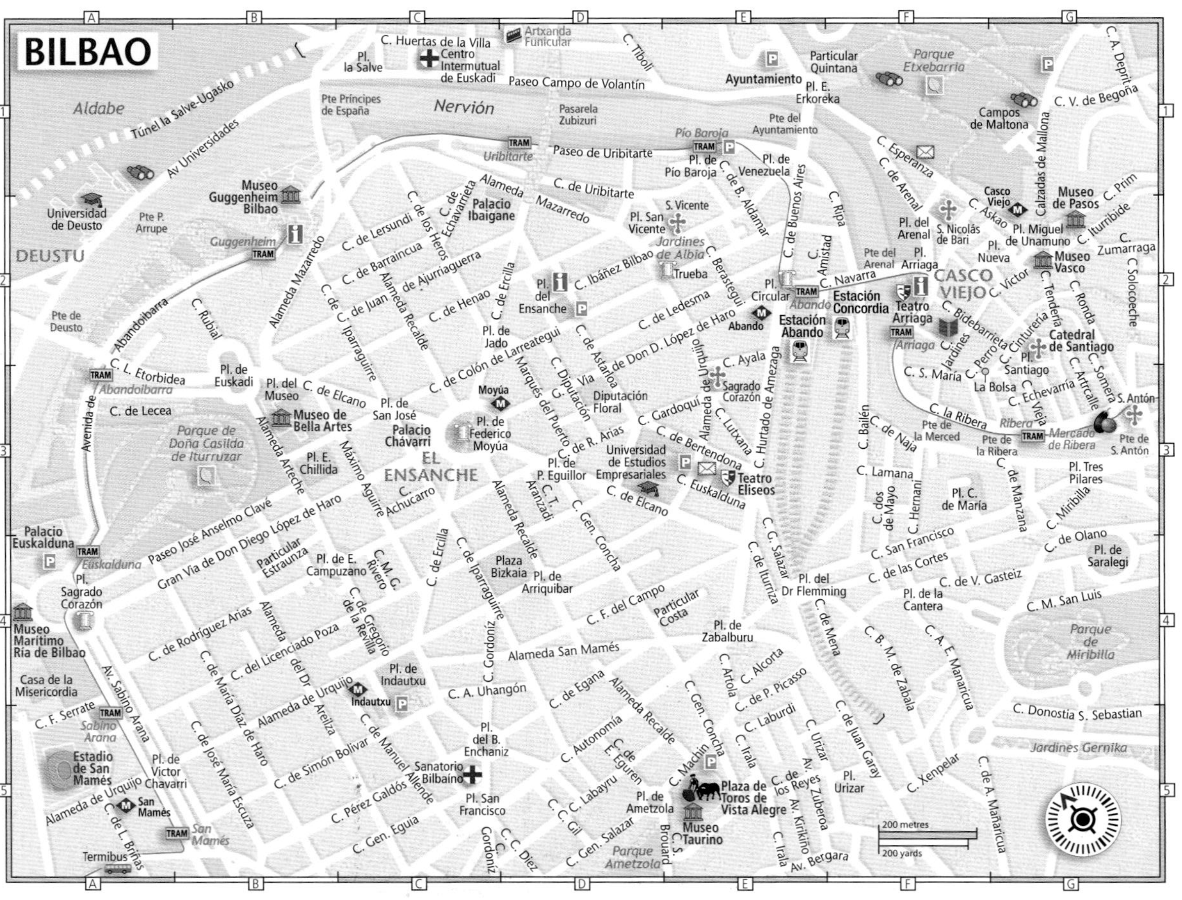

BILBAO
Aldabe
DEUSTU
Túnel la Salve-Ugasko
Av Universidades
Universidad de Deusto
Pte P. Arrupe
Pte de Deusto
Museo Guggenheim Bilbao
Guggenheim
Pl. la Salve
C. Huertas de la Villa
Centro Intermutual de Euskadi
Artxanda Funicular
Pte Príncipes de España
Nervión
Paseo Campo de Volantín
Pasarela Zubizuri
C. Tiboli
Uribitarte
Paseo de Uribitarte
Pío Baroja
Pl. de Pío Baroja
Ayuntamiento
Pte del Ayuntamiento
Particular Quintana
Pl. E. Erkoreka
Parque Etxebarria
Campos de Maltona
C. V. de Begoña
C. A. Deprit
Calzadas de Mallona
Museo de Pasos
C. Prim
C. Iturribide
C. Zumarraga
C. Solocoeche
C. Esperanza
C. de Arenal
Pl. del Arenal
S. Nicolás de Bari
Casco Viejo
C. Askao
Pl. Miguel de Unamuno
Pl. Nueva
Museo Vasco
Pte del Arenal
Pl. Arriaga
CASCO VIEJO
C. Víctor
C. Tendería
C. Ronda
Catedral de Santiago
C. Bidebarrieta
C. Cinturería
Teatro Arriaga
Arriaga
C. Jardines
C. Perro
Pl. Santiago
C. S. María
La Bolsa
C. Echevarría
C. Vieja
C. Artecalle
C. Somera
S. Antón
Pte de S. Antón
C. la Ribera
Ribera
Mercado de Ribera
Pte de la Merced
Pte de la Ribera
Alameda Mazarredo
Alameda Mazarredo
C. de Uribitarte
Pl. de Venezuela
C. de B. Aldamar
C. de Buenos Aires
C. Amistad
C. Ripa
C. Navarra
Pl. Circular
Abando
Estación Concordia
Estación Abando
Pl. San Vicente
S. Vicente
Jardines de Albia
Trueba
C. Berastegui
C. Ibáñez Bilbao
Pl. del Ensanche
C. de Lersundi
C. de los Heros
C. de Echavarrieta
Palacio Ibaigane
C. de Barraincua
C. de Juan de Ajurriaguerra
Alameda Recalde
C. de Henao
C. de Ercilla
C. de C. Iparraguirre
C. Rubial
Abandoibarra
C. L. Etorbidea
Pl. de Euskadi
Avenida de Abandoibarra
C. de Lecea
Pl. del Museo
C. de Elcano
Pl. de San José
Museo de Bella Artes
Parque de Doña Casilda de Iturrizar
Alameda Arteche
Pl. E. Chillida
Máximo Aguirre
Palacio Chávarri
EL ENSANCHE
C. Achucarro
Pl. de Jado
C. de Colón de Larreategui
Moyúa
Pl. de Federico Moyúa
Marqués del Puerto
C. Diputación
G. Vía de Don D. López de Haro
C. de Astarloa
C. de Ledesma
Diputación Floral
Alameda de Urquijo
C. Ayala
Sagrado Corazón
C. Hurtado de Amezaga
C. Lutxana
C. Gardoquí
C. de R. Arias
C. de Bertendona
Universidad de Estudios Empresariales
Pl. de P. Eguillor
C. T. Aranzadi
C. Euskalduna
Teatro Eliseos
C. de Elcano
C. Gen. Concha
Alameda Recalde
Palacio Euskalduna
Euskalduna
Paseo José Anselmo Clavé
Gran Vía de Don Diego López de Haro
Particular Estraunza
Pl. de E. Campuzano
C. M. G. Rivero
C. de Ercilla
C. de Iparraguirre
Plaza Bizkaia
Pl. de Arriquibar
Pl. Sagrado Corazón
Museo Marítimo Ría de Bilbao
Casa de la Misericordia
C. de Rodríguez Arias
C. de María Díaz de Haro
Alameda del Dr Areilza
C. del Licenciado Poza
C. de Gregorio de la Revilla
C. Gordoniz
Alameda San Mamés
C. F. del Campo
Particular Costa
Pl. de Indautxu
Indautxu
Alameda de Urquijo
C. A. Uhangón
C. F. Serrate
Sabino Arana
Av. Sabino Arana
Estadio de San Mamés
Pl. de Victor Chavarri
C. de José María Escuza
C. de Simón Bolívar
C. de Manuel Allende
Pl. del B. Enchaniz
Sanatorio Bilbaíno
Alameda de Urquijo
San Mamés
C. de L. Briñas
Termibus
C. Pérez Galdós
C. Gen. Eguia
Pl. San Francisco
C. C. Gordoniz
C. C. Diez
C. C. Gil
C. Gen. Salazar
Parque Ametzola
C. Labayru
C. de E. Eguren
C. Autonomía
C. de Egana
Alameda Recalde
Pl. de Ametzola
C. Machin
Plaza de Toros de Vista Alegre
Museo Taurino
C. S. Brouard
C. Gen. Concha
C. Artola
C. Alcorta
C. de P. Picasso
C. Laburdi
C. Irala
C. Irala
C. de los Reyes
Av. Kirikiño
Av. Zuberoa
Av. Bergara
C. Urizar
Pl. Urizar
C. de Juan Garay
Pl. de Zabalburu
C. G. Salazar
C. de Iturriza
Pl. del Dr Flemming
C. de Mena
C. B. M. de Zabala
C. A. E. Manaricua
C. Xenpelar
C. de A. Mañaricua
200 metres
200 yards
C. Bailén
C. de Naja
C. Lamana
C. dos de Mayo
C. Hernani
Pl. C. de María
C. de Manzana
Pl. Tres Pilares
C. Miribilla
C. de Olano
Pl. de Saralegi
C. San Francisco
C. de las Cortes
C. de V. Gasteiz
Pl. de la Cantera
C. M. San Luis
Parque de Miribilla
C. Donostia S. Sebastian
Jardines Gernika

Riverbank

The once-grim riverbank has been completely redesigned as the focus of Bilbao's regenerative leap into the 21st century. If you only take one stroll in Bilbao, make it an evening paseo along the Nervión from the Casco Viejo west to the Guggenheim Museum (see below). Highlights on the way include the fin de siècle **Teatro Arriaga**, *Tram Arriaga*, and Calatrava's eerily skeletal **Zubizuri footbridge**, *Tram Uribitarte*.

Beyond the Guggenheim the bizarre **Palacio Euskalduna** opened in 1998 on the site of the last Bilbao shipyard and is now a major venue for concerts, particularly classical. Nearby is the **Museo Marítimo**, *Muelle Ramón de la Sota, T902 131000, www.museomaritimobilbao.org. Tue-Fri 1000-1400, 1600-1800, Sat and Sun 1000-1400, 1600-2000, €4,*

Best of the rest

At the mouth of the Nervión, 20 km from the centre, Getxo has a pretty old harbour and good beaches. The impressive Puente Vizcaya, a UNESCO World Heritage Site, zips cars and passengers across the estuary via a hanging 'gondola'. The rugged coast to the east is lined with great surf beaches and appealing fishing towns, such as Mundaka, a laid-back little surf village with one of Europe's most famous waves, and Lekeitio, a Basque fishing port with a picturesque harbour and good eating. Inland is the unmissable and thriving town of Gernika, the symbolic home of Basque nationalism. Its **Museo de la Paz**, *Pl Foru 1, T946 270 213, www.museodelapaz.org, Tue-Sat 1000-1400, 1600-1900, Sun 1000-1400, no lunchtime closing Jul-Aug, €4*, is a moving but optimistic museum detailing the brutal aerial bombardment endured by the town on 26 April 1937.

Tram Euskalduna, a salty treat that includes a number of different boats as part of its exterior exhibition. Across the river from here is the university barrio of **Deusto**, while, just south, is **San Mamés stadium**, *C Felipe Serrate, T944 411 445, www.athletic-club.net. Metro/tram San Mames*, home of the fervently supported Athletico Bilbao.

Guggenheim Museum

Abandoibarra Etorbidea 2, T944 359 000, www.guggenheim-bilbao.es.
Tue-Sun 1000-2000, Jul-Aug also Mon. Around €13 including audioguide, combined ticket, €13.50 including Museo de Bellas Artes. Tram Guggenheim. Map B2.

More than anything else, it is this building that has thrust Bilbao firmly on to the world stage. Frank Gehry's exuberant Guggenheim brings art and architecture together. It sits among the older riverfront buildings like some unearthly vehicle that's just landed. The titanium panels are paper thin and malleable, making the whole structure shimmer like a writhing school of fish.

Outside, a pool and fog and fire sculptures interact fluidly with the river. Jeff Koons' giant floral sculpture, Puppy, sits eagerly greeting visitors at the entrance. Inside, while most exhibits are temporary, enormous Gallery 104 holds Richard Serra's magnificent and interactive The Matter of Time, eight monumental structures of curved oxidised-steel, centred around *Snake*, whose curved sheets will carry whispers from one end to another.

El Ensanche

Across the river from the Casco Viejo, the new town was laid out in 1876 and has an elegant European feel to it. The wealth of the city is evident here, with stately banks and classy shops lining its avenues. Here you'll find the **Museo de Bellas Artes**, *Pl del Museo 2, T944 396 060, www.museobilbao.com, Tue-Sun 1000-2000, €6, Wed free, Metro Moyua*, which houses modern Basque art, older pieces and temporary exhibits. On the edge of El Ensanche is the bullring (*www.plazatorosbilbao.com*) and museum of **Vista Alegre**, *C Martın Agüero, T944 448 698, Metro Indautxu.*

Below: Guggenheim museum.
Left: University Bridge, Duesto.
Opposite page: Euskadulna Bridge.

Sleeping

Gran Domine €€
Alameda Mazarredo 61, T944 253 300, www.granhoteldomine bilbao.com.
Tram Guggenheim.
Inspiring modern hotel opposite the Guggenheim with a façade of tilted glass panels and a delightful interior.

Indautxu €€
Pl Bombero Etxariz, El Ensanche, T944 211 198, www.hotelindautxu.com.
Metro Indautxu.
Comfortable Ensanche four-star with bags more character than most business-level establishments.

Petit Palace Arana €€
C Bidebarrieta 2, T944 156 411, www.hthoteles.com.
Metro Casco Viejo.
Sensitive conversion of historic building to a smart modern hotel with great facilities at the mouth of the Casco Viejo warren.

Apartamentos Atxuri €
Av Miraflores 17, T944 667 832, www.apartamentosatxuri.com.
Tram Atxuri.
These beautifully sleek apartments occupy a modern building just east of the Casco Viejo.

Hostal Begoña €
C Amistad 2, T944 230 134, www.actioturis.com.
Tram Casino.

Above: Bilbao square. Opposite page: Bilbao metro.

A welcoming modern hotel near Abando station, packed with flair and comfort.

Hotel Sirimiri €
Pl de la Encarnación 3, T944 330 759, www.hotelsirimiri.com.
Tram Atxuri.
Great hotel with a genial owner, gym, sauna and free parking.

Iturrienea Ostatua €
C Santa María, T944 161 500, www.iturrieneaostatua.com.
Tram Arriaga.
Beautiful pensión fitted out in stone, wood and idiosyncratic objects. Tasty breakfasts.

Eating

Casco Viejo is the best place to head for *pintxos* (bar snacks) and evening drinks, especially the Plaza Nueva and around the Siete Calles. In El Ensanche, there's concentrations of bars on Av Licenciado Poza, C García Rivero and C Ledesma. Restaurants are scattered throughout the Casco Viejo, Ensanche and Deusto.

Guria €€€
Gran Vía 66, El Ensanche, T944 415 780, www.restauranteguria.com.
Tram Euskalduna.
One of Bilbao's top restaurants; its stock-in-trade is bacalao. Menús are €41-62, otherwise it's €60 per head minimum. There are various degustation menus; budget at least €60 per head à la carte.

Victor €€€
Pl Nueva 2, Casco Viejo, T944 151 678.
Metro Casco Viejo.
An elegant but relaxed place to try Bilbao's signature dish, *bacalao al pil-pil.*

Kasko €€
C Santa María, Casco Viejo, T944 160 311, www.restaurantekasko.com
Tram Arriaga.
High-class but low-priced new Basque food in this spacious bohemian bar-restaurant in the heart of the action.

Serantes III €€
Alameda Mazarredo 75, T944 248 004, www.marisqueriaserantes.com.
Metro Moyua/Indautxu.
Opposite the Guggenheim, this is one of three excellent seafood restaurants that have notable reputations, great fresh fish and crustaceans and fair prices.

Café-Bar Bilbao €
Pl Nueva 6, Casco Viejo, T944 151 671.
Metro Casco Viejo.
Don't miss this sparky place with top service and a selection of some of the best *pintxos* to be had in the old town, all carefully labelled and irresistible. Try them with a *txakolí* (a slightly fizzy local wine).

El Globo €
C Diputación 8, T944 154 221,
Metro Moyúa.
There's an extraordinary variety of cold and cooked-to-order hot pintxos here; traditional bites take their place alongside wildly imaginative modern creations.

Mina €
Muelle Manzana s/n, T944 795 938, www.restaurantemina.es.
Perhaps the most enjoyable place to eat in town, this restaurant faces the Casco Viejo on the riverbank. Expect creative combinations that you haven't seen before and are unlikely to again.

Travel essentials

Getting there

Bilbao International Airport, T905 505505, designed by Santiago Calatrava, is 10 km northeast of the city. Buses run to the centre every 30 mins or so, taking 20-30 mins (€1.15). A taxi will cost about €20.

Getting around

Bilbao is reasonably walkable – the Guggenheim is an easy 20-min stroll along the river from the old town – but the re-established **tram** line is a handy alternative. It runs every 10-15 mins from Atxuri station along the river, skirting the Casco Viejo and El Ensanche, with stops at the Guggenheim and the bus station (Termibus) among other places.
A single costs E1. To reach destinations further afield, including Deusto, Getxo and the beaches, use the fast, efficient **metro**. A single fare costs €1.15; a day pass is €3. **Euskotren** (T902-543210) services from Abando and Atxuristations link Bilbao with coastal towns and Gernika. There are also buses from C Hurtado Amezaga, next to Abando station.

Tourist information

Bilbao Turismo, www.bilbao.net, is at Pl Ensanche 11, T944 795 760, Mon-Fri 0900-1400 and 1600-1930. There are information centres at **Teatro Arriaga**, on the edge of the old town, Mon-Fri 1100-1400 and 1700-1930, Sat 0930-1400 and 1700-1930, Sun 0930-1400; near the **Guggenheim** at Abandoibarra Etorbidea 2, Tue-Fri 1100-1800, Sat 1100-1900, Sun 1100-1400, and at the **airport**, T914 710 301. You can also phone for information, T944 710 301, daily until 2300.

Ratings

Art and culture ☆☆☆☆
Eating ☆☆☆☆☆
Nightlife ☆☆
Romance ☆☆☆☆☆
Shopping ☆☆☆
Sightseeing ☆☆☆☆☆
Value-for-money ☆☆
Overall city rating ☆☆☆

Bruges

Bruges is a miniature marvel, a perfectly preserved medieval city set upon a network of canals. Sometimes called the 'Venice of the North', it was, like its southern sister, at the centre of a huge trading empire during the middle ages. When the canals silted up, so did the trade, and Bruges was forced onto the sidelines of European history. Paradoxically, it was the centuries of neglect which preserved the old city intact, and made it the magical time capsule so beloved by travellers. From the top of the medieval belfry, you can still gaze down over a picture-postcard huddle of red-roofed gabled mansions and bridge-studded canals. Contemporary Bruges is now firmly on the tourist track, but there are numerous secret corners and quiet gardens to escape the hordes. After wandering the cobbled streets, taking a boat trip along the canals, or admiring the city's spectacular artworks (highlights include the Flemish Primitives at the Groeningemuseum, Memling at the Hospital Museum, or Michelangelo's Madonna in the Church of Our Lady), head to the city's cosy pubs to sample some famous Belgian beers. Gourmets are in for a treat, as Belgian cuisine is world-renowned. Bruges offers something for all budgets, from the punnets of golden chips (fries) dispensed from *frietkoten* (street stalls), to no less than six Michelin-starred restaurants.

Bruges at night.

Around the city

Astridpark (Queen Astrid Park)

Entrances on Gevangenisstraat and Minderbroedersstraat.
Map E3.

A small green lung in the heart of the city, this garden was laid out in the 19th century and boasts meandering paths, a serene pond with spouting fountain, and verdant lawns for picnicing and playing.

At a glance

The historic centre of Bruges is small and compact, an egg-shaped warren of medieval streets neatly contained within a ring of canals. The bus and train stations are found next to each other on the southeastern edge of the old city, close to the modern **concert hall** (Concertgebouw) which also contains the main tourist information office. Shop-lined **Zuidzandstrasse** and **Steenstrasse** will bring you to the **Markt**, the heart of the city, a grand ensemble of gabled townhouses set around a huge cobbled square. It's dominated by the **Belfry**, the city's most famous landmark. A two-minute stroll east will bring you to the Burg, the political and administrative centre of Bruges for more than a thousand years, and the location of the gilded **city hall** (Stadhuis) and the magnificent **Basilica of the Holy Blood** (Heilig Bloedbasiliek). Behind the Burg is the Vismarkt, the wonderful 18th-century fish market, and the pretty little café-lined square of the **Huidevettersplein**. The main museums, including the **Groeningemuseum** and the **Memlingmuseum**, in the **Sint-Jan Hospital**, are found just to the south, close to a picturesque canal where you can pick up boat tours. Also here is the **Church of Our Lady** (Onze-Lieve-Vrouwerk), with Michelangelo's sublime *Madonna and Child*. Follow the canal further south to the charming **Begijnhof**, a religious complex composed of whitewashed houses and a simple church, which provides a quiet retreat from the city bustle. On the opposite bank of the canal is the lush, watery expanse of the **Minnewater**, a dreamy park overlooking a lake. Another clutch of smaller sights and museums can be found northeast of the Markt: these include the **Kantcentrum**, where lace is still made according to ancient traditions, the **Folklore Museum** (Museum voor Volkskunde), and, near the old city gate of **Kruispoort**, a pair of traditional windmills, now a museum.

Begijnhof

Begijnhof 24-30, www.monasteria.org.
Open daily 0630-1830. Open Mon-Sat 1000-1700, Sun 1430-1700. Museum €2, €1.50 concessions. Complex or church free. Map G5.

The most serene and tranquil corner of old Bruges, the Begijnhof is a hushed, whitewashed monastic enclosure set around a tree-filled courtyard. The convent complex was established in 1245 for the Begijnen (Beguines in French), a lay order founded by the Countess of Flanders in the 12th century for the widows of crusaders, although most of the surviving buildings date from between the 16th and 18th centuries. It is now inhabited by a community of Benedictine nuns, but visitors are welcome to admire the gabled houses, the simple church, and to visit the museum which occupies one of the historic dwellings.

Belfort (Belfry)

Markt 7, T050 448 743.
Open 0930-1700. €8, €6/€4. Map D4.

The city's best-loved symbol is the medieval Belfry, which, at 83 metres, is visible from almost everywhere. Built between the 13th and 15th centuries, the Belfry once doubled as a watchtower and treasury: money and charters were stored in medieval 'safes' still visible behind 13th-century wrought-iron gates, and guards kept a careful eye

Begijnhof.

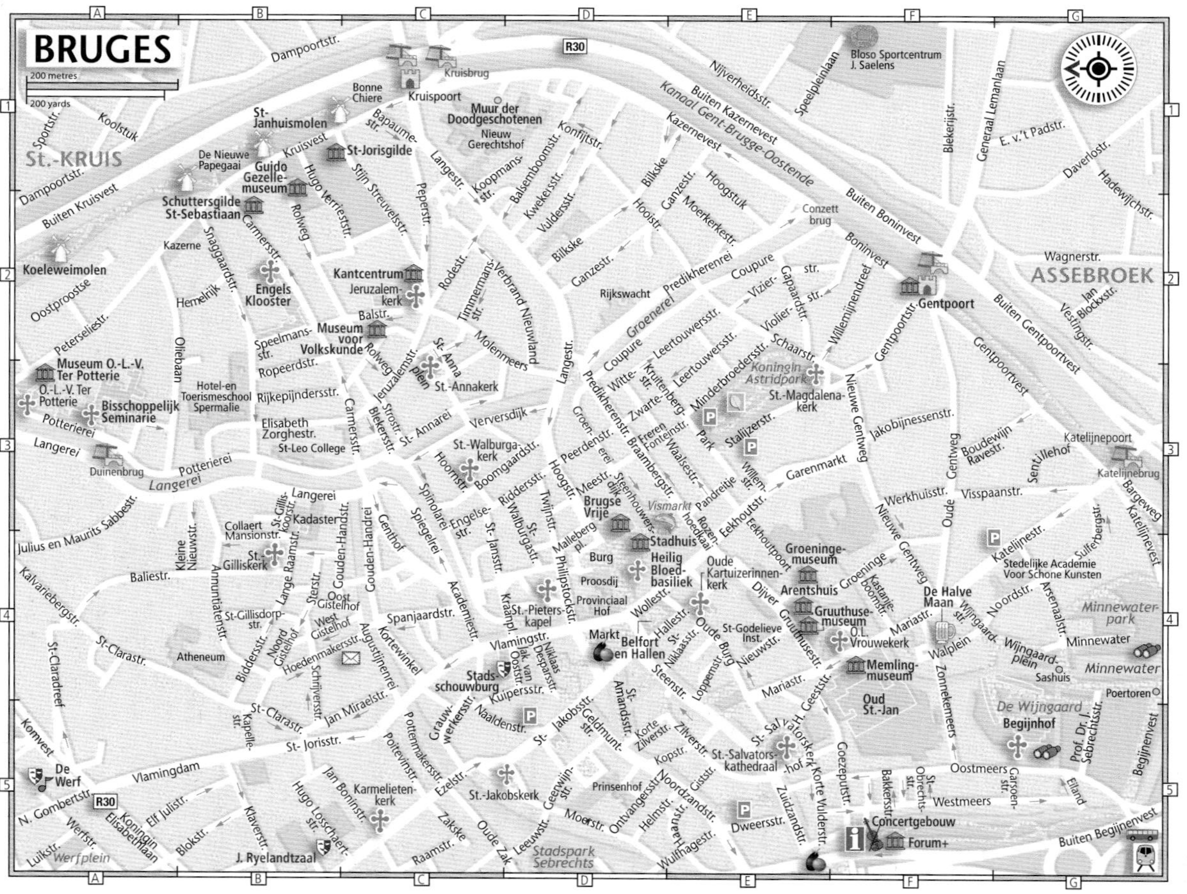

BRUGES
200 metres
200 yards
ST.-KRUIS
ASSEBROEK
R30
Kanaal Gent-Brugge-Oostende
Buiten Kazernevest
Buiten Boninvest
Buiten Gentpoortvest
Buiten Kruisvest
Buiten Begijnenvest
Begijnenvest
Katelijnevest
Gentpoortvest
Boninvest
Kazernevest
Dampoortstr.
Sportstr.
Koolstuk
Oostproosse
Peterseliestr.
Potterierei
Langerei
Duinenbrug
Julius en Maurits Sabbestr.
Kalvariebergstr.
St-Claradreef
St-Clarastr.
Komvest
De Werf
Werfplein
Vlamingdam
Koningin Elisabethlaan
Elf Julistr.
Blokstr.
Klaverstr.
J. Ryelandtzaal
Hugo Losschaertstr.
Jan Boninstr.
Karmelietenkerk
Raamstr.
Zakske
Oude Zak
St.-Jakobskerk
Leeuwstr.
Stadspark Sebrechts
Geerwijnstr.
Moerstr.
Ontvangersstr.
Prinsenhof
Noordzandstr.
Helmstr.
Haanstr.
Wulfhagestr.
Dweersstr.
Zuidzandstr.
Korte Vulderstr.
Goezeputstr.
Concertgebouw
Forum+
Bakkersstr.
St-Obrechtsstr.
Westmeers
Oostmeers
Garsoenstr.
Begijnhof
De Wijngaard
Wijngaardplein
Sashuis
Prof. Dr. J. Sebrechtstr.
Eiland
Poertoren
Minnewater
Minnewaterpark
Stedelijke Academie Voor Schone Kunsten
Arsenaalstr.
Noordstr.
Katelijnestr.
Sulferbergstr.
Bargeweg
Katelijnebrug
Katelijnepoort
Sentillehof
Visspaanstr.
Boudewijn Ravestr.
Oude Gentweg
Nieuwe Gentweg
Werkhuisstr.
Jakobijnessenstr.
Gentpoortstr.
Gentpoort
Willemijnendreef
Wagnerstr.
Jan Blockxstr.
Vestingstr.
Hadewijchstr.
Daverlostr.
E. v.'t Padstr.
Generaal Lemanlaan
Blekerijstr.
Bloso Sportcentrum J. Saelens
Speelpleinlaan
Nijverheidsstr.
Conzett brug
De Halve Maan
Wijngaardstr.
Walplein
Zonnekemeers
Mariastr.
O.L. Vrouwekerk
Memlingmuseum
Oud St.-Jan
Kastanjeboomstr.
Groeninge
Groeningemuseum
Arentshuis
Gruuthusemuseum
Gruuthusestr.
Dijver
Eekhoutpoort
Eekhoutstr.
Oude Kartuizerinnenkerk
Rozenhoedkaai
Oude Burg
St-Godelieve Inst.
Nieuwstr.
Loppemstr.
St.-Salvatorskerkhof
H. Geeststr.
St.-Salvatorskathedraal
Steenstr.
Zilverstr.
Korte Zilverstr.
Geldmuntstr.
St.-Amandsstr.
Kopstr.
Gistsstr.
Markt
Belfort en Hallen
Hallestr.
Wollestr.
St.-Niklaasstr.
Stadhuis
Heilig Bloedbasiliek
Vismarkt
Burg
Brugse Vrije
Proosdij
Provinciaal Hof
Philipstockstr.
St.-Pieterskapel
Niklaas Desparsstr.
Jak. van Ooststr.
Kuipersstr.
Naaldenstr.
Stadsschouwburg
Vlamingstr.
Kraanpl.
St-Jakobsstr.
Grauwwerkersstr.
Ezelstr.
Pottenmakersstr.
Poitevinstr.
St.-Jorisstr.
Jan Miraelstr.
Kortewinkel
Spanjaardstr.
Augustijnenrei
Academiestr.
St-Jansstr.
Engelsestr.
Walburgastr.
Twijnstr.
Hoogstr.
Meestr.
Mallebergpl.
Steenhouwersdijk
Groenerei
Peerdenstr.
Braambergstr.
Predikherenstr.
Zwarte Leertouwersstr.
Fonteinstr.
Freren
Waalsestr.
Pandreitje
Willemstr.
Stalijzerstr.
Park
Kruitenbergstr.
St.-Magdalenakerk
Koningin Astridpark
Schaarstr.
Minderbroedersstr.
Leertouwersstr.
Witte Leertouwersstr.
Coupure
Gapaardstr.
Vizierstr.
Violierstr.
Predikherenrei
Langestr.
Rijkswacht
Ganzestr.
Hooistr.
Moerkerkestr.
Hoogstuk
Bilkske
Konfijtstr.
Vuldersstr.
Kweekersstr.
Balsemboomstr.
Koopmansstr.
Muur der Doodgeschotenen
Nieuw Gerechtshof
Verbrand Nieuwland
Timmermansstr.
Molenmeers
Rodestr.
Kruisbrug
Kruispoort
Peperstr.
Bapaumestr.
St.-Jorisgilde
Stijn Streuvelsstr.
Bonne Chiere
St-Janhuismolen
Hugo Verrieststr.
Kruisvest
Rolweg
Guido Gezellemuseum
Carmersstr.
Engels Klooster
Schuttersgilde St-Sebastiaan
De Nieuwe Papegaai
Snaggaardstr.
Hemelrijk
Kazerne
Koeleweimolen
Oliebaan
Hotel-en Toerismeschool Spermalie
Museum O.-L.-V. Ter Potterie
O.-L.-V. Ter Potterie
Bisschoppelijk Seminarie
Kantcentrum
Jeruzalemkerk
Balstr.
Museum voor Volkskunde
Jeruzalemstr.
St- Anna plein
St.-Annakerk
St.-Annarei
Strostr.
Blekersstr.
Speelmansstr.
Ropeerdstr.
Rijkepijndersstr.
Elisabeth Zorghestr.
St-Leo College
Verversdijk
St.-Walburgakerk
Boomgaardstr.
Riddersstr.
Hoornstr.
Spinolarei
Spiegelrei
Genthof
Gouden-Handrei
Gouden-Handstr.
Kadaster
Sterstr.
Oost Gistelhof
West Gistelhof
Hoedenmakersstr.
Schrijversstr.
Lange Raamstr.
Noord Gistelhof
Biddersstr.
St-Gilliskoorstr.
St.-Gilliskerk
Collaert Mansionstr.
St-Gillisdorpstr.
Annuntiatenstr.
Atheneum
Kleine Nieuwstr.
Baliestr.
Kapellestr.
N. Gombertstr.
Werfstr.
Luikstr.

on fires and trouble-makers from their lofty vantage point. Nowadays, visitors climb the 366 steps to the top for panoramic views over the red-tiled rooftops and canals. The tower also contains the famous 47-bell Dumery carillon, which dates back to the mid-18th century, as well as the huge Triumphal Bell, which is only rung on special occasions.

Burg

Renaissance Hall of the Liberty of Bruges. Burg 11a, T050 448 711, www.museabrugge.be.
Adm €2. Map D4.

Bruges began in the Burg, an elegant square named for the fortified castle ('burg') built by Baldwin Iron Arm, first Count of Flanders, in the 9th century. The castle has long gone, but the Burg is still the administrative and political heart of Bruges, and its southern end is dominated by some of the city's most spectacular historic buildings. These include the Gothic Stadhuis, which is Belgium's oldest city hall, and the 12th-century Heilig Bloedbasiliek (Basilica of the Holy Blood, see below). Facing the basilica is the gorgeously gilded 16th-century Civil Registry, which incorporates the Renaissance Hall of the Liberty of Bruges. Here you can admire a lavish mantelpiece carved in honour of the Emperor Charles V, who visited Bruges in 1515.

De Halve Maan

Walplein 26, T050 332 697, www.halvemaan.be.
Open Apr-Oct Mon-Fri 1000-1600, Sat-Sun 1000-1700; Oct-Mar Mon-Fri 1100-1500, Sat-Sun 1100-1600. €5.50 including tasting. Map F4.

De Halve Maan (The Half Moon) is the only traditional brewery still operating in central Bruges, and is famous for its 'Brugse Zot' (which means 'Bruges Fool') and 'Straffe Hendrik' beers, which are produced on the premises. Visitors can enjoy an entertaining guided tour of the brewery, which includes a visit to the rooftop for bird's-eye views, and culminates with a sample of their brew.

Groeningemuseum

Dijver 12, T050 448 711. www.museabrugge.be.
Open Tue-Mon 0930-1700. €8, concessions €6. Map E4.

One of the finest museums in Europe, this contains a spectacular collection of Flemish and Belgian art spanning six centuries. The highlight is the collection of Flemish Primitives, particularly the outstanding works by Jan van Eyck (1395–1441), Rogier van der Weyden (1399–1464), and Dirk Bouts (1410–1475). Among them, look out for Jan van Eyck's *Madonna with Canon van der Paele* (1436), considered the jewel of the collection. Not merely a religious painting, the extraordinary level of detail in the rich robes and decorations offers a fascinating glimpse into the prosperous world of Bruges under the Dukes of Burgundy. Other celebrated pieces include a gory *Last Judgment* by Hieronymous Bosch, and a few Surrealist works by René Magritte and Paul Delvaux.

Heilig Bloedbasiliek (Basilica of the Holy Blood)

Burg 10, T050 336 792. www.holyblood.org.
Open Apr-Sep 0930-1200 and 1400-1800; Oct-Mar Thu-Tue 1000-1200 and 1400-1600, Wed 1000-1200. Museum €1.50. Map D4.

The 12th-century Basilica of the Holy Blood contains a crystal vial containing blood supposedly wiped from the body of Christ. Credited with miraculous powers, it is said to have been brought back to Bruges after the Second Crusade by the

Count of Flanders in the mid-12th century. Every year on Ascension Day it is paraded through the streets of the city in a tradition which was first chronicled in 1291. More than 1600 locals dressed in historic costumes take part in the procession, which attracts enormous crowds of visitors and pilgrims. The vial is displayed on Fridays in the basilica's upper chapel, built in flamboyant late-Gothic style in the early 16th century and thickly covered with statues by Flemish artist Lancelot Blondel. In contrast, the lower chapel preserves one of the finest Romanesque interiors in Belgium, with rounded arches and plain stone walls. A pocket-sized museum next door displays the jewel-encrusted reliquary used to transport the vial during the Procession of the Holy Blood.

Markt

Map D4.

The bustling, commercial heart of Bruges is the Markt, an enormous cobbled square enclosed by gabled former guildhalls and dominated by the celebrated Belfry (see above). The old guildhalls are now cafés and restaurants, most with large terraces which are perfect for a spot of people-watching. One of the nicest cafés is the Craenenburg at Markt 16, which occupies the oldest original building to survive on the square. At the centre of the square is a 19th-century statue depicting the heroic guild-masters Jan Breydel and Pieter de Coninck, who led a famous rebellion against the French in 1302.

Memling In Sint Jan Hospitaalmuseum (Memlingmuseum, St John's Hospital)

Mariastraat 38, T050 448 711, www.museabrugge.be.
Open Tue-Sun 0930-1700, pharmacy open Tue-Sun 0930-1145 and 1400-1700.
€8, concessions €6. Map F4.

St John's, established in the late 12th century, is one of the oldest and best preserved hospitals in Europe. The cavernous old wards, where monks and nuns once tended to sick travellers, now display furniture, paintings, gruesomely rudimentary medical instruments and even a medieval ambulance. The chapel contains six outstanding works by 15th-century artist Hans Memling, including the masterful *St Ursula Shrine*, a large reliquary illustrating the martyr's life and gruesome death.

Minnewater

Map G4.

This canalised lake, overhung by willow trees, is the focus of an idyllic park, perfect for a quiet stroll. The grassy banks are filled with ducks and swans and trees form a gauzy canopy. It's hard to imagine that once this was a busy dock, where ships from across Europe would unload their exotic cargoes of silks and spices, and exchange them for prized Flemish cloth.

Below: Minnewater.
Above left: Heilig Bloedbasiliek.
Above right: Memling In Sint Jan Hospitaalmuseum.
Opposite page: The Burg.

Onze Lieve Vrouwekerk (Church of Our Lady)

Mariastraat. T050 448 743, www.museabrugge.be.
Church open Mon-Fri 0930-1650, Sat 0930-1640, Sun 1330-1640. Museum open Tue-Fri 0930–1700, Sun 1330-1700. Church free, museum €2, concessions €1. Map A3.

This beautiful church of golden stone is adorned with a slender spire, which, at 122 metres, is one of the tallest in Belgium. It contains the city's most celebrated treasure: a tender depiction of the *Madonna and Child* sculpted by Michelangelo in 1504. The white marble statue has been stolen twice – first by the French during the Napoleonic Wars and then by the Nazis – but was recovered each time. The church is also remarkable for the handsome Renaissance tombs of Charles the Bold (1433–1477) and his daughter, Mary of Burgundy (1457–1482).

Sint-Salvator-kathedraal (St. Salavator's Cathedral)

Steenstraat, www.sintsalvator.be.
Cathedral open Mon-Fri 0900-1200 and 1400-1730, Sat 0900-1200 and 14001500, Sun 0900-1000 and 1400-1700; Treasury open Sun-Fri 1400-1700. Cathedral free; Treasury €2. Map E5.

The oldest church in Bruges, Saint Salavator's was begun in the 12th century and completed three hundred years later. It remained a simple parish church until the early 19th century, when it was raised to the status of cathedral and given a lavish neo-Gothic facelift. The city's first cathedral was demolished by French armies at the end of the 18th century. Its surviving treasures, including paintings, sculptures and tapestries, were transferred to St Salvator's and are displayed in the cathedral treasury.

Vismarkt (Fish Market)

Market Tue-Sat 0800-1300. Map D3.

Historically, the fishmongers of Bruges occupied a corner of the Markt square, but locals complained so bitterly about the stench that they were moved to splendid, purpose-built quarters in 1821. The elegant stalls, with their balustrades and broad counters, remain virtually unchanged, and stretch all the way around the square. Come in the mornings (except Sun and Mon) to catch the market in full swing, with stall-holders bellowing out their wares in time-honoured tradition. The arcades around the square are filled with terrace cafés, where you can watch the action in comfort.

Best of the rest

Arentshuis (Brangwyn Museum)
Dijver 16, T050 448 763. Tue–Sun 0930–1700. €2.
An appealing museum set in an elegant 18th-century mansion, featuring the eclectic works of British artist Frank Brangwyn (1867–1956).

Gruuthusemuseum (Gruuthuse Museum)
Dijver 17, T050 448 711, www.museabrugge. Tue–Sun 0930–1700. €6, concessions €5.
A magnificent 15th-century mansion, built for the Lords of Gruut, with rooms decorated in period styles, and a magpie collection of artworks, tapestries and historic tools.

Jeruzalem Kirk (Jerusalem Church) and Lace Centre
Peperstraat 3a, T050 330 072, www.kantcentrum.eu. Mon–Sat 1000–1700.
Watch lace being made the old-fashioned way, then head next door to the macabre Gothic church.

Museum voor Volkskunde (Folklore Museum)
Balstraat 43, T050 448 711, www.museabrugge.be. Tue–Sun 0930–1700. €2.
A cluster of 17th-century almhouses converted into a charming folklore museum.

Choco-Story
Sint-Jansstraat 7b, T050 612 237, www.choco-story.be. Daily 1000–1700. €6, concessions €5/4.
Learn about the history of chocolate and enjoy a special tasting.

Sleeping

Central Bruges is so compact that most hotels and guesthouses are located within a 15-minute walk of the Markt. Accommodation is generally pricy; if you're on a budget, consider one of the scores of delightful B&Bs. The tourist office has a comprehensive accommodation brochure, available in print, or online at www.brugge.be, which lists hotels, B&Bs and self-catering accommodation. There are few modern chain hotels, so expect plenty of character and charm, but fewer amenities.

Pand Hotel €€€
Pandreitje 16, T050 340 556, www.pandhotel.com.
This bijou boutique hotel is the chicest address in town and perfect for a romantic break. The 18th-century mansion contains 26 supremely elegant, antique-filled rooms and suites, yet the atmosphere remains one of a gracious private home rather than a hotel. Sip a cocktail by the fire in winter, or relax in the plant-filled patio in summer.

Prinsenhof €€€
Ontvangerstraat 9, T050 342 690, www.prinsenhof.com.
An enchanting luxury hotel in the city centre, the Prinsenhof is located in a mansion built for 13th-century merchants. Traditional furnishings are complemented by contemporary amenities such as plasma TVs and spacious bathrooms, but the hotel's greatest strength is its thoughtful and attentive staff. Good, varied breakfasts are served, and there are several excellent restaurants within a short stroll of the hotel.

Adornes €€
Sint-Annarei 26, T050 341 336, www.adornes.be.
If you're looking for tranquility, consider the appealing Hotel Adornes. It is tucked away on the banks of a canal in a quiet neighbourhood about a 10-minute walk to the Markt, and offers free parking and free use of bicycles to its guests. Friendly service, spotless rooms, and a copious buffet breakfast (included in the price) make this an excellent mid-priced option. Doubles €120–150.

Ter Duinen €€
Langeria 52, T050 330 437, www.hotelterduinen.eu.
Book early for a room at this captivating little hotel, set in a typical gabled mansion overlooking the canal. The hotel has an airy conservatory overlooking the garden, and tasteful guestrooms. It's located in a quiet neighbourhood about a 10-minute stroll from the main sights. An excellent buffet breakfast is served and the service is exceptional.

Hotel Fevery €
Collaert Mansionstraat 3, T050 331 269 , www.hotelfevery.be.
Comfortable, friendly and modestly priced, this family–run, eco-friendly hotel is about a ten-minute walk from the Markt. There are just ten simple guestrooms, and a decent breakfast is included in the price. The welcoming owners can arrange day trips or guided tours and are happy to make recommendations. Private parking is available for around €9 per day. Doubles €40–90.

Hotel 't Voermanshuys
Oude Burg 14, T050 341 396, www. voermanshuys.be.
A great budget option, this offers functional but quiet and perfectly comfortable rooms in a superb location just off the Markt. The friendly owner is full of useful advice, and a simple breakfast is included in the price.

Eating

Belgian cuisine is world famous, and you'll have plenty of options. Flemish and French cuisines dominate the local culinary scene, but there is a sprinkling of international restaurants if you're hankering for something different. Lunch is usually served between 1200 and 1400 and dinner from 1900 to 2100. Always reserve in advance: the most popular places fill up early. Sundays and Mondays are the most common closing days for restaurants, but it's always worth checking in advance.

De Karmeliet €€€

Langestraat 19. Tel050 338 259, www.dekarmeliet.be.

One of the finest restaurants in Belgium, with three Michelin stars and a host of other accolades, De Karmeliet excells on every front. The spectacular cuisine is complemented by the elegant, high-ceilinged dining room, superlative service, and magnificent wine list. Book early for a table on the romantic, ivy-covered terrace. For a real splurge, opt for the eight-course Brugge die Scone menu (€180 per person). If the prices are too daunting, consider chef Geert van Hecke charming bistrot, Der Refter (see below). Closed Mon.

Kardinaalshof €€€

St Salvatorskerkhof 14, T050 341 691, www.kardinaalshof.be.

The award-winning cuisine at this luxurious restaurant, which sits in the shadow of St Salvator's Cathedral, is complemented by elegant décor and charming service. Choose from a selection of set menus (from €52 for four courses to €88 for the eight-course option), and savour traditional local recipes like wild duck with chicory, pears and nuts, or lamb with olives.

Der Refter €€

Molenmeers 2, Tel050 444 900, www.bistrorefter.com.

Award-winning chef Geert van Hecke of De Karmeliet (see above) is behind this colourful, modern bistro, which occupies the old refectory of a former Carmelite convent. They serve a superb set price menu (€35 for three courses, or €25 for main course and desert), which changes according to what's freshest at the market. Great terrace. Closed Sun and Mon.

Les Malesherbes €€

Stoofstraat 3-5, Tel050 336 924

Tucked down an impossibly narrow side street, this cosy and romantic spot is a great address for tasty French favourites like cassoulet (a rich stew of beans, sausage and duck), magret du canard (duck breast, served here in a fruity sauce), or a selection of fresh fish. Tiny and family-run, it feels rather like invited to someone's house for dinner. Charming service.

Koek & Zopie €

Dweersstraat 3, Tel047 2504 626, www.koekenzopie.be

A laid-back, friendly café with magazines and free Wi-Fi for the grown ups, and toys, high chairs, and a play area for the little ones. Funky retro décor, including wild orange wallpaper, makes it a magnet for arty locals. The pastries, cakes, pies, juices, and smoothies are made with organic, free-trade ingredients where possible.

Salade Folle €

Walplein 13, Tel050 349 443, www.saladefolle.com.

This restaurant isn't strictly vegetarian, but veggies will find plenty to choose from among the long list of soups, salads, quiches and pasta dishes. Some are made with organic produce. There are well priced set menus available at lunchtimes (€13) and weekend evenings (€24–28), and it's also a lovely spot for afternoon coffee and cakes.

Cafés and tea rooms

De Medici Sorbetiere €

Geldmunstraat 9, T050 339 341, www.demedici.com.

One of the most famous cafés in town, justly lauded for its thick hot chocolate (which comes as a DIY package – frothy, hot milk with chunks of chocolate to stir in). Their home-made ice creams and sorbets are a treat in summer, while the cakes are delicious at any time. They also serve light lunches – salads, toasted sandwiches and a couple of pasta dishes.

De Proeverie Tea Room €

Katelijnstraat 5-6, T050 330 837, www.deproeverie.be.

Scrumptious cakes and hot chocolate are the fare of choice in this wonderful tea room, owned by the famous Sukerbuyc chocolate shop just across the street. The range of hot chocolates is enormous, with all kinds of unusual flavours – try the dark chocolate and orange. They are beatifully presented with a swirl of fresh cream and a little dish of chocolate treats.

Nightlife

If you're looking for nightclubs, best head to Ghent or Antwerp: the nightlife in Bruges is decidedy low-key, and focused largely on the city's traditional taverns. Try one of the hundreds of speciality beers, perhaps take in a little live music, and soak up the city's relaxing vibe. For a relatively small city, it packs a big cultural punch, with plenty of concerts, theatre and dance performances throughout the year. Most are held at the Concertgebouw (www.concertgebouw.be). To find out what's on, pick up a copy of the *Agenda Brugge* pamphlet from the tourist office.

De Republiek

St-Jakobsstraat 36, Tel050 3402 29, www.derepubliek.be.
Downstairs from the Cinéma Lumière, this big, buzzy café-bar is a favourite with young locals, particularly on summer weekends when everyone piles out into the huge courtyard. They often have DJs at weekends, and they also serve food.

Staminee de Garre

De Garre 1, Tel050 341 029.
This old-fashioned bar, with exposed brick walls, beams, and wooden furnishings is a mecca for beer aficionados, thanks to its carefully chosen list of exceptional Belgian beers, each served in its own special glass. The house speciality is Tripel de Garre, a fabulous – if incredibly strong – local brew. Order a platter of Flemish cheese as an accompaniment.

Cactus Club @ Ma/Z

Sint-Sebastiaan 4, T050 332 014, www.cactusmusicbe.
From the people behind the city's excellent contemporary music festivals (Cactus, Klinkers, Music in Mind), the Cactus Club enjoys a well deserved reputation for its eclectic live music programme. Anything goes, from jazz and blues to reggae and R&B, and they also host regular club nights. The promoters also organise events at the Concertgebouw.

Travel essentials

Getting there

The nearest **international airports** to Bruges are in Brussels (110 km northeast of Bruges) and Charleroi (150 km southeast of Bruges). Brussels is the main international airport (*www.brusselsairport.be*), while Charleroi is smaller and is mainly used by lowcost airlines (*www.charleroi-airport.com*). From Brussels airport, there are regular train and bus links to the centre of Brussels, where you can change for trains to Bruges (total journey time 90 mins). From Charleroi airport, take the bus to Brussels and then the train out to Bruges (total journey time 2 hrs). Train timetables are available at www.b-rail.be.

Eurostar (*www.eurostar.com, T08432 186 186*) operates an **international train service** between London and Brussels, where you can pick up local trains for Bruges. The journey time (London to Brussels) is 1 hr 50 mins, and fares start at £69 return.

Getting around

Bruges is compact, so few visitors will need to make use of the **bus** network, except for the shuttle bus between the train station and the centre. The main bus station is next to the train station, about a 10-minute walk from the city centre. Bus tickets cost €1.20 in advance (from tobacconists and newsstands), or €1.60 on the bus. A one-day bus pass costs €5 in advance, or €6 on the bus.

Bruges is a bike-friendly city. Ask your hotel for bike rental or contact the following: **Bruges Bike Rental**, *Niklaas Desparsstraat 17, T050 616 108, www.brugesbikerental.be*, or **Bicycles Popelier**, *Mariastraat 26, T050 343 2362, www.fietsenpopelier.be*. Average costs are around €4 an hour, or €10–12 per day.

Driving is not recommended in Bruges. Leave your car at the multi-storey car park next to the train station (€2.50 for 24 hrs) and forget about it during your visit. Show your car park ticket at the bus ticket window to get a pass for the shuttle bus. Taxis cannot be hailed in the street, but there are convenient taxi stands at the train station and the Markt.

Tourist information

Concertgebouw, *'t Zand. Open daily 10am–6pm. T050 444 646, www.bruges.be/tourism.*

Railway Station, *Stationsplain. Open Mon–Fri 10am–5pm, Sat–Sun 10am–2pm. T050 444 646, www.bruges.be/tourism.*

Ratings

Art and culture ☆☆☆☆
Eating ☆☆☆☆☆
Nightlife ☆☆☆
Outdoors ☆
Romance ☆☆
Shopping ☆☆
Sightseeing ☆☆☆
Value-for-money ☆☆☆
Overall city rating ☆☆☆

Brussels

With Brussels, it's rarely a case of love at first sight, but this is a city that soon gets under your skin. Despite its grey image, the 'capital' of Europe is not short of showpiece buildings or stunning works of art – and its shabby, slightly frayed feel could be regarded as part of its charm. The EU presence lends the city an upbeat, cosmopolitan atmosphere, while the Dutch-speaking minority adds a cultural cutting edge – and all the city's communities unite in their appreciation of the finer things in life. The cooking really is superlative, even in the humblest corner café; the beer is out of this world, and the local penchant for self-deprecating humour gives the nightlife an earthy, unpretentious vibe. Oh, and the frîtes are mighty fine, too.

Godfrey of Bouillon statue.

At a glance

The core of Brussels is the plectrum-shaped **Pentagone**, home to the Upper and Lower Towns. At the Lower Town's heart is the **Grand'Place**, an awe-inspiringly opulent square graced with gilt-strewn guildhouses and a Gothic town hall. Around it bustle bars and restaurants in a warren of medieval streets known as the **Ilôt Sacré** ('Sacred Isle'). The **Upper Town**, otherwise known as the Royal Quarter, is almost oppressively monumental, its wide boulevards, mansions and palaces still lofty and inaccessible. The view back across town makes the uphill trudge worthwhile, however, and the Fine and Modern Arts Museums are essential viewing. Down rue de la Régence, under the shadow of the preposterously grandiose Palais de Justice, is the chic **Sablon** district,its main square lined with elegant houses, smart cafés and swish antiques shops. For something a little earthier, head into the **Marolles**, a traditional working-class area with a fabulous flea market. East of the Pentagone is the **European Quarter**, where quiet squares of stunning art nouveau architecture nestle amid the concrete colossi that house the EU institutions. To the south lie **St Gilles** and **Ixelles**, two characterful communes, laced with leafy squares, belle époque buildings, ethnic eateries and cosy cafés.

24 hours in the city

The die-hard Bruxellois breakfasts on beer, but a coffee on a **Grand'Place** terrace may have more appeal. Once you've drunk it all in, amble through the Ilôt Sacré, visiting the **Galeries St Hubert**, one of the world's first covered shopping arcades, and, if you can't beat the urge, paying homage to the **Manneken Pis**. Head up the Mont des Arts to the Upper Town, stopping at the art nouveau Old England building to visit the marvellous **Musical Instruments Museum**: the top-floor café is a good spot for lunch with a view. See the Bruegels and Magrittes at the **Fine and Modern Arts Museums**, then stroll down to the Sablon for a spot of window shopping; or, if you're an architecture buff, take a tram to **St Gilles** and visit the house of Victor Horta, the master architect of art nouveau. In the evening, head to the streets around tranquil **Place Ste Catherine** for fine fish and moules-frîtes in any of a dozen wonderful places before hunkering down for some serious beer appreciation in the bountiful bars of the Old Town.

Grand'Place

Map D2.

On this jaw-droppingly gorgeous square, it's hard to know where to stare first – at the exquisite Gothic **Town Hall**, with its curlicued masonry and soaring spire, or the glorious baroque **guildhouses**, honey-coloured and dripping with gilt and leaded glass.

Jean Cocteau called the square "the greatest theatre in the world", and its story is nothing if not dramatic: Louis XIV's artillery razed the square in 1695, but the doughty burghers rebuilt it in just four years. Each house belonged to a guild, and identifying the trade from the golden statues atop each building is all part of the fun. Victor Hugo lived at **Nos 26-27** (known as '**The Pigeon**') during his exile from France; Marx brooded over the *Communist Manifesto* in the workers' café at **No 9**, '**The Swan**', now a swanky restaurant. The best terrace is at **Nos 1-2**, '**Le Roy d'Espagne**', formerly the bakers' guild. Drinks are not cheap, but the views are priceless.

Ilôt Sacré

The jumble of medieval streets around the Grand'Place has long been anything but sacred. Their names attest to intense mercantile activity – Butchers' Street, Herring Street, Spur-Makers' Street – and they remain a blur of shops, restaurants, bars and clubs. The eateries around rue des Bouchers,

Grand'Place.

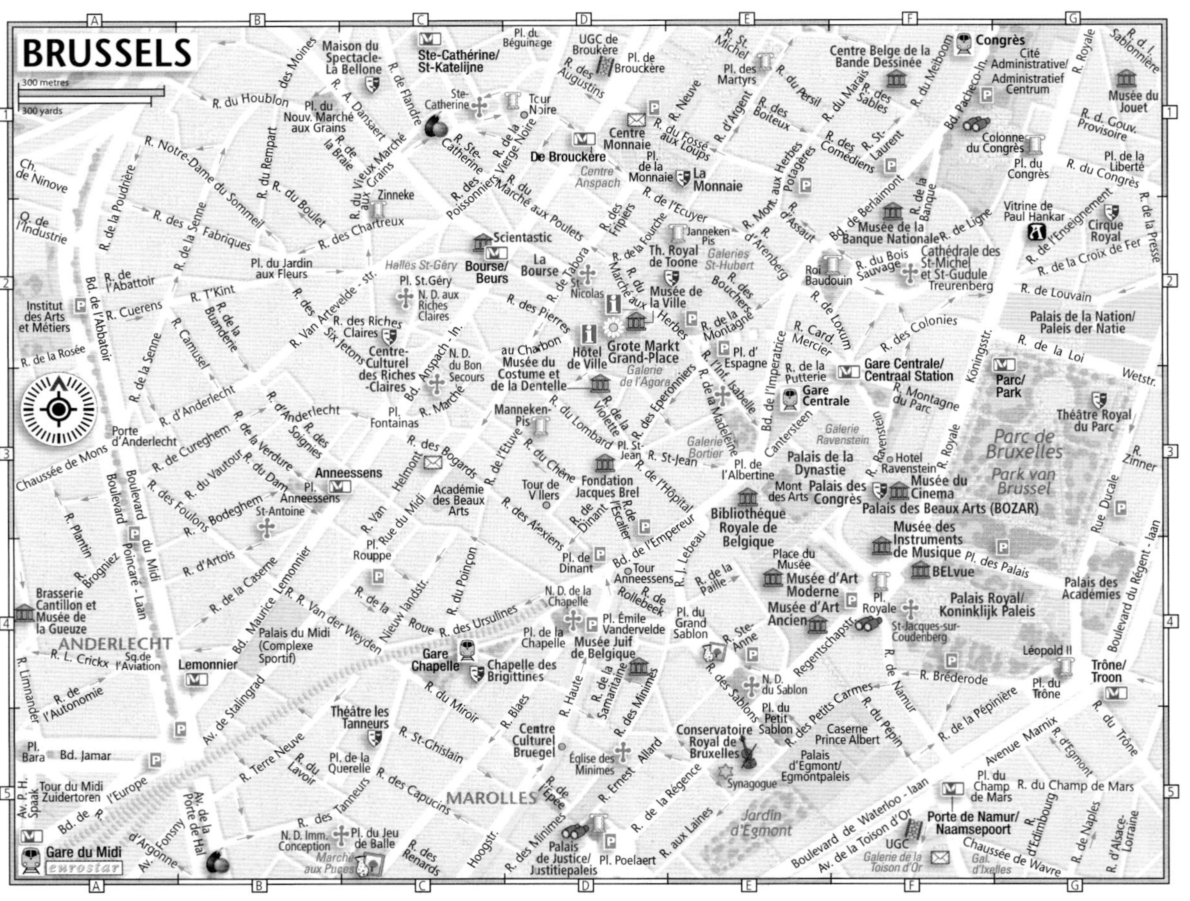

BRUSSELS
300 metres
300 yards
Grote Markt
Grand-Place
Hôtel de Ville
Musée de la Ville
Manneken-Pis
Bourse/Beurs
De Brouckère
Gare Centrale/Centraal Station
Parc de Bruxelles
Park van Brussel
Palais Royal/Koninklijk Paleis
Palais des Beaux Arts (BOZAR)
Musée des Instruments de Musique
Musée d'Art Ancien
Musée d'Art Moderne
Bibliothèque Royale de Belgique
Centre Belge de la Bande Dessinée
Cathédrale des St-Michel et St-Gudule
Colonne du Congrès
Congrès
Trône/Troon
Porte de Namur/Naamsepoort
Palais de Justice/Justitiepaleis
MAROLLES
Conservatoire Royal de Bruxelles
Jardin d'Egmont
Gare Chapelle
Chapelle des Brigittines
Palais du Midi (Complexe Sportif)
Lemonnier
Anneessens
Gare du Midi
ANDERLECHT
Ste-Cathérine/St-Katelijne
La Monnaie
Centre Monnaie
Galeries St-Hubert
Musée du Costume et de la Dentelle
Boulevard du Midi
Boulevard Poincaré - Laan
Bd. de l'Abbatoir
Boulevard du Régent - laan
Boulevard de Waterloo - laan
R. Royale
Rue Ducale

All hail the ale

Brewing is one of Belgium's grandest traditions, and the appreciation of a really good beer, poured reverently into its special glass, is one of the high points of any visit to Brussels. Even if you don't consider yourself an ale aficionado, you'll savour a trip to the **Brussels Gueuze Museum**, *Q Cantillon brewery, rue Gheude 56, T02 521 4928, www.cantillon.be, Mon-Fri 0830-1700, Sat 1000-1700, €5*, the capital's last bastion of traditional lambic production. The basis for Belgium's fabled fruit beers, lambic is the only brew to ferment spontaneously without yeast: the roof is left open to allow spores from the local atmosphere to infuse the liquid. Learn more on the brewery tour, marvelling at the musty ambience, the huge copper vats and the unbridled enthusiasm of the owner. Then it's tasting time: the kriek (cherry) and framboise (raspberry) beers are sharper, fruitier and more refreshing than the sweetened stuff on sale in most cafés. But the real deal is the gueuze, a complex blend of lambics that has a sharp, sour, almost vinegary taste. If you don't like it on the first try, buy 75cl bottles to take home and/or inflict on your nearest and dearest.

Above: Manneken Pis.
Opposite page: Inside the Galeries St Hubert.

with vast seafood displays outside, are expert at relieving unwary tourists of their cash and are best avoided. (If that sounds bad, night-time visitors in the 19th century were considered lucky to leave with their lives!) That said, there are other great places to eat and drink, and the atmosphere can be positively Bruegelian. The **Galeries St Hubert**, one of the world's first covered shopping arcades, is an oasis of calm amid the surrounding hubbub; a cool, airy glass structure erected in 1847, it houses a theatre, a cinema and cafés and restaurants.

Belgian Comic Strip Center (Centre Belge de la Bande Desinée)

Rue des Sables 20, T02 219 1980, www.comicscenter.net.
Tue-Sun 1000-1800. €8. Map F1.

Tintin fans are in for a treat here; but there's more to bande dessinée than the intrepid boy reporter. While this marvellous museum, converted from a Horta-designed art nouveau department store, gives Hergé ample coverage, it's a great place to catch up on Belgium's other memorable comic-book creations. And, more ignominiously, the origins of the Smurfs. Parents be warned: they take the 'ninth art' seriously in Belgium, and the top-floor displays show just how grown-up the genre can be.

Manneken Pis

Rue de l'Etuve.
Map D3.

Symbol of Bruxellois irreverence, anti-war icon or shamelessly tacky photo opportunity? Here's your chance to decide, if you can force your way through the camcorder- wielding crowd that surrounds Brussels's smallest tourist attraction. Mystery surrounds his origins, but the pint-size piddler's current incarnation is a copy of a statue fashioned by Jérôme Duquesnoy in 1619 and smashed into smithereens two centuries later. He's often decked out in costumes donated by visiting dignitaries, from the Elector of Bavaria, in 1698, to Elvis.

Fine and Modern Arts Museums

Place Royale 1-2, T02 508 3211, www.fine-arts-museum.be.
Tue-Sun 1000-1700. €5. Map E4.

These twin museums comprise the country's finest collection. The Fine is a conventional 19th-century gallery with a superb survey of works by the artists once grouped together as the 'Flemish Primitives': Van der Weyden, Memling, Bouts and, most important, Pieter Bruegel the Elder. It's full of vast Rubens canvases and superbly observed smaller works. The Modern is an unusual subterranean spiral with the world's largest collection of works by the star Surrealist René Magritte; there's also a good sample of 20th-century greats – Picasso, Matisse, Bacon, Dalí – and Belgian masters: Paul Delvaux, Leon Spilliaert and Constant Permeke.

Musical Instruments Museum

Rue Montagne de la Cour 2, T02 545 0130, www.mim.fgov.be.
Tue-Fri 0930-1700, Sat-Sun 1000-1700. €5. Map E5.

No prizes for guessing what's on show here – but the setting is a real surprise. The frills and flourishes of the ornate Old England building, a delightful art nouveau department store in glass and black iron, are an apt counterpoint to the exquisite craftsmanship of the exhibits. The painted pianos from pre- revolutionary France are a highlight, as are the weird and wonderful folk instruments. The top-floor restaurant has some of the best views in town.

Place du Grand Sablon

Map E4.

The Grand'Place may be the city's grandest square, but the Sablon has a little more, well, class. Although

Stained-glass window in Notre Dame du Sablon.

the baroque houses lack their counterparts' flamboyance, they're still drop-dead gorgeous. The antiques shops at street level are reassuringly expensive, the cafés and restaurants smart and perfect for observing how Brussels' other half lives. There's a wonderful Gothic church, Notre Dame du Sablon, at the square's southeastern side.

Place du Jeu de Balle

If you find the Sablon too stuffy, head downhill to the grittier, more ramshackle Marolles, a traditionally working-class district in the shadow of the preposterously overblown Palais de Justice. It sprawls around rues Blaes and Haute (on which Bruegel lived, at No 132), but its heart is the **flea market** on place du Jeu de Balle (daily 0700-1400). Amid the mountains of tat, there are some serious bargains, especially for early birds.

Horta Museum

Rue Américaine 25, T02 543 0490, www.hortamuseum.be.
Tue-Sun 1400-1730. €7. Tram 81 or 92. Off map.

Victor Horta was perhaps the greatest exponent of art nouveau, and the house he built in St Gilles is an eloquent reminder of his philosophy and craftsmanship. Horta believed in total design, right down to the door knobs, but he never let the swirls and curls get out of control. Inside, the house is a symphony of burnished wood, stained glass, delicate wrought iron and covetable antiques.

European Quarter

Home to the Commission, the Council of Europe and the European Parliament, as well as countless NGOs, lobby groups, media organizations and multinationals, this district east of the Old Town is like an entirely separate city, one where English is the lingua franca, but where you'll hear dozens of languages on every street. If possible, time your visit for a weekday; the area's deserted at weekends and the relentlessly functional post-war office blocks can deaden the soul. Amid the glass, steel and concrete boxes, however, are two lovely squares, **place Ambiorix** and **place Marie-Louise**. The Hôtel St-Cyr, at 11 place Ambiorix, is so ridiculously ornate, it's beyond parody.

Sleeping

Although there are plenty of characterful establishments, Brussels depends primarily on business. That's great news for short-breakers, as rates plummet at the weekend. Expect reductions of at least 30% and often much more. Summer prices are also extremely keen. The Old Town has a good concentration of hotels; there are also good options in the European Quarter and Ixelles. Try www.bookings.be for late deals; for B&Bs, visit www.bnb-brussels.be or www.bedandbreakfastbelgium.com.

Amigo €€€
rue de l'Amigo 1-3, T02 547 4747, www.hotelamigo.com.
Part of Rocco Forte's exclusive portfolio, this is an immensely stylish establishment near the Grand'Place. Once a prison (the poet Paul Verlaine was incarcerated here after shooting his lover, Rimbaud), it's now a liberating mix of ancient and modern, with lush tapestries and Flemish masters complemented by top-quality contemporary fabrics and fittings.

Le Dixseptième €€€
rue de la Madeleine 25, T02 517 1717, www.ledixseptieme.be.
Don't be fooled by the discreet façade – this was once the Spanish ambassador's residence. Now it's really spoiling us with a superbly restored 17th-century interior, relaxed service and 24 dreamily luxurious, classically kitted-out rooms.

Theater Hotel Brussels €€
Rue Van Gaver 23, T02 350 9000, www.theaterhotelbrussels.com.
A new addition to the city's range of boutique hotels, located, as the name suggests, in the theatre district. The building has been completely renovated, resulting in stylish but simple interiors with smooth lines and no frills. It's also handy for Rue Nueve, the city's main shopping area, so not too far to carry the bags!

Welcome €€
rue du Peuplier 5, T02 219 9546, www.hotelwelcome.com.
Amid the fish restaurants of Place Ste Catherine is this wonderful little hotel with 15 world-themed rooms. The Congo is all leopard-print fabrics; the Japan, sleek, stark and serene. It's too well done to be kitsch, and the owners have charm to spare.

Noga €€€
rue du Béguinage 38, T02 218 6763, www.nogahotel.com.
There's a nautical theme in this quiet place on a side street near Place Ste Catherine. The rooms are bright, boldly coloured and extremely comfortable, and the clincher is what the website calls "Noga's little extras": bike hire, a piano in the lounge, a snooker room. It's also great value.

2Go4 Hostel €
Boulevard Emile Jacqmain-laan 99, T02 219 3019, www.2go4.be.
A bright and cheerful 19th century building, situated in the heart of the city, making it a very popular choice for budget conscious travellers who like to be in the thick of things. New private rooms have recently been added, giving guests more choice when it comes to sleeping preferences. Friendly staff on hand 24/7 to help with tour bookings and orientation. No curfew so great for night owls.

Eating

Even the self-deprecating Bruxellois can't help being proud of their city's culinary prowess, and with good reason: it's almost impossible to have a bad meal here, unless you're foolish enough to succumb to the wiles of the waiters on rue des Bouchers. Brasseries and cafés usually have an all-day menu, with staples such as spaghetti bolognese, omelettes and a range of croques. Portions are enormous, so go easy on the starters.

Breakfast

Het Warm Water €
rue des Renards 25, T02 513 9159, www.hetwarmwater.be.
Thu-Tue 0800-1900.
For brekkie, brunch and Belgian specialities, with a side order of authentic Marollien atmosphere, you can't beat this place off place du Jeu de Balle. It serves earthy, homely cuisine – Brussels soup, pottekees, cheese and endive omelette – as well as croissants and muesli. Brunch on Sun (1100-1500) is a riotous affair.

Lunch

Le Paon Royal €€-€
Oude Graanmarkt 6, T02 513 0868, www.paonroyal.com.
Tue-Sat 0800- 2200.
Lunchtime special €8.50.
The Royal Peacock is the quintessence of Brussels bonhomie. Off Place Ste Catherine, it's homely with a country-pub feel, serving shrimp croquettes, veal cooked in cherry beer and eels in a pungent green sauce. Excellent beer too.

In 't Spinnekopke €€-€
Bloemenhofplein 1, T02 511 8695, www.spinnekopke.be.
A homely tavern, slightly off the beaten track, but worth seeking out. Belgian classics are the order of the day and the mussels are

a speciality (when in season). Wash your lunch down with one of the many Belgian Beers on offer. The atmosphere is warm and welcoming, so much so that you may not want to leave…

Dinner

Maison du Cygne €€€
Rue Charles Buls 2, T02 511 8244, www.lamaisonducygne.be.
One of Brussels finest restaurants, serving traditional French and Belgian cuisine. Step back in time and experience an elegant bygone era in stunning surroundings. The quality of the food matches the décor, so be prepared to settle down for the evening and enjoy. There are over 20,000 wines to choose from in the restaurant's cellar, so take your time.

Bij Den Boer €€
quai aux Briques 60, T02 512 6122, www.bijdenboer.com.
Mon-Sat 1200-1430 and 1800-2230.
There are posher and trendier places to eat fish in the Ste Catherine area but this resolutely old-fashioned restaurant has rugged charm aplenty. It's a sea of burnished wood and check tablecloths, with specials chalked up on mirrors. House specialities include mussels five ways, North Sea bouillabaisse and poached skate wing.

La Roue d'Or €€
rue des Chapeliers 26, T02 514 2554, www.resto.be.
Daily 1200-0000.
Although its striking decor tips a (bowler) hat to Magritte and the Surrealists, the polished wood and mirrors give the game away: the Golden Wheel is basically a brasserie, and a jolly good one at that. Just off the Grand'Place, it offers a mix of French (cassoulet, andouillette AAAAA) and Belgian dishes (sausage and stoemp, creamy fish or chicken waterzooi), handling both cuisines with aplomb. The double-fried chips are to die for.

Nightlife

With so many great beers to try, it's a good job Brussels is rammed with great bars. The expat crowd stick to the European Quarter's Irish joints; leave them to it and focus on the Old Town. Place St Géry's terraces are a magnet for the beautiful people, but rue du Marché au Charbon has more edge, with samba and salsa at **Canoa Quebrada** (No 53), the boho **Au Soleil** (No 86) and the LHB haven **Belgica** (No 32).

The intersection of rue Dansaert and rue des Chartreux is another good crawling point: on the former, **L'Archiduc** (No 6) is a seriously cool art deco jazz bar; on the latter, **Le Greenwich** (No 7) is a classic old café where chess players congregate; and on nearby rue Orts, the **Beurs Café**, is a super cool post industrial space.

Beyond the Old Town, chaussée de Charleroi (tram 91 or 92) is lounge central. Try **Chelsea** (No 85), **Le Living Room** (No 50) and Kolya (No 102). Off the main drag are two great conversions: **Khnopff**, rue St Bernard 1, a cooler-than-thou bar-restaurant; and the hugely romantic wine bar **Amadeus**, 13 rue Veydt, in Rodin's studio.

Beer buffs should head straight for **Chez Moeder Lambic**, 68 rue de Savoie; pré-Métro Horta, a loveably scruffy St Gilles institution that stocks every Belgian brew you can think of. Open till (at least) 0300 most nights.

Travel essentials

Getting there

Brussels is well served by international trains: **Eurostar** (www.eurostar.com) runs from London to Brussels Gare du Midi (2 hr 20 mins, returns from £69), while the high-speed Thalys service (www.thalys.com) links the city with Paris, Amsterdam and Cologne. The city has 2 airports. **Brussels International** (www.brusselsairport.be) is served by airlines from destinations throughout Europe. From the airport, there are 4 trains an hour to the city's 3 stations; the 20-min ride costs €2.80. A **taxi** costs €30 each way. **Brussels South (Charleroi)** (www.charleroi-airport.com) is used by some budget airlines and is a 1-hr bus ride from the capital. Alternative routes from the UK include ferry services to Zeebrugge, Ostend (both an hour's drive from Brussels) and Calais (1½-2hrs), or the EuroTunnel. See also pages 12 and 14.

Getting around

The Pentagone is easily negotiable on foot; for journeysfurther afield, there's an excellent tram, bus and metro network, run by **Societé des Transports Intercommunaux Bruxellois (STIB/MIVB)**, online at www.stib.irisnet.be. A day pass for all forms of transport costs €4.20. You get free public transport with the **Brussels Card** (www.brusselscard.be), available at the Gare du Midi, the main tourist office and from hotels and museums. It offers free access to 32 museums in the city, a city map and guide and 25% discounts in shops, restaurants and bars across the city. A card costs €24 for one day, €34 for two days or €40 for three days. Cycling in the city centre is not recommended (given the tramlines, cobbles and traffic-clogged boulevards).

Tourist information

The main **Brussels International** tourist office is located in the Town Hall, on the Grand'Place, T02-513 8940, www.brussels international.be. Open Mon-Sat 0900- 1800; Sun 0900-1800 in summer, 1000- 1400 in winter, closed Sun Jan-Easter. It sells the **Brussels Card** (see above), maps and guides. There's also a room-finding service for visitors who arrive in the city without a hotel reservation.

Note that most museums are closed Mon; some are also closed at lunchtime on other days.

Ratings

Art and culture ☆☆☆☆
Eating ☆☆☆☆
Nightlife ☆☆☆☆
Romance ☆☆☆
Shopping ☆☆☆
Sightseeing ☆☆☆☆
Value-for-money ☆☆☆
Overall city rating ☆☆☆

Budapest

Although some investment has flowed into Budapest since Hungary's EU accession in 2004, prosperity is yet to reach the doors of ordinary Hungarians. Still, the city bears the imprint of its communist years pretty lightly and shares much of the imposing grandeur of its Hapsburg neighbour, Vienna, although it is more derelict and more charming for it. The two cities Buda and Pest, joined administratively in the 19th century, are still kept apart by the grey sweep of the Danube. Above its waters lie belle époque buildings and the weathered stone of neoclassical and baroque mansions. The home of Liszt and Bartók has a rich musical heritage, as well as an underground arts and bar scene, not to mention beautiful mosaic Turkish baths where you can steam yourself back to life after a night on the town.

Budapest sign.

At a glance

Buda's Castle Hill rises just over 180 m on the west side of the Danube to offer brilliant views of both the neighbouring hilltop, **Gellért**, to the south, and the low-level sprawl of **Pest** across the river to the east. Pest incorporates two-thirds of the city and is more dynamic and grimy than its west bank rival. The **Chain Bridge** links Castle Hill with **Belváros** on the east bank. This is where the medieval city grew up. It is bordered by a semicircular series of roads (József Attila ut, Károly körút, Múzeum körút and Vámház körút), which together are dubbed the **'Little Boulevard'**. Cutting straight through the inner city, parallel to the Danube, is the shopping street-cum-tourist zone, **Váci út**. To its northeast is **Deák Ferenc tér**, the starting point for the city's most important and grandiose thoroughfare, **Andrássy út**, which runs northeast for over 2 km to the city park, **Városliget**, and **Heroes Square** (Hösök Tere), focal point of the 1956 anti-Soviet uprising.

The **Great Boulevard** is a broader arc that apes the semicircle of the Little Boulevard, running from Margit Hid (Margaret Bridge) at the toe-tip of Margit Island in the north, crossing Andrássy út at Oktogon, then looping back to the river at Petöfi Híd to the south of the city.

24 hours in the city
For an early morning view of Budapest's World Heritage status head for Buda's Castle District. Enter through the northern **Vienna Gate** (Bécsi kapu tér) and stroll past the ceramic roof of the **National Archives**, before exploring the cobblestone sidestreets and ducking west for a leafy walk along the ramparts. Have a late breakfast at **Ruszwurm**, then head on towards Holy Trinity Square to see the **Mátyás Church** and the **Fishermen's Bastion**. Take the funicular down the hill to the river and then take a tram south to the **Gellért** thermal spa for a swim and a pummel. After a snack lunch at the **Central Market** in Pest, head up Váci út, to reach **Szent István Bazilika**, then stroll along Andrássy út to the **House of Terror**. Recover from the horrors of the 20th century by contemplating the achievements of the Spanish masters at the **Museum of Fine Arts** on Heroes Square. Head back to the river for an early evening **cruise** before enjoying a recital at the **Opera House** or **Liszt Academy**. Supper could be something modishly Hungarian at Vörös és Fehér, followed by table football and a nightcap at a trendy kerts. Too down-at-heel? Try a Liszt Ferenc Square bar, or the A38 boat on the river between Petöfi and Lágymányosi bridges, Buda.

Várhegy and Király Palota (Castle Hill and Royal Palace)

Map A3/B4.

A fortress was first built on Buda's unmistakable World Heritage hilltop following the Mongol invasion of 1241, which almost razed the settlements of low-lying Obuda and Pest. The Royal Palace occupies the southern slopes of the hill and commands regal views over the quays and boats of Pest but, although the site was successfully defended over the centuries, its buildings proved to be less resilient. The palace was destroyed first in battle with the Turks in the 17th century and, again, during the German retreat at the end of the Second World War, and each time it was rebuilt in the architectural vernacular of the day. Today, its stately neoclassical buildings and stone parapets house a rash of cultural institutes: the **Hungarian National Gallery**, *T020 439 7325, www.mng.hu, Tue-Sun 1000-1800, HUF900 (temporary exhibitions HUF1900)*; the **Budapest History Museum**, *T01 225 7809, www.btm.hu, Tue-Mon 1000-1800, HUF1300*; the **National Széchényi Library**, *T01 224 3700, www.oszk.hu, Tue-Sat 1000-2100*; and the **Ludwig Museum**, *T01 555 3444, www.ludwig museum.hu, Tue-Sun 1000-2000, from HUF700 (prices vary with exhibitions)*. Look out for the bronze sculpture of King Mátyás at the hunt, looking every inch like Errol Flynn. A funicular, the **Budavári Sikló** (HUF800) is a good way to climb to the top of the hill.

Castle Hill and Royal Palace.

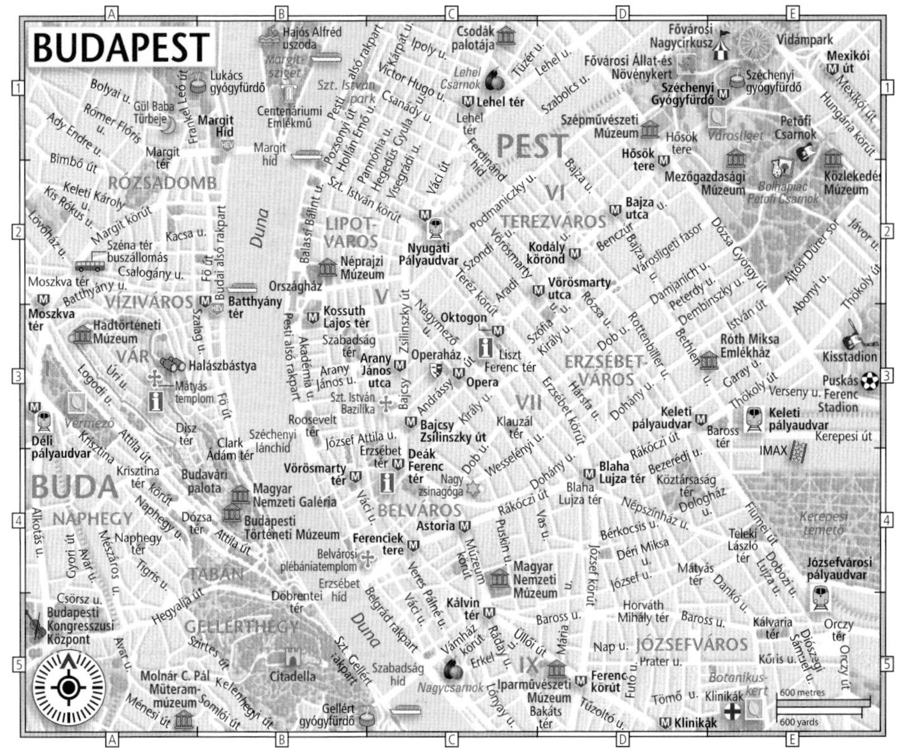

Mátyás Templom, Fishermen's Bastion and Várnegyed

Szentháromság tér, District 1, T01 355 3657. Daily 0600-2000. HUF270-550 in summer. Map A3.

The two-thirds of Buda that wasn't taken up with palace buildings was left to the civilians. At the centre of this area is **Holy Trinity Square** (Szentháromság tér) and the lovely **Mátyás Church**, *www.matyas-templom.hu, Mon-Fri 0900-1500, Sat 0900-1300, Sun 1300-1700, HUF650.* Painted with Asian and Turkish-influenced geometric heraldic motifs, the church has had to wear a number of religious hats down the ages. It was shared between Catholics and Protestants and became a Mosque during the Turkish occupation of 1541. The Gothic body of the church was built in the 13th century, the tower in the 15th. A facelift, timed to coincide with the 1896 millennium celebration, gave it back its eye-popping frescoes, medieval-style tiles and stained glass. The whole project was overseen by Frigyes Schulek, who also designed the neo-Romanesque trim to the church, the Halászbástya, known as the **Fishermen's Bastion**.

North of the square, in **Várnegyed**, are the squat merchants', noblemen's and courtiers' residences, painted umber, olive, yellow, ochre and cream. Heavy doors open on to courtyards, with wells and plane trees, and shallow stone reliefs decorate the façades. Parts of the area are medieval but much was rebuilt in the baroque and Louis XVI styles when the Turks left after the 1686 siege.

Orszaghaz (Parliament)

Kossuth Lajos tér, District 5, T01 317 9800.
Visits by guided tour only (tickets from the gate), daily 1000, 1200, 1400, 1800. Map C3.

The puffed-up Parliament building on the Pest embankment is a splendid piece of pomp, modelled on the Palace of Westminster, and it's as impressive inside as out: full of frescoes and sculptures, deep red carpets, stained-glass windows, hundred-bulb chandeliers, four-tonne monolithic granite colonnades and the crown, sceptre, orb and sword of the Hungarian coronation.

Szent István Bazilika (St Stephen's Basilica)

Szent István tér, District 5, T01 317 2859
Summer 0900-1700; winter 1000-1600. Map C3.

Budapest's largest church, completed in 1905, is a fat neoclassical building perfumed with the myrrh of its votive candles and dominated by marble

(15 different types), mosaics and paintings. If Matyas Church is Budapest's fussy Westminster Abbey, then St Stephen's is the city's St Paul's. It is named after the founder of the Hungarian state, Catholic King Szent István, whose mummified arm is kept on the left side of the chapel, and who sits carved from Italian marble on the high altar. Go up to the dome for amazing rooftop views of the Postal Savings Bank, designed by Ödön Lechner. What appears at

street level to be an unremarkable white building, reveals itself from above to be a perfect aesthetic expression of the building's function: the bank's roof is embroidered with bees, the symbol of saving.

Magyar Állami Operaház (State Opera House)

Andrássy út 22, District 6, T01 332 7914, www.opera.hu.
Map C3.

Hungary punches well above its weight in terms of musical virtuosity, and the Hungarian State Opera House is an appropriate physical representation of the country's acoustic refinement. The sphinx-flanked entrance gives onto a Fabergé-egg of an interior. Built in 1884 in neo-Renaissance style to Miklós Ybl's design, the architecture is best enjoyed during a ballet or opera performance. Tickets are decidedly affordable by London standards.

Andrássy út

This UNESCO-protected boulevard runs for 2½km, like a grandiose spoke, from inner-city Pest at Szent István's to the Hösök Tere and City Park in the northeast. It was built in the late 19th century at the time of the administrative union of Buda, Óbuda and Pest, after the Austro-Hungarian Compromise. Its buildings are almost absurdly beautiful and can be divided loosely into three sections: closest to the Danube are four-storey residential blocks, then two-storey mansions give way to palaces and gardens the further out you get. Modelled on the Champs-Elysées and designed by Ybl, it is one of the world's finest urban landscapes. Look out particularly for the Postamúzeum, the **Postal Museum**, *Andrássy út 3, T01 269 6838, www.postamuzeum.hu, Tue-Sun 1000-1800, HUF500*, which is notable for its architecture rather than its exhibits, and Kodály Köröndd, a series of mansion blocks with amazing frescoed façades.

Right: Adrássy út.
Opposite page top: Fishermen's Bastion.
Opposite page left: Parliament building.
Opposite page right: St Stephen's Basilica.

Buda bath time

Residents on the Buda side of the city have water pressure sloshing from their taps with the force of a hardly-harnessed Niagara: Budapest lies on top of somewhere between 80 and 120 active springs and wells from which 70 million litres of water burst forth daily. The medicinal properties of the city's naturally hot springs were recognized during the Turkish occupation and, by 1500, the Turks had bequeathed their Hungarian subjects some beautiful Ottoman baths, featuring high domes with shafts of light searing through the steam, and tile mosaics lining the 18°C plunge pools. Today, the baths remain a brilliant way to atone for a night on the Buda or Pest tiles, despite the off-putting appearance of most bathhouse staff. Baths tend to be single sex, although swimming pools are usually mixed. Specific treatments for rheumatism, physiotherapy and inhalation are available, but on weekends from April to September, most people head outside to lounge around and sunbathe with the papers, stirring only to complete extremely lackadaisical laps of the swimming pool. The best baths in town are: **Gellért**, *Kelenhegyi út 4-6, T01 466 6166, www.gellertbath.com, Mon-Sat 0600-1900, Sat-Sun 0600-1700, HUF3500*, which is full of art nouveau furnishings, mosaics and stained-glass windows; the neo-baroque **Széchenyi Spa**, *Állatkerti út 11, District 14, T01 363 3210, May-Sep 0600-1900, Oct-Apr 0600-1700, HUF3100-3400*, which has chess boards in its pool, and the gay favourite, **Király Medicinal**, *Föutca 82-84, T01 202 3688, Mon, Wed, Fri 0700-1800 for women, Tue, Thu, Sat 0900-2000 for men, all day HUF2100, afternoon HUF1570.*

Best of the rest

Gellérthegy (Gellért Hill)
District 6.
A symbol of Austrian supremacy, this citadel was built after the 1848 revolution.

Chain Bridge
The oldest bridge to span the Danube (1849) was designed by the engineer of Hammersmith Bridge, William Tierney Clark, and built by Scotsman, Adam Clark.

Dohány Street Synagogue
Dohány utca 2, Mon-Thu 1000- 1700 (winter 1500) Fri, Sun, 1000-1400, HUF400-1000.
Central Europe's largest Jewish community gave rise to its largest synagogue. The Holocaust tree in the garden has metal branches and dog-collar leaves, bearing the names of Jewish lives lost.

Liszt Ferenc Zeneakadémia (Franz Liszt Academy of Music)
Liszt Ferenc tér 8, District 6, T01 462 4600, www.lfze.hu.
Amazing art nouveau building and one of the city's main concert halls.

Margitsziget (Margaret Island)
The lungs of the city, a favourite destination for romantics and joggers.

Szoborpark (Statue Park)
Balatoni út/ Szabadkai utca, District 22, T 01 424 7500, www.szoborpark.hu. 1000-sunset. HUF1500. From Ferenciek tér: No 7 or No 173 buses to Etele tér, then Volan Bus (yellow to Diosd-Erd).
'The Disneyland of Communism' displays the vast statues that once lined the city's streets: Marx, Engels, Lenin, Hungarian labour movement heroes, plus the hammer and sickle.

Hósök Tere (House of Terror)

Andrássy út 60, District 6, T01 374 2600, www.terrorhaza.hu.
Tue-Sun 1000-1800, closed Mon. HUF1800. Map D1.

Brace yourself: this is sightseeing as harrowing 20th-century history lesson. Number 60 Andrássy út was, from 1939 to 1944, the House of Loyalty, party HQ of the Hungarian Nazi Arrow Cross Party. Between 1945 and '56 it went on to become the head of the Soviet terror organizations ÁVO and ÁVH. Both were remarkable for institutionalized brutality and the torture of subjects. The emphasis is on experience over mere exhibition. Nagging music and newsreel footage make this document of the crimes of the successive terror regimes so vivid as to turn your stomach. Documentary footage contrasts the order and iconography of the Nazi regime with the relative scrappiness of Soviet rule but the museum has also been criticized for describing the atrocities of the latter in detail, while providing only relatively cursory treatment of the Nazi genocide.

Szépm vészeti Múzeum (Museum of Fine Arts)

Dózsa György út 41, Heroes Sq, District 4, T01 469 7100, www.szepmuveszeti.hu.
Tue-Sun 1000-1730. Map D1.

This imitation Greek temple at the City Park end of Andrássy út houses a collection of Spanish masters including seven El Grecos and five Goyas. Its walls also carry bleary oil paintings of saints, acts of martyrdom, beheadings and sermons. Outside, the **Millennium Monument** marks the 1000th anniversary of the Magyar Conquest, with archangel Gabriel on top of a column and the seven tribal chieftains below. Across Heroes Square, the showcase for political gatherings and displays of Communist and Soviet might, sits the **Palace of Arts**. Behind is **City Park**, home to **Széchenyi spa** and the winter ice-skating rink.

Left: The Chain Bridge.

Sleeping

Budapest has its share of charmless Soviet-style business hotels but there are some treats too. The city also has a strong homestay tradition, as well as serviced apartments, which are available for both long-term rental and short lets.

Art'Otel €€€
Bem Rakpart 16-19, T01 487 9487, www.artotel.de.
On the Buda side of the Danube, overlooking Parliament, this hotel is spruce, slick and more minimalist than the Gresham. The 148 rooms in four baroque townhouses have floor-to-ceiling windows and snappy service.

Four Seasons Hotel Gresham Palace €€€
Chain Bridge, Roosevelt tér 5-6, T01 268 6000, www.fourseasons.com/budapest.
The art nouveau/secessionist Gresham Palace was built to accommodate wealthy British aristocrats. Today, this landmark building is home to Budapest's most luxurious hotel. Rooms have huge fluffy pillows, giant bathrooms and the best views in Pest. There's also an infinity pool, gym, spa and a flawlessly polished service ethic.

Danubius Hotel Gellért €€
Szent Gellért tér 1, T01 889 5500, www.danubiushotels.com/hu.
The grand dame among Budapest's hotels. Its carpets can be dank and it reeks of the Soviet era but the views across the Liberty Bridge are splendid, and it has character in spades. Rates include admission to the excellent onsite Gellért Thermal Baths (see page 69).

Hotel Pest €€
Paulay Ede u. 31, District 6, T01 343 1198, www.hotel pest.hu.
An 18th-century apartment building just a stone's throw from the Opera House is now an elegant, 3-star hotel with 25 immaculate rooms overlooking an ivy-clad courtyard.

Residence Izabella €€
Izabella út/ Andrássy út, T01 475 5900, www.mamaison.com.
This residential apartment in a 19th-century building has been exactingly refurbished. Thirty-eight Suites have one-three bedrooms, plus kitchen, lounge and dining room. Room service, breakfast, laundry, concierge, AV system, sauna, pool room and home theatre are all available.

Kalmar Bed & Breakfast €
Kelenhegyi út 7-9, T01 430 0831.
Something of a time warp, Kalmar is a 1900-mansion-turned-idiosyncratic pension sitting in its own garden on the southeast slope of Gellért hill, a few hundred yards back from the Danube. It's a family-run concern, with large, clean rooms. There are double rooms, suites, plus a top-floor apartment that can sleep 4; all have antique furniture, high ceilings, large windows and TVs.

Eating

Hungarians know their way round a knuckle of ham, but the country that gave us goulash hasn't earned a place at the top table of global cuisine. Stout, artery-thickening dishes are the norm; most come soused in thick creamy sauces. That said, there is a lively metropolitan restaurant scene at the top end, serving fish fresh from Lake Balaton, and the countryside seems to produce so much fruit that the Hungarians have no option but to use it in spiced soups – a cool cinnamon-spiked peach broth is not uncommon in late summer. Cakes are a strong suit, as are lángos, a pizza-like dough that's fried, then smeared with sour cream and garlic.

Menza €€€
Liszt Ferenc ter 2, T01 413 1482, www.menzaetterem.hu.
Funky retro floral wallpaper sets the tone for this funky recreation of Soviet-era canteen style. Modern international touches influence the Hungarian dishes on the menu and there's a good wine list. An oh-so-cool compilation album is also available.

Café Kör €€
Sas utca 17, Szent István Bazilika, T01 311 0053, www.cafekor.com.
Mon-Sat 1000-2200, closed Sun.
A cosy, ochre-walled bistro on the heels of the Basilika that, in a glut of high-price showy restaurants, still attracts locals as much as passing sightseers. Flavours are Hungarian (goulash and goose liver, aubergine cream, cottage cheese dumplings with hot forest fruit sauce) with some lighter European notes. Booking is strongly recommended. Also serves breakfast.

Gerbeaud €€
Vörösmarty tér 7, Deák Ferenc tér, District 5, T01 429 9000, www.gerbeaud.hu.
Daily 0900-2100.
A 150-year-old institution dripping with chandeliers. The café's signature dessert is a cake with nuts, jam and apricot, covered in chocolate. Once part of the weekend ritual of the middle classes, it is now firmly etched on the tourist's itinerary.

Café Gusto €
Frankel Leó utca 12, District 2, T01 316 3970.
Closed Sun.
One of the tiniest cafés in Budapest has, in its relatively short lifespan, become a real local institution. Although it has only just acquired a gas cooker (so now you can get lasagne along with beef carpaccio), Gusto has a loyal fanbase among the city's intelligentsia. On match days, a TV is slapped on a centre table.

Ruszwurm Cukrászda €
Szentháromság utca 7, Várhegy, District 1, T01 375 5284, www.ruszwurm.hu.
A glory clock hangs behind the old-world cherrywood counter at this perfect Biedermeier relic. Gilt chandeliers, velvet banquettes, 19th-century ornaments and chinaware – this is the place for strudels, gingerbread and salt cakes.

Central Market Hall
Fövám Krt 1-3, District 4.
Pile 'em high is the philosophy at the cheap food counters ranged around the top of the grand Market Hall built in 1890. Mounds of cabbage, stews of butter beans, stringy pickles and plenty of sordid looking sausages. Sophisticated it ain't.

Nightlife

There are the chichi metropolitan sit-outs at **Liszt Ferenc Square**, or slightly seedier coffee shops along **Raday utca** and, in summer, there are chic and dressy clubs on **Margit Island**. The cool **A38** boat, moored on the Buda side between Lágymányosi and Petőfi bridges, *T01 464 3940, www.a38.hu*, is a Ukrainian stone carrier ship that stages cutting-edge concerts.

Ten out of ten for hipness, though, goes to the **kerts**, Budapest-style late-night speakeasies that set up in the disused courtyards of the city's derelict housing squares. Unpopular with sleep-deprived neighbours, they squat in uninhabitable dwellings until local opposition forces the fridge, chairs, tables and, invariably, fussball tables, to move a few doors down to the next condemned and neglected ghost house. Understandably shy of publicity, they seldom have street signs or set addresses, so ask a local to direct you through the medieval district or look out for a doorman propped on a bar stool outside an otherwise unassuming doorway. The two longest-running venues are: **Szoda** in District 5; and **Szimpla** in the Jewish district, *Kazinczy utca 14, T01 321 9119, www.szimpla.hu.*

Tüzraktér Independent Cultural Centre, *Tüzoltó u 54-56, District 9, http://tuzrakter.hu*, is the place for VJ festivals, avant-garde art, jazz and performance, while

Festivals

Kis West-Balkán, *Kisfaludy utca 36, District 8, T01 371 1807, www.west-balkan.com*, is an open-air drink and dance hall.

Classical and opera

The city has fistfuls of concert venues, from the **National State Opera** house and the art nouveau **Liszt Ferenc Academy** to the state-of-the-art Russell Johnson-designed **National Concert Hall** at the Palace of Art, *Komor Marcell u 1, T01 455 9000, www.muveszetekpalotaja.hu*, home of the National Philharmonic Orchestra. Tickets are available from T06 303 030999, www.tex.hu.

There's a quick marching parade of week-long festivals throughout the year, from the highbrow opera, ballet and folklore-themed **Budapest Spring Festival**, www.festivalcity.hu, to glass-clinking champagne and wine fests, and Central Europe's answer to Woodstock or Glastonbury: the island festival of **Sziget**, www.sziget.hu.

Right: Restaurant door.
Opposite page: Famous goulash soup.

Travel essentials

Getting there

Ferihegy International Airport (*www.bud.hu*) is 16 km southeast of the city, T01 296 9696. Terminal 1 serves low-cost airlines, while Terminal 2 serves most other airlines, including Hungary's **Malev**. A handy **airport minibus**, T01 296 8555, runs to any address in the city 0600-2200 (HUF2990 one way, HUF4990 return); it's cheaper than a taxi but you must book your return journey 24 hrs in advance. You can also travel by bus 200E to Kőbánya-Kispest metro station (HUF320).

Most international express trains plus domestic trains to and from the north use **Keleti pályaudur**, VIII Kerepesi út 2-6 (M3 metro); other main stations are **Deli pályaudur**, I Krisztina körút 37 (M2 metro), and **Nyugati pályaudur**, VI Teréz körút (M3 metro). T01 461 5400, www.mav.hu, for domestic services and T01 461 5500, www.elvira.hu, for international links, including Vienna, every 3 hrs (2½ hrs), Berlin (12 hrs) and Paris (16 hrs).

Getting around

Walking around Budapest is a pleasure but the public transport network of buses, trams and trolleybuses, plus 3 metro lines, is excellent, cheap and runs 0430-2310. You can buy single journey tickets (HUF320) or booklets at newsagents, stations and stops. A 24-hour pass costs HUF1550. Tickets must be validated once on board; you face a HUF6000 on-the-spot fine if you travel without a ticket. The tourist office's Budapest Card gives you access to unlimited public transport in the city for 48 hrs (HUF6300) or 72 hrs (HUF7500), as well as discounts on sights, activities and thermal baths.

Bikes can be rented from many of the city's hotels and from **Velo-Touring**, T01 319 0571, www.velo-touring.hu. **Taxis** have yellow number plates and run on a meter; drivers will expect a 10% tip on top of the fare. Booking by phone is cheaper than hailing a cab on the street: try **Budataxi**, T01 233 3333; **Rádió Taxi**, T01 377 7777; **Főtaxi** T01 222 2222, or **City Taxi** T01 211 1111.

Tourist information

Budapest's **Tourinform** office is at Deák tér/Sütő utca 2, T01 438 8080, www.budapest info.hu, daily 0800-2000. **Budatours**, T01 374 7070, www.budatours.hu, run a 2-hr bus city tour, HUF4500, from outside Bajcsy-Zsilinkszky út metro (M1).

Exchange rate

Hungarian Forint (HUF): £1 = HUF321. €1 = HUF273.

Ratings

Art and culture ☆☆☆
Eating ☆☆☆☆
Nightlife ☆☆☆☆
Outdoors ☆☆☆
Romance ☆☆☆
Shopping ☆☆☆☆
Sightseeing ☆☆☆
Value-for-money ☆☆
Overall city rating ☆☆☆

Copenhagen

What can we say about Copenhagen, capital of the land that gave us Lego, Lurpak and the egg chair? To say it is 'understated chic' hardly raises the blood pressure. We know it's Scandinavian and that hints at the sensual and the liberated. An existentialist philosopher called Kierkegaard hailed from the city, and isn't there some statue of a mermaid that keeps getting decapitated? All this is true but it hardly opens a window on the city's soul. Surprise is the bonus that comes with a city that is not presented in tourist cellophane. Sightseeing here becomes a more personal odyssey, and Copenhagen's world-class museums and art galleries, the city's ever- so-literate awareness of architecture and design, and the everyday style and pace of life all become something to discovered and experienced as new.

Copenhagen house.

Tivoli Gardens

Vesterbrogade 3, T3315 1001, www.tivoli.dk.
Open for summer season, mid Apr-late Sep daily 1100-2300. Open for Halloween and Christmas holidays daily 1100-2300. Kr75. S-tog København H. Map A7.

First opened in 1843, Tivoli pleasure gardens remain Denmark's most visited attraction and a national institution (most visitors are Danes). The tweeness has encouraged Disneyfication, but a glimmer of the original Orient-inspired magic still pervades. There is an ancient rollercoaster amongst the modern fair-ground rides, as well as fainter echoes of times past, such as the 1949 spiral lamp by Poul Henningsen near Tivoli Lake. Henningsen also designed the stunning Glassalen, with its hint of camp. When twilight descends, the Turkish facade of *Restaurant Nimb* is subtly illuminated, while outside is the silent fountain inspired by Niels Bohr, Danish winner of the Nobel Prize for physics. The Chinese-style Pantomime Theatre plays host to a genuine ghost of *commedia dell'arte*.

At a glance

Rådhuspladsen is Copenhagen's Times Square, with the **Tivoli Gardens** and Central Station to the southwest. The capital's major shopping street, **Strøget**, runs northeast from here to Kongens Nytorv and **Nyhavn**. To the north are royal residences and grand boulevards in Frederiksstaden and Rosenborg. Southeast of Strøget is Slotsholmen, an oblong-shaped island enclosed by narrow canals that forms the historical heart of Copenhagen. Immediately west of Central Station, multicultural and semi-gentrified **Vesterbro** is good for accommodation. The tree-lined boulevards and elegant gardens of Frederiksberg are further to the west, while, to the north, a string of artificial **lakes** separates the city centre from gritty **Nørrebro**, where the sharp edge of contemporary Copenhagen is revealed. The 'free city' of bohemian **Christiania** lies on the island of Christianshavn to the east of the centre.

NyCarlsberg Glyptotek

Dantes Plads 7, T3341 8141, www.glyptoteket.dk.
Tue-Sun 1100-1700. Kr 60, Sun free. S-tog København H. Map B7.

This is one of Copenhagen's must-see galleries, founded by the Carlsberg brewing magnet Carl Jacobsen at the end of the 19th century. Like other world-class museums, it contains too much to take in on a single visit, including extensive ancient Near East and Mediterranean collections. At its heart is the magnificent glass-domed Winter Garden, where Roman sarcophagi and contemporary Danish sculptures share the space with giant tropical palm trees. The 19th-century French Impressionists are housed in a purpose-built wing, added in 1996.

Nationalmuseet

Ny Vestergade 10, T3313 4411, www.natmus.dk.
Tue-Sun 1000-1700. Free. S-tog København H. Map B7.

Denmark's National Museum showcases four floors of world cultural history and, although the emphasis is on Denmark, it also has an expansive ethnographical collection and a floor devoted to Near Eastern and Classical antiquities. Highlights include some astounding 3000-year-old artefacts, Viking silver ornaments, jewellery, coins and skin cloaks, an Eskimo hunter's anorak made of sealskin and a metope from the outer frieze of the Parthenon, purchased by a Danish naval officer in the 17th century.

Tivoli Gardens.

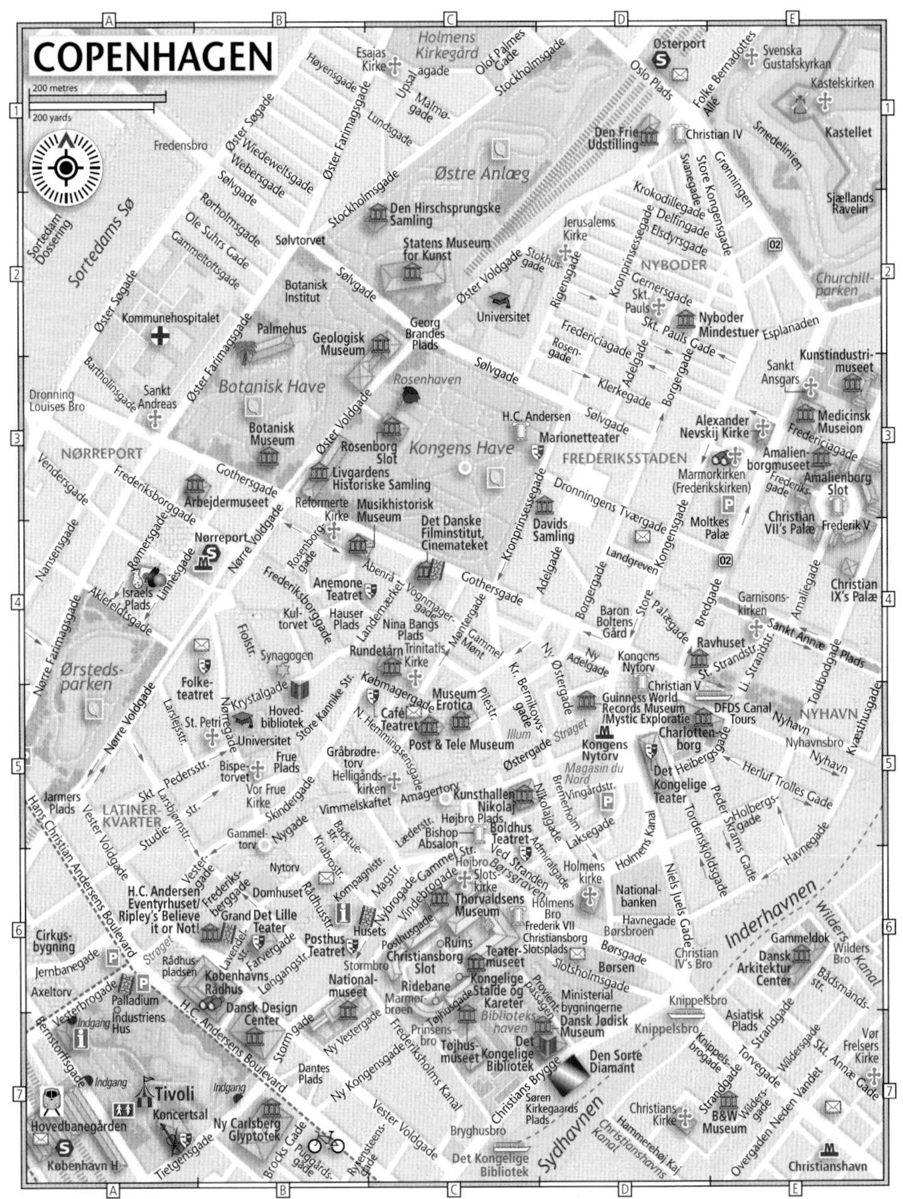
COPENHAGEN
Tivoli
Kongens Have
Botanisk Have
Østre Anlæg
Nyhavn
Inderhavnen
Sydhavnen

Slotsholmen

The island of Slotsholmen (www.ses.dk) is where Bishop Absalon first built a stone castle in 1167. Today it is crowded with buildings that chart the evolution of the city from the 12th century to the present. At its heart is **Christiansborg Slot**, *Christiansborg Slotsplads, T3392 6492, www.ses.dk, map C6, May-Sep daily 1000-1600 (tours 1100-1500), Oct-Apr Tue-Sun 1000-1600 (tours 1200-1500), ruins Kr40, reception rooms Kr70*, the 20th-century incarnation of a palace first built by Christan VI in the 1730s. It now houses the Danish parliament, Royal Reception Rooms and an absorbing exhibition on the excavation of Absalon's original fort.

Among the many other museums and interesting buildings here, seek out the 17th-century Børsen (stock exchange), with its whimsical decorations; **Den Sorte Diamant (Black Diamond)**, *Søren Kierkegaards Plads 1, T3347 4747, www.kb.dk, map D7, daily 0800-2300 (tours available)*, a stunning black granite and smoked glass extension to the Royal Library, and the peaceful enclave of the Bibliotekshaven (Royal Library Garden).

Strøget and the Latin Quarter (Latiner Kvarter)

The wide open space of Rådhuspladsen is best explored before mid morning, when there's only a gentle buzz of commuters. Dominating the late 19th- and early 20th-century square is the brown-brick **Rådhuset (City Hall)**, *T3366 2582, map D4, access to tower Oct-May Mon-Sat 1200; Jun-Sep Mon-Fri 1000-1400, Sat 1200, Kr20, S-tog Vesterport*. Check out the fine views from the tower and the intricate cogs and wheels of Jen Olsen's World Clock near the entrance.

Copenhagen's most hyped street, pedestrianized Strøget, runs northeast from here. By lunchtime, its cafés, restaurants and cobbled squares heave with people and street performers. To get away from the crowds, explore the narrow side streets where medieval Copenhagen developed. For a more tangible feel of the past, move on a few centuries and explore the Latin Quarter around the university with some grand 19th-century churches and a studious atmosphere. Strøget continues its long, shop-laden route along Østergade to Kongens Nytorv, while the small streets to the north are filled with speciality stores and restaurants. Købmagergade caters to hedonists and consumers, with more prestigious shops and the unique **Museum Erotica**, *Købmagergade 24, T3312 0311, map C5, May-Sep daily 1000-2300, Oct-Apr daily 1100-2000, Kr69, Metro Kongens Nytorv*. Also here is the **Rundetårn**, *Købmagergade 52a, T3373 0373, www.rundetaarn.dk, map C4, May-Sep daily 1000-2000, Sep-May daily 1000-1700. Mid-Oct-mid Mar, Tue and Wed Tower and Observatory 1900-2200, Kr25, Metro/S-tog Nørreport*, built as an observatory by Christian IV. Ascend the spiral walkway for good views of the city centre.

Slotsholmen.

Museum Erotica.

The polis and the politics

Across the water from Slotsholmen is the island of Christianshavn and the multi-faceted community of Christiania (www.christiania.org). Much more than a bohemian social experiment, Christiania is a buzzing area that mixes anarchists with hard-nosed dealers, and canny careerists with 21st-century hippies. It came into existence over 30 years ago, when hippies and activists moved into abandoned military buildings. Over the years, it has experienced numerous clashes with the authorities but now up to 1000 people work or live here tax-free, in homes most have designed and built themselves. Christiania attracts visitors intrigued by the possibility of an alternative community flourishing in the heart of a modern bourgeois state. The makeshift entrance and a few down-and-outs can be off putting but, around Pusher Street, you'll find cafés and stalls selling jewellery and T-shirts. A few years ago numerous types of cannabis were on sale here but a major clean-up campaign has stopped the open selling of drugs on the streets. While you're here, don't miss the baroque splendour of Vor Frelsers Kirke, with its wacky external staircase that twists around a spiral tower.

Frederiksstaden

A populist atmosphere characterizes the north side of the Nyhavn canal, where colourful Dutch-style houses and a cluster of eateries encourage visitors to sit on the quayside and soak up the sun. Around the corner, on stately Bredgade, the mood changes abruptly amidst the many reminders of inherited influence. Frederiksstaden, laid out by Frederik V in the mid-18th century, has many palaces and churches, such as the Danish royal residence at Amalienborg Slot and the remains of an old fortress, Kastellet. The most absorbing museums are **Frihedsmuseet**, *Churchillparken, T3313 7714, www.natmus.dk, Oct-Apr Tue-Sun 1000-1500, May-Sep Tue-Sun 1000-1700, free, S-tog Østerport*, chronicling Danish resistance to Nazi occupation, and **Kunstindustrimuseet**, *Bredgade 68, T3318 5656, www.kunstindustrimuseet.dk, map E3, Tue-Sun 1100-1700, Kr60, Kr40*, with its exquisite collections of decorative art.

Top: Colourful houses and populist atmosphere along Nyhavn canal. Above: Art on Copenhagen's streets.

Rosenborg

West of Frederiksstaden lies the much-visited **Rosenborg Slot**, *Øster Voldgade, T3315 3286, www.dkks.dk, map C3, Nov-Apr Tue-Sun 1100-1600, May daily 1100-1600, Jun-Aug daily 1000-1700, Sep and Oct daily 1100-1600, Kr75, Metro/S-tog Nørreport*, built by Christian IV in the 17th century. The castle is stuffed full of overblown furniture, tapestries and trinkets and is surrounded by the manicured greenery of the Kongens Have (Royal Gardens).

To the northwest are two top-notch art galleries: the esteemed **Statens Museum for Kunst**, *Sølvgade 48, T3374 8494, www.smk.dk, map C2, Tue-Sun 1000-1700, Wed 1000-2000, closed public hols, free, S-tog Østerport*, which houses the national collection of major works of European art; and the lesser-known but highly rewarding **Den Hirschsprungske Samling**, *Stockholmsgade 20, T3542 0336, www.hirschsprung.dk, map C2, Wed-Mon 1100-1600, Kr 50, free Wed, S-tog Østerport*, a veritable treasure trove of Danish art from the last two centuries.

Sleeping

The main hotel areas are Vesterbro and Frederiksberg, where smart and comfortable double rooms can be found for below Kr1000. Classier hotels tend to be around Nyhavn and Kongens Nytorv.

Hotel D'Angleterre €€€
Kongens Nytorv 34, T3312 0095, www.dangleterre.com.
Over 250 years old, this luxurious five-star hotel is definitely the city's finest. Steeped in tradition and oozing with elegance, it occupies a prime spot on King's Square and offers guests a fabulous spa experience and top notch dining options.

71 Nyhavn €€€-€€
T3343 6200, www.71nyhavnhotel.com.
Two warehouses have been converted into this smart, 150-room hotel. Original beams lend a rustic touch to the luxury interior, including the bar and the above-average restaurant.

DGI-byens €€
Tietgensgade 65, T3329 8070, www.dgi-byen.dk.
A hotel that fulfils one's expectations of Scandinavian style and Danish modernism – sleek and uncluttered. Superb swimming pool and sports facilities adjoin the hotel.

Hotel CPH Living €€
1C Langebrogade, T6160 8546, www.cphliving.com.
A unique and stylish floating boutique hotel, located in the city's harbour area. The maritime theme is continued throughout the interior and up top is a private sun deck for taking in the harbour views on a sunny day.

Cab Inn City €
Mitchellsgade 14, T3539 8400, www.cabinn.com.
Pristine, budget rooms: tiny but perfectly formed with all you need contained in an amazingly small space. Very central, with a good coffee bar and 24-hour reception. Possibly the best value in town.

Eating

Gammel Strand opposite Slotsholmen has some upmarket fish restaurants and cafés. Nyhavn offers a more democratic mood for wining and dining, while in Vesterbro you'll find everything from Danish bakeries to kebab shops to specialist eateries. Værnedamsvej, off Vesterbrogade, has several non-touristy places.

Noma €€€
Strandgade 93, Christians-havn, T3296 3297, www.noma.dk.
Tue-Sat 1200-1330 and 1830-2200.
Set in a converted 18th-century warehouse overlooking the harbour, this ultra-minimalist room is offset by the excellent and creative modern Scandinavian cuisine.

Restaurant Godt €€€
Gothersgade 38, T3315 2122, www.restaurant-godt.dk.
Tue-Sat 1800-0000.
A small and intimate venue so booking essential. Husband and wife team, Colin and Marie-Anne, serve up some of the city's finest Scandinavian cuisine to rave reviews. The menu changes on a daily basis using the best locally sourced ingredients.

Nørrebro Bryghus €€
Ryesgade 3, Nørrebro, T3530 0530, www.noerrebro bryghus.dk.
Mon-Sun 11.30-1500, Mon-Thu 1730-2200, Fri and Sat 1730-2300.
An old factory converted into a stylish restaurant and microbrewery with live music in the basement, superlative service in the great dining hall and sleek steel vats and pipes gurgling away beside you in the brewery itself. Inventive modern Californian-Danish food.

Nytorv Restaurant and Café €€-€
Nytorv 15, T3311 7706, www.nytorv.dk.
Daily 1100-2200.
One of the city's oldest restaurants, this is one of the few places left specializing in the much-heralded open sandwich. At lunch, it's full of Danes enjoying this *smørrebrød*.

Rizraz €
Kompagnistræde 20, T3315 0575, www.rizraz.dk. Daily 1130-2400.
A vast warren of a place with a huge vegetarian all-you-can-eat Mediterranean buffet and tasty meat dishes. Possibly the best value in town.

Nightlife

Copenhagen boasts a lively, ever- changing bar and club scene, based around Vesterbro, Nørrebro, Østerbro and the centre. The great thing is that the city is small enough to allow you to sample a selection of several venues in any one night. The most popular club in town is **Vega**, *Enghavevej 40, T3325 7011, www.vega.dk*, in Vesterbro, which incorporates a nightclub at weekends, plus a lounge bar, concert venue and cocktail bar. In Nørrebro head to **Rust**, *Guldbergs gade 8, T3524 5200, www.rust.dk*, another multi- venue place where good music takes precedence over the weekly cattle market. In the city centre, **Park Café**, *Østerbrogade 79, T3542 6248, www. parkcafe.dk*, has three dance floors and attracts an upwardly mobile crowd. For some of the best R&B and hip hop in town, head to **Club Mantra**, *Bernstorffsgade 3, T3311 1113*, located in a basement next door to Tivoli. Minimalist décor but with an exciting line up of guest DJs.

Travel essentials

Getting there

Copenhagen International Airport, T3231 3231, flight information T3247 4747, www.cph.dk, is 9 km from the city and 13 mins from Central Station by train every 10 mins (Mon-Fri 0500-2400, Sat 0530- 2400, Sun 0630-2400, Kr28.50). Some stop at Nørreport, where a metro links with Kongens Nytorv for accommodation around Nyhavn. A city bus service, 250S, costs about the same as the train but takes 25 mins. Night bus 96N runs every 30 mins-1 hr to the centre (Kr45). A taxi from outside the arrivals hall will cost about Kr180-200. International trains arrive at Central Station, T7013 1415, www.dsb.dk; long-distance coaches also arrive here.

Getting around

Public transport tickets cover buses, S-Tog trains and the metro, within designated zones. The basic ticket costs Kr23 and is valid for up to 1 hr within any 2 zones (which covers most of the sights and places of interest). Tickets and maps showing the zones are available from machines or ticket offices in train stations and from bus drivers. A new electronic Travel Card system that does away with the current zones is due to be introduced in the near future. If you intend to do a lot of travelling about the city you can buy a *klippekort*, valid for 10 rides or a 24-hr unlimited travel card (Kr125). Another alternative is to buy a **Copenhagen Card**, which offers unlimited travel in greater Copenhagen and free admission to some museums and sights. It's valid for 24-72 hrs and costs Kr229-449. It is also easy to get around the various sights on foot. From Central Station it takes about 30 mins to walk the length of Strøget and reach Nyhavn. From around Istedgade or Vesterbrogade it takes 20 mins to reach Slotsholmen.

Tourist information

Wonderful Copenhagen tourist office, T7022 2442, www. visitcopenhagen.dk, is on the corner of Vesterbrogade and Bernstorffsgade, close to Central Station. May-Jun and Sep Mon-Sat 0900-1800; Jul-Aug Mon-Sat 0900-2000, Sun 1000-1800; Oct-Apr Mon-Sat 0900-1600, Sat 0900-1400. There is a smaller tourist office at the airport.

Exchange rate

Danish Kroner (Kr). £1 = Kr8.77. €1 = Kr7.45.

Copenhageners don't start to kick their heels until at least 2400-0100, particularly at weekends, but lounge bars (glam cocktail joint **Ruby**, Nybrogade 10, T3393 1203, and **Stereo Bar**, *Linnesgade 16A, T3313 6113*, in Nørrebro, are among the best) will keep you in an intimate and inviting atmosphere until then. Special one-off and try-out club and bar nights are plentiful. The weekly Copenhagen Post's *In & Out* guide contains a good day-by-day rundown in English.

Ratings

Art and culture ☆☆☆
Eating ☆☆☆
Nightlife ☆☆☆☆
Outdoors ☆☆☆
Romance ☆☆
Shopping ☆☆
Sightseeing ☆☆☆
Value-for-money ☆☆
Overall city rating ☆☆☆

Dublin

From struggling provincial backwater to the city that never sleeps, Dublin has been riding one hell of a roller coaster in recent years. Ireland's capital has regained a European presence that it last experienced in the 18th century. Every day plane-loads of visitors arrive in this city ready to party. While Temple Bar ladles on the blarney as thick as the head on a pint of Guinness, the statue of the 19th-century nationalist Daniel O'Connell overlooks wood-panelled Edwardian pubs, designer bars and clubs, chic shops and high-tech arts centres. Yet, amid the sophisticated gloss, the fiddly-diddly music and the political wheeler-dealing is a city whose secrets are still waiting to be explored. And through the heart of it all snakes the Liffey: dark, unfathomable and just a little bit muddier than we'd like to admit.

Oscar Wilde statue in Merrion Square.

Trinity College

College Green, www.tcd.ie.
Campus tours May-Sep daily 1015-1540, 30 mins, €10 with Book of Kells. Map D4.

Trinity College is a time capsule of smooth lawns, cobblestones, statuary and formal buildings, looking more like Oxford's dreaming spires than some of the Oxford colleges themselves. It was founded in 1592 by Elizabeth I, in an attempt to prevent young Protestant intellectuals of the Pale going to Europe and discovering Catholicism. Its squares are dominated by the campanile tower, beside which is a Henry Moore statue, Reclining Connected Form. To the right is the finest building on the campus, the 18th-century Old Library, home to the Book of Kells Exhibition, *T01 896 2320, Mon-Sat 930-1700, May-Sep Sun 0930-1630, Oct-Apr Sun 1200-1630, closed over Christmas and New Year, €8.50.* Two pages of the ninth-century illuminated manuscript are on show each day, accompanied by displays explaining its religious symbolism and manufacture. Upstairs is the magnificent 65-m Long Room, where 200,000 of the library's oldest books are held.

Across Fellowes Square is the Arts Block, built in 1980, and showing collections of conceptual and avant-garde art in its Douglas Hyde Gallery, *T01 896 1116, www.douglashydegallery.com, map D4, Mon-Fri 1100-1800, Thu 1100-1900, Sat 1100-1645, free.*

School of Natural Sciences, Trinity College.

At a glance

Georgian **Grafton Street** runs from Trinity College south to St Stephen's Green. This area and the streets to the east are the centre of tourist Dublin, where you'll find most of the most significant sights and the city's best restaurants and hotels. **Temple Bar**, with its ancient, redeveloped streets, Dublin Castle and Christchurch Cathedral lie to the west, while to the southwest is an odd mishmash of areas, loosely defined as the **Liberties** and barely touched by the previous decade's Celtic Tiger phenomenon.

North of the Liffey, **O'Connell Street**, one of the city's oldest and grandest boulevards, is now cluttered with shop signs and statuary. It's less tourist-focused than areas south of the river but has a great deal to offer thanks to its powerful historical associations and impressive literary connections. You'll also find much of the city's cheapest accommodation here. Northwest of the Liffey is a relatively unvisited area with a long history, an ancient church, the city's Four Courts and **Smithfield market**. Further west still are the old **Collins Barracks**, which house a branch of the National Museum, and, beyond that again, is **Phoenix Park**, the largest enclosed public space in Europe. Victorian and Edwardian **Ballsbridge**, southeast of the centre, is the poshest part of Dublin with some good restaurants and lively bars.

24 hours in the city

Start your day with a full Irish breakfast at the **Kingfisher** on Parnell Street. Here you'll find a mix of locals and tourists all tucking in to a hearty spread. Spend the morning marvelling at the collection of gold in the **National Museum**, followed by a quick peek at the Picasso in the **National Gallery** and a really classy lunch at The Commons. In the afternoon stroll around the shops and alleys of Temple Bar before hopping on a bus to the **Guinness Storehouse** to enjoy a bird's eye view of the city – and a pint of Guinness to boot. In the evening head back to Temple Bar to sample modern Irish cuisine at Eden. After dinner enjoy a drink at Oliver St John Gogarty's, where you've a good chance of catching some traditional Irish music, or grab a cab over to the Brazen Head, Dublin's oldest bar. The next port of call for nightowls should be **Old Harcourt Street**, where the clubs get going around 2300. POD, Crawdaddy and Tripod are some of the hippest joints in town.

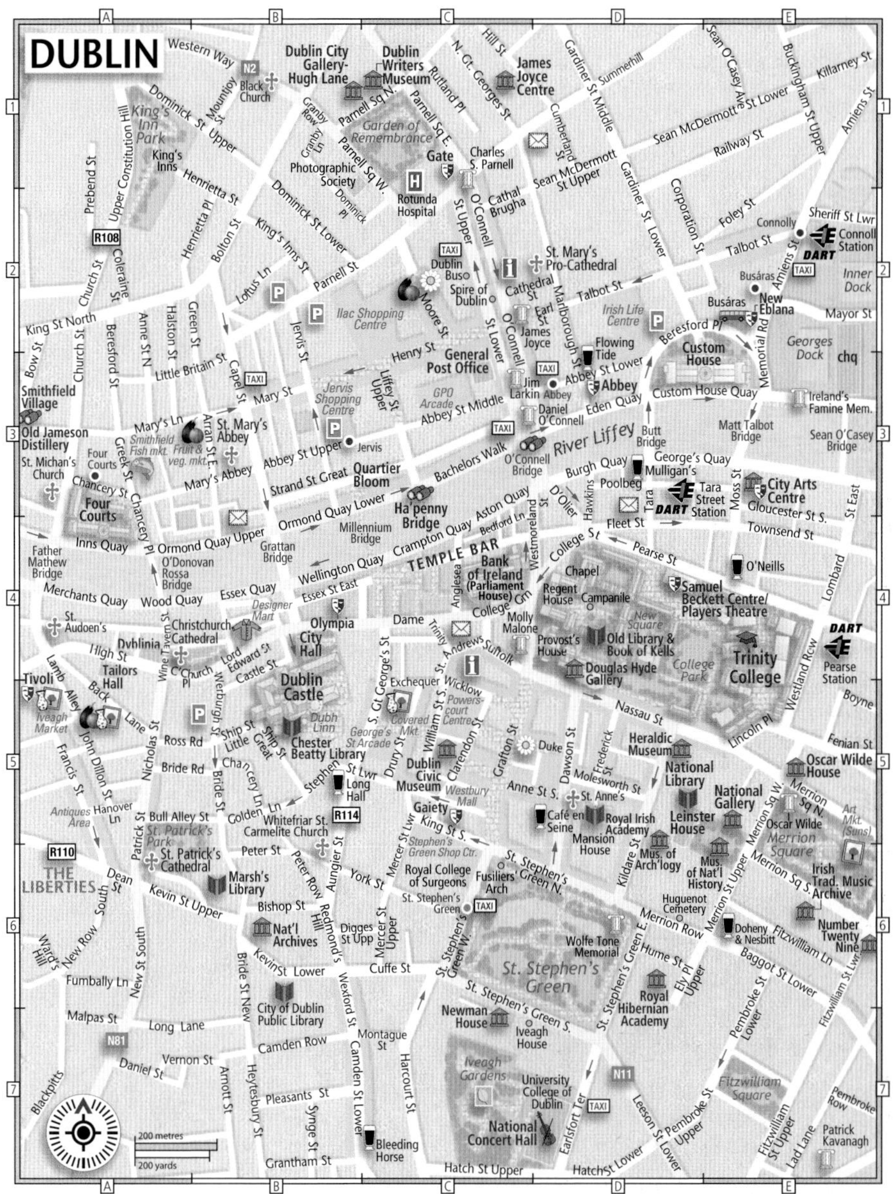
DUBLIN
Dublin City Gallery-Hugh Lane
Dublin Writers Museum
James Joyce Centre
Garden of Remembrance
Gate
Rotunda Hospital
Photographic Society
King's Inns
King's Inn Park
St. Mary's Pro-Cathedral
Spire of Dublin
Ilac Shopping Centre
General Post Office
Irish Life Centre
Custom House
Connolly Station
Busáras
Inner Dock
Georges Dock
chq
Smithfield Village
Old Jameson Distillery
St. Michan's Church
Four Courts
St. Mary's Abbey
Jervis Shopping Centre
Abbey
Flowing Tide
River Liffey
Ha'penny Bridge
Quartier Bloom
O'Connell Bridge
Butt Bridge
Mulligan's
Tara Street Station
City Arts Centre
Ireland's Famine Mem.
TEMPLE BAR
Bank of Ireland (Parliament House)
Trinity College
Old Library & Book of Kells
Douglas Hyde Gallery
Samuel Beckett Centre/ Players Theatre
O'Neills
Pearse Station
Christchurch Cathedral
Dvblinia
Tailors Hall
Tivoli
City Hall
Olympia
Dublin Castle
Chester Beatty Library
Powerscourt Centre
Dublin Civic Museum
Long Hall
Gaiety
Heraldic Museum
National Library
Leinster House
National Gallery
Oscar Wilde House
Merrion Square
Irish Trad. Music Archive
Number Twenty Nine
Royal Irish Academy
Mansion House
Café en Seine
St. Patrick's Cathedral
Marsh's Library
THE LIBERTIES
Whitefriar St. Carmelite Church
Royal College of Surgeons
Fusiliers' Arch
St. Stephen's Green
Wolfe Tone Memorial
Nat'l Archives
City of Dublin Public Library
Newman House
Iveagh House
Royal Hibernian Academy
Iveagh Gardens
University College of Dublin
National Concert Hall
Bleeding Horse
Fitzwilliam Square
Patrick Kavanagh
200 metres
200 yards

National museums

The area south of Trinity College and east of Kildare Street is tightly packed with museums and other places to visit. At its heart is Leinster House, which is home to the Republic's two Houses of Parliament: the Dáil and the Seanad. The house was built around 1745 by James Fitzgerald, Earl of Kildare (later Duke of Leinster), as an escape from Parnell Square in north Dublin, which had become a little too nouveau riche for his liking. In the 19th century, Leinster House was sold to the Royal Dublin Society, which added two new wings on either side, designed in 1884-1890 by Deane and Son, to form the **National Library**, *Kildare St, T01 603 0200, www.nli.ie, map D5, Mon-Wed 1000-2100, Thu and Fri 1000-1700, Sat 1000-1300, free,* and the **National Museum of Ireland**.

The museum is full of wonderful things, including a stunning hoard of Bronze Age gold, guarded by two stone sheela-na-gigs. Upstairs, you'll find Viking and medieval artefacts, a display of ancient Egyptian embalming techniques and 'The Road to Independence' exhibition.

National Gallery

Merrion Sq, T01 661 5133, www.nationalgallery.ie.
Mon-Wed, Fri and Sat 0930-1730, Thu 0930-2030, Sun 1200-1730. Free. Map E5.

Merrion Square, the Georgian heartland of Dublin, was one-time home to Daniel O'Connell at No 58, W B Yeats at 82 and Oscar Wilde at No 1. On its western side is the country house façade of Leinster House and the entrance to the National Gallery, where the big names of European art are well represented. There are works by Caravaggio, Degas, El Greco, Fra Angelico, Goya, Mantegna, Monet, Picasso, Rembrandt, Tintoretto, Titian, Velasquez and Vermeer for starters. Then there is also a decent display of English art and a marvellous collection by Irish artists. Although the gallery always functioned on a hand-to-mouth basis, more prosperous times saw the opening of a Millennium Wing in 2002.

St Stephen's Green

Map C/D6.

Nowadays the city's playground, and great for a picnic on a sunny day with occasional music from the bandstand, St Stephen's Green, south of Trinity College, has had many incarnations over the centuries. Until the 1660s it was an expanse of open ground where people grazed their cattle and public executions took place. As the surrounding area began to be developed the green was partly fenced in and became a park. In 1814 the public were excluded and only residents of the grand houses overlooking the park could use it. In 1877 Lord Ardilaun, one of the Guinness family, introduced a bill to Parliament making it a public park again and put up the cash to make it happen.

Dublin Castle

Dame St, T01 645 8813, www.heritageireland.ie.
Open for pre-booked guided tour only (45 mins) Mon-Sat 1000-1645, Sun 1400-1645; Last admission 1645. €4.50; Dublin Castle can be closed at short notice for Government business. Map B5.

It is difficult to surmise from the hand-tufted carpets and 18th-century plasterwork that this was once Dublin's biggest stronghold, built in 1204 to defend the city against the native Irish. It must have looked the part, too, because, apart from a Fitzgerald attack in 1534 and an aborted attempt at seizing it in 1641, the castle has seen very little

Above: Dublin Castle.
Opposite page: St Stephen's Green.

Republican city

Built in 1792 and opened just in time to incarcerate any surviving rebels of the 1798 uprising, Kilmainham Gaol saw hundreds of men suffer and die for their belief in independence in the uprisings of 1798, 1803, 1848, 1867, 1916 and 1922. Most of the big names in Republican history spent time in here and some of them died here. The last man to walk out was Eamon de Valera at the end of the Civil War in 1923, whereupon the gaol was closed. Forty years later a group of history buffs decided to restore it and Kilmainham was opened to the public. A museum covers the early 20th-century political history of Ireland, prison memorabilia and a guided tour. It takes you around the dungeons, tiny cells, the chapel where Joseph Plunkett was married three hours before his execution and the grim yard where Connolly, Plunkett and 15 other leaders of the 1916 uprising were executed. *Inchicore Rd, T01 453 5984, www.heritageireland.ie. Apr-Sep Mon-Sun 0930-1645, Oct-Mar Mon-Fri 0930-1600, Sun 1000-1645. €6.*

action. The most exciting thing to take place here must have been the night during the Black and Tan War, when Michael Collins infiltrated the records office. In 1922 the castle was officially handed over to him as commander in chief of the Irish army. The guided tour explores the State Apartments then passes into the Upper Yard, where you can see the Statue of Justice over the gateway, unblindfolded and with her back to the city she should have been defending. Until she was mended in the 1980s, her scales of justice regularly tipped when they filled with rainwater. From here you visit the **Undercroft**, where you can see the remains of Viking fortifications, part of the old medieval city wall, the moat, postern steps for deliveries and a dribble of the River Poddle itself.

Housed in a beautifully converted clocktower within the castle walls is the stunning **Chester Beatty Library**, *T01 407 0750, www.cbl.ie, map B5, Oct-Apr Tue-Fri 1000-1700, Sat 1100-1700, Sun 1300-1700, May-Sep also Mon 1000-1700, closed public hols, free*, a priceless collection of cultural and religious treasures – icons, papyrus texts, Buddhas and ancient copies of the Bible and the Koran – bequeathed to the state by the Irish-American mining magnate, Chester Beatty.

Christchurch Cathedral

Christchurch Pl, T01 677 8099, www.cccdub.ie. Jun-Aug Mon-Sat 0945-1815, Sun 1230-1430, 1630-1815, Sep-Oct Mon-Sat 0945-1715, Sun 1230-1430, Nov-May Mon-Sat 0945-1615, Sun 1230-1430, 1630-1715. €6. Map A4.

This is Dublin's oldest building, pre-dating the castle by a century or so. However, the original wooden construction is long gone and, although the crypt, north wall and south transept date from the 12th century, most of what you see is 19th-century stone cladding. Inside there are lovely faux ancient floor tiles, a 16th-century replica of the tomb of Strongbow (Richard de Clare, the Norman conqueror of Ireland) and lots of stuff to admire in the 'Treasures of Christchurch' exhibition in the crypt. If you stand in the choir by the bishop's throne and look back towards the entrance, you'll notice that the north wall (to your right) is seriously out of kilter.

Temple Bar

Map C4.

The landmark Ha'penny Bridge over the River Liffey is a cast-iron footbridge built in 1816 and named after the toll levied on it until 1919. On the south side of the bridge, Merchant's Arch leads into the hub of streets and alleys that define Temple Bar. Nowadays a vibrant tourist ghetto, this network of narrow lanes, named after its 17th-century developer, Sir William Temple, criss-crosses between the river and Dame Street and from Fishamble Street to Fleet Street. Despite all the redevelopment, a few remnants of the old city are still intact. Look out for Sunlight Chambers, on the corner of Parliament Street and Essex Quay, with multi-coloured terracotta reliefs displaying the benefits of soap.

The Gallery of Photography, *Meeting House Sq, T01 671 4654, www.galleryofphotography.ie, Tue-Sat 1100-1800, Sun 1300-1800, free*, is a carefully-lit, purpose-built venue with a permanent collection of 20th-century Irish photographs, plus changing monthly exhibitions by Irish and International artists. The Irish Film Centre on Eustace Street shows art house films in a post-modern conversion of a Quaker Meeting House.

Best of the rest

St Patrick's Cathedral
Patrick's Cl, T01 453 9472, www.stpatrickscathedral.ie.
Despite its ugly exterior, the national cathedral of the Church of Ireland is the more interesting of Dublin's two cathedrals.

Guinness Storehouse
St James' Gate, T01 408 4800, www.guinnessstorehouse.com. Sep-Jun daily 0930-1700; Jul-Aug daily 0930-1900. €13.50.
A temple to the famous Irish drink and brand.

National Museum of Decorative Arts and History
Collins Barracks, Benburb St, T01 677 7444, www.museum.ie. Tue-Sat 1000-1700, Sun 1400-1700. Free.
A former military barracks houses exquisite pieces from the Museum of Ireland's decorative arts collection.

James Joyce Museum
Sandycove, 13 km south of the centre, T01 280 9265. Apr-Aug Tue-Sat 1000-1700 (closed 1300-1400), Sun 1400-1800. Closed on Mon. €6.
A Martello tower houses literary memorabilia associated with Joyce and Ulysses.

O'Connell Street and around

Most of the hyped tourist spots are in the southern half of the city but the north has lots to offer and fewer crowds; there is also a more genuine, earthy feel to it because it is less geared up to the tourist market. The area has strong historical and literary associations and boasts some of the city's earliest Georgian buildings.

The General Post Office, O'Connell Street's most famous building, was gutted by fire and shelling in 1916 and suffered further damage in 1922 during the Civil War before being rebuilt in 1929. Inside the functioning post office is a series of paintings depicting scenes from the 1916 Easter Rising.

At the north end of O'Connell Street are the excellent Hugh Lane Gallery, *Charlemont House, Parnell Sq North, T01 222 5550, www.hughlane.ie, map B1, Tue-Thu 1000-1800, Fri and Sat 1000-1700, Sun 1100-1700, free*, with its fine collection of modern art, and the attractive Dublin Writers' Museum, *18-19 Parnell Sq, T01 872 2077, www.writersmuseum.com, C1, Mon-Sat 1000-1700, Sun and public holidays 1100-1700, later opening Jun-Aug, €7.50.*

Nearby, homage can be paid to Dublin's most famous writer at the James Joyce Centre, *35 North Great George St, T01 878 8547, www.jamesjoyce.ie, map C1, Tue-Sat 1000-1700, Sun 1200-1700, closed Christmas and New Year, €5.*

Below: Ha'penny Bridge.

Sleeping

Hotel rooms in Dublin don't come cheap. Grafton St and Temple Bar form Dublin's chief accommodation area and prices here are pretty high, with no B&Bs. North of the river is a concentration of more affordable guesthouses – the top end of O'Connell St, around Parnell Sq, has some interesting options – but the central location and proximity of the bus and railway station mean they tend to fill up most quickly. Ballsbridge, southeast of the city centre, has a great range of top-notch hotels, quality guesthouses and a cluster of good restaurants.

The Clarence €€€
6-8 Wellington Quay, T01 407 0800, www.theclarence.ie.
Owned by U2, the Clarence has preserved its original wood panelling amidst modish embellishments like leather-clad lifts, Egyptian cotton on the king-size beds, and CD players in the individually designed bedrooms. Friendly staff, a bookless lounge called the Study and original artwork contribute to the strange mix of the spartan and the sybaritic.

Morrison €€€
15 Ormond Quay, T01 887 2400, www.morrisonhotel.ie.
This classy building sits unobtrusively on the bank of the river and vies with the Clarence for Dublin's hippest hotel award. The decor is refreshingly un-Irish,

with plenty of interesting touches waiting to be noticed, not least of which is the restaurant Halö. In the chic, air-conditioned bedrooms you'll find CD players, mood lighting, quality fabrics and original artwork.

Dylan €€€-€€
Eastmoreland Place, T01 660 3000, www.dylan.ie.
A relatively new addition to the city's ever increasing list of chic 5 star boutique hotels (voted the city's best in 2008). With only 44 bespoke bedrooms it manages to retain an intimacy sometimes lost in larger hotels. The décor is funky yet elegant and the Dyaln restaurant offers a menu of sumptuous contemporary Irish cuisine. Only a short stroll from the RDS and the Aviva Stadium makes it an upmarket choice for sports enthusiasts.

Merrion Hall €€
56 Merrion Rd, T01 668 1426, www.halpinsprivate hotels.com.
A quiet, welcoming place with four-poster beds, an ample lounge area, private gardens and a library of tourist literature. Award-winning breakfasts are served in the serene, sunny breakfast room.

Ariel House €€-€
50-54 Lansdowne Rd, T01 668 5512, www.arielhouse.net, 3 mins on foot from Lansdowne Rd DART station.
Built in the 1860s, this listed red-brick Victorian building is a classy guesthouse with a choice of no-smoking rooms, all with bath and shower; three have four-poster beds. American visitors adore the decor and antiques. Car park available.

Bewley's Hotel €
Merrion Rd, T01 668 1111, www.BewleysHotels.com.
Smart, spacious and comfortable accommodation in the Ballsbridge area. The red-brick Victorian building has been converted from a convent school and the original entrance opens into a roomy public area with

the O'Connell's restaurant downstairs and a café. The Aircoach stop is right outside. Rooms cost around €99 for up to three adults or a family of four.

Castle Hotel €
2-4 Gardiner Row, T01 874 6949, www.thecastlehotelgroup.com.
A real find, this is a lovingly restored Georgian building that offers so much more, and at better value, than some of the faceless hotels in town. Elegant lounge and comfortable rooms. Michael Collins is said to have used room 201, originally No 23, when sleeping in one of his familiar safe houses during the War of Independence. Parking available.

Eating

While many of Temple Bar's restaurants are fun, fashionable and relatively inexpensive places to enjoy a meal, the area from St Stephen's Green to Merrion Square is where the real money tends to eat. Don't even look at the menus if you're on a tight budget but for seriously fine dining and splashing out, this is the place to eat.

Thorntons €€€
Fitzwilliam Hotel, St Stephen's Green, T01 478 7000, www.fitzwilliamhoteldublin.com.
Considered by many of Ireland's foodies to be one of the city's finest restaurants. Acclaimed chef, Kevin Thornton, serves up his innovative signature dishes in a contemporary setting overlooking the Green. Thorntons is Michelin starred and has an extensive wine list with dozens of fine wines available by the glass.

Peploe's €€€
16 St Stephen's Green, T01 676 3144, www.peploes.com.
People seem to love or hate this place. It has been listed among the world's best places to eat by prestigious journals and has a growing band of addicted visitors. You can order simple, inexpensive dishes in the wine bar or snuggle into the main restaurant for an imaginative and lovingly prepared meal. Book well in advance.

Gallagher's Boxty House €€
20-21 Temple Bar, T01 677 2762, www.boxtyhouse.ie.
Sells the eponymous filled potato pancakes, plus lots more Irish-sourced edibles. Vegetarians will do well here. It has an old-fashioned country-kitchen feel to it, with newspapers and books to read.

Tante Zoe's €€
1 Crow Street, T01 679 4407, www.tantezoes.com.
Established over 20 years ago in Temple Bar and still going strong. A lively Cajun/Creole restaurant with a legion of fans.

The best gumbo and jambalaya this side of the Atlantic!

Mermaid Café €€
70 Dame St, T01 670 8236, www.mermaid.ie.
One of Dublin's better restaurants, the Mermaid has an American-influenced changing menu, featuring mussel and smoked fish chowder and pecan pie with maple ice cream. The wine list is above average.

Nico's €€
53 Dame St, T01 677 3062.
Ask anyone involved in the food business in Dublin where they like to eat and they'll mention here. Good traditional Italian food, white cloths, Chianti bottles and bustling waiters.

Gruel €
68a Dame St, T01 670 7119, www.gruel.ie.
Very popular inexpensive restaurant that serves hearty

hot meals, such as beef hotpot and pan-fried sea trout, as well as simpler filled rolls and soups. Bare boards and plain tables inside.

Nightlife

Pubs, bars and clubs are what Dublin does best. Tourists flock to Temple Bar to party well into the early hours every night of the week. Elsewhere, the liveliest streets are South Great George's and Camden, which, from Thu evening, turn into a huge street party. Old Harcourt Street is the centre of clubland. Most clubs serve drinks until 0200 and close around 0300. For up-to-date entertainment listings, check on noticeboards or consult the excellent *Event Guide*. Live music pours out of several pubs and bars in Dublin: try **Bruxelles**, *7/8 Harry Street*; **The Porterhouse**, *16-18 Parliament Street*; **Whelan's**, *25 Wexford St*; **Eamon Doran's**, *3A Crown Alley*; or the **Cobblestone**, *North King St*. There are also great venues for comedy and drama, including iconic names **Abbey Theatre**, *26 Lwr Abbey St, T01 878 7222, and Gate Theatre, 1 Cavendish Row, T01 874 4045.* See **Jameson Dublin Film Festival** (www.jdiff.com) in spring and **Dublin Theatre Festival** (www.dublintheatrefestival.com) in autumn.

Travel essentials

Getting there

Dublin International Airport, T01 814 1111, www.dublin-airport.com, is 12 km north of the city centre. **Aircoach**, www.aircoach.ie, runs to and from city centre hotels 24 hrs daily. Tickets can be bought on board and cost €7 single or €12 return, journey time 35 mins. A taxi costs about €25. At the mouth of the Liffey, Dublin Port is used by ferries to and from Holyhead (Terminal 1) and Liverpool (Terminal 3); bus 53/53A runs into the centre. Other ferry services use Dun Laoghaire harbour, 30 mins south of the city and accessible on the DART.

Getting around

The centre of Dublin is easy enough to negotiate on foot but if you get tired, local buses run by **Dublin Bus**, T01 873 4222, www.dublinbus.ie, are frequent and cheap. Bus stops are green and fares (exact change only to the driver) start at 95c for a short hop within the city. A new bus corridor has recently opened with a city centre zone for public transport only that operates during rush hours. Fares within the zone at these times of day are only 50c. A 1-day pass costs €5 (3- and 5-day passes €10 and €16.50 respectively). An excellent bus map of the city is available free from Dublin Bus or the tourist office. Dublin Bus also operates the hop-on, hop-off Dublin City Tour, which starts on O'Connell Bridge. The complete tour takes over an hour and visits 16 sights around the city. A ticket (€16) includes discounts at each of the sights and is valid for a day. The electric tram system, the Luas, www.luas.ie, is designed for commuters but the red line, from Connolly Street through the shopping streets north of the river and then along the quays to Phoenix Park and Heuston station, can be useful. Tickets are available at each stop; a single ticket is valid for only 90 mins, a return for the whole day. The all-zone combi ticket for bus and Luas costs €7.50 for 1 day. The **DART** (Dublin Area Rapid Transit), T01 850 366222, www.irishrail.ie, is a suburban rail service that links the coastal suburbs with the city centre. It is useful for travel between the south and north of the city and for transport to some suburban areas. There are taxi ranks on O'Connell Street, Dame Street and St Stephen's Green.

Tourist information

Dublin Tourism Centre, St Andrew's Church, Suffolk St, www.visitdublin.com, Jan-Dec Mon-Sat 0900-1730, Sun (all year round) 1030-1500, Jul-Aug Mon-Sat 0900-1900, offers accommodation advice and bookings, ferry and concert tickets, car hire, bureau de change, free leaflets and guidebooks for sale. There's also a **Temple Bar information centre** at 12 East Essex St, www.visit-templebar.ie.

Ratings

Art and culture ☆☆☆☆
Eating ☆☆☆☆
Nightlife ☆☆☆
Outdoors ☆☆☆☆
Romance ☆☆☆
Shopping ☆☆☆
Sightseeing ☆☆☆☆
Value-for-money ☆☆☆
Overall city rating ☆☆☆☆

Edinburgh

Few cities make such a strong impression as Edinburgh. Scotland's ancient capital is undeniably one of the most beautiful cities in Europe, with a grandeur to match Paris or Prague, Rôme or Vienna. Fittingly, such a setting provides the stage for the Edinburgh Festival, the biggest arts event on the planet. But Edinburgh is more than just the sum of its arts. Its Hogmanay party is the largest celebration in the northern hemisphere and the arrival of the new Scottish Parliament has brought confidence and vitality to a city that was always thought of as being rather straight-laced. Edinburgh's famous pursed lip has gone, replaced by a broad smile. The city is learning how to have fun, how to be stylish and, heaven forfend, how to be just a wee bit ostentatious.

Walter Scott Monument.

Edinburgh Castle

T0131 225 9846, www.edinburghcastle.gov.uk. Apr-Sep daily 0930-1730; Oct-Mar daily 0930-1630. £15. Map C3.

The city skyline is dominated by the castle, sitting atop an extinct volcano and protected on three sides by steep cliffs. Until the 11th century the castle was Edinburgh, but with the development of the royal palace from the early 16th century, it slipped into relative obscurity. Though mobbed for much of the year, and expensive, the castle is worth a visit. It encapsulates the history of a nation, and the views from the battlements are spectacular. The highlight is the **Crown Room**, where the 'Honours of Scotland' are displayed, along with the Stone of Destiny, the seat on which the ancient kings of Scotland were crowned.

The Royal Mile

Map C/D3.

Running down the spine of the Old Town, from the castle to the Palace of Holyroodhouse, is the Royal Mile. The 1984 regal yards comprise four separate streets: Castlehill, Lawnmarket, the High Street and the Canongate. Along its route is a succession of tourist attractions – some more worthy of the description than others – as well as many bars, restaurants, cafés and shops selling everything from kilts to Havana cigars. This is the focus of the

Edinburgh Castle.

At a glance

South of Princes Street is the **Old Town**, a medieval Manhattan of high-rise tenements running from the castle to the Palace of Holyroodhouse. This dark and sinister rabbit warren of narrow alleys and wynds is still inhabited by the ghosts of the city's past. North of Princes Street is the elegant, neoclassical **New Town**, built in the late 18th and early 19th centuries to improve conditions in the city. The eastern New Town is bordered by **Broughton Street**, which forms one side of the so-called 'Pink Triangle', the pumping heart of the city's gay scene. Here you'll find hip bars and clubs as well as a neighbourly, laid-back atmosphere. Looming over the Pink Triangle is **Calton Hill**, whose summit and sides are studded with sublime Regency terraces and bizarre monuments. The **West End** is a seamless extension of the New Town, with perfect neoclassical symmetry and discreet old money.

Northeast of the city centre is **Leith**, Scotland's major port until the shipbuilding and fishing industries decanted south. Neglected and ignored for years, Leith has undergone a dramatic transformation and now warehouse conversions, gourmet restaurants, bars and bistros jostle for position along its waterside.

24 hours in the city

Plan your day over breakfast at Café Hub, then take a leisurely stroll down the length of the historic **Royal Mile** before landing back in the present with a bump at the award-winning **Scottish Parliament** building. Head back up the Royal Mile for lunch at Off The Wall, then stretch your legs with a walk up **Calton Hill** for the stupendous views of Arthur's Seat, the Castle and across the Firth of Forth to the hills of Fife. Afterwards, indulge in some indoor aesthetic appreciation at the **National Gallery of Scotland**, then hop on a bus down to Ocean Terminal for a fascinating tour of the **Royal Yacht Britannia.** From here it's a short stroll to **Leith** for an alfresco aperitif on the quayside, followed by a superb dinner at Martin Wishart. Then take a cab back to the centre for a nightcap in your hotel or some late-night action in one of the many bars on or around George Street in the **New Town**.

city's tourist activity, especially during the festival when it becomes a mêlée of street performers, enthralled onlookers and alfresco diners and drinkers. One of the main points of interest is the medieval **High Kirk of St Giles**, conspicuously placed on the High Street.

Palace of Holyroodhouse

www.royalcollection.org.uk.
Apr-Oct daily 0930-1800; Nov-Mar daily 0930-1630. £10.50. Map D3.

At the foot of the Royal Mile lies Edinburgh's royal palace. The present structure largely dates from the late 17th century when the original was replaced by a larger building for the Restoration of Charles II, although the newly crowned monarch never set foot in the place. Opposite the Palace of Holyroodhouse is the **Scottish Parliament building**, *www.scottish.parliament.uk*, which finally opened in October 2004 after years of delay and spiralling costs.

Holyrood Park

Map D/E3.

Edinburgh is blessed with many magnificent open spaces but Holyrood Park tops them all. The main feature is the 237-m-high **Arthur's Seat**, the igneous core of an extinct volcano. It is a genuine bit of wilderness right in the centre of Scotland's capital and well worth the climb for the stupendous views. Another dominant feature on the skyline are the precipitous Salisbury Crags, directly opposite the south gates of Holyrood Palace.

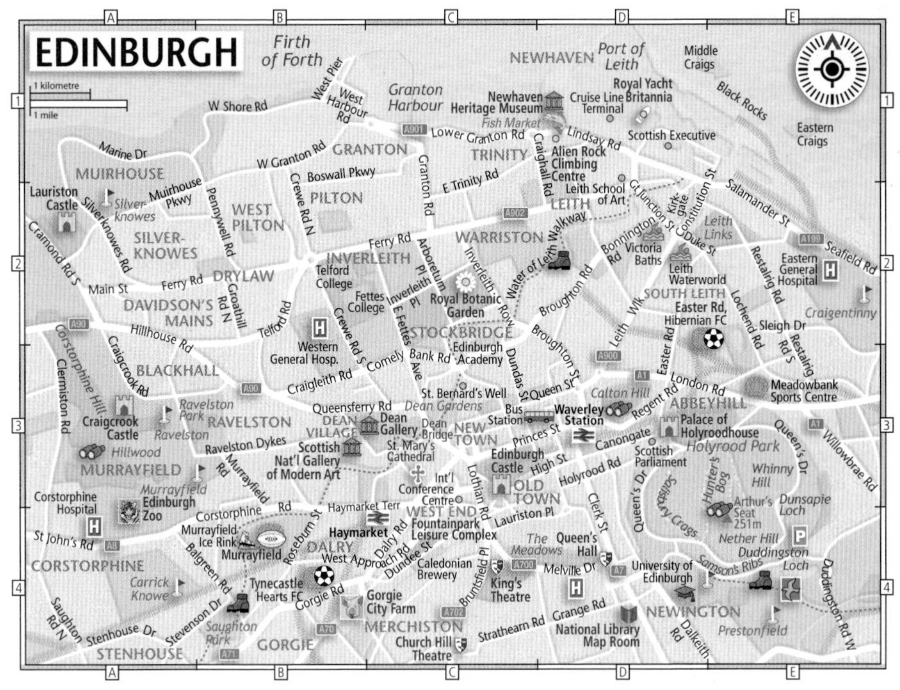

Secret city

The spirits who haunt the vaults and tunnels of old Edinburgh have long drawn tourists to the capital. Recent research has revealed that there may be something really going on beneath the city's streets. A detailed study into paranormal activity was carried out as part of the **Edinburgh International Science Festival**. Volunteers entered the network of ancient tunnels and reported greatly increased paranormal activity, such as hearing loud breathing, seeing figures and being touched or grabbed. **Mercat Tours** (www.mercattours.com) runs tours of the 200-year-old haunted vaults, Apr-Sep daily at 1200, 1400 and 1600; Oct-Mar at 1400 and 1600, £8. If that isn't enough to frighten the living daylights out of you, check out the **City of the Dead Haunted Graveyard Tour** (www.blackhart.uk.com), which involves being locked in a haunted graveyard at night with a bloodthirsty poltergeist; Apr-Oct daily at 2030 and 2200, Nov-Mar daily at 1930 and 2030, £9.50. Tours start from the Mercat Cross, next to St Giles Cathedral on the High Street.

Museum of Scotland and Royal Museum of Scotland

Chambers St, T0300 123 6789, www.nms.ac.uk.
Daily 1000-1700. Free. Map D3.

The Museum of Scotland is a treasure trove of intriguing and important artefacts, displayed chronologically from the basement up to the sixth floor. Though coverage is at times patchy and incomplete, the museum does help to take the mystery out of Scottish history and makes for a pleasurable few hours.

Its elderly neighbour, the Royal Museum, holds an extensive and eclectic range of artefacts, from Classical Greek sculptures to stuffed elephants and Native North American totem poles, all housed in a wonderful Victorian building.

Above: Edinburgh from Calton Hill.
Opposite page: Museum of Scotland.

National Gallery

The Mound, T0131 624 6200, www.nationalgalleries.org.
Daily 1000-1700, Thu till 1900. Free. Map C3.

At the junction of The Mound and Princes Street are two of Edinburgh's most impressive neoclassical buildings, the National Gallery and the Royal Academy, connected by the WestonLink, which provides more exhibition space and a striking café that overlooks Princes Street Gardens. The former houses the most important collection of Old Masters in the UK outside London and boasts many masterpieces from almost every period in Western art.

National Portrait Gallery

1 Queen St, T0131 624 6200, www.nationalgalleries.org.
Daily 1000-1700, Thu till 1900. Free. The gallery is currently closed but will reopen in Autumn 2011. Map D3.

The first of its kind in the world, this gallery houses a collection of the great and the good of Scottish history in a fantastical French Gothic medieval palace, modelled on the Doge's Palace in Venice.

Calton Hill

Map D3.

Calton Hill, at the east end of Princes Street, is another of Edinburgh's extinct volcanoes and well worth climbing for some of the best views in the city as well as for the monuments at the top. These form the four corners of a precinct and make for a strange collection. The most famous is the **National Monument**, built to commemorate the Scots who died in the Napoleonic Wars.

Scottish National Gallery of Modern Art

75 Belford Rd, T0131 624 6200, www.nationalgalleries.org.
Daily 1000-1700. Free. Map B3.

About 20 minutes' walk from the West End is the Scottish National Gallery of Modern Art, featuring

The world's greatest arts festival

Every year Edinburgh plays host to the world's biggest arts festival, when the capital bursts into life in a riot of entertainment unmatched anywhere else. Over a million tourists descend on the city to experience a brain-sapping variety of acts performed in a frightening variety of venues. The **Edinburgh Festival** is actually a collection of different festivals running alongside each other, from the end of July through to the beginning of September. The **International Festival** (T0131 473 2000) tends to be a fairly highbrow affair and features large-scale productions of opera, ballet, classical music, dance and theatre performed in the larger venues. **The Fringe** (T0131 226 0000) features everything from top-class comedy to Albanian existentialist theatre performed in a lift. Also coming under the festival heading are the **International Jazz and Blues Festival, International Book Festival, International Film Festival** and **Military Tattoo**. For details of all the events and links to other websites see www.edinburghfestivals.co.uk.

everything from the Impressionists to Hockney. It's particularly strong on Expressionism, with works by Picasso, Cézanne, Matisse, Magritte, Mondrian, Kandinsky, Klee, Giacometti and Sickert all displayed, as well as the big names from Fauvism, Surrealism, Abstract Expressionism and Cubism. Alongside these are British greats like Francis Bacon, Helen Chadwick and Damien Hirst. Opposite, the **Dean Gallery** houses one of the most complete collections of Dada and Surrealist art in Britain.

Best of the rest

Our Dynamic Earth
Holyrood Rd, www.dynamicearth.co.uk. Apr-Oct daily 1000-1730; Jul-Aug 1000-1800; Nov-Mar Wed-Sun 1000-1730. £11.90, children £7.95.
Hi-tech virtual journey through time with strong environmental message.

The Real Mary King's Close
Warrinston's Close, High St, T0845 070 6244, www.realmarykingsclose.com. Apr-Oct daily 1000-2100; Aug daily 0900-2300; Nov-Mar Sun-Thu 1000-1700, Fri-Sat 1000-2100. £11.50.
Authentic and spooky insight into 17th-century town life.

Surgeon's Hall Museums
9 Hill Sq, T0131 527 1649, www.rcsed.ac.uk. Mon-Fri 1200-1600. £5.
Fairly grotesque but fun look through the keyhole of surgical history.

Talbot Rice Gallery
Old College, www.trg.ed.ac.uk. Tue-Sat 1000-1700 (daily during the festival). Free.
The University's collection of Renaissance paintings, housed in a wonderful neoclassical building.

Stockbridge
One of the city's most beguiling corners, with a jumble of antique shops and second-hand bookstores.

Rosslyn Chapel
7 miles south, www.rosslynchapel.org.uk. Mon-Sat 0930-1700, Sun 1200-1645. £7.70.
This 15th-century chapel is in the Da Vinci Code and is said to be the last resting place of the Holy Grail.

Cramond
On the northwestern fringes is this 18th-century coastal village. Head along the Almond river to the Cramond Inn for some liquid refreshment.

Water of Leith and the Botanic Gardens

If the weather's fair, one of the finest pleasures this city has to offer is the walk along the bucolic Water of Leith. The Water of Leith Walkway runs from the western outskirts of the city, all the way to the docks at Leith, but the most beautiful section starts from below Belford Bridge, by the Scottish National Gallery of Modern Art and Dean Gallery, and takes you to the gorgeous **Royal Botanic Gardens**, *East gate, Inverleith Row, T0131 552 7171, map C2; Mar daily 1000- 1800; Apr-Sep daily 1000-1900; Oct daily 1000-2000. Free.*

Royal Yacht Britannia

Ocean Terminal, Leith, T0131 555 5566, www.royalyachtbritannia.co.uk.
Apr-Jun & Oct daily 1000-1600; Jul-Sep 0930-1630; Nov-Mar 1000-1530. £11. Britannia Tour bus from Waverley Bridge or buses 11, 22, 34, 35 and 36 from Princes St. Map D1.

The Britannia is a fascinating attraction and shows the Windsors in a strangely downbeat manner. The relatively steep entrance fee is well worth the outlay. The tour offers a genuine insight into the lives of Britain's best-known family and the sight of Her Majesty's bedroom, more in keeping with a Berkshire guesthouse than a Head of State's private quarters, comes as a real shock.

Leith waterfront.

Sleeping

Edinburgh has a huge selection of places to stay. Most of the upscale accommodation is in the New Town, West End and around Calton Hill. Many city centre hotels offer good low-season deals, especially at weekends, and also offer a standby room rate throughout the year. You'll need to book well in advance during the festival or at Hogmanay. The tourist office has a free accommodation brochure or their Central Reservations Service, T0131 473 3855, centres@eltb.org, will make a reservation for a fee of £5. Also check www.laterooms.com for last-minute deals.

Hotel Missoni €€€
1 George IV Bridge, T0131 220 6666, www.hotelmissoni.com.
Those who find bright colours and angles interrupt their sleep might want to give it a miss. But for those who love modernity and clever design, the Missoni the ultimate Edinburgh hotel. The bar and restaurant, Cucina, are so good, you won't want to leave but most charmingly, the thoughtful extras thrown make you feel genuinely treated rather than like they're squeezing every last penny out of you.

The Rutland €€€
1-3 Rutland St, T0131 229 3402, www.therutlandhotel.com.
This historic Edinburgh Townhouse has had an oh-so stunning refit, bringing together handsome original features with gorgeous colours and fittings. Its bar, genuinely good restaurant and luxe cocktail bar – The One Below – feel more like NYC than Edinburgh: it's only the burr of the staff's voices and the haggis and porridge served for breakfast that tells you otherwise.

Scotsman Hotel €€€
North Bridge, T0131 556 5565, www.thescotsmanhotel.co.uk.
The former offices of *The Scotsman* newspaper have been transformed into this state-of-the-art boutique hotel. Each room is distinctive and has been furnished with great attention to detail, with original art, DVD and internet. Services and facilities include valet parking, screening room, bar, brasserie and restaurant, breakfast room, private dining rooms and health club and spa.

Apex Waterloo Place €€
27 Waterloo Place, T0131 523 1819, www.apexhotels.co.uk.
Just up the stairs and round the corner from Waverly train station, it offers superb value for money which means the money-conscious needn't skimp on quality or style. A king-sized bed, soft fluffed up bedding, flat screen TV, free Wi-Fi, a breakfast fit for a king and a little rubber duck to take home all come as standard. Check for deals.

Ten Hill Place €€
10 Hill Place, T0131 662 2080, www.tenhillplace.com.
Close to the Festival Theatre, this hotel is technically a three-star but you'd never know it. Large, bright rooms with big beds and spotless bathrooms (although the glass doors on these may panic some). Breakfasts are bountiful and the staff eager to keep everyone happy.

Eating

Edinburgh has a wide range of culinary options. Most of the upmarket restaurants are in the New Town, though there are also some excellent places to be found around the Royal Mile and in Leith, which has fish restaurants and dockside bistros. During busy periods such as the festival it's best to book ahead.

Breakfast

Valvona & Crolla €€

19 Elm Row, T0131 556 6066.

Great home cooking and the best cappuccino in town. The perfect place for a big Saturday brunch and very popular. Authentic Italian deli.

Vin Caffé €€

11 Multrees Walk, T0131 557 0088.

Right next door to Harvey Nicks. It serves really great coffees, panini and drinks downstairs whilst upstairs, the swanky dining room – complete with its own film projector - serves authentic classic Italian dishes and the wines that other Italians seem to want to keep to themselves.

Lunch

Doric Tavern €€

15/16 Market St, T0131 225 1084.

Close to the train station this pub has an atmospheric dining room upstairs that's all creaky floorboards, fast service and an interestingly mixed clientele (especially during the festival). The menu is offer simple gourmet pub stuff at very decent prices.

Petit Paris €€

38-40 Grassmarket, T0131 226 2424.

The checked tablecloths, French staff and accordion music will kid you into believing you are in Paris rather than the Grassmarket. The menu includes authenticities such as cocotte (stew) and saucissces de Toulouse. They even hold fondue and moule parties!

Dinner

Dubh Prais €€€

123b High St, T0131 557 5732.

Dubh Prais (pronounced doo prash) understated grandeur makes for a fine but not overly pricey dinner, with wood panelling, starchy white tablecloths and staff that appear and disappear just when you want them to. Serving all manner of beasts that have fed on Scottish grass or swam in its seas, there really is no better place to sample the finest game, salmon, beef and lamb.

The Kitchin €€€

78 Commercial Quay, T0131 555 1755.

Tom Kitchen, one of the UK's most celebrated chefs, slept on Paris floors to learn his trade. Edinburgh's all the better for his return with this chic but cheerful restaurant that serves sumptuous, inventive dishes. Bookings essential. 3

Nightlife

Edinburgh has more pubs and bars per square mile than any other European city. The prime drinking venue is George St and the streets running north and south of it. Another good destination is the area at the top of Leith Walk known as the 'Pink Triangle'. For more raucous boozers, head to Lothian Road and the Grassmarket. The club scene has improved dramatically and any self-respecting raver will be supplied with the latest dance floor tunes spun by some of the UK's top DJs.

For movie fans, the legendary Filmhouse, *88 Lothian Rd, T0131 228 2688*, is the UK's most famous regional cinema and the hub of Edinburgh's International Film Festival. The café-bar is a good place to hang out. The Jazz Bar, *1A Chambers St, T0131-220 4298*, was voted 2010 UK Jazz venue of the Year. Gigs and jam sessions seven days a week. Expect a varied programme – including blues, soul, funk and acoustic – alongside some emerging and established jazz artists.

The Traverse Theatre, *Cambridge St, T0131 228 3223, www.traverse.co.uk*, is the city's most exciting theatre venue, which commissions works from contemporary playwrights from Scotland and all over the world.

Travel essentials

Getting there

Edinburgh International Airport, T0844 481 8989, is 8 miles west of the city centre. An **Airlink** bus (www.flybybus.com) to and from Waverley Bridge leaves every 10-20 mins, takes 25 mins and costs £3.50 one way, £6 return. A taxi to Prices St costs around £20.

There are direct trains to **Edinburgh Waverley** from London King's Cross (4½ hrs), Birmingham (5 hrs) and Manchester (3½ hrs). Fares vary widely depending on the time of travel; for times, fares and bookings T0845 748 4950, www.thetrainline.co.uk. **Scotrail**, T0845 601 5929, www.scotrail.co.uk, runs the overnight Caledonian Sleeper service from London Euston (7 hrs).

Getting around

Most of what you'll want to see lies within the compact city centre, which is easily explored on foot. **Public buses** are generally good and efficient. Princes Street is the main transport hub and you can get a bus to any part of the city from here. An excellent way to see the sights is to take one of the guided bus tours on board an open-top double-decker bus with a multilingual guide. These depart every 20 mins from Waverley Bridge, the first one leaving around 0930 and the last one between 1600 and 1730, depending on the time of year. Tickets are valid for the full day and you can hop on and off any of the company's buses at any of the stops. Tickets cost £12 from **Guide Friday Tours**, www.stuckonscotland.co.uk, or **Edinburgh Tour**, T0131 220 0770, www.edinburgh tour.com.

Taxis are not cheap, costing from around £4 for the very shortest of trips up to around £10 from the centre to the outskirts. They also tend to be scarce at weekends so book ahead if you need one.

Tourist information

Main tourist office, 3 Princes St, on top of Waverley Market, T0845 225 5121, www.edinburgh.org. Mon-Sat 0900-1700, Sun 1000-1700 (Jul-Aug till 1900). It has a full range of services, including currency exchange, and will book hotel rooms, provide travel information and book tickets for various events and excursions. There's also a tourist information desk at the airport T0845 225 5121, in the international arrivals area.

For details of entertainment listings in the city, pick up a copy of *The List* from any newsagent.

Ratings

Art and culture ☆☆☆☆☆
Eating ☆☆☆
Nightlife ☆
Outdoors ☆☆
Romance ☆☆☆☆
Shopping ☆☆☆
Sightseeing ☆☆☆☆☆
Value-for-money ☆☆☆
Overall city rating ☆☆☆

Florence

For all its reputation as one of the world's most beautiful cities, Florence can seem impenetrable to the first-time visitor: a city of cramped traffic, swarms of tourists, street-hawkers and markets selling enormous quantities of leather belts and aprons decorated with the anatomy of Michelangelo's David. But it's a city that people come back to. There's good Tuscan food and wine (if you know where to look), beautiful countryside all around and a history that includes the birth of the Renaissance. But it's the art and architecture that, rightly, are most celebrated. From Michelangelo's David and Botticelli's Venus to the marginally less well known but no less impressive cloisters in Santa Croce and frescoes in Santa Maria Novella, Florence has it all. And, if you need a new belt, there are few better places.

Ponte Santa Trinita.

At a glance

Florence sits mostly on the northern bank of the river Arno. Many arrive in the city at **Santa Maria Novella**, the city's train station and main transport hub. The city centre spreads out southeast beyond it. To the immediate east, the area of **San Lorenzo** has streets crowded with market stalls. Just northeast of here is the **Galleria dell'Accademia**, home to many of Florence's statues. The **Duomo**, Florence's biggest landmark, lies a little further south, below which a regular grid of streets stretch towards the river and make up the heart of the antique district. At the western edge of this grid, **Palazzo Strozzi** is a hulking Renaissance building, while to the south **Piazza della Signoria** competes with the Duomo to be the city's centre point; it's surrounded by grand buildings including the **Palazzo Vecchio** and the **Uffizi**, Florence's great art gallery. Nearby, the **Ponte Vecchio**, Florence's oldest bridge, leads to the enormous Palazzo Pitti and elegant Giardino di Boboli. Also here are the churches of Santo Spirito and, up a steep hill, San Miniato al Monte. Back on the northern bank of the Arno, to the east of Piazza della Signoria, is the spectacular Gothic basilica of **Santa Croce** and an area of interesting narrow streets and considerably fewer visitors.

24 hours in the city

Start with a coffee and a pastry from a café (stand at the bar to drink it – many of Florence's cafés will charge you a small fortune to sit down) and allow a little time to wander across the **Ponte Vecchio** before the crowds descend. You can also stop off in **piazza della Signoria** for the obligatory photo of Michelangelo's *David*. If you plan to visit the **Uffizi**, start early to get a good place in the queue and allow the whole morning. Alternatively, the **Galleria dell'Accademia**, **Bargello** or museums and galleries of the **Pitti Palace** will give a taste of Renaissance art with less queuing time involved. Find a restaurant in the **Oltrarno**, on the other side of the river, for lunch and follow it up with a stroll in the **Giardino di Boboli**, or a climb up the hill to **San Miniato al Monte**. In the late afternoon, visit the spectacular **Duomo** and the Battistero and climb to the top of either the Campanile or the Cupola and survey the city from above, ideally with the sunshine glowing off the rooftops. Head to **Santa Croce** in the evening – if you can get there before it closes at 1730 have a look around the interior and the cloisters. Otherwise sit for a while on the steps while people gather for aperitivi before drinking one or two of your own. There are some good eating options around here, too, and you shouldn't miss an ice cream from **Vivoli**. If you want to keep going into the night, bars around Piazza Santa Croce are a good place to start, followed by a nearby club in which you can dance until dawn.

Duomo and Battistero

piazza del Duomo, T055 230 2885, www.operaduomo.firenze.it.
Duomo: Mon-Wed and Fri 1000-1700, Thu 1000-1530, Sat 1000-1645 (1st Sat of month 1000-1530), Sun 1330-1645; free. Campanile: daily 0830-1930; €6. Cupola: Mon-Fri 0830-1900, Sat 0830-1740; €8. Battistero: Mon-Sat 1200-1900, Sun 0830-1400; €4. Map C2.

Florence's tallest building is still its pink-and-white, marble-clad cathedral. Filippo Brunelleschi's dome was completed in 1463 and, at the time, was the biggest in the world with a span of 42 m. Brunelleschi constructed the octagonal ribbed dome without scaffolding, using bricks inside a marble skeleton. Both the cupola and the separate campanile can be climbed; there are 414 steps up the belltower and 463 steps to the top of the dome. The campanile was designed by Giotto in 1334 but not completed until after his death.

The interior of the Duomo doesn't quite match the extraordinarily beautiful exterior, although Vasari's 16th-century frescoes of the Last Judgement on the inside of the dome are spectacular.

Just to the west of the Duomo, the **Battistero** (baptistry) may date from as early as the fourth century and is the city's oldest building. The interior has 13th-century mosaics and a font where Dante was baptized. The highlights, however, are the famous 14th- and 15th-century brass doors, by Pisano and Ghiberti. Those in situ are now copies; the originals are in the **Museo dell'Opera del Duomo**, *piazza del Duomo 9, T055 230 2885, Mon-Sat 0900-1930, Sun 0900-1345, €6.*

Piazza della Signoria

At the heart of the city, piazza della Signoria is a busy square which buzzes with tourists milling around the Renaissance and Roman statues and fountains. A replica of Michelangelo's *David* gets the most camera clicks but there is also the *Fontana di Nettuno* (Neptune Fountain) by Ammannati (1575) and the *Rape of the Sabine Women* by Giambologna (1583), carved, remarkably, from a single block of marble.

On the southern edge of the piazza, opposite the 14th-century, statue-filled Loggia dei Lanzi,

Looking past the Uffizi to Piazza della Reppublica.

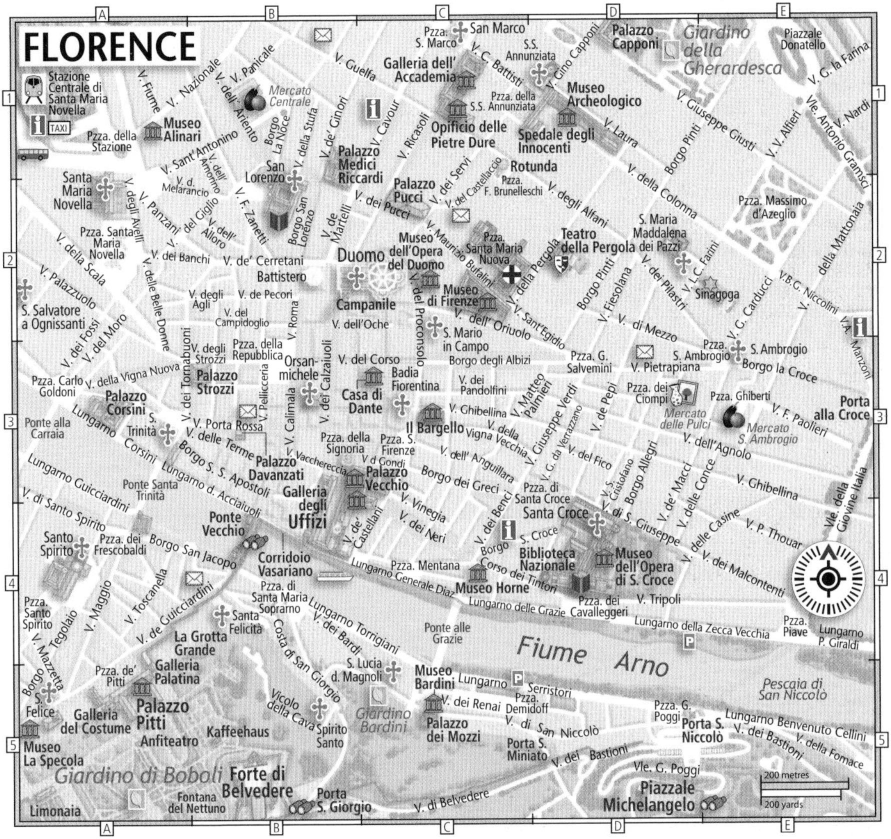

is the **Palazzo Vecchio**, *T055 276 8224, Fri-Wed 0930-1730, Thu 0930-1230, €6.* Originally the town hall, it also served as the residence of Duke Cosimo de Medici. Nowadays visitors can wander through some of its grand rooms.

Galleria degli Uffizi

piazzale degli Uffizi, T055 238 8651, www.polomuseale.firenze.it.
Tue-Sun 0815-1850. €10. Map D3/4,

Some of the longest queues in the art world are to be found outside the Uffizi gallery, so allow several hours to get in. Booking ahead is highly recommended but even this is unlikely to mean you will be able to swan straight in.

Once inside the hallowed halls of Renaissance art, highlights include: Sandro Botticelli's *Birth of Venus*, Titian's *Venus of Urbino*, Artemisia Gentileschi's *Judith Beheading Holofernes*, Michelangelo's *Holy Family*, three Caravaggios, three Leonardos and two Giottos.

The Giorgio Vasari-designed building was finished in 1581, originally intended to be offices (hence the name) of Florentine magistrates. It suffered significant damage as a result of a car bomb in 1993.

Ponte Vecchio

Best known for the jewellers' shops which line its sides, the Ponte Vecchio is the only Florentine bridge to have survived the Second World War. There have been shops on the bridge since it was built in 1345 – possibly originally in order to escape taxes. These days the shops are expensive tourist traps but the bridge itself remains one of the city's iconic symbols.

Palazzo Pitti and Giardino di Boboli

piazza Pitti.
Tue-Sun 0815-1850 (closing time of gardens varies with dusk). Combined ticket to museums and garden, €10. Map A5.

Started in 1457, the Palazzo Pitti was built by a banker, Luca Pitti as a conscious effort to outdo the Medicis, the most powerful family in Renaissance Florence. However, the enormity of the project practically bankrupted the Pitti family and the Medicis themselves moved into the palace in 1550. Already grandiose, the palace was further extended over the years, the most recent additions being the wings added in the 18th century. During Florence's brief position as capital of Italy in the 19th century, the Palazzo Pitti served as the main royal residence.

The contemporary palace houses several museums. The *Galeria Palatina, T055 238 8614*, contains many great works of Renaissance art, including paintings by Titian, Botticelli and Veronese. The **Appartamenti Monumentali** are examples of overblown opulence, and there are also museums dedicated to costume, porcelain and gold and silver.

Behind the Palazzo Pitti, **Giardino Boboli** is a large formal garden offering a peaceful, relaxed and often pleasantly cooler counterpoint to the stresses of the city centre. The gardens are the setting for musical and theatrical events in summer.

San Miniato al Monte

via Monte alle Croci. Summer daily 0800-1930.
Daily 0800-1230 and 1500-1730. Free.

High on a hill to the southeast of the city centre, the church of San Miniato is one of Italy's most beautiful Romanesque buildings. Construction began in 1013 and the church has changed little in the last 1000 years. The striking exterior is decorated with green and white marble. Inside the choir is raised above the crypt, creating a two-tier design, all of which is bathed in light. The nave is inlaid with mosaics and the walls have faded frescoes.

Just down the hill, **piazzale Michelangelo**, an otherwise unremarkable car park, affords great views over the Arno and across the city. The place fills with tourists and local couples around sunset.

Santa Croce

piazza Santa Croce, T055 246 6105.
Mon-Sat 0930-1730, Sun 1300-1730. €5. Map D4.

Containing the tombs of several famous Florentines, including Michelangelo, Galileo and Machiavelli, the Gothic basilica of Santa Croce is one of Florence's most important churches.

To the right of the altar, Giotto's frescoes of the Bardi and Peruzzi chapels are the highlights of the interior. Brunelleschi's 15th-century Secondo Chiostro (second cloister) is serenely beautiful and the Capella dei Pazzi (also by Brunelleschi) is another fine example of Renaissance architecture. There is a statue of Dante outside the basilica and a funerary monument to him inside, although he was actually buried in Ravenna.

Right: Orsanmichele.
Opposite page left: Palazzo di Bianca Capello.
Opposite page right: Florentine houses with washing hanging out to dry.

Excursions: Fiesole

In the hills to the northeast of Florence, Fiesole was once a more important power base than Florence itself and still likes to think of itself as a little bit superior. Certainly a little cooler, Fiesole is also more laid-back and has great views down over Florence in the valley below as well as some sights of its own. The town has a duomo which dates back to the 11th century as well as the archeological remains of a Roman theatre. The **Museo Archeologico**, *via Portigiani 1, T055 5961293, summer Wed-Mon 1000-1900, winter Thu-Mon 1000-1600, €12)*, contains pieces that were uncovered at this site. The winding walk along via Vecchia Fiesolana to San Domenico is a scenic one but many choose not to move far from the central piazza Mino, which has plenty of good bars and restaurants. Bus No 7 goes between Santa Maria Novella train station in Florence and Fiesole every 15 minutes.

Best of the rest

Capella Brancacci
piazza del Carmine, T055 276 8558. Mon and Wed-Sat 1000-1700, Sun 1300-1700, reservation required. €4.
This small chapel contains some of Masaccio's 15th-century frescoes, belonging to the church of Santa Maria del Carmine.

San Lorenzo
piazza San Lorenzo, T055 216634. Mon-Sat 1000-1730. €3.50.
In the middle of Florence's market district and so surrounded by Leonardo aprons and fake designer belts, San Lorenzo was the Medici's church in the 15th century. Brunelleschi, Donatello and Michelangelo all worked on it and it remains one of the city's most important buildings.

Oltrarno
One of the most satisfying areas of the city to wander around, the south bank of the Arno has a more laid-back feel than the rest of Florence. There's a market in Piazza Santo Spirito on some days of the week.

Bargello
via del Proconsolo 4, T055 238 8606. Daily 0815 1400, closed 2nd and 4th Mon in month. €4.
Built in 1255, the Bargello was later used as a prison but now holds Renaissance sculpture by Michelangelo, Donatello, Sansovino and others.

Museo di Storia della Scienza
piazza dei Giudici 1, T055 265 311, www.imss.fi.it. Wed-Mon 0930-1800, Tue 0930-1300. €8.
Explores the Renaissance from a scientific viewpoint.

Above: Via delle Terme.
Below: Via de Tornuoni.

Santa Maria Novella

piazza Santa Maria Novella, T055 219 257.
Mon-Thu 0900-1730, Fri 1100-1730, Sat 0900-1700. €3.50

Built by the Dominicans in the 13th and 14th centuries, the church of Santa Maria Novella holds a startlingly colourful fresco cycle by Ghirlandaio, illustrating the life of John the Baptist. Other highlights include Masaccio's *Trinità*, famous for its pioneering use of perspective, and the *Chiostro Verde*, so-called because of the green pigment used for the frescoes by the artist, Paolo Uccello. The Romanesque-Gothic façade (by Leon Battista Alberti) was added in 1470.

Galleria dell'Accademia

via Ricasoli 60, T055 238 8609.
Tue-Sun 0815-1850. €10.

Famously containing Michelangelo's masterful statue of David, sculpted in 1504 (when the artist was 29 years old), the Accademia also holds unfinished Michelangelo sculptures intended for the tomb of Pope Julius II.

Sleeping

Hotels in Florence tend to be expensive and, with notable exceptions, service can be below standard; the city's popularity means that it is a seller's market and standards tend to suffer.

Gallery Hotel Art €€€
vicolo dell' Oro 5, T055 27263, www.lungarnohotels.com.
A contemporary luxury hotel near the Ponte Vecchio, Gallery Hotel Art has over 70 elegant rooms and suites and has a well-stocked library and a trendy international bar serving fusion food. The place is decorated in muted tones and holds photography and art exhibitions.

JK Place €€€
piazza Santa Maria Novella 7, T055 264 5181, www.jkplace.com.
A real fire and antique furniture meet hip design in coffee and caramel tones in this 20-room hotel on piazza Santa Maria Novella. There's an immaculate roof terrace, cakes are served in the courtyard and you'd be hard-pushed not to feel eminently fashionable, in a refined Florentine kind of way.

Casa Howard €€
Florence, via della Scala 18, T06 6992 4555, www.casahoward.com.
The elegant recipe of the well-known Rome hotel has been repeated in Florence – a handful of individually designed (and loosely themed) rooms, creating an intimate and homely feel. The owners have a personal and idiosyncratic style, with plenty of quality fabrics and artefacts from around the world.

Torre Guelfa €€
borgo Santi Apostoli 8, T055 239 6338, www.hoteltorreguelfa.com.
Draped four-poster beds, wooden floors, a roof terrace (at the top of the eponymous 13th-century tower) with views over the Florentine rooftops make Torre Guelfa good value. Its location near the Ponte Vecchio makes it an even better choice.

Orchidea €
via borgo degli Albizi 11, T055 248 0346, www.hotelorchideaflorence.it.
A small, friendly place with 7 rooms on one floor of a palazzo just to the east of the Duomo. Some of the large, simple rooms overlook an internal garden. It tends to fill up quickly, so book ahead.

Pensione Scoti €
via De' Tornabuoni 7, T055 292 128, www.hotelscoti.com.
Almost opposite Palazzo Strozzi, Pensione Scoti is a smart, friendly, antique place with frescoes and large, simple, old-fashioned rooms.

Residenza Johanna 1 €
via Bonifacio Lupi 14, T055 481896, www.johanna.it.
The cheapest of a group of five residenze in Florence (the others are Johanna II, Johlea I and II and Antica Dimora Firenze). Johanna is especially good value, with antiques and parquet floors. Service is friendly, though staff all go home at 1900.

Eating

An abundance of good quality fresh produce lies at the heart of Tuscan cuisine and Florence's restaurants do well from it. Eating out is not especially cheap, although there are still some traditional trattorias to be found, which cater to a local market rather than the tourists.

Alla Vecchia Bettola €€
Vila e Ariosto 32-33, T055 224 158.
Closed Sun and Mon.
Communal eating on benches at marble-topped tables is the style at this excellent traditional trattoria just off piazza Tasso near Santo Maria del Carmine. A daily changing menu offers top Tuscan food.

Cibreo Trattoria €€
via dei Macci 122/r, T055 234 1100.
Closed Sun and Mon.
Also known as 'Il Cibreino', this is the little sibling of the altogether smarter Cibreo next door. It's cheaper and the style is more rustic, but the food is the same inventive, occasionally idiosyncratic, take on Tuscan classics.

Fuori Porta €€
via del Monte alle Croci 10/r, T055 234 2483.
Perfectly placed for those who plan to visit San Miniato al Monte but never make it up the hill, Fuori Porta is a wine bar that serves excellent light meals too. The outside tables are popular and, inside, you can gaze on (and of course consume) some of the enormous selection of wine on offer.

Da Benvenuto €
via della Mosca 16/r, T055 214833.
Closed Sun.
Simple but reliably good (and reliably good-value) Tuscan food in the centre of Florence.

Da Nerbone €
1st floor Mercato Centrale di San Lorenzo, T055 219 949.
Closed Sun.
Well-known for its tripe rolls (see Tripperia da Sergio e

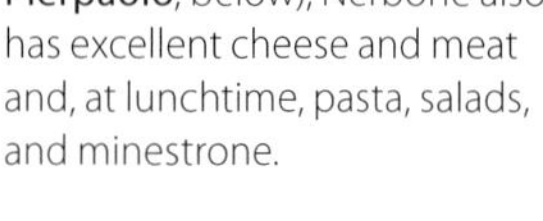

Pierpaolo, below), Nerbone also has excellent cheese and meat and, at lunchtime, pasta, salads, and minestrone.

Il Pizzaiuolo €
via dei Macci 113, T055 241171.
Closed Sun.
An authentic Neapolitan pizza place in Santa Croce, Il Pizzaiuolo fills up quickly in the evenings with those eager for their mouthwatering discs of tomato and mozzarella. In a city not renowned for its pizzas, this is a beacon of excellence.

Osteria Santo Spirito €
piazza Santo Spirito 16/r, T055-238 2383.
A friendly and colourful place in the corner of the attractive piazza, which has attempted to reinvent the traditional osteria in a contemporary style. Popular with travellers.

Tripperia da Sergio e Pierpaolo €
via dei Macci.
To the east of the city centre, some of Florence's most traditional food is served from Italy's most traditional agricultural vehicle – with no compromises to tourism or mad cow disease. From a specially adapted *Ape*, usually to be found at lunchtimes near Cibreo Trattoria on the corner of Piazza Sant'Ambrogio (see above), tripe is cooked and served fresh to an increasingly

Renaissance team

Twice Italian champions and six times cup winners, Fiorentina were, for a long time, big fish in the Italian football pond. In 2002 they were declared bankrupt and became one of the biggest casualties of a financial crisis in Italian football. However, as 'ACF Florentia', they made their way back up from the lower leagues and were conveniently allowed to skip one division. They bought back the rights to their old name and re-entered Serie A in 2004. Their involvement in the calciopoli match-fixing scandal in 2006 meant they were deducted 15 points at the beginning of the 2006/07 season and only avoided relegation back to Serie B after an appeal. They have since been one of Italy's strongest sides, qualifying for the Champions League in 2009/10. The club plays at the Stadio Artemio Franchi Iviale Manfredo Fanti, T055 503 0190, www.acffiorentina.it.

young and fashionable Florentine crowd. And, to wash it down, you can help yourself to a plastic cup of wine. It's very good value and it tastes better than you might expect.

Vivoli
Via Isole delle Stinche 7, T055 292 334.
Closed Mon.
Quite rightly one of Italy's most celebrated gelaterias, serving ice cream of the highest quality in generally old-fashioned flavours.

Travel essentials

Getting there
Florence's **Amerigo Vespucci Airport**, T055 306 1300, www.aeroporto.firenze.it, is 4 km from the centre of Florence. A taxi to the centre will cost you €25; alternatively the Volainbus (every 30 mins, €5) connects with Santa Maria Novella railway station. Vespucci is a small airport, so flying to Pisa's Gallileo Galilei Airport, T050 849 111, www.pisa-airport.com, or even Bologna's Marconi Airport, T051 647 9615, www.bologna-airport.it, may be cheaper (onward travel by train to Florence is not difficult from either). The main station is Santa Maria Novella, Piazza Stazione, T892 021, www.trenitalia.it, which also serves as the hub for the city's buses. A new high-speed train station is being built on the site of the city's ex-slaughterhouse at Belfiore at a cost of hundreds of millions of Euros.

Getting around
The city centre is small and doing anything other than walking has little to recommend it. Taxis can be found at ranks but they are notoriously few and far between. Buses work reasonably well but traffic is often snarled up in jams. Cars are not allowed in some parts of the centre and trying to park is next to impossible.

Tourist information
Azienda Promozionale Turistica, via Cavour 1, T055 290 832, www.firenzeturismo.it, Mon-Sat 0815-1915, is helpful and has free maps as well as information on opening hours, prices and tours. There are also offices at **Santa Maria Novella station**, T055 212 245, Mon-Sat 0830-1900, Sun and public holidays 0830-1400, and at the airport, T055 315 874, daily 0830-2030.

Nightlife

Bars and clubs

Much of Florence's nightlife takes place around piazza Santa Croce, with other lively pockets in the Oltrarno. Clubs loosen up a little and move outside in the heat of summer but for the rest of the year, well-dressed chic predominates.

Aperitivi, usually drunk between 1900 and 2100, are often accompanied by generous buffets of complimentary snacks. Drinks are correspondingly more expensive but at places like **Negroni**, via dei Renai 17, you can just about nibble your way to an evening's sustenance.

After *aperitivi*, cocktails (or, increasingly, wine bars) take over, followed by dancing the night away at locations such as **Maramao**, via dei Macci 79/r, usually a refined rather than a raucous experience.

Live music

The pop, rock and jazz scenes have become livelier in recent years, belying Florence's conservative reputation. Record shops are the best places to find out what's going on. Tourist offices have details of classical concerts at the **Accademia Bartolomeo Cristofori**, *via di Camaldoli 7/r, T055 221 646, www.accademiacristofori.it*, and other venues. For opera and ballet head to the **Teatro del Maggio Musicale Fiorentino**, *via Solferino 15, T055 27791, www.maggiofiorentino.com.*

Ratings

Art and culture ☆☆☆☆
Eating ☆☆☆☆☆
Nightlife ☆☆☆
Romance ☆☆☆☆
Shopping ☆☆☆☆☆
Sightseeing ☆☆☆☆
Value-for-money ☆☆☆
Overall city rating ☆☆☆☆

Istanbul

With over 25 centuries of uninterrupted history, including periods as the capital of three world empires – Roman, Byzantine and Ottoman – Istanbul is an undisputed cultural heavyweight. Castles, mosques, churches, seminaries, bazaars and palaces, plus some world-class museums: it has them all. Add to that a superb backdrop, cleaved by the waters of the Continent-dividing Bosphorus and the Golden Horn, with minarets and domes puncturing the skyline and the taste of salt in the air. The cosmopolitan human landscape with its vibrant café culture is no less beguiling, as modernity and tradition rub shoulders at this ancient meeting place of east and west. Istanbul has taken on the mantle of one of Europe's coolest cities with confident aplomb . Be prepared – Istanbul will surprise, amaze, entertain and confound you, all in the space of an afternoon.

Egyptian Mosque.

At a glance

Home to the Byzantine Emperors and Ottoman Sultans, **Sultanahmet** is Istanbul's historic heart. If you are only visiting for a few days, much of your time will be spent here. The area has a concentration of the city's main sights within a short stroll of its most atmospheric accommodation – think boutique Ottoman. Within walking distance are the **Grand Bazaar** and the teeming streets of **Eminönü** (where the Bosphorus ferries dock) and the **Spice Bazaar**. It's easy to spend several days exploring this part of the city, although a lot more awaits north of the Golden Horn. Across the Galata Bridge, in what was the European quarter in Ottoman times, **Galata** and **Beyoglu** have many of the city's best bars and restaurants. Formerly seedy and run-down, the narrow backstreets off pedestrianized **Istiklal Caddesi**, Istanbul's main shopping street, are dotted with atmospheric eateries, galleries and bars. At the north end of Istiklal Caddesi is **Taksim Square**, centre of the modern city but with little of interest besides its bland modern hotels. A short cab ride north is Nisantasi, an upmarket shopping district ideal for a spot of retail therapy. Down beside the Bosphorus, a string of suburbs are great to explore. The cobbled streets of **Ortaköy** lead to a waterside square overlooked by lively cafés and bars. Beyond the continent-spanning Ataturk Bridge, things get progressively more exclusive, as you head towards the upmarket Bosphorus 'village' of **Bebek**, with its diminutive mosque, cafés and restaurants overlooking the expensive yachts moored offshore. Nearby is the Ottoman castle of Rumeli Hisar, built in preparation for the conquest of Constantinople, while a string of equally bucolic villages lining the Asian shore can be reached by ferry.

24 hours in the city

Have a lazy breakfast on your hotel roof terrace while drinking in the fantastic view. If your lodgings are one of the few in the Old City that don't have one, then try the Hotel Uyan. Be enthralled by the soaring symmetry of the Sultanahmet (Blue) Mosque, before jumping on a tram to shopaholic heaven – the Grand Bazaar. With lightened wallet and bag of souvenirs in hand, weave your way down through the backstreets to Eminönü and the Spice Market. Take refuge from the hustle and relax over a late lunch at the Pandeli Restaurant. Afterwards, wander past the fishermen on the Galata bridge before catching the Tünel funicular up to Galata and the other main shopping hub of Istanbul, Istiklal Caddesi. The Genoese watchtower in Galata is a great place to enjoy the sunset and a well-earned beer. After dark, jump in a taxi to Ortaköy, where in summer you can dine alfresco on the main square. Alternatively, the bars and clubs of Beyoglu await those wanting to imbibe or boogie until the wee hours.

Topkapı Palace (Topkapi Sarayi)

Topkapı Sarayi, Sultanahmet, T0212 512 0480.
Wed-Mon 0900-1700. TL20. Harem Tour TL15. Map C5.

Home of the Ottoman sultans and centre of their empire, the Topkapı Palace is one of the world's most important historical collections, as well as being one of the most popular sights in the whole country. Each year tens of thousands wander through its many halls, apartments and pavilions. Entered through the imposing **Imperial Gate** (Bab-i Humayun), the palace sprawls over a series of large courtyards, with the Harem, inviolate residence of the Sultans, their wives and concubines, at its core. Things can get very crowded so it is wise to visit early in the day and buy your ticket for the Harem tours, which depart every 30 minutes, as soon as you arrive. With so many other things to see, you should allow at least half a day for your wanderings. Highlights include the newly renovated palace kitchens and the dazzling artefacts in the Imperial Treasury.

Haghia Sophia (Aya Sofya)

Sultanahmet Meydani, T0212 520 7742.
Tue-Sun 0900-1700. TL20. Map C6.

The pinnacle of Byzantine architectural achievement was built in AD 537 at the behest of Emperor Justinian, eager to prove the pre-eminence of his 'New Rome'. Towering over the city's rooftops and topped by a whopping 30 m-wide dome, the cathedral enthralled Byzantine visitors then and continues to do so today. Despite a sacking by the Crusaders in 1204, its conversion into a mosque in 1453, then a museum in 1935,

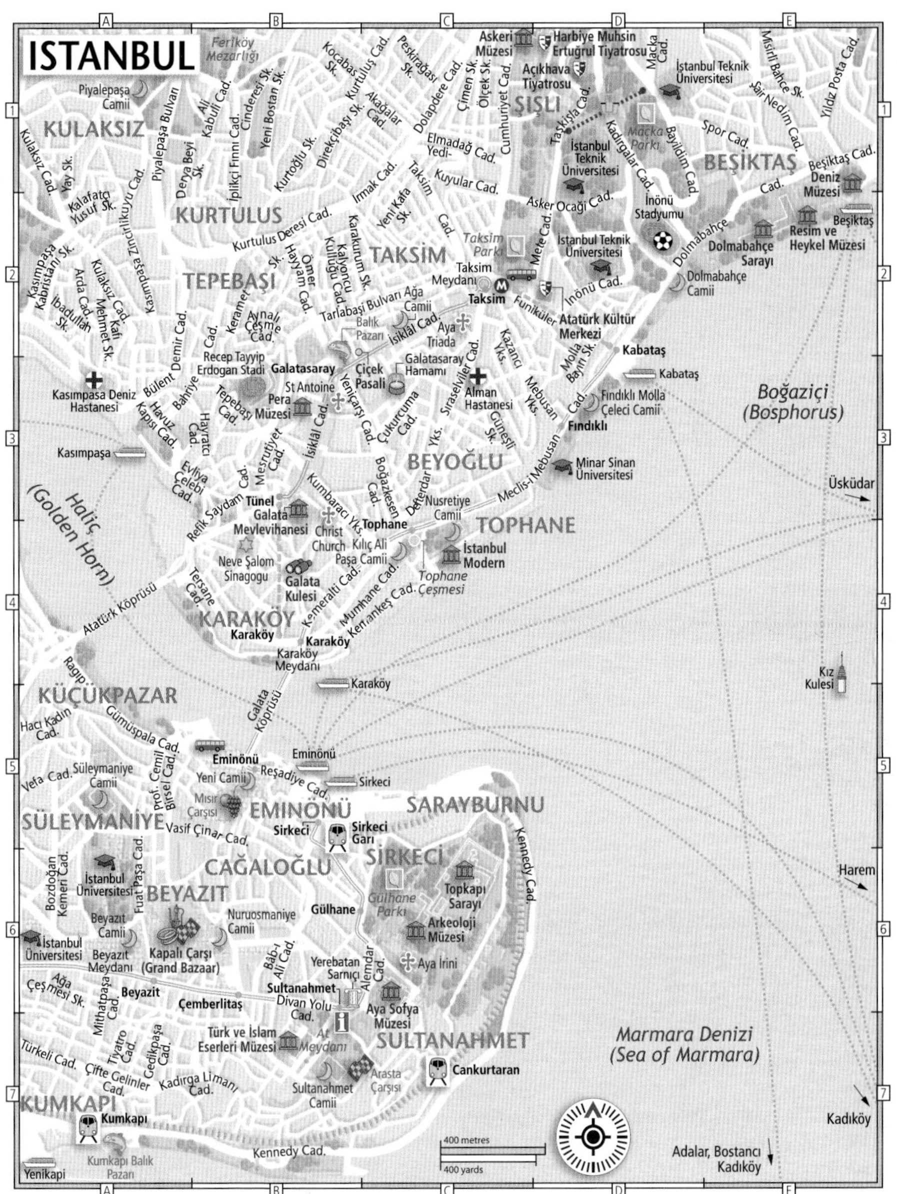
ISTANBUL
KULAKSIZ
KURTULUS
TEPEBAŞI
TAKSİM
ŞIŞLI
BEŞİKTAŞ
BEYOĞLU
TOPHANE
KARAKÖY
KÜÇÜKPAZAR
SÜLEYMANIYE
EMINÖNÜ
SARAYBURNU
SIRKECI
CAĞALOĞLU
BEYAZIT
SULTANAHMET
KUMKAPI
Haliç (Golden Horn)
Boğaziçi (Bosphorus)
Marmara Denizi (Sea of Marmara)
Taksim Meydanı
Taksim
Atatürk Kültür Merkezi
Dolmabahçe Sarayı
Galata Kulesi
Topkapı Sarayı
Arkeoloji Müzesi
Aya Sofya Müzesi
Kapalı Çarşı (Grand Bazaar)
Üsküdar
Harem
Kadıköy
Adalar, Bostancı Kadıköy
Kız Kulesi
400 metres
400 yards

the building has a great collection of precious and ancient mosaics, some only recently rediscovered beneath Ottoman plaster. But it is the venerable atmosphere that can't help but impress.

Sultanahmet Mosque (Sultanahmet Camii)

Daily 0900-1900. TL5-10 donation suggested. Map B7.

Gracefully cascading domes and sharp, soaring minarets, the Sultanahmet Mosque, better known as the **Blue Mosque**, rises evocatively above the well-kept gardens of Sultanahmet Square. Built by Sultan Ahmet in 1616, it was the last of the great imperial mosques, an architectural milestone marking the beginning of the Ottoman Empire's long, inexorable decline. Controversially, the Sultan had six minarets built, instead of the usual four, an act that many saw as a mark of disrespect to the Mosques of the Prophets in Mecca, which were also graced with a half-dozen towers. As a functioning mosque you enter through a special entrance and must be dressed appropriately – shawls can be borrowed to cover exposed arms and female heads at the door. Inside, the walls are gaudily decorated with 20,000 patterned Iznik tiles, hence the building's western name.

Poorer palace?

Istanbul's most famous hotel is the Pera Palas, Mesrutiyet Caddesi 98, Tepebasi, Beyoglu, **built in 1892 to accommodate travellers stepping off the glittering Orient Express. The visitor's book is filled with the names of heads of state, politicians, poets, movie stars and spies: Greta Garbo, Mata Hari, Alfred Hitchcock and Jackie Onassis among them. Agatha Christie penned part of *Murder on the Orient Express* while staying, and Ataturk, the country's founder and first president, rested his head in room 101, which is kept as a mini-shrine to the great man. Small brass plaques on many of the doors identify other famous occupants. Curiosity value aside, little of the Pera Palas' original splendour survived after the hotel reopened its doors in late 2010 following a thorough renovation. Touches of majesty still remain in the original cage lift and the Orient Bar. The chic new Agatha restaurant is one of Istanbul's hippest dining spots.**

Museum of Turkish and Islamic Art (Turk ve Islam Eserleri Muzesi)

At Meydani 46, Sultanahmet, T0212 518 1805. Tue-Sun 0900-1700. TL4. Map B7.

Overlooking what was once the Byzantine Hippodrome, an arena where ceremonies, parades and races were held, and which is now known as **At Meydani**, the museum boasts a fascinating collection covering the Middle East and Central Asia, from earliest Islamic times through to the present day. The exhibits range from ivory to calligraphy to mosaics and ceramics, and are well labelled and organized. All are housed in a 16th-century palace constructed by Ibrahim Paþa, the Grand Vizier to Suleyman the Magnificent, before he was strangled at his master's behest.

Below left: Haghia Spohia.
Below right: The Blue Mosque.

Above left: Spice Bazaar.
Above right: Archaeological Museum.

Grand Bazaar

www.grandbazaarturkey.com.
Mon-Sat 0830-1930. Map B6.

With over 5000 shops connected by a maze of covered streets and passage-ways, the Grand Bazaar is the largest retail area of its kind in the world. Surrender yourself to the inevitability of getting lost and just wander, browsing shops selling clothes, carpets, gold and silver, household goods and souvenirs, stopping to practice your haggling skills. Each type of shop is concentrated in a particular area, with silver and antique merchants occupying the Ic Bedestan, the historic heart of the bazaar. If you need a break there are several cafés within the bazaar.

Çemberlitaş Hamamı

www.cemberlitashamami.com.tr.
0600-2400. TL60, plus 10% tip. Map B6.

The perfect antidote to a day's sight-seeing is a steam clean, followed by a massage in one of the city's many Turkish baths. Built in 1584 by master architect Mimar Sinan, and with separate sections for men and women, the Çemberlitaş Hamamı is one of the most atmospheric, as well as being close to the Grand Bazaar and Sultanahmet. Towels and cloths to wrap around you while bathing are provided, and refreshments are also available. Pricey, but a real experience.

Best of the rest

Museum of Innocence
Arasta Sokak, Beyoglu, www.masumiyetmuzesi.com. Tue-Sun 1000-1800. TL10.
This vintage nick-knack collection inspired by the novel by Nobel prize-winning author Orhan Pamuk opened in early 2011.

Yerebatan Sarnic
Yerebatan Caddesi 13, Sultanahmet, T0212 522 1259, www.yerebatan.com. Daily 0900-2000. TL10.
Underground cistern featured in *From Russian With Love.*

Suleymaniye Mosque
Tiryakiler Çarsisi, Suleymaniye. Sat-Thu 0900-1900.
The city's grandest mosque reopened greatly refreshed in 2010.

Galata Tower
Galata Sq. Daily 0900-1900, T212 293 8180, www.galatatower.net. TL5.
A medieval Genoese watchtower with a great view.

City Walls
The historic city walls have been restored and you can walk much of their 6.5 km length, although it's best not to do it alone.

Dolmabahçe Palace
Dolmabahçe Caddesi, Beşiktaş, T0212 236 9000, www.dolmabahce.gov.tr. Tue-Sun 0900-1600. TL20.
Ostentatious home of the last Ottoman sultans.

Nişantaşi
An upmarket shopping and residential district north of Taksim, which has designer clothes stores, pavement cafés and domestic chains aplenty.

Santralistanbul
Kazım Karabekir Caddesi 2, Golden Horn, T0212 311 7809, www.santralistanbul.org. TL7. Daily 1000-1700.
Groundbreaking digital design museum housed in Istanbul's old power station. Immense.

Leander Tower (Also called the Maiden's Tower)
Salacak Caddesi. Daily 1000-1900.
Catch ferry from Kabataş to this tiny tower bobbing in the Bosphorus. Photo opportunities aplenty and Bond fans may recognise it from *The World Is Not Enough.*

Egyptian Bazaar and Eminönü

Mon-Sat 0800-1900. Map B5.

Also known as the **Spice Market**, this busy arcade lined with shops selling spices, imported foods, souvenirs and herbal remedies, such as the somewhat dubious 'Turkish Viagra', gets its name from a time when it was endowed with the custom duties from Cairo. The market is part of the **Yeni Camii** (New Mosque) complex, which is surrounded by the bustling district of Eminönü. Bosphorus ferries dock at the quayside and the air is filled with the smell of juicy kebabs and the sound of itinerant traders hawking their wares from the pavements.

Istiklal Caddesi and Beyoglu

In Ottoman times Beyoglu was home to the city's Greek, Armenian and European communities, and many of their churches and consulates remain. With the departure of these communities after the establishment of the Turkish Republic, the area fell on hard times, though it has enjoyed a Bohemian renaissance in recent times. Beyoglu's narrow streets, running off the main shopping thoroughfare of Istiklal Caddesi, are studded with cutting edge restaurants, cafés and bars.

Ortaköy

Ortaköy is the first of the Bosphorus 'villages' on the European shore. Cobbled streets lined with cafés, shops and market stalls lead down to a small square overlooked by the baroque **Mecidiye mosque**, which looks like a wedding cake when lit up at night. On sunny days, the cafés are crowded, as are the bars at night. Further north, some of the city's most upmarket nightspots overlook the straits.

Rumeli Hisar and Bebek

Tue-Sun 0900-1630. TL8. Bus 25E from Eminönü or bus 40 from Taksim.

In preparation for his attack on Constantinople in 1453, Sultan Mehmet had castles built on either side of the Bosphorus to prevent supply ships reaching the city. The larger of these was Rumeli Hisar, on the European shore north of Bebek, overlooking a bend in the Bosphorus. Today you can walk the restored 15 m-thick battlements and take imaginary pot-shots at passing ships. There are several excellent little cafés nearby or stroll along the coastal path to the genteel Bosphorus 'village' of Bebek, which attracts a well-heeled crowd.

Below: European Istanbul.

Excursion: Prince's Islands

Off Istanbul's Asian shore are a collection of nine islands, which were a place of exile in Byzantine and Ottoman times, later becoming home to wealthy families from the city's Greek and Armenian minorities. The islands are graced with many beautiful wooden houses, churches and a Greek Orthodox monastery. They also remain blissfully car-free, with horse carts the only means of transport. The largest, **Buyukada**, is the most interesting and you can explore it by rented bicycle or hire a horse-drawn phaeton. A tour of the island takes a couple of hours on foot, taking in Leon Trotsky's home – he wrote *The History of The Russian Revolution* while living here – and the hilltop St George's Monastery.

There is a beach club on the far side of the island with a small beach for cooling off. Ferries depart from Eminönü and Kabataş's Adalar Piers regularly for the hour-long crossing. Tickets cost TL4.5.

Sleeping

Istanbul has an excellent choice of accommodation from budget hotels to atmospheric Ottoman boutique places and luxury international chains. Prices are competitive in comparison with other European cities, although there are plenty of places to pamper yourself if you wish. Booking in advance is advisable at any time of year as the most popular hotels fill up quickly. Many of the city's top-notch beds are found along the Bosphorus.

Çiragan Palace €€€
Çiragan Caddesi 32, Beşiktaş, T0212 326 4646, www.kempinski.com.
This five-star on the edge of the Bosphorus is truly glorious, and is housed inside the former Turkish parliament building. It has the city's finest swimming pool, as well as a spa and several excellent restaurants including Tuğra, widely considered Istanbul's best.

Four Seasons €€€
Tevfikhane Sokak 1, Sultanahmet, T0212 638 8200, www.fourseasons.com.
Formerly a prison, this is now one of Istanbul's most exclusive and luxurious hotels. Its 54 high-ceilinged rooms have every possible mod con. The great restaurant comes into its own at brunch. New sister hotel sits next to the Çiragan Palace.

Empress Zoe €€
Adliye Sokak 10, Sultanahmet, T0212 518 2504, www.emzoe.com.
Incorporating the ruins of 15th-century Turkish Baths, the Zoe is exquisitely decorated, with modern frescoes and wall hangings and small but comfy and well-furnished rooms. There is a scenic roof terrace bar and a lovely garden.

The House Hotel €€
Bostanbaşı Caddesi 19, Beyoglu, T0212 244 3400, www.thehousehotel.com.
Perfectly located inside a century-old four-storey mansion in Istanbul's coolest quarter. Composed of 20 ultra-hip suites, rooftop bar and art deco interiors, all blessed with top-notch service.

Istanbul Sweet Home €€
Various locations in Beyoglu, www.istanbulsweethome.com.
This neat concept involves 10 or so designer apartments, most with awesome views over Istanbul, rented out by the week in hip Beyoglu locations. Flats range from the sophisticated to the sumptuously traditional. All have great kitchens, while some have Turkish baths and vast outdoor terraces.

Hotel Uyan €€-€
Utangac Sokak 25, Sultanahmet, T0212 516 4892, www.uyanhotel.com.
A good choice for a budget hotel. It's set in a converted corner house with clean en suite rooms. The scenic roof terrace has stunning views.

Side Hotel €
Utangac Sokak 20, Sultanahmet, T0212 517 2282, www.sidehotel.com.
A well-managed place with a selection of simple pension rooms, or more expensive hotel suites, most with their own bathrooms.

Eating

Istanbul's restaurant scene has come on leaps and bounds in recent years, with a crop of talented new Turkish chefs adding to the existing mix of superb traditional *meyhane* (the city's equivalent of a taverna), kebab houses and fish restaurants. Dining out is generally great value for money, though prices in some of the top-notch establishments are on a par with prices in other European cities. Alcohol is available in the vast majority of the city's dining spots.

For a great evening out visit the raucous area of Kumkapi, on the coast south of Beyazit, and the Grand Bazaar, which is crowded with meze and fish restaurants, where diners are entertained by gypsy street musicians. The *meyhane* of Nevizade Sokak, reached down the Balik Pazari from Istiklal Caddesi, are very popular with local diners.

Breakfast

Fes Café €
Halýcýlar Caddesi 62, Grand Bazaar, T0212 528 613.
At the heart of the bazaar, this trendy café is a good spot for a cappuccino and a snack.

Dârüzziyafe €€
Şifahane Sokak 6, Fatih, T0212 511 8414.
Set in the grand old gardens and kitchens of the Süleymaniye Mosque, this is classic Ottoman dining at its most atmospheric. Choose from around 60 classics, from chicken and walnut stew to lamb shish. Sherbets and juice only, no hard stuff.

Lunch

Haci Abdullah €€
Sakizagaci Caddesi 17, T0212 293 8561, www.haciabdullah.com.tr.
In a sidestreet off Istiklal Caddesi, this is a grandfather of the Istanbul restaurant scene, having served Ottoman-Turkish cuisine for over 110 years. It's also known for its pickles and preserves which are displayed in colourful jars along the walls. No alcohol served.

Pandeli €€
Misir Carþisý (Egyptian Bazaar), Eminönü, T0212 527 3909.
This atmospheric restaurant, housed in century-old dining room above the entrance to the Spice Market, serves traditional Turkish dishes at lunchtime only.

Dinner

Vogue €€€
BJK Plaza, A Blok, Beşiktaş, T0212 227 4404.
Hip rooftop dining. Lord it over

Travel essentials

Getting there
Ataturk Airport, www.ataturkairport.com, is 25 km west of the city centre. The journey by taxi into Sultanahmet or Taksim takes 30-60 mins depending on the traffic, and costs TL40-55 (taxis are metered). Havas operates an airport bus into Taksim (every 30 mins, TL10). The cheapest way to Sultanahmet is by tram (TL3, every 5 mins), change at Zeytinburnu.

Getting around
To get around the Old City all you need is your feet and an occasional ride on the modern **tram**, which passes Aksaray, Beyazit and the Covered Bazaar, Sultanahmet Square and Topkapı Palace (Gülhane) before terminating in Eminönü. Tokens can be bought at each station and cost TL1.50.

The 19th-century **funicular railway**, known as the Tünel, climbs steeply up to Istiklal Caddesi from the north side of the Galata bridge (straight on at the end of the bridge and then bear left at the first main junction). Tokens can be bought from the ticket booths in either station, TL1.10. There's also a picturesque little tram that will take you the length of Istiklal Caddesi, from Tünel to Taksim Square, without stopping. For longer journeys, taxis are fast and cheap, but avoid road travel during rush hour, and don't fall for the old taxi driver ruse where your TL50 note is swapped for a TL5 note!

Ferries regularly cross the Bosphorus from Eminönü and Karaköy to the suburbs of Uskudar and Kadiköy on the Asian shore. Tickets cost TL1.50 and the crossing takes about 15 mins. There are also 3 daily cruises up and down the Bosphorus to the Black Sea. These depart at 1030 and 1330 from Eminönü's Bogaz Hatti pier,with an extra sailing at 1200 during the summer. Tickets cost TL10 and the trip takes over 6 hrs, including a stop for lunch.

Tourist information
The most convenient offices are in the arrivals hall at Ataturk Airport, T0212 663 0793; Sultanahmet Sq, at Divan Yolu 3, T0212 518 1802; and in Sirkeci Station, Eminönü, T0212 511 5888. They can provide maps, brochures and information on current events, although not much else. For listings and city information buy a copy of *Istanbul: The Guide*.

Exchange rate Turkish Lira (TL). £1 = TL2.25. €1 = TL1.95.

Visas These can be bought at the airport before customs. It's £10 for Brits, or €15 for most other nationalities. Remember to have cash ready to pay for it.

all Istanbul from 13 storeys up as you gorge on harbour-fresh sushi, accomplished Mediterranean bites or the city's best Sunday brunch offering.

Imroz €€
Nevizade Sokak 19-29, T0212 249 9073.
One of the best fish and meze restaurants on a street crowded with excellent meyhane.

Nightlife

You certainly won't be bored after dark in Istanbul. Beyoglu has a diverse collection of bars and clubs, catering for tastes from jazz to Turkish folk and techno. Pick up a copy of *Time Out Istanbul* for details of the best nightspots.

Ataturk Cultural Centre
Taksim Sq, T0212 251 5600, www.idobale.com.
The city's premier performing arts venue reopened in 2010 to host concerts, ballet and opera.

Babylon
Seybender Sokak 3, Asmalimescit, Beyoglu, www.babylon-ist.com.
A live venue which hosts top international and Turkish acts, as well as club nights.

If you want to see where Istanbul's rich and famous strut, visit one of the super-clubs overlooking the Bosphorus in Kuruçeþme. Try **Reina**, *Muallim Naci Caddesi 44, Kuruçeşme, T0212 259 5919 www.reina.com.*tr, but dress up and be prepared for a vertiginous bar bill. Call ahead to get on the guest list.

Shopping

Istanbul has to be one of the great shopping cities of the world, up there, in its own unique way, with New York and Milan. The **Grand Bazaar** is of course a good place to start, but there are other areas to check out including **Arasta Bazaar**, beside Sultanahmet Mosque, for carpets, handicrafts and Iznik tiles. The **Istanbul Handicraft Centre**, *Kabasakal Caddesi 7, Sultanahmet Sq*, has artisans onsite producing various traditional Ottoman crafts.

Istaklal Caddesi, the city's main drag, has a mix of department stores, clothing shops (like Mavi Jeans) and some good bookshops. For antiques, the Beyoglu district of Çukurcuma, east of Istiklal Caddesi, is dotted with little treasure troves, though remember there are restrictions on exporting real antiquities. **Nişantaşi** has international and home-grown fashion labels along Abdi Ipekci Caddesi and Tesvikiye Caddesi.

Across the Bosphorus in **Kadiköy**, the city's largest street market is held on Tue and Sun along Kusdili Sokak. Ask for the Salý Pazan, then follow the crowd.

Grand Bazaar.

Ratings

Art and culture ☆☆☆
Eating ☆☆☆
Nightlife ☆☆☆☆☆
Romance ☆☆☆☆
Shopping ☆☆☆
Sightseeing ☆☆
Value-for-money ☆☆☆☆
Overall city rating ☆☆☆☆

Lisbon

With its back to Europe and its soul in the 15th century, scrupulously self-effacing Lisbon has long kept a low profile while its neighbours strutted their stuff. During nearly 50 years of solitude, Salazar smothered the city in a conservative mantle but now it has emerged from its cocoon. Thanks to European funding, a stint as City of Culture in 1994 and Expo '98, which saw the arrival of the futurist Parque das Nações, Lisbon is flourishing. Appropriately, given Portugal's sea-faring, imperialist history, old and new worlds sit comfortably side by side in the capital. Lisboetas emerge from riverside warehouse conversions and flash fashion boutiques to board arthritic trams that still chug up ludicrous gradients, zigzagging past squat dwellings, hole-in-the-wall grocers and ancient Roman walls.

Elevador da Bica.

At a glance

Square and spare, Lisbon's downtown, **Baixa**, is the city's commercial nexus, a grid of thrusting thoroughfares built in the wake of the 1755 earthquake. Pedestrianized **Rua Augusta** is the Rambla-esque central promenade, which funnels south to handsome **Praça do Comércio**, Lisbon's Whitehall and medieval city gateway. To the north, Baixa's main square and the city's central reference point is **Rossio**. To the west, straddling one of Lisbon's seven hills, is gentrified **Chiado**. North of Rossio is the grand **Avenida da Liberdade**, which ends at **Praça Marques de Pombal**. Beyond it is Lisbon's largest park **Parque Eduardo VII** and, further north, the unassailable **Museu Calouste Gulbenkian**. West of Chiado, the **Bairro Alto** has always been Lisbon's Latin quarter, where sleek bars and fado houses line labyrinthine alleyways. Chiado's backyard to the west is the earthy neighbourhood of **São Bento**, which gives way to smarter **Estrela** and, further west still, streets climb to haughty, diplomatic **Lapa**. East of Baixa is **Alfama**, a maze of medieval Moorish streets and where it all began. A few kilometres west of Baixa, stretching along the Tagus, **Belém** sees Portugal's imperial triumphs made stone and its pastries made delicious. To the northeast, suburban sprawl gives way to sleek modernism at **Parque das Nações**, site of Expo '98.

Baixa and Rossio

Surrounded by whizzing traffic, all roads seem to lead to Rossio, Baixa's central square, formally known as Praça Dom Pedro IV. The neoclassical **Teatro Nacional de Dona Maria II**, built in 1846 by Fortunato Lodi, occupies the north side of the square. During the 18th century this was the site of the Palace of the Inquisition. To the northwest stands the interlocking horseshoe arches of **Rossio station**, designed in 1887 and betraying a late 19th-century nostalgia for the period of the Discoveries. Adjacent to Rossio, **Praça da Figueira** retains more endearing old-world charm.

Southbound from Rossio, **Rua Augusta** is lined with touristy pavement cafés, international chain stores and leather emporiums. This climaxes with the overarching splendour of the **Arco de Vitória**, gateway to **Praça do Comércio** – the culmination of an enlightened despot's vision for a model city and designed to out-pomp the most regal of Europe's squares. The showpiece is a bronze equestrian statue of King Dom José I and, on the north side of the square, nestling beneath the arcaded colonnades is one of Lisbon's most famous literary landmarks, **Café Martinho do Arcado**.

On Rua Santa Justa, just south of Rossio, **Elevador de Santa Justa**, *Daily 0900-2100, map C2, €1.50*, is one of Lisbon's most iconic and memorable images. Designed by an apostle of Eiffel, Raoul Mesnier du Ponsard, the 45-m vertical wrought-iron structure was built to link the Baixa with Largo do Carmo, via a 25-m walkway.

Alfama

Alfama is Lisbon's spiritual heart. It's the old Moorish quarter where ribbons of alleyways coil into blind alleys and crooked alcoves. Dominating the skyline is the iconic, if a little Disneyfied, **Castelo de São Jorge**. Ancient trams take you to **Miradouros de Santa Luzia** and **Largo Portas de Sol** from where the view of city below is breathtaking. The pristine baroque **Panteão Nacional de Santa Engrácia** and the twin bell towers of the **Igreja de São Vicente da Fora** rise amidst clusters of squat houses stacked on top of each other. Encircling the church on Saturday or Tuesday is the 'thieves' **flea market**, Feira da Ladra; buy your own piece of crumbling Lisbon, a fireman's T-shirt, or a traditional basket. Surrounded by seafood restaurants, tour group-orientated fado houses and neighbourhood grocers, the **Casa do Fado e da Guitarra Portuguesa**, *Largo do Chafariz de Dentro, 1, T21 882 3470, daily 1000-1300 and 1400-1800, €2.50*, tells the history of the national song. A short bus ride away, set in the tranquil Madre de Deus Convent, the **Museu Nacional do Azulejo**, *Rua de Madre de Deus 4, T21 810 0340, www.mnazulejo.imc-ip.pt, Tue 1400-1800, Wed-Sun 1000-1800, €5, free on Sun 1000-1400*, houses the finest collection of azulejo tiles in the country. For more authentic exposure to Portugal's art forms,

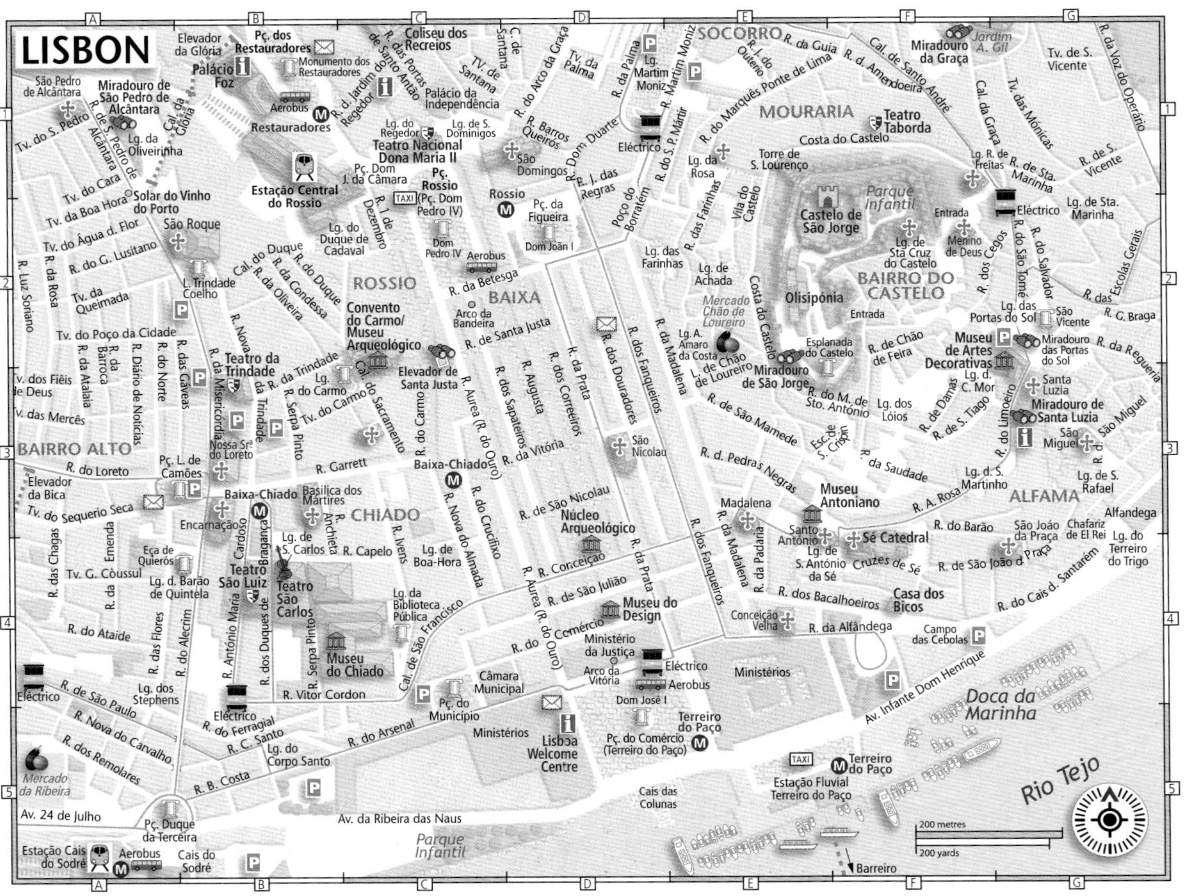
LISBON
Rio Tejo
Doca da Marinha
200 metres
200 yards
ALFAMA
BAIRRO DO CASTELO
MOURARIA
SOCORRO
BAIXA
ROSSIO
CHIADO
BAIRRO ALTO
Castelo de São Jorge
Sé Catedral
Casa dos Bicos
Museu Antoniano
Museu de Artes Decorativas
Miradouro de Santa Luzia
Miradouro da Graça
Miradouro de São Jorge
Miradouro de São Pedro de Alcântara
Teatro Taborda
Olisipónia
Museu do Design
Núcleo Arqueológico
Convento do Carmo/Museu Arqueológico
Elevador de Santa Justa
Museu do Chiado
Teatro São Carlos
Teatro São Luiz
Teatro da Trindade
Teatro Nacional Dona Maria II
Coliseu dos Recreios
Palácio da Independência
Estação Central do Rossio
Palácio Foz
Solar do Vinho do Porto
São Roque
Lisboa Welcome Centre
Câmara Municipal
Ministérios
Arco da Vitória
Pç. do Comércio (Terreiro do Paço)
Estação Fluvial Terreiro do Paço
Terreiro do Paço
Cais das Colunas
Estação Cais do Sodré
Mercado da Ribeira
Av. Infante Dom Henrique
Av. da Ribeira das Naus
Av. 24 de Julho
R. Aurea (R. do Ouro)
R. Augusta
R. da Prata
R. dos Fanqueiros
R. dos Correeiros
R. dos Douradores
R. Garrett
R. Nova do Almada
R. do Crucifixo
Rossio
Baixa-Chiado
Restauradores
Barreiro

stroll around earthy **Mouraria** to the north, the cradle of fado, or **Graça**, to the northwest, where fragments of lustrous 16th-century azulejos peel from façades.

Chiado

In Chiado, 19th-century old-world elegance prevails. **Rua Garrett** is studded with high fashion boutiques and art nouveau jewellery stores. The literary legacy of cryptic genius Fernando Pessoa still hangs in the air, his spirit immortalized in stone at Café A Brasileira (see page XX). Devastated by fire in 1988, Chiado has been born again and now Soho-style wrought-iron architecture is juxtaposed with the rococo elegance of the **Teatro Nacional de Sao Carlos**, *Rua Serpa Pinto, map B4, T21 325 3045/6, www.saocarlos.pt.*

From Rua Garrett, Calçado do Sacramento leads to the peaceful **Largo do Carmo**, site of one of the most enigmatic buildings in the city, the cavernous **Convento do Carmo**, *T21 347 8629, map C3, Oct-Apr Mon-Sat 1000- 1700, May-Sep Mon-Sat 1000-1800, €3*. Heading south along Rua Serpa Pinto towards the river, the **Museu do Chiado**, *T21 343 2148, www.museudochiado-ipmuseus.pt, map B/C4, Tue-Sun 1000-1800, €4, free on Sun 1000-1400*, is one of the finest exhibition spaces for Portugal's 19th- and 20th-century artists.

Bairro Alto

In Lisbon's 'High Town', peeling doorways reveal sleek bars, gritty tascas and fado houses. Seductive samba mingles with deep techno and black-shawled divas sing out the nation's woes. Here you'll also find baroque magnificence in the Jesuit **Igreja de São Roque**, *Largo Trindade Coelho, www.museu-saoroque.com, T21 323 5381, map A/B2, Tue-Sun 1000-1700, museum €2.50*, free Sun until 1400, and exotic gardens at the **Jardim Botânico**, *Rua da Escola Politécnica, www.jb.ul.pt, May-Oct 0900-2000, Nov-Apr daily 0900-1900, €1.50.* Connecting the Baixa with Bairro Alto, the **Elevador da Glória** wheezes up to the stunning Miradouro de São Pedro de Alcântara.

On the southern edge of the Bairro Alto, Santa Catarina has some of the most endearing streets in the city. The **Miradouro de Santa Catarina** offers views across the Tagus and is the new site of the acclaimed **Design and Fashion Museum (MuDe)**, which moved here in 2009, *Rua Augusta 24, T21 888 6117, www.mude.pt; Tue-Thu and Sun 1000-2000.*

Belém

Belém, spreading west along the banks of the inky blue Tagus, is a tremendous heap of 15th- and 16th-century marvels, built to celebrate Vasco da Gama's discovery of the sea route to India. It is also one of the loveliest places in the city. There are breezy riverside walkways, super-sleek yachts, coloured fishing boats, and kites and frisbies flying across expansive parks. The **Mosteiro dos Jerónimos**, *Praça do Império, T21 362 0034, www.mosteiro jeronimos.pt, Oct- Apr Tue-Sun 1000-1730, May-Sep Tue-Sun 1000-1830, church free, cloisters €4.50, free Sun 1000-1400*, astounds with its sublime cloister where fantastical sea creatures and maritime emblems writhe in milky stone. By the river, the Torre de Belém, *Av de Brasília, T21-362 0034, www.torrebelem.pt, Oct-Apr Tue-Sun 1000-1700, May-Sep Tue-Sun 1000-1830, €3, free Sun 1000-1400*, looks more like a chess piece washed ashore than a defensive fort.

Museu Calouste Gulbenkian

Av da Berna, 45a, T21 782 3000, www.gulbenkian.pt.
Tue-Sun 1000-1800. €5, free Sun. Metro São Sebastião. Off map.

Lisbon's number one attraction, as monumental in its scope as in its quality, is the Museu Calouste Gulbenkian, lying in its own serene, 17-acre garden and housing an outstanding collection of Western and Eastern art of the major periods from 2800 BC onwards.

Also north of the city centre is the decorative art museum, Casa-Museu Dr Anastácio Gonçalves, *Av 5 de Outubro, T21 354 0823, www.cmag-ipmuseus.pt, Tue 1400-1800, Wed-Sun 1000-1800, €3, Metro Saldanha/Picoas*. It's worth visiting for its swirling art nouveau façade alone.

Parque das Nações

This industrial wasteland has been transformed into a modernist playground, united by the theme 'The Oceans, a Heritage for the Future'. Cable cars glide up to the city's highest viewpoint, the Torre de Vasco da Gama, *Cais das Naus, T21 891 8000, daily 1000-2000, €2.50.*

The Oceanarium, *T21 891 7002, www.oceanario.pt, Mar-Oct 1000-2000, Nov-Mar 1000-1900, last entry 1hr before closing, €12*, is the largest in Europe and there is also the Interactive Science museum (Pavilhão do Conhecimento Ciência Viva), *Alameda dos Oceanos, T21 891 7100, www.pavconhecimento.pt, Tue-Fri 1000-1800, Sat-Sun and holidays 1100-1900, €7.*

Excursion: Sintra

About 30 km from Lisbon is the UNESCO World Heritage site of Sintra. Poets have raved and pagans have revelled in its Elysian Fields, recaptured from the Moors in 1147. It's an ethereal landscape where castles rise from emerald mountain ranges. On sloping terraces, carpeted with lush pine forests, erupts a rhapsody of Bavarian kitsch in the form of the slapstick **Palácio da Pena**, *T21 910 5340, Jul-mid Sep Tue-Sun 1000-1900; mid Sep-Jun Tue-Sun 1000-1730, last entry 30 mins before closing*, the epitome of 19th-century decadence. In the valley are the cobble-stone streets and Moorish courtyards of **Sintra Vila**, the old quarter – all very chocolate box, but nonetheless alluring. The tourist magnet, however, is the sublime **Palácio Nacional**, *Largo Rainha D Amélia, T21 910 6840, www.pnsintra.imc-ip.pt, Thu-Tue 0930-1730, last admission 30 mins before closing, €7*, a 14th-century royal palace steeped in Arabian myths and the imprint of cavorting kings. Trains run from Sete Rios to Sintra every 15 minutes (journey time 45 minutes; €3.60 return). The Scotturb bus No 434 runs every 20 minutes from Sintra train station through Sintra Vila to the Palácio da Pena (€4.50). A combined one-day train and bus ticket costs €12. It takes a good hour to walk up to the palace. For further information visit the tourist office at **Sintra station**, *www.cm-sintra.pt, daily 0900-1900.*

Right: Rua do Comercio, Lisbon.
Opposite page: Lisbon doors.

Sleeping

The most idiosyncratic places to stay are in Alfama, with its charming guest houses, arty pensões and a few sleeker four-star options. Bairro Alto is in the heart of the night-time action. Many rooms overlook Rossio and Praça da Figueira, but this area is noisy. Avenida da Liberdade has most of the really swanky choices.

Tiara Park Atlantic €€€
Rua Castilho, off Parque Eduardo VII 149, T21 381 8700, www.tiara-hotels.com.
Contemporary rooms and the highest standards. Sweeping views out over the Tagus.

Hotel Lisboa Plaza €€
Travessa Salitre 7, off Av da Liberdade, T21 321 8218, www.heritage.pt.
A warm hotel with an understated, luxurious atmosphere and a home-from-home feel.

Hotel Metrópole €€
Praça do Rossio, 30, T21 321 9030, www.almeidahotels.com.
Unrivalled views over Rossio, a stately 1920s classic with characterful rooms. Great value.

Pensão Ninho das Águias €
Costa do Castelo, 74, Alfama, T21 885 4070.
Just below the walls of Castelo de São Jorge is one of the best pensãos in the city. Comfortable rooms, some en suite. Proud owner Luís is utterly charming and devoted to the history of the place and the city in general.

Pensão Residencial Santa Catarina €
Rua Dr Luís de Almeida e Albuquerque, 6, T21 346 6106.
This temple to 1960s kitsch is just 10 minutes from Bairro Alto bars and restaurants on a tranquil and picturesque street.

Travel essentials

Getting there

Lisbon's **Portela Airport**, *T21 841 3700, www.ana-aeroportos.pt*, is 6.5 km from the city centre. The **AeroBus** is the cheapest and most convenient way to reach the city centre, departing every 20 mins (0745-2015) making stops en route, including Saldanha, Marquês de Pombal, Praça dos Restauradores, and arriving in Rossio in around 20-25 mins, before terminating at Cais do Sodré railway terminal. A ticket costs €3.50 and is valid on the transport network for 1 day. Buses 22, 44, 45 and 83 also operate 0600-2130 to the centre (€1.40), and bus 45 runs until 0010 from outside the Cais de Sodré terminal. Bus 5 links the airport to Oriente Station. A taxi to the city centre costs €12-15 on the meter or €13 for a pre-paid taxi voucher bought in the terminal.

Getting around

Most of the main sights of the Baixa, Bairro Alto, Chiado and Alfama can be reached on foot but there's also an efficient network of orange buses run by **Carris**, *T21 361 3000, www.carris.pt*. A simple (1-way) ticket bought on board costs €1.45. A ride on one of Lisbon's ancient emblematic trams is the most enjoyable way to get around. Tram 28 is an unofficial tourist tram. The super tram No 15, runs from Praça da Figueira to Belém and then on to Ajuda Palace. Bright yellow Carris booths provide maps of bus and tram routes. Lisbon's metro, with 4 lines, is fast and efficient. It's best used if you are going to the north and west of the old city. A rechargeable card, '7 Colinas' costs an initial 50c and can then be credited to cover Carris buses and trams (eg one zone for 81c or a day for €3.75) or the entire network including the metro. Taxis are cheap; a trip from Rossio to the northern suburbs should be no more than €5. Fares are higher after 2200. There are ranks near Baixa-Chiado Metro station and Largo de Camões, or call Radio Taxis, T21 792 756.

Tourist information

The main office is the **Lisboa Welcome Centre**, *Praça do Comércio, T21 031 2810, www.visitlisboa.com, daily 0900-2000*, with other information points around the city. **Ask Me Lisboa**, *www.askmelisboa.com*, has information on sports, the arts, palaces and museums.

Eating

Chiado offers Portuguese traditional cuisine, Alfama is fado tour group territory and Bairro Alto has hip food, soul food, Portuguese staples and poly-cultural delicacies. Dinner is eaten late; in Bairro Alto restaurants stay open until around 0200.

Gambrinus €€€
Rua Portas de Santo Antão 23e 25, Baixa, T21 342 1466, www.gambrinuslisboa.com.
Daily 1200-0130.
One of Portugal's best seafood restaurants and a local institution. Tantalizing flavours, served by knowledgeable and friendly staff.

100 Maneiras €€
Rua do Texeira 35, T21 099 14 75, www.restaurante100maneiras.com.
The 10-course, prix-fixe menu features inventive international cuisine using local ingredients in a low-key setting.

Bota Alta €€
Travessa da Queimada 35, Bairro Alto, T21 342 7959.
Mon-Fri 1200-1430, 1900-2245, Sat 1900-2245.
Eccentric wood-panelled tavern with a faultless repertoire of Portuguese classics. Favourites include steak in red wine and cod with port and sausages.

Casa do Alentejo €€
Rua das Porta de S Antão 58, Baixa, T21 346 9231.
Daily 1200-1430, 1900-2200.

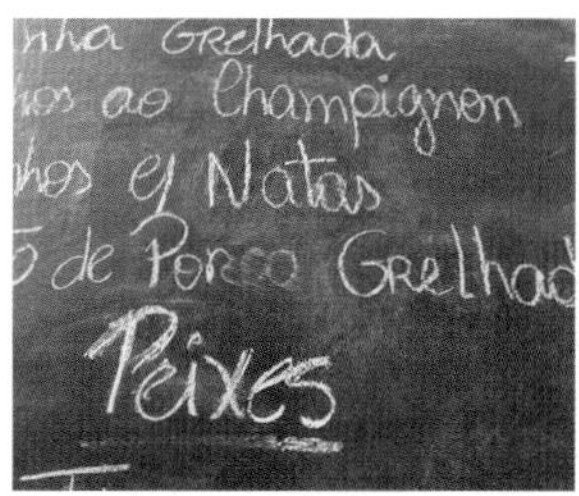

Cross the Arab patio to this gem, serving delicacies from the Alentejo region.

Antiga Pastelaria de Belém €
Rua de Belém 90, www.pasteisdebelem.pt.
Daily 0800-2300.
Around 10,000 salivating locals come to worship each day at the shrine of the most famous bakery in Portugal. The best way to spend 75c in Lisbon.

Café A Brasileira €
Rua Garrett, Chiado, T21 8346 9541.
Mon-Fri 0800-0000, Sat and Sun 0800-0200.
The best place for a *bica and pastel de nata*. The former stomping ground of Lisbon's literati is now a popular gay meeting point.

Café Martinho da Arcada €
Praça do Comércio, 3, T21 886 6213.
Mon-Sat 0800-2300.
The oldest café in Lisbon, dating from 1782, is an essential stop on the trail of Fernando Pessoa. There's an expensive restaurant or you can simply order a *bica and a pastel de nata.*

Nightlife

Bairro Alto is the best place to kickstart an evening. Its cobbled streets hold hundreds of bars, eateries, clubs and shops. Start along the main Rua da Atalaia and explore down-to-earth tascas, sleek gay joints (Sétimo Céu), jazz bars (Catacombas), lounge clubs (Caffe Suave, Clube da Esquina) and funky discos (Bicaense) that come to life after 2200. Miradouro de Santa Catarina has the best views, on the terrace or at the Noo Bai rooftop bar. B.leza has the best African rhythms, with live music every night in Largo Conde Barão. Av 24 de Julho holds the larger, more commercial venues, like Kremlin or Kapital with pop-rock and house. East of 25th April Bridge, the Docas district of renovated warehouses on a marina has bars and clubs serving up latino sounds and tall drinks. Finally, the nightclub of Lisbon, Lux Frágil, (www.luxfragil.com), in the docks opposite Santa Apolonia train, is high- tech and spacious and offers the best in DJs, concerts, performance and video.

Finding authentic fado is tricky. Still, you can stumble across raucous amateur fado vadio, with no formal programme, only an orgy of catharsis.

Ratings

Art and culture ☆☆☆☆☆
Eating ☆☆☆☆☆
Nightlife ☆☆☆☆☆
Romance ☆☆☆
Shopping ☆☆☆☆☆
Sightseeing ☆☆☆☆
Value-for-money ☆☆
Overall city rating ☆☆☆☆☆

London

Somewhat to its own surprise, London is still one of the world's great cities. It's not the loveliest in the world, nor the most antique, romantic, or mysterious. Far from exotic, it's not the richest, largest, or even the most happening place on the planet either. Notwithstanding all of this, it's impossible to resist. Civilized, improvised, sophisticated and alive, London wins everyone over in the end. Most definitely the capital of the UK, and very British, it's also a global city that has grown up thanks to other nations. Perhaps the world's best advert for multiculturalism, London's fusion of flavours is an invigorating one, with little discord and enormous cultural energy. It's not Gotham or even Paris. The Romans, who founded Londinium in the first century AD, failed to pass any of their order on to their successors, who have developed various centres of power, commerce and entertainment over the centuries. London's streets, despite their enormous extent, are small, haphazard and human in scale. But they hold a world of artistic wonder within their mixed-up planning. The city still does tradition, with its Tower, Buckingham Palace and Trooping the Colour, but there's a new London too: the London Eye, Tate Modern, Millennium Bridge, St Pancras International, Wembley and a new-found self-confidence afforded by the successful Olympic bid. With such magnificent trees, river views and murky weather, with its thriving culture and driven soul, this teeming muddle works its way into your heart.

The British Museum.

At a glance

Trafalgar Square is usually considered to be the centre of the city, with **Whitehall** and **Westminster**, the seat of government, immediately to the south. From the square, **The Strand** runs east to **St Paul's Cathedral** and the **City**. Just north of the Strand is **Covent Garden** and, to the northwest of Trafalgar Square, **Leicester Square** and **Shaftesbury Avenue** are the showbiz centre of the West End with **Chinatown** next door. Beyond, **Soho** is the West End's late-night party zone, with Oxford Street forming its northern boundary. **Regent Street** separates **Soho** from **Mayfair** to the west, the swankiest end of town with the gentleman's clubland and royal stamping ground of **St James**'s next door. Between these two areas, **Piccadilly** heads west to Hyde Park Corner with panache. West of here, **Knightsbridge** and **South Kensington** boast luxury shopping and a trio of great museums. **Regent's Park** and **London Zoo** are northeast of Hyde Park, above **Marylebone** with its low-brow tourist attractions around **Baker Street. Bloomsbury**, to the east, is the academic heart of London, home to the British Museum. Further east are **Holborn**, with its Law Courts, and buzzing **Clerkenwell**. South of the river, **Southwark**, **Bankside** and **Borough** are laden with attractions and reached from St Paul's across the Millennium Bridge, or along the river from the **South Bank** and the London Eye. Out in the East End, some of London's most happening nightlife is in **Shoreditch**, **Hoxton**, **Brick Lane** and **Spitalfields**, while **Greenwich**, across the river from **Docklands**, has the National Maritime Museum and Royal Observatory.

24 hours in the city

In order to see as much of London as possible in a day, it's best to avoid public transport. An easy three-mile stroll takes in several of the major sights. From **Trafalgar Square**, walk down Northumberland Avenue to the Embankment and cross over the Golden Jubilee footbridge to the **South Bank**, from where there are great views of Big Ben and Houses of Parliament. Unless you want a closer look at the attractions of **County Hall**, turn left to walk along the river, past the Royal Festival Hall and **Waterloo Bridge**, to **Tate Modern** and Shakespeare's **Globe Theatre** before heading over the Millennium Footbridge to **St Paul's Cathedral**. After a look around St Paul's, the restaurants and clubs of **Clerkenwell** and **Smithfield** or **Shoreditch** are close at hand for an evening's entertainment.

Trafalgar Square

WC2.
Tube Charing Cross, Leicester Sq. Map D4.

Trafalgar Square is the centre of London, traditionally used by Londoners when, unless they want to make their voices heard at demonstrations and celebrations. Linked to Westminster and Parliament by the breadth of Whitehall, this is where the administrative offices of government meet the people. **Nelson's Column**, **Landseer's Lions** and the two large fountains give the square some dignity, inspiring a sense of occasion. The pedestrianization of the north side of the square has transformed access to the **National Gallery**, *T020 7747 2885, www.nationalgallery.org.uk, map D3, daily 1000-1800, Wed 1000-2100, free, guided tours from Sainsbury Wing Level 0 daily at 1130 and 1430, also Wed 1800 and 1830, Sat 1230 and 1530, Fri 1000-2100, free*, one of the world's most comprehensive fine art collections, with more than 2000 Western European paintings dating from the 13th century to 1900. Behind it is the **National Portrait Gallery**, *St Martin's Pl, T020-7306 0055, ext 216, www.npg.org.uk, W, Mon-Wed, Sat-Sun 1000-1800, Thu-Fri 1000-2100, free.*

Below: The National Gallery at Trafalgar Square.

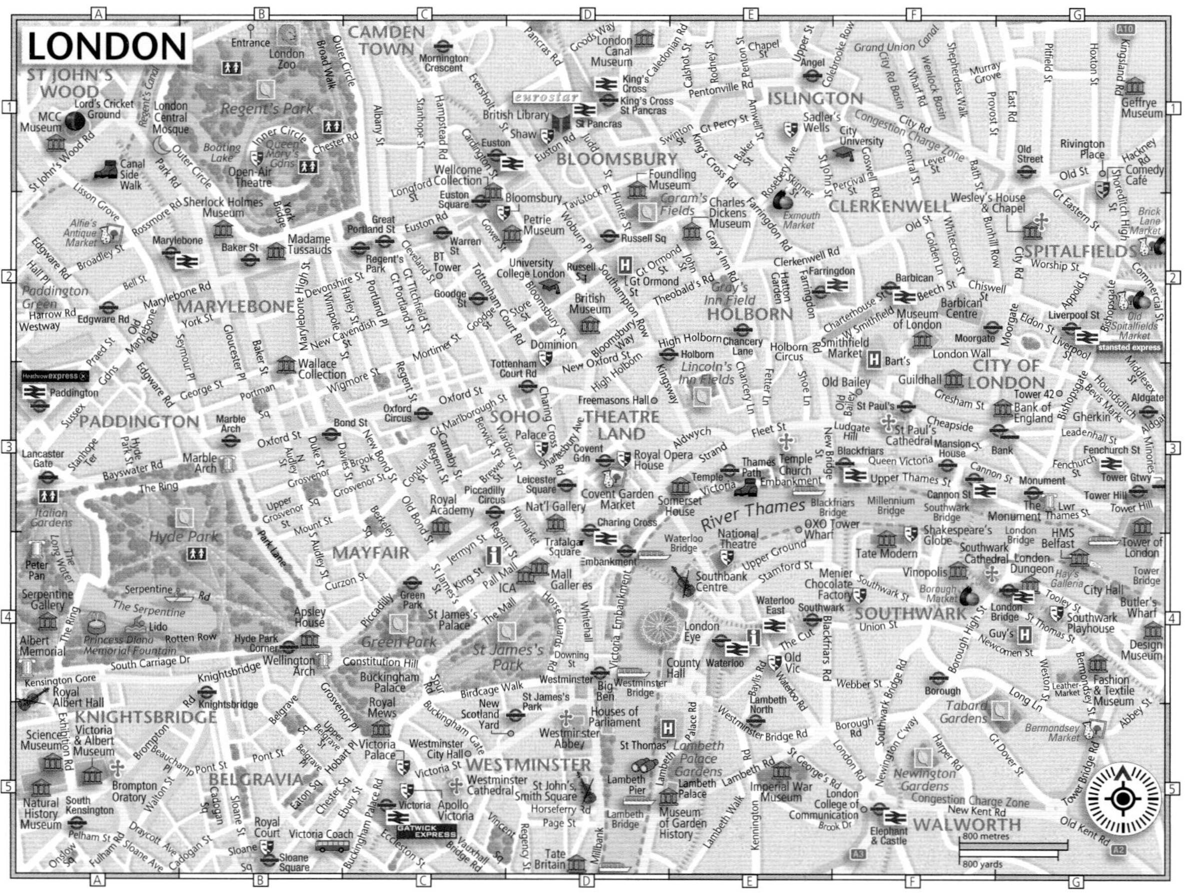
LONDON
ST JOHN'S WOOD
CAMDEN TOWN
ISLINGTON
CLERKENWELL
SPITALFIELDS
BLOOMSBURY
MARYLEBONE
HOLBORN
CITY OF LONDON
PADDINGTON
SOHO
THEATRE LAND
MAYFAIR
SOUTHWARK
KNIGHTSBRIDGE
BELGRAVIA
WESTMINSTER
WALWORTH
River Thames
Regent's Park
Hyde Park
Green Park
St James's Park
The Serpentine
The Long Water
Italian Gardens
Lord's Cricket Ground
MCC Museum
London Central Mosque
London Zoo
Open-Air Theatre
Queen Mary's Gdns
Boating Lake
Sherlock Holmes Museum
Madame Tussauds
Wallace Collection
British Library
British Museum
Foundling Museum
Charles Dickens Museum
Petrie Museum
Wellcome Collection
University College London
London Canal Museum
Geffrye Museum
Wesley's House & Chapel
Museum of London
Barbican Centre
Guildhall
Bank of England
Tower 42
Gherkin
Tower of London
Tower Bridge
HMS Belfast
Design Museum
Fashion & Textile Museum
London Dungeon
Southwark Cathedral
Shakespeare's Globe
Tate Modern
Millennium Bridge
Vinopolis
Borough Market
Imperial War Museum
London Eye
County Hall
Southbank Centre
National Theatre
Houses of Parliament
Big Ben
Westminster Abbey
Westminster Cathedral
Tate Britain
Museum of Garden History
Lambeth Palace
Buckingham Palace
Royal Mews
St James's Palace
Apsley House
Wellington Arch
Marble Arch
Royal Academy
Nat'l Gallery
Trafalgar Square
Covent Garden Market
Royal Opera House
Somerset House
Royal Albert Hall
Albert Memorial
Victoria & Albert Museum
Science Museum
Natural History Museum
Brompton Oratory
Serpentine Gallery
Peter Pan
Princess Diana Memorial Fountain
eurostar
Heathrow express
stansted express
GATWICK EXPRESS
800 metres
800 yards

Westminster Abbey

SW1, information and tours T020 7654 4834, www.westminster-abbey.org.
Mon, Tue, Thu, Fri 0930-1630; Wed 0930-1900, Sat 0930-1430. Sun entry is for services only. £15. Tube Westminster. Map D5.

Of enormous significance to the Anglican faith and British state, Westminster Abbey (oldest parts are from 13th century). Once inside, the length and especially the height (over 30.5 m) of the nave are awe-inspiring. Highlights include the **Coronation Chair**, made to order for Edward I and used to crown every English monarch except three since 1308; **Henry VII's Chapel** (or Lady Chapel), dating from the early 16th century; and **Poet's Corner**, with its monuments to Shakespeare, Chaucer and other poets and actors, as well as scientists, architects and historians.

Buckingham Palace and St James's Park

T020 7766 7300, www.royalcollection.org.uk.
Aug-Sep daily 0945-1830. £17.50. Tube Green Park, St James's Park, Hyde Park Corner. Map C4.

The Queen's official London residence is open to the paying public for two months of the year and, despite the high admission prices and long queues, it attracts thousands of people from all over the world. Next door to the palace visitors' entrance and open year round, the **Queen's Gallery**, *T020 7766 7301, daily 1000-1730 (last admission 1630), £8.50*, displays changing selections from the Queen's collection of Old Masters and portraiture, an extraordinary array founded by Charles II. The **Changing of the Guard** takes place daily on the Palace forecourt at 1130 from 1 April to the end of July and on alternate days for the rest of the year.

St James's Park, stretching out east from the palace, is the finest and most carefully laid out of the Royal parks (others include Hyde Park, Green Park, Regent's Park and Kensington Gardens). A wander around reveals surprising but carefully orchestrated vistas at every turn. Guided tours are given by its warden from April to September.

South Kensington Museums

SW7.
Tube South Kensington. Map A5.

Although they are located tantalisingly close together, the temptation to 'do' all three of these great museums in a day should definitely be resisted. Even two could prove too rich a treat.

The **Science Museum**, *Exhibition Rd, T0870 870 4868, www.science museum.org.uk, daily 1000-1800, free*, prides itself on being one of the most forward-thinking, interactive and accessible museums in the country. The Wellcome Wing is particularly worth visiting, with its four floors dedicated to cutting- edge science, incorporating an IMAX cinema and the first Virtual Voyage simulator in Europe.

The **Natural History Museum**, *Cromwell Rd, T020 7942 5000, www.nhm.ac.uk, daily 1000-1750, free*, housed in an extraordinary orange and blue terracotta building, is an academic research institution that is now seriously fun packed. Divided into Life Galleries and Earth Galleries, it tells the history of our planet through a successful combination of venerable artefacts and child-friendly attractions, including stuffed mamals and an animated, life-sized tyrannosaurus rex.

The **Victoria and Albert Museum**, *Cromwell Rd, T0870 906 3883, www.vam.ac.uk, Sat-Thu 10-1745, Fri 1000-2200, free*, was founded in 1857 with the aim of educating the populace in the appreciation of decorative art and design by exhibiting superb examples of these. Not a narrow nationalistic enterprise, its remarkable collection was gathered, like the British Museum's, from all corners of the globe. In recent years the V&A has shrugged off a slightly fusty reputation with some cutting edge modern exhibits.

British Museum

Great Russell St, WC1, T020 7323 8000, www.thebritishmuseum.ac.uk.
Sat-Wed 1000-1730, Thu-Fri 1000-2030 (late view of main floor and some upper floor galleries only); Great Court Mon-Wed 0900-2100, Thu-Sat 0900-2300, Sun 0900-1800. Free (donations appreciated), prices of temporary exhibitions vary. Tube Tottenham Court Rd. Map D2.

Open to the public for free since 1753, the British Museum is one of the world's greatest cultural institutions. Norman Foster's redevelopment of the **Great Court** in 2000 turned the museum's long-hidden central quadrangle into the largest covered square in Europe. A beautiful lattice-work canopy of 3312 unique panes of glass wraps itself around the dome of the famous **Reading Room**, free-standing once again at the heart of the museum.

Opposite page top: Green Park in the early morning.
Opposite page bottom: Westminster Abbey.

Best of the rest

Royal Academy of Arts
Piccadilly, T020-7300 8000, map C3.
Mon-Thu, Sat and Sun 1000-1800, Fri 1000-2030.
Attention-grabbing exhibitions of contemporary art.

Cabinet War Rooms
King Charles St, T020 7930 6961.
Daily 0930-1800 (last admission 1700). £11.
Nerve centre of Churchill's morale-boosting war effort.

London Zoo
Regent's Park, T020 7722 3333, www.zsl.org, map B1.
Summer daily 1000-1730, winter daily 1000-1630 (last admission 1 hr before closing). £13.50.

Museum of London
150 London Wall, T0870 444 3852, events T020 7814 5777, www.museumoflondon.org.uk, map F2.
Mon-Sat 1000-1750, Sun 1200-1750. Free.
A refreshing visual approach to the social history of the city.

Imperial War Museum
Lambeth Rd, T020-7416 5320, www.iwm.org.uk, map E5.
Daily 1000-1800. Free.
Dedicated to the history and consequences of all 20th-century warfare.

Somerset House
Strand, T020 7845 4600, www.somerset- house.org.uk, map E3. Daily 1000-1800 (last admission 1715).
1 collection £5, any 2 collections £8, all 3 £12.
An ice rink in winter and fine art and antiques all year in the Courtauld and Gilbert Collections or Hermitage Rooms.

Tate Britain
T020 7887 8888, www.tate.org.uk/britain, map F4.
Daily 1000-1750, free, but special exhibitions £10.
Ancient and contemporary British art.

Sex and clubs and rock 'n'roll

Soho has long been associated with sex and vice. Central London's notorious one square mile district was home to some 300 prostitutes in the 1950s and, when they moved elsewhere in the 1960s, the number of strip clubs and drinking clubs increased dramatically, though most have now closed. From the late 1960s Soho became the centre of the porn industry. While pornographic publications were whipped over from the continent in Danish bacon lorries, the Obscene Publications Squad (OPS) was being bribed to turn a blind eye. But in 1972 a new commissioner of the Metropolitan Police was appointed to clean up Soho and the OPS was suspended. In the early 1980s new legislation requiring all sex shops to be licensed came into effect. Soho was also one of the centres of British bohemia. **The Groucho Club**, once the epitome of Thatcherite excess, still serves the inflated egos of medialand and the **French House**, London centre of the French resisitance, continues to ooze Gallic charm in half-pint glasses. Newcomers such as **Milk and Honey** pursue a slightly more democratic version of exclusivity. Soho also has mighty impressive music credentials: **Ronnie Scott**'s was the first outlet in the capital for modern jazz, while **Ain't Nothin' But... The Blues Bar** is one of the best blues venues around. Soho's most recent incarnation as the capital's big, gay heart, with venues centring around Old Compton Street, only confirms its status as London's Left Bank or Greenwich Village.

On entering the Great Court from the south, pick up a floorplan and get your bearings. Head to the **west wing** for Ancient Egypt, the Ancient Near East and Ancient Greece; the **east wing** for the Enlightenment and the King's Library; and the **north wing** for ethnography, Asia and the Americas. The upper floors are devoted to Ancient Rome, Europe, prehistory, Ancient Egypt, the Ancient Near East and the Japanese and Korean collections. It would be quite impossible to see everything in one day, so, apart from the guided and audio tours, it's worth joining one of the free daily 30- to 40-minute eyeOpener Gallery Talks.

St Paul's Cathedral

T020 7236 4128, www.stpauls.co.uk.
Mon-Sat 0830-1630. £12.50 including cathedral crypt and galleries. Organ recitals Sun 1700, free. Tube St Paul's. Map F3.

Standing proud at the top of Ludgate Hill is St Paul's Cathedral. At least the fifth church on the site, construction started in 1675 and took about 35 years to complete. Hemmed in by other buildings, Sir Christopher Wren's colossal church still impresses. The redevelopment of Paternoster Square has opened up new views of St Paul's, reflecting its cleaned Portland stone in plate-glass office blocks, while the **Millennium Bridge** now provides a neat approach from Tate Modern. It's definitely worth climbing up to the **Whispering Gallery**, around the base of the inner dome, and then continuing up the dizzying cast-iron stairway to the open-air **Golden Gallery** to soak up the tremendous wraparound views.

South Bank

SE1.
Tube Westminster, Waterloo. Map E4.

The **British Airways London Eye**, *T0870 500 0600, www.ba-london eye.com, E, Jun-Sep daily 1000-2100, Oct-May daily 1000-2000, £17.95, private capsule £440 (advance booking available online)*, is a vast spoked white observation wheel beside Westminster Bridge that dominates the London skyline. Over 100 m in diameter, it's visible from unexpected places all around the city. There's no denying its novelty value or even, perhaps, its beauty. The half-hour 'flight' in one of its surprisingly roomy capsules, moving at 25 cm per second, provides superb 25-mile views over the city.

Next door to the Eye, the magisterial **County Hall** now houses the highly acclaimed **London Aquarium**, *T020- 7967 8000, www.londonaquarium.co.uk, daily 1000-1800 (last admission 1700), £18*, while downstream is the **South Bank Centre**, the largest arts complex of its kind in Europe. Apart from the main Royal Festival Hall (page 110), it also houses other concert venues, an exhibition space, the Poetry Library, the National Theatre (page 111), the National Film Theatre (page 109) and the cutting-edge **Hayward Gallery**, *T020 7928 3144, www.southbankcentre.co.uk, Sat-Wed 1000-1800, Thu and Fri 1000-2000, price varies.*

Tate Modern

Bankside. SE1.
Ticket bookings T020 7887 8888; information T020 7887 8008, www.tate.org.uk.
Sun-Thu 1000-1800, Fri and Sat 1000-2200 (last admission 45 mins before closing). Free (charges for special exhibitions around £12). Tube Southwark or Blackfriars. Map F4.

Tate Modern is one of the most spectacular and popular of London's attractions. The converted Bankside Power Station houses the Tate's collection of international modern art from 1900 to the present. A great solid box of brick with a single free-standing square chimney front centre, the power station was decommissioned in 1986 and left desolate until Swiss architects Herzog and de Meuron were appointed to adapt the building to its current role. The immense **Turbine Hall** is an astonishing space for specifically commissioned artworks on a grand scale, with the rest of the main collection permanently arranged in galleries along one side. Free guided tours leave from Level 3 at 1100 (Poetry and Dream) and 1200 (Material Gestures), and from Level 5 at 1400 (States of Flux) and 1500 (Energy and Process).

Tower of London

EC3, T0870-756 7070, www.hrp.org.uk.
Mar-Oct Tue-Sat 0900-1800; Mon, Sun 1000-1800; Nov-Feb Tue-Sat 0900- 1700, Mon and Sun 1000-1700. Last entry 1 hr before closing. £15. Tube Tower Hill. Map G3.

The Tower was built 900 years ago not to protect Londoners but to subdue them, a role it played until the mid-19th century. Nowadays, some dismiss it as a tourist trap, but it makes an enormous effort to elucidate its wealth of historical associations and bring the old buildings to life with a mix of bare Norman stonework and 21st-century three- dimensional virtual tours. Highlights include the Norman **White Tower**, the **Royal Armouries** and the **Crown Jewels**. Nearby is the neo-Gothic extravagance of **Tower Bridge**.

Greenwich

SE10.
Cutty Sark DLR or overland train from Charing Cross or London Bridge to Greenwich train station.

With its 18th-century architecture, expansive views and royal associations, Greenwich has attracted visitors for centuries. Flanking the Renaissance Queen's House, the **National Maritime Museum**, *Park Row, T020 8858 4422, www.nmm.ac.uk, daily 1000-1700, free*, is dedicated to Britain's sea-faring history. Uphill from here, in Greenwich Park, is the **Royal Observatory**, *T020 8858 4422, www.nmm.ac.uk, daily 1000-1700, free*, home of Greenwich Mean Time. Explore antique shops and market stalls in the village, and, on the waterfront, the 19th-century tea clipper **Cutty Sark**, *T020 8858 3445, www.cuttysark.org.uk*, closed for restoration and fire damage repair.

Left: The South Bank.

Sleeping

Accommodation doesn't come cheap in London – even at the budget end – but, if it's luxury, pampering and romance you're after, you'll be spoilt for choice. We've left out the really obvious big-hitters, like Claridge's, The Dorchester and The Savoy, in favour of more intimate, cosy or romantic options. All are centrally located.

Dukes €€€
St James's Pl, SW1, T020 7491 4840, www.dukeshotel.com.
With 90 comfortable, old-fashioned rooms and a health club, this is a very discreet luxury hotel with a cosy bar that mixes devastating Martinis.

Hazlitt's €€€
6 Frith St, W1, T020 7434 1771, www.hazlittshotel.com.
Many people's London favourite with 23 individual period rooms of great character, in memory of the London essayist. No restaurant or bar but plenty nearby in the liveliest streets of Soho.

Malmaison €€€
18-21 Charterhouse Sq, EC1, T020 7012 3700, www.malmaison.com.
With 97 differently shaped rooms, this hotel is comfortable, easygoing but quite flash.

The Rookery €€€
Peter's Lane, Cowcross St, T020 7336 0931, www.rookeryhotel.com.
A renovated old-fashioned townhouse hotel with 33 rooms in an antique building and a crow's nest of a penthouse.

St Martin's Lane €€€
45 St Martin's Lane, WC2, T020 7300 5500, www.morganshotelgroup.com.
Formerly Ian Schrager's media favourite, designed by minimalist Philippe Starck. The restaurant does classic French and modern European on the side and, for drinking, there's the awesome Light Bar and the Seabar.

B&B Belgravia €€
64-66 Ebury Street, SW1, T020 7259 8570, www.bb-belgravia.com.
Slick and minimalistic in a way that you wouldn't usually associate with a B&B; cut-price contemporary chic.

The Claverley €€
13-14 Beaufort Gdns, SW3, T020 7589 8541, www.claverleyhotel.co.uk.
Classy and comfortable small hotel. All rooms are different, with marble bathrooms, decorated in a romantic English way. Breakfast is included.

Number Sixteen €€
16 Sumner Pl, SW7, T020 7589 5232, www.numbersixteenhotel.co.uk.
Forty-two rooms in four small townhouses. Elegant privacy and the most salubrious (and expensive) of the set in this dainty little stucco street. Part of the successful Firmdale group.

Tophams Belgravia €€
28 Ebury St, SW1, T020 7730 8147, www.tophamshotel.com.
A charming, small country house-style hotel, family-run with very friendly service.

Eating

London's restaurant scene continues to mature at a heady rate. The range of excellent food on offer in almost every setting and price bracket can be baffling. A good meal has become an integral part of a top night out. But the city is a notoriously pricey place in which to eat compared to much of Europe. This is partly compensated by the sheer variety of cuisines available – from Africa to Yemen via Poland and New Zealand.

Andrew Edmonds €€€
46 Lexington St, W1, T020 7437 5708.
Excellent modern European cooking at reasonable prices is served up in a cosy, candlelit atmosphere. Booking ahead strongly recommended.

Hakkasan €€€
8 Hanway Pl, W1, T020 7927 7000.
Probably the funkiest Chinese in the capital, with its blue-lit banquettes, stylish decor and a Michelin star to boot.

Moro €€€
34-36 Exmouth Market, EC1, T020 7833 8336.
A modern Spanish restaurant that wows the area's hipsters with its artful dishes and super-fresh ingredients.

Nobu €€€
Metropolitan Hotel, 19 Old Park Lane, W1, T020 7447 4747.
Robert de Niro et al's venture at the super-fashionable Metropolitan Hotel. Sample some ultra-light Japanese- cum-South American food. Make dinner bookings up to a month ahead.

The Eagle €€
159 Farringdon Rd, T020 7837 1353.
One of the first pubs to go gastro, cooking up excellent modern European food.

Maze €€
10 -13 Grosvenor Square, W1, T020 7107 0000, www.gordonramsay.com.
One of the most stylish of Gordon's Ramsay's restaurants, Maze serves Asian-influenced French cuisine in Spanish tapas-sized portions.

St John €€
26 St John St, T020 7251 0848.
Especially good offal and freshly baked bread are served up in a stark former smokery celebrating 'nose to tail' eating. St John Bread and Wine, 94-96 Commercial St, T020 7251 0848, is the cheaper, no-frills version.

India Club €
143 Strand, WC2, T020 7836 0650. Closed Sun.
Pay up to £10 for old-style curries at formica tables on linoleum floors with yellow walls. A very Indian institution, since 1950. Bring your own booze.

Lahore Kebab House €
2 Umberston St, E1, T020 7488 2551. Daily till 2330.
A 30-year-old family-owned informal restaurant set in the Pakistani and Bangladeshi quarters of East London. Delicious and authentic Pakistani dishes attract a multicultural crowd. Bring your own alcohol.

Nightlife

Buy *Time Out* (www.timeout.com), the weekly magazine, for the latest entertainment listings.

Bars and clubs

Some traditional pubs boast genuine Victorian interiors (The Salisbury, *90 St Martin's Lane, W1*) while others thrive as straightforward local boozers (Coach and Horses, *29 Greek St, W1*; Dog and Duck, *18 Bateman St, W1*). Music bars are still jumping into the wee small hours, particularly in Shoreditch (Big Chill Bar, *Dray Walk, off Brick Lane, E1*; Shoreditch Electricity Showrooms, *39a Hoxton St, N1*), as are the gay bars in Soho (Freedom, *60-66 Wardour St, W1*) while others are branching out (The Book Club, *100 Leonard St, EC2*). There are also hundreds of candlelit wine bars, swish brasseries, elegant hotel bars, sweaty dives and designer cocktail lounges. Many of the best clubs are around Old Street and Shoreditch.

Cinema

BFI London IMAX
Waterloo, SE1, T0870 787 2525, www.bfi.org.uk.

Curzon Soho
99 Shaftesbury Avenue, W1, T020-7292 1686, www.curzoncinemas.com.
Middle to highbrow mainstream movies on three screens.

Aubin Cinema
64-66 Redchurch Street, E2, T0845 604 8486, www.aubincinema.com.
Sofas and wine-coolers make this London's most chic movie house.

ICA Cinema
Nash House, The Mall, SW1, T020 7930 3647, www.ica.org.uk.
The place for very rare or independent films, especially world cinema.

National Film Theatre (NFT)
South Bank, SE1, T020 7928 3535, www.bfi.org.uk.
Home to the British Film Institute.

Travel essentials

Getting there

London Heathrow Airport, T0844 335 1801, is 15 miles west of central London. Piccadilly Line tube trains run every 5-9 mins (roughly 0630-0100), journey time 50 mins. Heathrow Express, T0845 600 1515, www.heathrowexpress.co.uk, runs to Paddington Station, every 15 mins (0510-2340), journey time 15 mins, £18 single, £32 return. A black cab costs £45-75 (45 mins-1 hr).

London Gatwick Airport, T0870 000 2468, 28 miles south of the capital. Gatwick Express, T0845 850 1530, to and from London Victoria every 15 mins (hourly at night), £16.90 single, £28.70 return. Taxi around £75-100, about 1 hr.

London Luton Airport, T01582-405100, 30 miles north of central London. Regular trains to and from London Bridge, Blackfriars, Farringdon and King's Cross stations. A taxi takes 50 mins and costs around £75-100.

Stansted Airport, T0870 000 0303, 35 miles northeast. Stansted Express, T0845 850 0150, every 15 mins to Liverpool Street, 45 mins, £20 single, £29 open return. A taxi takes 1-1½ hrs and costs about £75-100.

There are 4 main train stations: King's Cross from Scotland and northeast England; Euston from the northwest; Paddington from Wales and the west; and Waterloo International for the south. **Eurostar**, www.eurostar.com, operates from the new St Pancras International, adjacent to King's Cross. For train times and ticket prices call **National Rail Enquiries**, T08457-484950, or www.nationalrail.co.uk.

Getting around

London's public transport network consists of mainly buses and the underground (known as the Tube). It is fairly efficient, but expensive. Single Tube fares in Zone 1 (most of central London) cost £4, and single bus fares £2. Daily travelcards, for buses and the Tube, cost £7.20 (peak) and £5.60 (off-peak). Or buy an Oyster card, for the cheaper single fares on public transport. For 24-hr information on public transport and tickets call T020-7222 1234, or visit www.tfl.gov.uk. The Tube is faster, but buses are good for sightseeing as you travel around town. Car drivers must pay a congestion charge (£8) in central London Mon-Fri 0700-1800; see the website above.

Tourist information

Britain and London Visitor Centre (BLVC), 1 Lower Regent St, SW1 (Piccadilly Circus tube), Mon 0930-0630, Tue-Fri 0900-0630, Sat-Sun 1000-1600; Jun-Sep Sat 0900-1700, Sun 1000-1600. **London Information Centre**, in Leicester Sq, T020 7292 2333, www.londontown.com, daily 0800-2300. **City Information Centre**, St Paul's Churchyard, south side of the cathedral, T020 7332 1456, Apr-Sep daily 1000-1800; Oct-Mar Mon-Fri 0930-1700, Sat 0930-1230.

Classical music and dance

Barbican Centre
T020 7638 8891, www.barbican.org.uk.
Home of the London Symphony Orchestra.

Royal Albert Hall
Kensington Gore, T020 7589 8212, www.royalalberthall.com.
This is a grand setting for a wide-ranging variety of entertainment spectacular.

Royal Opera House
Bow St, T020 7304 4000, www.royaloperahouse.org.
Bastion of high culture, seats from under £5 to £125. Also home to the Royal Ballet.

Sadler's Wells and Lilian Baylis Theatre
Rosebery Av, T020 7863 8198, www.sadlerswells.com.
Superb state-of-the-art base for dance and opera.

South Bank Centre
T0870 380 4300, www.southbankcentre.co.uk.
The Royal Festival Hall stages large-scale orchestral and choral concerts, while the Queen Elizabeth Hall and Purcell Room host chamber music groups.

Wigmore Hall
36 Wigmore St, T020 7935 2141, www.wigmore-hall.org.uk.
Chamber music and song.

Jazz, rock and pop

Koko
1a Camden Road, NW1, T0870 432 5527, www.koko.co.uk.
Ex-theatre, now a multi-floor club and top-notch music venue for big-name and on-the-way-up acts.

O2 Academy Brixton
211 Stockwell Rd, T020 7771 2000, www.o2academybrixton.co.uk.
Rock and pop acts.

The Jazz Café
3 Parkway, Camden, NW1, T020 7916 6060, www.jazzcafe.co.uk.
An eclectic mix of world, funk and folk, as well as jazz.

Ronnie Scott's
47 Frith St, W1, T020 7439 0747, www.ronniescotts.co.uk.
Classic jazz venue enjoying a revival after refurbishment in 2006.

Theatre

The heart of theatreland is still the West End, with its diet of hit musicals and popular drama. Discount tickets are sold from a booth in Leicester Sq. Off-West End theatres are often a better bet for thought-provoking productions or new drama. Those with a particular good reputation include the National Theatre, *South Bank, SE1, T020 7452 3000, www.nationaltheatre.org.uk*, which has three stages for all styles and sizes of production; the Almeida, *Almeida St, Islington, N1, T020 7359 4404, www.almeida.co.uk*; the Donmar Warehouse, *41 Earlham St, WC2, T020-7240 4882, www.donmar warehouse.com*; the Royal Court Theatre, *Sloane Sq, SW1, T020 7565 5000, www.royalcourttheatre.com*; the Old Vic, *The Cut, SE1, T0844 871 7628, www.oldvictheatre.com*; and the Young Vic, *The Cut, SE1, T020 7922 2922 , www.youngvic.org.* The Globe Theatre, *21 New Globe Walk, SE1, T020 7401 9919, www.shakespeares-globe.org*, is also worth visiting for its authentic Elizabethan architecture and innovative open-air productions.

Shopping

The difficulty is knowing where to begin. Oxford St and Regent St have Selfridges, Hamleys, Liberty and other large department stores and big brand shops. Tottenham Court Rd is good for computers and electronics. Head to Charing Cross Rd and Bloomsbury for new and second-hand books and Soho and Carnaby St for urban streetwear. Covent Garden is good for clothes, specialist foods, toys, toiletries and gifts. Visit Bond St and Mayfair for couture fashion and expensive jewellery. For bespoke boots, suits, smoking requisites, wine and other clubby male accessories, go to St James's and Savile Row. For crafts and independent designers, visit Clerkenwell. Knightsbridge has high street fashion and Harrods. Chelsea and Notting Hill are good for one-off, independent fashion labels, second-hand clothes, music, books and gifts. See also Markets, below.

Markets

London's markets often show the city at its best: lively enclaves of character and creativity. Here are the main ones: **Berwick Street,** W1, Mon-Sat 0900-1700), fabrics and food; **Borough**, SE1, Fri 1200-1800, Sat 0900-1600, organic food; **Brick Lane**, E1, Sun 0700-1400, just about everything; **Camden**, NW1, daily 0900-1800, furniture, gifts, clothes, accessories and general mayhem; **Columbia Road**, E1, Sun 0800-1400, flowers; **Leather Lane**, EC2, Mon-Fri 1030-1400, cheap clothes, accessories, fruit and veg; **Portobello Road**, W11, Sat 0800-1800, antiques, second-hand clothes and bric-a-brac; **Spitalfields**, E1, Mon-Fri 1000-1600, Sun 0900-1700, clothes, books, organic food, jewellery and bric-a-brac.

Ratings

Art and culture ☆☆☆☆☆
Eating ☆☆☆☆
Nightlife ☆☆☆☆☆
Outdoors ☆
Romance ☆☆
Shopping ☆☆☆
Sightseeing ☆☆☆☆
Value-for-money ☆☆☆
Overall city rating ☆☆☆☆

Madrid

Madrid is not a city of half-measures: Europe's highest, youngest, sunniest capital likes to boast Desde Madrid al Cielo ('from Madrid to Heaven'), with a matter-of-fact assumption that when you've seen Madrid, the only place left is Heaven. The city is as famous for what it lacks as for what it boasts – there's no great river, no architectural marvels, no immediate picture- postcard charm. But what it does have, it has in spades: a fabulous collection of western art held in the Prado, the Thyssen and the Reina Sofía; a crooked old centre where almost every alley is stuffed with excellent tapas bars and restaurants; a famously intense blue sky; and an even more intense nightlife that makes most other cities look positively staid.

Statue and flag.

Museo del Prado

Paseo del Prado, T91 330 2800, www.museoprado.mcu.es.
Tue-Sun 0900-2000 (last entry 1930). €8, free Tue–Sat 1800-2000, Sun 1700–2000; Abono Paseo del Arte (for the Prado, Reina Sofía and Thyssen-Bornemisza) €17.60. Metro Banco de España. Map D3.

The Prado houses one of the world's greatest art collections, a dazzling display of European art spanning seven centuries. When it opened in 1819, it was one of the very first public art museums, infused with the spirit of the Enlightenment and shored up by royal whim (Queen Isabel of Braganza had been impressed with the Louvre and wanted one for Spain). The collection encompasses several thousand works of art, and the sheer scale can make it a daunting prospect. Pick out some highlights or favourite painters rather than trying to see it all in one go. The museum's strength is its magnificent collection of Spanish masterpieces dating from the 12th to the 19th centuries, including works by Zurbarán, Velázquez and Goya. A contemporary extension by Rafael Moneo has added more galleries, including a striking space which incorporates a 16th-century cloister.

Museo Thyssen-Bornemisza

Paseo del Prado 8, T91 420 3944, www.museothyssen.org.
Tue-Sun 1000-1900. €8, temporary exhibitions €5-8; Abono Paseo del Arte €17.60. Metro Banco de España. Map C3.

Across Plaza de Cánovas del Castillo from the Prado is the **Thyssen-Bornemisza**, which perfectly complements its 'big brother'. It plugs the gaps left by the Prado, with a vast collection of western European art spanning eight centuries, as well as offering a dazzling selection of early 20th-century masters, from Braque to Kandinsky, to whet your appetite for the Reina Sofía. There's a charming garden café and a fabulous rooftop restaurant, El Mirador.

At a glance

The leafy, elegant **Paseo del Prado** sits on the eastern side of the city, where the three big museums – the Prado, the Centro de Arte de Reina Sofía and the Thyssen-Bornemisza – are conveniently clustered. West of here is **Puerta del Sol**, Madrid's crossroads, and the cheerful, bohemian barrio of **Santa Ana**, which slopes downhill back towards the Prado. **Plaza Mayor**, west down Calle Mayor is the grand heart of old Madrid. The area around it, sprinkled with old palaces and monasteries, is known as **Madrid de los Austrias** (Hapsburg Madrid). To the west is the enormous Bourbon **Palacio Real** and the city's beautifully restored Opera House. South of Plaza Mayor are the multicultural, edgy, traditionally working class districts of **La Latina** and **Lavapiés**, with a great flea market on Saturdays. North of the **Gran Vía**, **Chueca** and **Malasaña** are sweetly old-fashioned by day and unstoppably wild by night. Swanky **Salamanca**, east of here, is an elegant 19th-century grid scattered with upmarket restaurants and designer boutiques.

24 hours in the city
Have breakfast on the **Plaza de Oriente**, with views of the Palacio Real. Spend a few hours seeing the highlights at one of the big three museums – the Goyas at the **Prado**, Picasso's *Guernica* at the **Reina** Sofía or the Italian Primitives at the **Thyssen**. Trawl around the old-fashioned tapas bars in the **Plaza Santa Ana** for lunch, followed by a siesta under the trees in the **Parque del Retiro**. Take a look at some of the new galleries springing up in trendy **Chueca** or go shopping at its quirky fashion boutiques. Soak up the atmosphere at a traditional restaurant like Casa Paco followed by flamenco at Casa Patas. Alternatively, check out the Madrid club scene: celebrity spot at Gold, or hop onto a podium at Kapital. Finish up with some traditional *churros con chocolate* at the *Chocolatería San Ginés*.

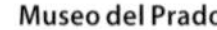
Museo del Prado.

Museo Nacional Centro de Arte Reina Sofía

C Santa Isabel 52, T91 467 5062, www.museoreinasofia.es.
Mon, Wed-Sat 1000-2100, Sun 1000-1430. €6 for permanent collection and temporary exhibitions, €3 for temporary exhibitions only, free Sat 1430-2100 and Sun 1000-1430; Abono Paseo del Arte €17.60. Metro Atocha. Map C/D4.

Housed in a former hospital close to Atocha station, Reina Sofia has been beautifully remodelled to hold the nation's collection of 20th-century art. A stunning new extension by Jean Nouvel, with glossy red curves, has added a library and a superb café-restaurant. It's a graceful, light-filled building set around a quiet, interior courtyard, with a pair of panoramic glass lifts which are almost an attraction in themselves. The second and fourth floors are devoted to the permanent exhibition and the first and third floors are used for temporary exhibitions which are usually excellent. The undoubted highlight is Picasso's celebrated *Guernica* (second floor), whose sheer scale and emotional power cannot fail to impress.

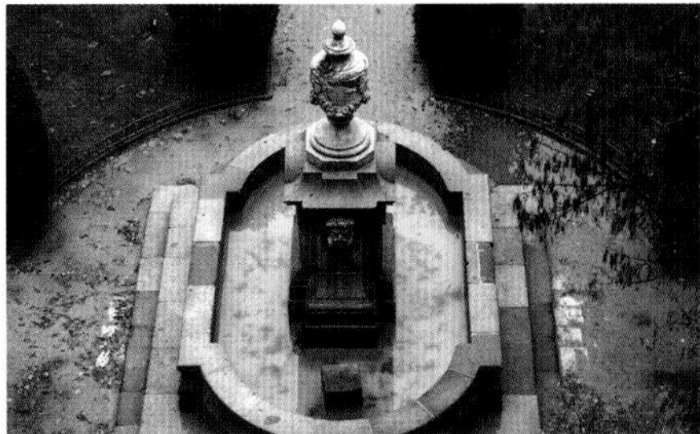

Museo Nacional Centro de Arte Reina Sofía gardens.

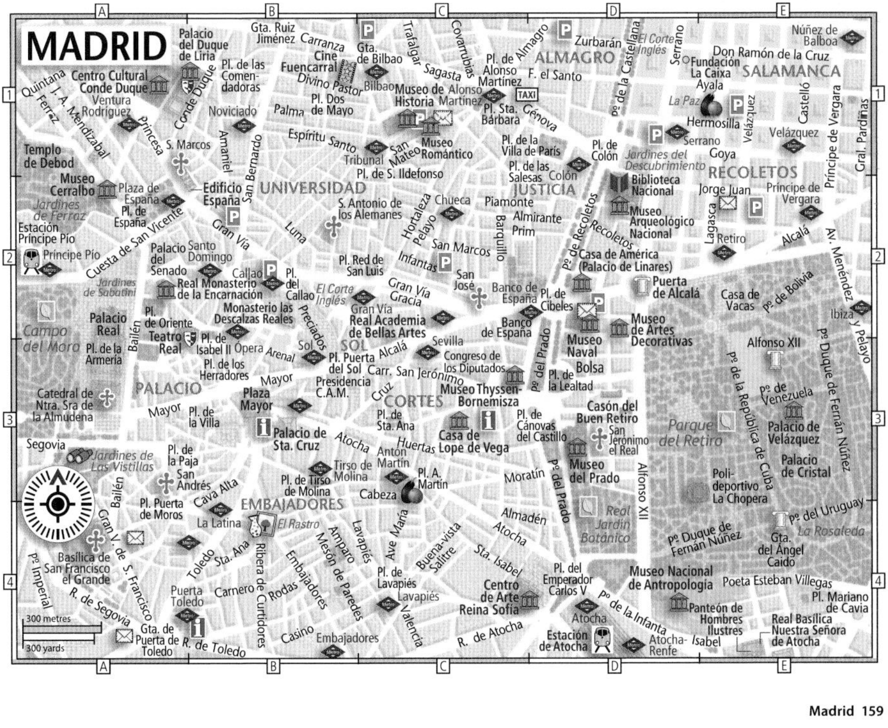
MADRID
A
B
C
D
E
1
2
3
4
Palacio del Duque de Liria
Gta. Ruiz Jiménez
Carranza
Gta. de Bilbao
Trafalgar
Covarrubias
Almagro
Zurbarán
El Corte Inglés
Serrano
Núñez de Balboa
Quintana
Centro Cultural Conde Duque
Pl. de las Comendadoras
Cine Fuencarral
Sagasta
Pl. de Alonso Martínez
ALMAGRO
F. el Santo
Fundación La Caixa
Don Ramón de la Cruz
SALAMANCA
J. A. Ferraz
Mendizábal
Ventura Rodríguez
Conde Duque
Noviciado
Divino Pastor
Bilbao
Museo de Historia
Alonso Martínez
TAXI
Pº de la Castellana
Ayala
La Paz
Palma
Pl. Dos de Mayo
Pl. Sta. Bárbara
Génova
Hermosilla
Velázquez
Castelló
Príncipe de Vergara
Gral. Pardiñas
Princesa
Espíritu Santo
San Mateo
Museo Romántico
Tribunal
Pl. de la Villa de París
Pl. de Colón
Serrano
Jardines del Descubrimiento
Goya
Templo de Debod
S. Marcos
Amaniel
San Bernardo
Pl. de S. Ildefonso
Pl. de las Salesas
Colón
RECOLETOS
Museo Cerralbo
Plaza de España
Edificio España
UNIVERSIDAD
JUSTICIA
Biblioteca Nacional
Jorge Juan
Príncipe de Vergara
Jardines de Ferraz
Pl. de España
S. Antonio de los Alemanes
Chueca
Piamonte
Museo Arqueológico Nacional
Lagasca
Estación Príncipe Pío
Cuesta de San Vicente
Gran Vía
Luna
Hortaleza
Pelayo
Almirante
Prim
Barquillo
Recoletos
Retiro
Alcalá
Príncipe Pío
Palacio del Senado
Santo Domingo
San Marcos
Pº de Recoletos
Casa de América (Palacio de Linares)
Av. Menéndez y Pelayo
Callao
Pl. del Callao
Pl. Red de San Luis
Infantas
San José
Puerta de Alcalá
Pº de Bolivia
Jardines de Sabatini
Real Monasterio de la Encarnación
El Corte Inglés
Gran Vía
Gracia
Banco de España
Pl. de Cibeles
Casa de Vacas
Campo del Moro
Palacio Real
Bailén
Pl. de Oriente
Monasterio las Descalzas Reales
Preciados
Gran Vía
Real Academia de Bellas Artes
Banco de España
Museo Naval
Museo de Artes Decorativas
Ibiza
Teatro Real
Pl. de Isabel II
Ópera
Pl. de la Armería
Arenal
Sol
SOL
Pl. Puerta del Sol
Alcalá
Sevilla
Congreso de los Diputados
Pº del Prado
Bolsa
Alfonso XII
Pº Duque de Fernán Núñez
Pl. de los Herradores
Carr. San Jerónimo
Pl. de la Lealtad
Pº de la República de Cuba
Catedral de Ntra. Sra de la Almudena
PALACIO
Mayor
Plaza Mayor
Presidencia C.A.M.
Cruz
Museo Thyssen-Bornemisza
Pº de Venezuela
CORTES
Casón del Buen Retiro
Mayor
Pl. de la Villa
Pl. de Sta. Ana
Pl. de Cánovas del Castillo
Parque del Retiro
Palacio de Velázquez
Palacio de Sta. Cruz
Atocha
Casa de Lope de Vega
San Jerónimo el Real
Segovia
Jardines de Las Vistillas
Pl. de la Paja
Huertas
Antón Martín
Tirso de Molina
Museo del Prado
Palacio de Cristal
San Andrés
Pl. de Tirso de Molina
Pl. A. Martín
Moratín
Pº del Prado
Polideportivo La Chopera
Bailén
Cava Alta
EMBAJADORES
Cabeza
Real Jardín Botánico
Pl. Puerta de Moros
La Latina
El Rastro
Almadén
Pº del Uruguay
Gran V. de S. Francisco
Lavapiés
Ave María
Atocha
Pº Duque de Fernán Núñez
Gta. del Ángel Caído
La Rosaleda
Pº Imperial
Basílica de San Francisco el Grande
Toledo
Sta. Ana
Ribera de Curtidores
Mesón de Paredes
Amparo
Embajadores
Buena-vista
Salitre
Sta. Isabel
Pl. del Emperador Carlos V
Museo Nacional de Antropología
Poeta Esteban Villegas
Pl. de Lavapiés
Centro de Arte Reina Sofía
Pl. Mariano de Cavia
R. de Segovia
Puerta Toledo
Carnero
Rodas
Lavapiés
Pº de la Infanta Isabel
Panteón de Hombres Ilustres
Real Basílica Nuestra Señora de Atocha
300 metres
300 yards
Gta. de Puerta de Toledo
R. de Toledo
Casino
Embajadores
Valencia
R. de Atocha
Estación de Atocha
Atocha
Atocha-Renfe
Isabel

Parque del Retiro

Metro Banco de España/Retiro.

This dreamy expanse of manicured gardens, lakes, shady woods and pavilions was once the garden of the Palacio Real del Buen Retiro and is the perfect escape from the city bustle. At the centre is a vast lake (*estanque*), with a sprinkling of cafés and boats for hire. At the southern end of the park, take a peek at the bizarre *Ángel Caído* (Fallen Angel), one of only three monuments in the world to Satan, caught midway in his fall from Paradise. Ricardo Velázquez designed the elegant **Palacio de Velázquez** and **Palacio de Cristal** in 1882. The pavilions are now used for the Reina Sofía's temporary art exhibitions.

Plaza Santa Ana

Metro Antón Martín. Map C3.

This square, flanked by restaurants, bars, theatres and hotels, has been the heart of the *Barrio de los Literatos* for centuries. It's been overhauled a dozen times and the latest restoration confirms Madrid's predilection for public squares.

Although not especially pretty, the square's charm lies in its vibrancy and constant animation; the pavements are lined with dozens of tapas bars complete with turn-of-the-20th-century fittings; it's one of the most popular places in Madrid for a tapas crawl (*tapeo*). On summer nights the pavements are dense with tourists, locals walking their dogs and elderly *Madrileños* sitting on benches. There are few reminders that this neighbourhood was once home to Cervantes, Lope de Vega, Quevado and other great writers of the Golden Age, but you can visit Lope de Vega's delightful home, the **Casa-Museo Lope de Vega**, *C Cervantes 11, T91 429 9216, guided tours (in Spanish) only, Tue-Fri 0930-1400, Sat 1000-1400; €2, free Sat.*

Plaza Mayor

Metro Sol. Map B3.

The Plaza Mayor is vast, a huge cobbled expanse surrounded by elegant arcades and tall mansions topped with steep slate roofs. When it's bright and sunny, it's packed with terrace cafés, souvenir shops and sun-worshipping tourists; the only time you might see a *Madrileño* in the Plaza Mayor is on a Sunday morning when a stamp and coin market is held here.

Building of the square started in 1617 to designs by Felipe II's favourite architect, Juan de Herrera. This was the ceremonial centre of Madrid, a magnificent backdrop for public spectacles, coronations, executions, markets, bullfights and fiestas. (It is riddled with the subterranean torture chambers of the Inquisition, which used the square for *autos-da-fé*, the trial of suspected heretics.) Before the square was built, a market was traditionally held in front of the **Casa de la Panadería**, the old bakery, which is now the most eye-catching building on the square. It was repainted in 1992 by Carlos Franco who covered it with a hippy-trippy fresco of floating nymphs. Arched passages lead off from here to some of 17th-century Madrid's most important thoroughfares – **Calle Toledo**, **Calle Mayor**, and **Calle Segovia**. Other street names still echo the trades that were once carried out here, such as **Calle Cuchilleros** (Street of the Knife Sharpeners), which incorporates part of the old city walls. This is where you'll find the traditional *mesones* (inns), which grew up to cater to merchants and travellers arriving at the city gates. Casa Botín, at Cuchilleros 17, opened in the 16th century and claims to be the oldest restaurant in the world.

Palacio Real

C Bailén s/n, T91 454 8803, www.patrimonionacional.es.
Oct-Mar Mon-Sat 0930-1700, Sun 0900-1400; Apr-Sep Mon-Sat 0900-1800, Sun 0900-1500. €8 (€10 with guided tour in English) for official salons with Pharmacy and Royal Armoury, €11 with Picture Gallery; €2 Picture Gallery only; €3.40 Royal Armoury only free to EU citizens on Wed. Metro Opera. Map A2.

In 1734, after a fire destroyed the original Moorish alcázar, Felipe V saw a chance to build something grander and commissioned the most prestigious architects of the day to create this monumental pile. Early plans for a palace four times the size of

Above: Palacio Real.
Opposite page top: Plaza Mayor.
Opposite page bottom: The Fallen Angel in the Parque del Retiro.

All about Almodóvar

Pedro Almodóvar arrived in Madrid in the late 1960s; he was just 16 but he already knew that he wanted to be a film-maker. Franco had closed Spain's only film school, so Almodóvar started making shorts on super-8. In 1978, three years after Franco's death and the year Spain signed a new democratic constitution, he made his first full-length film and began work on *Pepi, Luci, Bom*, whose subsequent success allowed Almodóvar to found his own production company. The Movida Madrileña was just getting into its stride: the city's youth, making up for decades of repression, turned music, fashion, design and art upside down, and no one knew the city's anarchic subculture better than Almodóvar. Madrid has been a recurrent feature of his work ever since, appearing in his movies as regularly as the 'las chicas de Almodóvar', the select band of actresses he favours. In 2000, Almodóvar hit the big time, winning an Oscar for *Todo Sobre Mi Madre* (All About My Mother). The subversive director became the toast of the Hollywood establishment, cementing his success with a string of successful films including *Hable con ella* (Talk to her, 2002), *La Mala Educación* (Bad Education, 2004), *Volver* (2006), *Los Abrazos Rotos* (Broken Embraces, 2009), and *La Piel que Habito* (The Skin I Live In, 2011).

the current one were rejected but the finished structure is still built on a staggering scale; it's no surprise that Juan Carlos I and family have chosen to live in the more modest Palacio de Zarzuela on the city's outskirts. The visit includes the offical salons, the historic pharmacy, the Royal Armoury and the Picture Gallery. The Royal Palace is used for official functions and can be closed at short notice; if two flags are flying, the King is at home and you won't be allowed in.

El Rastro

C Ribera de Curtidores.
Metro Tirso de Molina or Puerta de Toledo. Map B4.

South of Plaza Mayor, the districts of La Latina and Lavapiés have traditionally been home to Madrid's poorest workers and immigrants. It's here that Madrid's famous flea market, El Rastro, takes place every Sunday morning. Stalls wind all the way up **Calle Ribera de Curtidores** and sell everything from tacky clothes and souvenirs to leather goods, underwear, arts and crafts and kites. The street name means Tanner's Alley and recalls the pungent trades which took place down here, out of sight (and smell) of the smart neighbourhoods at the top of the hill. Rastro itself refers to the sticky trail of blood left when the meat carcasses were hauled through the streets. The surrounding shops are mainly devoted to antiques and bric-a-brac, although you'll still find plenty of leather goods, and, although the neighbourhood is still a little shabby, it's in the process of regeneration. The atmosphere on a Sunday is wonderful; after the stallholders have packed up, everyone heads to the surrounding bars for tapas and a well-earned cold beer. Watch out for your bags, though; El Rastro is notorious for pickpockets.

El Rastro.

Best of the rest

Museo del Traje
Avda de Juan de Herrera 2, T91 550 4700, www.museodeltraje.mcu.es. Metro Moncloa or Ciudad Universitaria. Tue-Sat 0930–1900, Sun 1000–1500, until 2130 Thu in July and Aug. €3, free Sat 1430–1900, Sun.
A slick modern museum dedicated to the history of fashion, set in beautiful gardens and with a stylish café-restaurant.

Monasterio de las Descalzas Reales
Reales 1 Pl de las Descalzas, T91 454 8800, www.patrimonionacional.es. Guided tour only Tue-Thu, Sat 1030-12.30, 1600-1730, Fri 1030-1230, Sun and hols 1100-1330. €5. Metro Sol.
A 16th-century convent for blue-blooded nuns, with a remarkable collection of tapestries and other artworks.

Parque del Oeste
C Ferraz s/n. Metro Ventura Rodríguez.
This cool, shady park spreads along the western flank of the city, north of the Plaza de España. It's most surprising sight is the Templo de Debod, a 2000-year-old gift from Egypt.

Museo Arqueológico
C Serrano 13, Salamanca, T91 577 7912, www.man.mcu.es, Tue-Sat 0930- 2030, Sun 0930-1500, free. Metro Serrano.
Spain's most complete archaeological museum, with a collection spanning millennia.

Plaza de Toros Monumental de las Ventas
C Alcalá 237, T91 725 1857, www.las-ventas.com. Museum Mar-Oct Tue-Fri 0930-1430, Sun and fight days 1000-1300; Nov-Feb Mon-Fri 0930-1430. Free. Metro Ventas.
The 1930s 'Cathedral of Bullfighting' has a 25,000-strong capacity.

Sleeping

Madrid has few hotels that are truly charming, although it has plenty of swanky upmarket places to attract the fashion crowd at one end of the spectrum, and a good selection of old-fashioned, spotless – if often soulless – pensiones at the other. Book as far in advance as possible and bring industrial strength earplugs – Madrid is noisy.

Hotel Urban €€€
Cra de San Jerónimo 34, T91 787 7770, www.derbyhotels.com.
Metro Sevilla.
Currently the city's hottest hotel, in a striking glassy contemporary building, with ultra-luxurious rooms, a pool, gym, sauna and excellent restaurant.

Orfila €€€
C Orfila 6, Salamanca, T91 702 7770, www.hotelorfila.com.
Metro Alonso Martínez.
A luxurious 19th-century mansion offering discreet five-star luxury. It has a beautiful, flower-scented terrace, a charming salón de té, and a renowned restaurant.

Galiano €€
C Alcalá Galiano 6, Salamanca, T91 319 2000, www.hotelgaliano.com.
Metro Colón.
Delightful, antique-filled hotel housed in a (much modernized) former palace, with spacious rooms and a leafy, central location.

Hostal Gala €€
Hostal Gala, Costanilla de los Ángeles , T91 541 9692, www.hostalgala.com.
Doubles €55-125.
A handsomely modernised hostal, with charming staff, and stylish rooms, some with their own sitting rooms. The amenities include air-conditioning, free Wi-Fi, and use of a microwave and fridge.

Hotel Mario €€
C Campomanes 4, T91 548 8548, www.room-matehoteles.com.
Metro Opera.
Part of a small chain of slickly designed hotels, all offering minimalist decor, friendly service, good central locations and excellent value. Highly recommended.

Hostal Cervantes €
C Cervantes 34, Santa Ana, T91 429 8365, www.hostal-cervantes.com.
Metro Antón Martín.
A great favourite. Friendly owners have made it feel like a home from home. There's a cosy lounge, each room has been decorated with pretty blue prints and all have en suite bathrooms.

EMonaco €
C Barbieri 5, T91 522 4639.
Metro Chueca.
This enjoyably louche former brothel is now distinctly shabby, even dilapidated, but still worth checking out. To really soak up the atmosphere, ask for room 20 or 123.

Eating

The streets around the Plaza Santa Ana – just five mins' walk from the Prado – are densely packed with all kinds of bars and restaurants. There are lots of traditional restaurants around the Plaza Mayor (although it's best to avoid the touristy ones on the square), as well as excellent gourmet tapas bars. Some of the cheapest and best tapas bars are in La Latina and Lavapiés.

Cafés and tapas bars

Café de los Austrias
Pl de Ramales 1, T91 559 846.
Daily 0900-0100, Fri and Sat 0900-0300. Metro Opera.
This old-fashioned café/bar is a perfect spot to while away an afternoon.

Lolina Vintage Café
Lolina Vintage Café, C/Espiritu Santo 9, www.lolinacafe.com.
A bright, colourful café-bar in the Malasaña neighbourhood, with retro furnishings, including original handpainted wallpaper from the 1950s. On the menu are salads, quiches, tarts, soups and cakes.

Taberna de la Dolores
Pl de Jesús 4, T91 429 2243.
Daily 1100-0100, Fri and Sat 1100-0200. Metro Antón Martín.
Beautiful, century-old tiled tapas bar – one of the most típico in the city.

Restaurants

La Terraza de Casino €€€
La Terraza de Casino, C Alcalá 15, T91 521 8700, www.casinodemadrid.es.
Mon-Fri 1330-1600 and 2100-2345, Sat 2100-2345. Closed Aug and public hols.
This sumptuous 19th-century building has a stunning panoramic terrace and contains one of Madrid's most spectacular restaurants – part of the legendary El Bulli group. The cuisine is as exciting and creative as you would expect. Be prepared to pay around €100 per head for an unforgettable experience.

Zalacain €€€
C Álvarez de Baena 4, T91 561 4840.
Mon-Fri 1300-1600, 2100-2400, Sat 2100-2400. Metro Gregorio Marañón.
Madrid's most celebrated restaurant holds all kinds of stars and awards under the direction of chef Benjamín Urdiaín. The Basque cuisine is complemented by a refined setting, perfect service and a spectacular wine list. Jacket and tie obligatory for men.

Casa Paco €€
Pl Puerta Cerrada 11, T91 366 3166.
Mon-Sat 1330-1600 and 2000-2400. Metro La Latina.
A resolutely old-fashioned bar with a restaurant at the back. Waiters in long aprons serve hearty stews, Madrileña classics, and good wines.

El Negro de Anglona €€
C Segovia 13, T91 366 3753.
Fri and Sat until 0200. Metro La Latina.
Fashionable restaurant in a 19th-century palace, with sleek, decor. Grilled meats and pasta.

Arrocería Gala €
C Moratín 22, T91 429 2562.
Mon-Thu 1330-1600 and 2030-2300, Fri-Sun 1330-1630 and 2030-2400. Metro Antón Martín.
Valencian rice dishes, including great paella, served in a glassy patio. No credit cards.

La Isla del Tesoro €
C Manuel Malasaña 3, T91 593 1440. Daily 1330-1600 and 2000-2400. Metro Bilbao.
A wonderfully romantic spot for vegetarian food. The *menú del día* (€11) features the cuisine of a different country each day.

Nightlife

In Madrid it's possible to start dancing on Fri night and not stop until Mon morning. Some of the best clubs are: *Low Club*, Fri at **De Nombre Publico** (Pl Mostenses 11); the gay party, *Ohm*, Sat and Sun at **Bash** (Pl de Callao 4); and *The Room*, Fri at stylish **Stella** (C Arlabán 7). There's tango or salsa Mon- Fri at the **Palacio Gaviria** (C Arenal 7) and dance music or electro-pop at weekends.

Elsewhere, the Paseo de Castellano is famous for its summer terrazas where you can drink and dance outside. Madrid also has hundreds of *discobares* spread all over the city. Santa Ana and Huertas get packed, especially in summer, and though not especially fashionable *barrios*, you are guaranteed a good time. The streets around Plaza de la Paja, in the Plaza Mayor and Los Austrias area, are packed with fancy tapas joints but there's also a healthy sprinkling of down-to-earth bars. There are some very funky bars tucked away in the old working-class districts of La Latina and Lavapiés, while to the north of Gran Vía are two formerly run-down neighbourhoods that have become the focal point of the city's heady nightlife: Chueca is the heart of the gay district and stuffed with some ultra-stylish places – such as **Acuarela** (*C Gravina 10*), **El Liquid** (*C Barquillo 8*) and the non-gay **Star's Café** (*C Marqués de Valdeiglesias 5*) – while Malasaña is popular with students and younger people looking for a good time. For the latest news, see www.clubbingspain.com.

Shopping

As a general guide, you can find almost anything you want in the streets around C Preciados: department stores, chain stores and individual shops selling everything from hams to traditional Madrileño cloaks. The northwestern neighbourhoods of Argüelles and Moncloa, particularly around C Princesa, are also good for fashion chains. Smart Salamanca has plenty of designer boutiques and interior decoration shops, while Chueca is full of hip, unusual fashion and music shops.

Travel essentials

Getting there

Madrid's **Barajas Airport** is 12 km northeast of the city (airport information T902 404704, www.aena.es). The most useful local bus lines into the city centre include No 828 for the Metro de Canillejas, and the No 200 (from all terminals) for Av de América; each costs €2. The yellow Exprés Aeropuerto (€2) runs 24 hours a day from Plaza de Cibeles, Atocha station, and terminals T1, T2 and T4. Metro line 8 runs from Terminal 2 and Terminal 4 to Nuevos Ministerios in the city centre (€2). If you'll be using public transport during your stay it's best to get a **Metrobús ticket** (see below), but you'll have to pay a €1 supplement for journeys to and from the airport. Taxi ranks are outside all arrival halls. A taxi into the city costs around €25. Long-distance trains (including an overnight service from Paris d'Austerlitz) arrive at Atocha station (metro line 1), T902 320 320, www.renfe.com.

Getting around

Almost all Madrid's sights are clustered in the centre, an enjoyable stroll from each other. However, if you're in a hurry, the **buses** and **metro** are cheap, efficient and user-friendly. A few places – the museums dotted around the Salamanca district and the Ventas bullring, for example – are a bit further afield but are all accessible by public transport. A single trip by bus or metro costs €1; the **Metrobús ticket** (which can be shared) costs €9 for 10 journeys. Tourist passes cost €5.20- €23.60 for 1-7 days' unlimited use of the bus and metro in Zone 1 (the most useful for visitors). You can buy tickets at metro stations; the Metrobús ticket is also sold at tobacconists (estancos). Pick up free bus and metro maps from tourist offices, metro and bus stations. Information in English is available by calling T010 or online at **www.ctm-madrid.es**. Good bus routes for sightseeing include: No 2 from Plaza España, along the Gran Vía to the Retiro; No 3 for an overview of the centre, from Puerta de Toledo to Chueca; No 5 from Puerta del Sol up Paseo de la Castellana to Plaza de Castilla; No 21 down Pintor Rosales in the northeast, through Chueca and to the Ventas bullring.

Tourist information

The main office is in the Casa de la Panadería, Pl Mayor 27, T91 588 1636, daily 0930-2030. There are other branches (all open daily 0930–2030, T91 588 1636) at Plaza de Colón (underground); Plaza de Cibeles; Plaza de Callao; Paseo del Arte on the corner of C/Santa Isabel; **Barajas Airport**, Terminals 2 and 4 (open daily 0900-2000). Staff can provide a basic map of the city and a copy of *Es Madrid Magazine*, a pocket-sized magazine with helpful local information and listings. There's also a free English-language monthly newspaper *InMadrid* (www.in-madrid.com), with plenty of bar and club listings. Useful websites include: www.madrid.org, www.descubremadrid.com and www.esmadrid.com.

Ratings

Art and culture ☆☆
Eating ☆☆☆☆
Nightlife ☆☆☆☆
Outdoors ☆☆
Romance ☆☆
Shopping ☆☆☆☆☆
Sightseeing ☆☆
Value-for-money ☆
Overall city rating ☆☆

Milan

The epitome of style and sleek design, Milan's often grey, polluted streets are an unlikely backdrop for its population of models, designers and chic businessmen. This is a functional modern Italian metropolis of football, Alfa Romeo, money and separatist politics, where industriousness is held in high esteem. Milan, however, is a city with hidden beauty. The city's courtyards, if you can get a glimpse of them, are famously attractive. The most impressive spot in the city is on the roof of the cathedral and there is a lively Milanese cultural life, too – from the grand opera of La Scala to hip modern music venues. As a city, Milan goes against what its fashion industry might suggest: in the end, it's what's under the surface that counts.

Restaurant table on the street in the Navigli.

The Duomo, *Piazza del Duomo, T02 7202 3375, www.duomomilano.it, daily 0700-1900, free; access to roof daily 0900-1645 (until 2200 in summer), €8 lift, €5 steps, Metro Duomo*, is the centrepoint of the city. Started in 1386, the mammoth cathedral was not completed until Napoleon ordered the addition of the façade in the 19th century. Intricately Gothic, the pale marble building has over 3000 statues, many on tall slender spires, best appreciated from the roof. Inside, a nail purportedly from Christ's cross, hangs from the ceiling.

A cathedral to the gods of shopping sits right beside the Duomo. The grand Galleria Vittorio Emanuele II links the northern side of the piazza del Duomo with the piazza della Scala. A vast, cross-shaped, vaulted arcade, it was opened by the eponymous first king of Italy in 1867.

It is now filled with pricey cafés and equally expensive shops. Milanesi come to strut and tourists come to marvel at the enormity of the place and, near the centre, to spin on the balls of the mosaic bull (a symbol of nearby Turin) for good luck.

Radiating out from here are several pedestrianized shopping streets, such as corso Vittorio Emanuele II, though the highest concentration of designer togs is to be found in the Quadrilatero della Moda, an area to the northeast around via Manzoni, via della Spiga, via Monte Napoleone and via Sant'Andrea. Further northeast again are the **Giardini Pubblici** and the **Galleria d'Arte Moderna**, *Villa Reale, Via Palestro 16, T02 8844 5947, www.gam-milano.com, Tue-Sun 0900-1300 and 1400-1730, free, Metro Palestro*, where works by Van Gogh, Picasso and Matisse hang in Napoleon's one-time residence. Beyond the Giardini Pubblici is the central train station.

To the northwest of the Duomo is the hulk of the **Castello Sforzesco**, *Piazza Castello 3, T02 8846 3700, www.milanocastello.it, various museums Tue-Sun 0900-1730, €3, free Fri after 1400, Metro Cairoli, Cardorna Triennale or Lanza*, with the Parco Sempione beyond.

Between the castle and the Giardini Pubblici, the area of Brera has some of the city's oldest and most interesting streets and an excellent gallery in the **Pinacoteca di Brera**, *Via Brera 28, T02 8942 1146, www.brera.beniculturali.it, Tue-Sun 0830-1915,*

€5, Metro Lanza. Highlights include paintings by Raphael, Caravaggio and Bellini.

Leonardo da Vinci's Last Supper, known as the **Il Cenacolo Vinciano**, *T02 8942 1146, www.vivaticket.it, Tue-Sun 0800-1900, €8, book by telephone or online at least 1 day in advance, Metro Conciliazone, Cadorna Triennale*, is located in the refectory of the Convent of Santa Maria delle Grazie, to the west of the centre. The already enormous popularity of Leonardo's innovative and dramatic masterpiece has been enhanced by the success of *The Da Vinci Code* and visitors must book ahead for their chance to see it. Most hotels in Milan will be happy to make a booking by telephone on behalf of their guests.

To the south of the centre, the Navigli still has remnants of Milan's old canal system and has become one of the best areas of the city for eating, drinking and shopping.

Above: Milanese shopping. Opposite page: Roof of the Duomo.

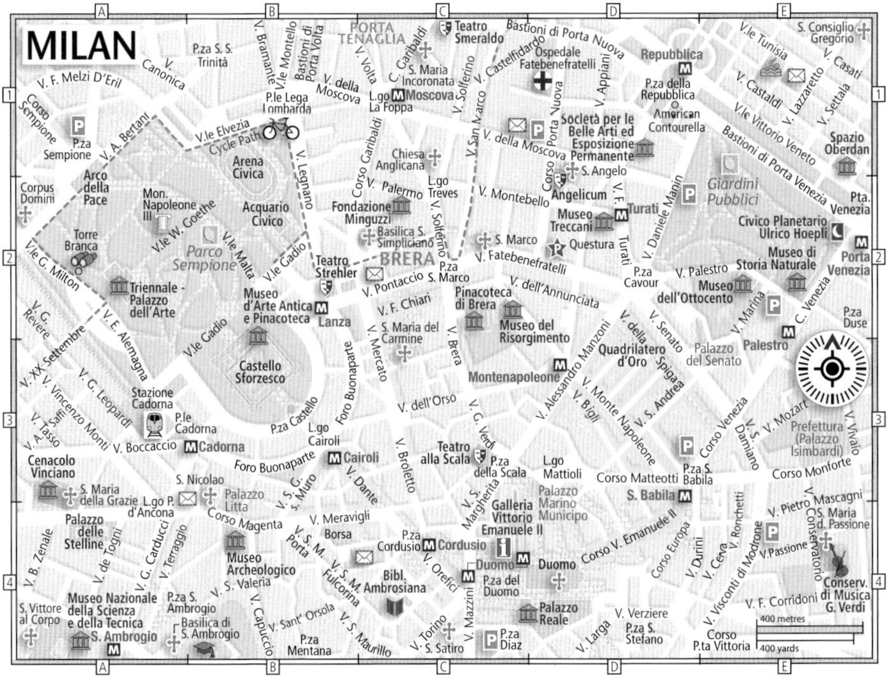

MILAN

A B C D E
1 2 3 4
Porta Tenaglia
Teatro Smeraldo
Bastioni di Porta Nuova
Ospedale Fatebenefratelli
Repubblica
S. Consiglio Gregorio
P.za S. S. Trinità
V. Canonica
V. F. Melzi D'Eril
V. Bramante
V.le Montello
Bastioni di Porta Volta
V. della Moscova
V. Volta
C. Garibaldi
S. Maria Incoronata
V. Solferino
V. Castelfidardo
V. Appiani
P.za della Repubblica
V.le Tunisia
V. Casati
V. Castaldi
V. Lazzaretto
V. Settala
Corso Sempione
P.le Lega Lombarda
L.go La Foppa
Moscova
American Contourella
V.le Vittorio Veneto
Bastioni di Porta Venezia
P.za Sempione
V. A. Bertani
V.le Elvezia Cycle Path
Arena Civica
Corso Garibaldi
V. San Marco
V. della Moscova
Corso di Porta Nuova
Società per le Belle Arti ed Esposizione Permanente
Spazio Oberdan
Chiesa Anglicana
S. Angelo
Corpus Domini
Arco della Pace
Mon. Napoleone III
V. Legnano
V. Palermo
L.go Treves
V. Montebello
Angelicum
V. F. Turati
Giardini Pubblici
Pta. Venezia
Acquario Civico
Fondazione Minguzzi
Museo Treccani
Turati
V. Daniele Manin
Civico Planetario Ulrico Hoepli
Torre Branca
V.le W. Goethe
V.le Malta
Parco Sempione
Basilica S. Simpliciano
V. Solferino
S. Marco
Questura
Museo di Storia Naturale
Porta Venezia
V.le G. Milton
V.le Gadio
Teatro Strehler
Brera
P.za S. Marco
V. Fatebenefratelli
P.za Cavour
V. Palestro
Triennale - Palazzo dell'Arte
Museo d'Arte Antica e Pinacoteca
Lanza
V. Pontaccio
V. F. Chiari
Pinacoteca di Brera
V. dell'Annunciata
Museo dell'Ottocento
V. Marina
C. Venezia
P.za Duse
V. G. Revere
V. E. Alemagna
V.le Gadio
S. Maria del Carmine
V. Mercato
V. Brera
Museo del Risorgimento
V. della Spiga
V. Senato
Quadrilatero d'Oro
Palazzo del Senato
Palestro
V. XX Settembre
Castello Sforzesco
Foro Buonaparte
Montenapoleone
V. Alessandro Manzoni
V. Monte Napoleone
V. S. Andrea
V. Vincenzo Monti
V. G. Leopardi
Stazione Cadorna
P.za Castello
V. dell'Orso
V. G. Verdi
V. Bigli
Corso Venezia
V. S. Damiano
V. Mozart
Prefettura (Palazzo Isimbardi)
V. Vivaio
V. Saffi
V. A. Tasso
P.le Cadorna
L.go Cairoli
V. Boccaccio
Cadorna
Cenacolo Vinciano
Foro Buonaparte
Cairoli
V. Broletto
Teatro alla Scala
P.za della Scala
L.go Mattioli
Corso Matteotti
P.za S. Babila
Corso Monforte
S. Maria della Grazie
L.go P. d'Ancona
S. Nicolao
Palazzo Litta
V. S. G. S. Muro
V. Dante
V. S. Margherita
Galleria Vittorio Emanuele II
Palazzo Marino Municipio
S. Babila
V. Pietro Mascagni
S. Maria d. Passione
Palazzo delle Stelline
Corso Magenta
V. Meravigli
Borsa
Corso V. Emanuele II
V. Ronchetti
V. Conservatorio
V. B. Zenale
V. de Togni
V. G. Carducci
V. Terraggio
Museo Archeologico
V. S. M. Porta
P.za Cordusio
Cordusio
Corso Europa
V. Durini
V. Cerva
V. Visconti di Modrone
V. Passione
V. S. Valeria
V. S. M. Fulcorina
Bibl. Ambrosiana
V. Orefici
Duomo
P.za del Duomo
Conserv. di Musica G. Verdi
Museo Nazionale della Scienza e della Tecnica
P.za S. Ambrogio
V. Mazzini
Palazzo Reale
V. F. Corridoni
S. Vittore al Corpo
Basilica di S. Ambrogio
S. Ambrogio
V. Capuccio
V. Sant' Orsola
V. S. Maurillo
V. Torino
V. S. Satiro
P.za Diaz
V. Larga
V. Verziere
P.za S. Stefano
Corso P.ta Vittoria
P.za Mentana
400 metres
400 yards

Sleeping

Many of the cheaper places to stay are in the area east of the station. Central hotels tend to be on the expensive side and often cater to a business clientele.

Straf €€€
via San Raffaele 3, T02- 805 081, www.straf.it.
A minimalist 21st-century design hotel in slate, brass and glass with vivid splashes of contemporary art, a stone's throw from the Duomo.

Antica Locanda Leonardo €€
corso Magenta 78, T02 4801 4197, www.anticalocandaleonardo.com.
A traditional, smart and friendly place west of the centre, with wooden floors, a garden and contemporary art.

Antica Locanda Solferino €€
via Castelfidardo 2, T02 657 0129, www.anticalocandasolferino.it.
Stylish 19th-century bohemian hotel in the laid-back Brera area of town.

Ariston €€
Largo Carrobbio 2, T02 7200 0556, www.aristonhotel.com.
Bio-architecturally designed, though a little blandly, the Ariston purifies the Milanese air and even the carpet glue is non-toxic. Bicycles are available for guests to use and it's only 400 m from the Duomo.

Hotel Charly €€-€
via Settala 76, T02 204 7190, www.hotelcharly.com.
Bargain elegance in two adjacent villas with a garden, near the station. The cheapest rooms lack en suite bathrooms.

Eating

The Brera area has many of Milan's best restaurants. The Navigli, to the south, has traditional, down-to-earth places.

10 Corso Como €€€
corso Como 10, T02 653 531.
Closed Mon.
A complex incorporating a café, photography gallery (Galleria Carla Sozzani, www.galleriacarlasozzani.org), bookshop, and fashion and perfume boutiques, Corso Como 10 really comes into its own in the evenings, when the who's who of Italian fashion troop into its courtyard restaurant to consume trendy food. It's also good for breakfast.

Al Pont de Ferr €€
ripa di Porta Ticinese 55, T02 8940 6277.
Closed Sat and Sun in winter and Sat and Sun lunch in summer.
A traditional, good-value, canal-side osteria lined with wine bottles. Offers country cooking and a good range of cheeses.

Joia €€
via P Castaldi 18, T02 2952 2124, www.joia.it. Closed Sun.
A rarity in Italy: a hip, inventive vegetarian eatery, despite ludicrous names of the dishes.

Latteria San Marco €
via San Marco 24, T02 659 7653.
Closed Sun.
A small traditional place in an ex-dairy in Brera serving a changing menu of Milanese food. Popular with locals and good for lunch; be prepared to wait.

Spontini €
via Spontini 4, T02 204 7444.
Closed Mon.
With lots of oil and copious mozzarella, the enormously thick and tasty pizza slices in this popular and noisy place only come in two versions – big and bigger. There's good beer on tap and it's handy for hotels near the station.

Nightlife

The tourist office produces the bilingual monthly *Mese Milano*, with details of events and concerts. You can download a copy from their website.

Bars and clubs

At aperitivo time, many bars compete with each other by offering ever more generous buffets of free nibbles with your drink and these can sometimes constitute a meal in themselves. Later on, Milan has a wider selection of nightclubs than most Italian cities, as well as some hip bars. Club opening hours vary with demand and the seasons but most stay open until at least 0400. Bars tend to close between midnight and 0200. The best areas for bars are **Brera** (the most unconventional), the **Navigli** (the cheapest, good on summer evenings when the area is closed to traffic) and **Corso Como** (the hippest). Notable nightspots include the immaculately smart and hip **Café Atlantique**, viale Umbria 42, www.cafe atlantique.com; and the lively, left-wing **Leoncavallo**, via Watteau 7, www.leoncavallo.org. In summer much of the nightlife decamps to Idroscalo, a lake near Linate airport.

Opera

La Scala
T02 7200 3744, www.teatroallascala.org.
Probably the world's most famous opera house, La Scala has a Dec-Jul opera season, with classical concerts at other times. Tickets, costing €20-170, can be booked online.

Travel essentials

Getting there

Malpensa, T02 7485 2200, www.sea-aeroportimilano.it, Milan's main airport, is connected to the central station by bus every 20 mins (journey time around 50 mins, €7.50 one-way, €12 return); buy tickets in arrivals or online. A taxi costs around €75, or you can travel by train every 30 mins (40 mins to Cadorna station, €11 single, €14.50 return). **Linate airport**, T02 7485 2200, www.sea-aeroportimilano.it, the most central, is connected to San Babila station by city bus 73 every 10 mins (about 30 mins, €1). Alternatively, Starfly buses run between Linate and the central station every 30 mins (€3). A taxi to the centre costs around €20. **Orio al Serio**, www.orioaeroporto.it, just outside Bergamo and used by Ryanair, has 3 bus connections to Milan central station, approximately every 30 mins, with Autostradale (€9.90, pay in advance at their airport office) and Locatelli Air Pullman (€7, pay on the bus). Austostradale also go, less frequently, to Lambrate station (€6.60). Or take a local bus (€1.70) into Bergamo and catch the train from there (1 hr, €4.05). International trains (including TGVs and sleeper services from Paris) arrive at Milano Centrale, Piazza Duca d'Aosta, www.trenitalia.com.

Getting around

Much of the city centre's main sights are within easy walking distance of the Duomo. The **metro** is an efficient way of getting to and from the station, or down to the Navigli. There are 4 colour-coded lines; red, blue, green and yellow. Single tickets (€1) allow travel on buses and trams for 75 mins but only one metro journey. Day tickets (€4) give the freedom to use any mode of transport.

Tourist information

The main tourist office, T02 7252 4301, www.visitamilano.it, is in piazza del Duomo, on the southern side of the cathedral.

Shopping

The line between Milanese street and catwalk is a fine one and it's not hard to spot the fashion set striding with hauteur around the city centre. The most famous area for Milan's designer clothing industry is the **Quadrilatero della Moda** or **Quadrilatero d'Oro** (Golden Square), an area just to the north of piazza della Scala. Quadrilatero has all the big names from Armani to Zenga and should be visited just for some window gazing even if you have no intention of making any purchases. There are, however, other parts of the city also worth visiting for the shops: the more leftfield **Navigli** is good for bargains, as is **corso Buenos Aires**, east of the station. And, if the clothes don't do it for you, on **via Durini** there are some pretty slick Italian designer kitchenware and furniture stores.

Ratings

Art and culture ☆☆☆☆
Eating ☆☆☆
Nightlife ☆☆☆
Outdoors ☆☆☆☆
Romance ☆☆☆
Shopping ☆☆☆
Sightseeing ☆☆☆
Value-for-money ☆☆
Overall city rating ☆☆☆

Munich

Munich knows how to have a good time. This is, after all, the beer capital of Europe. But while the merriment continues year-round in the city's bounteous beer halls, Munich manages somehow to shake off its hangover and retain a surprisingly sensible reputation for hard work and innovation. This is the home of BMW and Siemens, and is the location of some of Germany's finest museums, art galleries and theatres, lending it a rather refined and prosperous air. All this marries well with its elegant Bavarian palaces and grand churches. But look past the sharp suits and flash cars and you'll find another beer hall pounding with oompah music – an appealing reminder of Munich's mischievous side.

Munich panorama.

Marienplatz

S-Bahn/U-Bahn Marienplatz, bus 52 to Marienplatz, Tram 19 to Theatinerstrasse. Map C3.

The pulsing heart of Munich is this broad square, centred around the 17th-century **Mariensäule**, a column topped by a statue of the Virgin Mary. Flanking the north side is the gargoyled façade of the **Neues Rathaus** (New Town Hall), which holds the tourist office and has an 85-m tower offering impressive views of the city. A rather tuneless glockenspiel springs into action daily (at 1100, 1200 and 1700 in summer). Also here is the **Fischbrunnen** (Fish Fountain) and the **Altes Rathaus** (Old Town Hall), which was almost entirely destroyed during the Second World War. Today, its rebuilt bulk houses the **Spielzeugmuseum** (Toy Museum), *www.spielzeugmuseum-muenchen.de, daily 1000-1730, €3,* a vast collection of antique toys. In December, a traditional Christmas market takes place on the square. Overlooking Marienplatz from the west are the unmistakable domed towers of the Gothic **Frauenkirche** (Cathedral Church of Our

At a glance

Munich's centre radiates out from **Marienplatz**, the Gothic heart of the **Altstadt** (Old Town). Just to the north is the **Residenz**, a former palace, surrounded by grand town houses, churches, theatres and elegant shops, while to the east is **Platzl**, home to the city's most famous beer hall, the Hofbräuhaus. Further east is **Museumsinsel** (Museum Island), an island on the Isar River, site of the Deutsches Museum. Back at Marienplatz, the **Viktualienmarkt**, a bustling outdoor food market, sprawls to the south of the square, while to the west is the main pedestrian shopping district, leading to **Karlsplatz** and on to the main train station. A few blocks to the north of the station is a cluster of excellent art galleries, known collectively as the **Pinakothek**, while to the south is the **Theresienwiese**, the purpose-built area that holds the huge tents of the Oktoberfest each year. Munich's best-known suburb is **Schwabing**, the lively student district, stretching to the north of the centre. The tranquil, grassy **Englischer Garten** can also be found here. Further north still is **Olympiapark**, site of the 1972 Olympics, and out to the west are the sculpted grounds of **Schloss Nymphenburg**, Munich's summer palace.

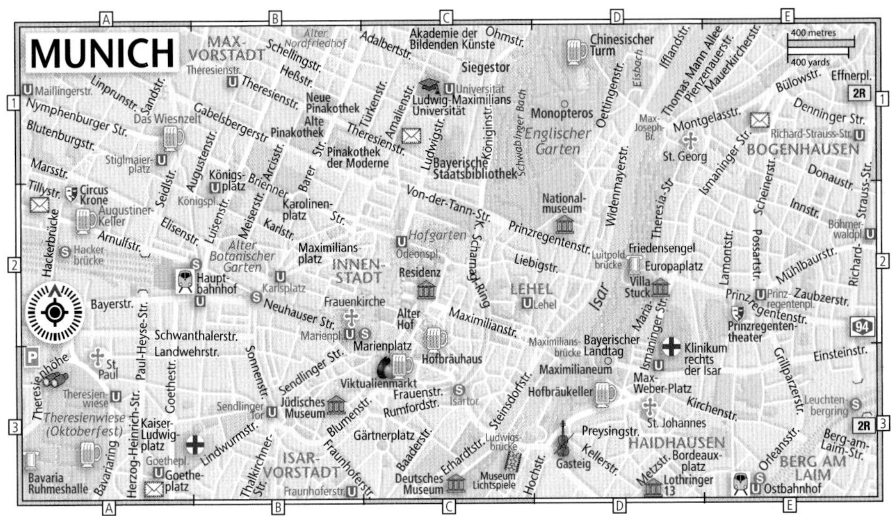

Beloved Lady); the Alps can be seen from the top of the south tower on a clear day. South of the square is **St Peterskirche** (St Peter's Church) and **Viktualienmarkt**, a huge open-air food market. The futuristic but basic Jewish synagogue opened in November 2006 on nearby St-Jakobs Platz, joined by the Jüdische Museum (Jewish museum) in March 2007, *T089 2339 6096, www.juedisches-museum-muenchen.de, Tue-Sun 1000-1800.*

Münchener Stadtmuseum

Sankt-Jakobs-Platz 1, T089 2332 2370, www.stadtmuseum-online.de.
Tue-Sun 1000-1800. €4.
S-Bahn/U-Bahn Marienplatz.

Near Viktualienmarkt is this excellent local history museum, which covers Munich from its official foundation in 1158 to the present, and also includes sections on fashion, musical instruments, puppets and film, with a cinema showing German and arthouse films.

Opposite page: Marienplatz.

Residenz and around

Residenzstr 1, T089 290 671, www.residenz-muenchen.de.
Apr-mid Oct daily 0900-1800; mid Oct-Mar daily 1000-1700. €6 (€9 with Schatzkammer) S-Bahn/U-Bahn Marienplatz, bus 52 to Odeonsplatz. Map C2.

Munich's most photographed sight is this magnificent Renaissance palace, the seat of Bavaria's rulers, the Wittelsbachs, until 1918. It is split into two sections: one open in the morning, the other in the afternoon, so you'll need a full day to take it all in. A total of 130 rooms are filled with art, period furnishings and decorations, including the ancestral portrait gallery and the extravagant royal apartments. The highlight is the **Antiquarium**, a vast, arched hall resplendent with rococo swirls and murals. A separate ticket allows entry to the **Schatzkammer**, the royal treasury, crammed with jewellery and artworks from the late Greco-Roman period to the Middle Ages.

To see their modern-day counterparts, head just south to **Maximilianstrasse**, where Munich's well-heeled spend their dosh in glamorous

boutiques. At the other end of Max-Joseph Platz is the baroque façade of **Theatinerkirche**, its ochre walls and green dome making a splash of colour in the pale stone surroundings.

Deutsches Museum

Museumsinsel 1, T089 21791, www.deutsches-museum.de. Daily 0900-1700. €8.50. U-Bahn Fraunhofer- strasse, S-Bahn Isartor, tram 17 to Isartor or tram 18 to Deutsches Museum. Map C3.

Claiming to be the world's largest science and technology museum, this is certainly a gargantuan collection, covering everything from seafaring and space probes to the car industry and chemistry. The 55,000 sq m museum can be exhausting, but it is a sure-fire hit with children.

Pinakothek

Barer Str, www.pinakothek.de. U-Bahn Theresienstrasse, Odeonsplatz or Universität, tram 27 to Pinakothek, bus 154 to Schellingstrasse. Map B1.

This series of art galleries is exceptional and regarded as one of the finest in Europe. The **Alte Pinakothek**, *No 27, T089 2380 5216, Tue 1000-2000, Wed-Sun 1000-1800, €7*, is a vast treasure trove of German art from the Middle Ages to the end of the rococo period. Its highlight is the exceptional collection by Dürer; look out for The Four Apostles, and his defining self portrait from 1500.

The **Neue Pinakothek lentrance on Theresienstrasse**, *T089 2380 5195, Thu-Mon 1000-1700, Wed 1000-2000, €6*, holds a fine collection from the late 18th century to the early 20th century, including the private collection of King Ludwig I.

Open since 2002 and worth visiting for its architecture as much as its collections, is the newest addition, the **Pinakothek der Moderne**, *No 40, T089 2380 5360, wwww.pinakothek-der-moderne.de, Tue and Wed 1000-1800, Thu 100-2000, Fri-Sun 1000-1800, €10.* The airy concrete and glass structure has works by Dalí, Picasso and German greats such as Beckman and Polke, and architecture and design exhibits.

Englischer Garten

Map D1.

Wedged between the Altstadt and Schwabing is the Englischer Garten, a large city park of rolling lawns and lakes. Don't be shocked by the nude sunbathers during summer – Munich is known for its liberal views on naturism. Bare sunbathing aside, the park is a wonderful area for a stroll or picnic. The **Chinesischer Turm**, a pagoda-shaped tower, is a good landmark, set above a popular beer garden.

At the southeast corner of the Englischer Garten is the **Bayerisches Nationalmuseum**, *T089 211 2401, www.bayerisches-nationalmuseum.de. Tue, Wed, Fri-Sun 1000-1700, Thu 1000-2000, €5, U-Bahn Lehel.* Although at times rambling, it provides a worthwhile overview of the region's history. Exhibits include a fine collection of porcelain from Nymphenburg and art nouveau glassworks.

Schloss Nymphenburg

T089 179 080, www.schloesser. bayern.de. Daily Apr-mid Oct 0900-1800, mid Oct-Mar 1000-1600. €5 museum only or €10 for museum and Marstallmuseum. Tram 17, bus 51.

Northwest of the city centre is the summer residence of the Wittelsbachs, built in the Italian style from 1664. The main building includes the **Schönheitsgallery** (Gallery of Beauties) collected by Ludwig I, which is filled with portraits of many of the women that he considered beautiful. The **Steinerner Saal** has an elaborate frescoed ceiling and the **Marstall-museum**, housed in the court stables, includes the coronation coach of Emperor Karl VII. Most attractive, however, are the beautiful formal gardens and pavilions surrounding the palace. Take some time to stroll around and get a feel for the place.

Right: Oktoberfest ferris wheel.
Opposote page top: Deutsches Museum.
Opposite page middle: Englischer Garten.
Opposite page bottom: Schloss Nymphenburg.

Wish you were beer?

Oktoberfest, the world's largest beer festival, attracts a staggering – often literally – six million-plus visitors each year, who manage to knock back around six million litres of beer over two weeks. The festival actually begins in September, to much pomp from various processions and brass bands, and takes over the 'Wiesn' – the nickname for the Theresienwiese to the southwest of the city centre. Fourteen vast tents spring up along custom-built avenues, surrounded by around 200 fairground rides and sideshows. Each tent is filled with rows of wooden tables where visitors down litre-sized Steins of beer and link arms to the pounding of oompah bands. The best time to visit is at lunch, when the tents are busy but not packed and it's possible to enjoy a big meal in relative peace (roast chicken and plates of sausages are the norm). In the evening, the pace picks up, the tents get crammed, and revellers take to dancing on the tables. Outside, the fairground rides do their best to churn the stomachs of those stumbling between tents. Although the festival attracts a fair contingent of Brits and Aussies, the majority of visitors are still Bavarian – you'll still see plenty of punters in Lederhosen and feathered caps. For more information, see **www.oktoberfest.de.**

Sleeping

Prices for accommodation tend to be high and, be warned, they rise further during Oktoberfest, when most hotels and guesthouses get booked up months in advance.

Bayerischer Hof €€€
Promenadeplatz 2-6, T089 21200, www.bayerischerhof.de.
Munich's leading hotel since 1841, Bayerischer Hof has a great central location, with a grand marble lobby and huge rooms, many with four-poster beds. There's also a roof garden with pool and spa, several bars and a nightclub.

Hotel Vier Jahreszeiten Kempinski €€€
Maximilianstrasse 17, T089 2125 2799, www.kempinski.com.
One of Munich's finest and most luxurious hotels located on one of the city's most desirable streets. Timelessly elegant with a fabulous spa and pool area. Perfect for a relaxing city break.

Advokat €€
Baaderstr 1, T089 216 310, www.hotel-advokat.de.
Claiming to be Munich's first boutique hotel, the Advokat is stylish and low-key, with scathingly cool staff. Excellent breakfasts served in the trendy café-bar.

Hotel Uhland €€
Uhlandstr 1, T089 543 350, www.hotel-uhland.de.
Friendly guesthouse in a beautiful neo-Renaissance villa on a quiet street close to the Oktoberfest site. Extremely helpful staff, free bikes for rent, and cosy rooms – some with waterbeds.

Wombat's City Youth Hostel €
Senefelderstrasse 1, T089 5998 9180, www.wombats-hostels.com/munich
In a side street next to the city's main train station you'll find the modern glass fronted Wombat's. It's a cool and funky place to lay your head with its own 'womBar' hosting nightly events. Great for meeting fellow travelers.

Eating

Tantris €€€
Johann-Fichte-Str 7, T089 361 9590, www.tantris.de.
One of the city's finest restaurants, with a moodily-lit interior, cool retro touches and a stylish lounge bar upstairs. The menu is a mix of contemporary French and Italian, with some good value (but not cheap) lunchtime menus.

Restaurant 181 €€€
Olympic Tower, T089 3509 48181, www.drehrestaurant.de
A culinary experience with a twist. Here you're guaranteed the most spectacular view of Munich as you enjoy fine dining at the top of the Olympic Tower. The restaurant sits 181 m above the city, revolving 360 degrees, giving you a different outlook with every course!

Brotzeitstüberl €
Viktualien Markt.
In the heart of the outdoor food market, this beer garden is a real social hub in summer, when locals flock here for a bout of people-watching, a cold beer and plate of the local Weisswurst and sweet mustard. Open until 2200 in summer.

Fraunhofer €
Fraunhoferstr 9, T089 266 460.
Students flock to this refreshingly tourist-free beer hall for big portions of good Bavarian food and the usual selection of beers. There's live music some nights, and a small theatre at the back.

Hofbräuhaus €
Platzl 9, T089 2901 3610, www.hofbraeuhaus.de.
Munich's most famous beer hall has been serving for over four centuries, although it's suffered from its popularity and can feel very touristy. Still worth a quick visit to soak up a bit of history – and half a litre of excellent beer, of course.

Café am Beethovenplatz €
Goethestrasse 51, T088 5529 110, www.hotelmariandl.de
Said to be the oldest café in town, locals and tourists alike flock here to indulge in the city's

finest Apfelstrudel. Served in shabby chic surroundings with its high vaulted dining room (complete with chandelier), it epitomises the Viennese Kaffehauses of old.

Nightlife

Munich's nightlife has something of a split personality. On the one hand, the city is famous for its down-to-earth beer halls, where locals gather for their huge litre-glasses of beer and spill out into leafy beer gardens in summer. On the other hand, Munich has a thriving yuppie class with a correspondingly flash nightlife scene, centred on cocktail lounges and thumping clubs dotted around the centre and suburbs. The studenty area of Schwabing has good laid-back bars, while the gay and lesbian bar scene is based around Gärtnerplatz. Also worth seeing are some of the jazz and classical music venues; the city has three first-rate symphony orchestras, several major theatres and numerous fringe theatres.

A good source of information is the monthly *Go München* magazine, www.gomuenchen.com, which also produces München Geht Aus, a useful guide to restaurants and bars.

Travel essentials

Getting there

Flughafen München, T089 97500, www.munich-airport.de, is 28 km northeast of the city centre. The Airport Bus runs to the centre every 20 mins and takes 45 mins. The S-Bahn (lines S1 and S8) connects the airport to the main train station and takes 45 mins. International trains (including sleeper services from Paris) arrive at the Hautbahnhof central station, T+49 1805 996 633, www.bahn.de.

Getting around

Munich has an excellent integrated public transport system, including underground (**U-Bahn**) and overground (**S-Bahn**) trains, **trams** and **buses.** The Altstadt is easily explored on foot but the wider city will require you to jump on a train or tram. One ticket system covers all public transport; tickets can be bought from machines at U-Bahn/S-Bahn stations and from some bus and tram stops. A day ticket costs €5.20 for the inner city or €9.40 for up to five adults. A 3-day ticket costs €12.80 (€22 for up to 5 adults). A single trip ticket costs €2.30, depending on the distance travelled. All tickets must be validated in the blue machines before travel. Strip tickets are useful for more than one trip; two strips need to be validated for each zone crossed.

Tourist information

The main **Munich Tourist Offices**, T089 2339 6500, www.muenchen-tourist.de, are in the main railway station (Mon-Sat 0930-1830, Sun 1000-1800) and in the Neues Rathaus on Marienplatz (Mon-Fri 1000-2000, Sat 1000-1600). The **CityTourCard**, www.citytourcard.com, is a 1- or 3-day ticket for public transport in the city centre as well as discounts of up to 50% at over 30 attractions. Cards cost €9.80 (€18.80 for 3 days) and are available from vending machines at U- and S-Bahn stations, at some bus and tram stops, at dedicated kiosks displaying the City Tour Card sign and from many hotels.

Shopping

The main shopping district is the pedestrian zone in the Altstadt, with streets such as Kaufingerstrasse between Marienplatz and Karlsplatz, lined with chain shops and department stores. The best place for food is the large open-air Viktualienmarkt. Also check out Schrannenhalle, rebuilt in 2005, with food and craft stalls and cultural events. The city's most exclusive boutiques are on Maximilianstrasse; nearby is trendy Theatinerstrasse and Fünf Höfe, a series of smart courtyards filled with shops. For more off-the-wall purchases, head to the second-hand shops in Schwabing.

Ratings

Art and culture ☆☆☆☆
Eating ☆☆☆☆
Nightlife ☆☆
Outdoors ☆☆☆
Romance ☆☆☆
Shopping ☆☆
Sightseeing ☆☆☆☆
Value-for-money ☆☆☆☆
Overall city rating ☆☆☆

Naples

Naples, wedged between the world's most famous volcano and the deep blue sea, is beautiful and ugly in equal measure. A world away from the genteel islands of Ischia and Capri that grace its bay, the city can be intimidating: anarchic and only sporadically law-abiding, the traffic is terrible and peace and quiet is hard to find. But it's an extraordinarily vivacious city, the pizzas are fantastic, music is ingrained in its culture and the treasure trove of historical and artistic sights hidden away in its narrow streets is overwhelming. More like Marrakech than Milan, ask an Italian from the north about Naples and they will throw up their hands in despair. But probe these gentrified folk a little more and they may start to reveal a siren-like fascination with the capital of the south: a city of pizza, of the Comorra, and of an extraordinary natural setting.

Maradona mural.

Santa Lucia

The grandest part of the city is around the giant and slightly barren **piazza del Plebiscito**. With its curved colonnade and vast, imposing space dotted with kids playing football, Vesuvius can be glimpsed between the grand 17th- and 18th-century buildings. The **Palazzo Reale**, *T848 800 288, www.palazzorealenapoli.it, Thu-Tue 0900-1900, Royal Apartments €4, palace courtyard and gardens free*, was built at the beginning of the 17th century for Spanish viceroys and extended by the Bourbons in the 18th century. Behind the church on the hill of **Monte di Dio**, tightly packed housing is stacked on the area where the original Parthenope was founded in around 680 BC by Greeks from nearby Cuma. **Via Chiaia**, running north of the hill, is one of Naples' smartest shopping areas. In piazza Trento e Trieste, **Teatro di San Carlo**, *T081 553 4565, www.teatrosancarlo.it, Mon-Sat 1000-1730, Sun 1100-1230, €5*, tours throughout the day except during performances, is Naples' great opera house. If you like castles, **Castel dell Ovo**, *Mon-Sat 0830-1930, Sun 0830-1345, free*, jutting out into the bay, is worth a wander round. And Borgo Marinari, the collection of houses and (mainly) restaurants and bars surrounded by jetties beside the castle, is heaving on summer evenings.

Centro Storico

This is the true heart of Naples; its dark, narrow streets greasy, irregularly paved and overflowing with scooters, people and noise. Now a UNESCO World Heritage Site, the area still follows the ancient Greek and Roman layout of Neapolis, with three main east-west streets, or decumani. Long, straight **Spaccanapoli** ('Split Naples', vias Benedetto Croce, San Biagio dei Librai and Vicaria Vecchia), was once the decumanus inferior of the Greek city, while **via dei Tribunali** was the decumanus major.

The most interesting part of Spaccanapoli begins at piazza del Gesù, with late 16th-century **Gesù Nuovo**, *T081 551 8613, daily 0630-1300, 1600-1900*. Its brutal armoured exterior gives little

Top: Castel dell Ovo.
Above: Galleria Umberto I.

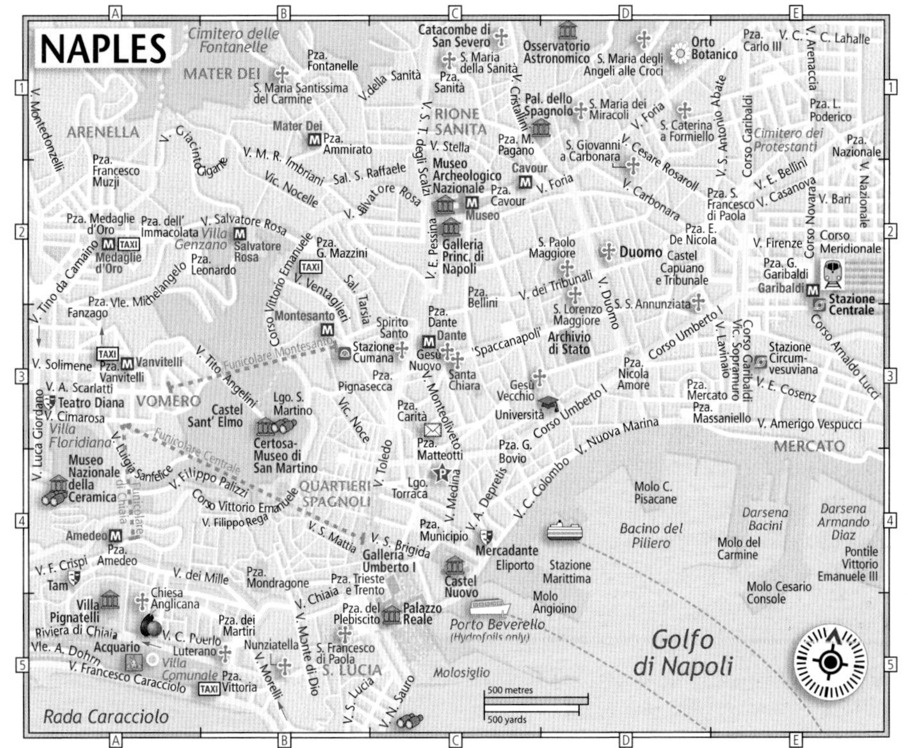

hint of its spectacular interior. Next up, away from the chaotic plethora of bars, restaurants and small shops, are the city's inconceivably peaceful and colourfully tiled 14th-century cloisters of **Santa Chiara**, *via Santa Chiara 49/c, T081 551 6673, www.monasterodisantachiara.com, Mon-Sat 0930-1730, Sun 1000-1430, €5.*

Other highlights of the Centro Storico include three 17th- and 18th-century spires, looking like enormously elongated wedding cakes: **Guglia dell'Immacolata**, piazza del Gesù, **Guglia di San Domenico Maggiore**, in a piazza of the same name, and **Guglia di San Gennaro**, in piazza Riario Sforza, adjacent to the Duomo. The 13th-century **Duomo**, *via del Duomo 149, Mon-Fri 0800-1230, 1630-1900, Sun 0800-1330, 1700-1930, Scavi del Duomo €3*, is slightly less of a focus than cathedrals in other Italian cities but still a grand building. Its chapels are especially interesting, one holding the famous remains of San Gennaro, the city's patron saint. Another, the fourth-century Cappella di Santa Restituta, is one of the city's oldest buildings. Under the building, in the Scavi del Duomo, some fascinating ancient remains have been unearthed.

Cappella Sansevero, *via de Sanctis 19, T081 551 8470, www.museosansevero.it, Wed-Sat and Mon 1000-1740, Sun 1000-1310, €7*, originally built in 1590 but remodelled in the 18th century, is also worth a visit for some virtuoso allegorical marble sculptures, notably Disillusion, by Francisco Queirolo (1704-1762), and an amazingly lifelike Veiled Christ (1753) by Giuseppe Sanmartino.

Amongst numerous places to wander, via San Gregorio Armeno, running north perpendicular to Spaccanapoli, is worth a visit. All year round, shops spill their wares out onto the pavements: thousands upon thousands of nativity scene figures, vie for space with models of fruit baskets, mini electrically pumped water features and the occasional mechanized man-drinking-beer, or butcher-chopping-meat. Above you, angels suspended from ceilings and doorways stare down lovingly.

Quartieri Spagnoli and Via Toledo

Via Toledo, Naples' bustling high street, runs between piazza del Plebiscito and piazza Dante. To its west, the narrow streets of the Quartieri Spagnoli are one of the city's poorest areas, and the Camorra heartland. There's a fascinating **market** every day up via Pignasecca and towards piazza Montesanto, while via Toledo heads north to the **Museo Archeologico Nazionale di Napoli**, *piazza Museo 19, T081 440 1466, www.marcheo.napolibeniculturali.it, 0900-1930, closed Tue, €6.50.* From enormous grandiose marble statues to small homely paintings, and from erotic oil lamps to a mosaic made of a million pieces, this is a staggering collection and gives an amazing idea of the look and feel of the ancient Roman world.

Mercato di Porta Nolana

Just to the west of the Circumvesuviana Terminal, this extraordinary piece of Neapolitan theatre spills out every morning onto via Cesare Carmignano and via Sopramuro. It's a heady mix of fish, fruit and veg, pirated DVDs, bread, olives, contraband cigarettes, cheap beer, toy helicopters and fishing rods.

La Sanità and Capodimonte

Beyond the Museo Archeologico the road continues to the fine, green Parco di Capodimonte, where the **Reggia di Capodimonte**, *via Capodimonte, T081 749 9111, www.museo-capodimonte.it, Thu-Tue 0830-1930, €7.50 (1400-1700, €6.50)*, houses the Bourbon and the

Farnese art collections. On a bus there you might not even notice Dickensian La Sanità. Home to the city's ancient catacombs, it lies below and is bypassed by the bridge built by the French in 1808.

Chiaia, Mergellina and Posillipo

To the west of the centre the genteel Caracciolo seafront curves around to the yacht-filled marina of Mergellina, beyond which the exclusive residential area of Posillipo rises. Chiaia in particular is a more laid-back area of bars, cafés and restaurants and some green spaces, notably the **Villa Comunale** park.

Certosa di San Martino

Largo San Martino 5, T081 558 5942, www.polomusealenapoli.beniculturali.it. Thu-Tue 0830-1930. €6.

Perched high above Naples, in Vomero, with exceptional views is this 14th- century Carthusian monastery. It now contains the excellent **Museo di San Martino** and is one of Naples' most satisfying sights, containing interesting paintings, an elegant cloister, an exhibition of presepi (nativity scenes), one of Naples' most spectacular churches and terraced gardens. The hulking **Castel Sant'Elmo** is next door.

Pompeii and Herculaneum

There's a reason why **Pompeii** is the most famous of Vesuvius' victims. It may not be as well preserved as Herculaneum, but its sheer scale is staggering. Here is an entire Roman town, once home to as many as 20,000 people, ruined yes, but in many ways extraordinarily intact; a city stopped dead in its tracks in AD 79. Much of the wonder of the place is to be had simply by wandering around, looking into ordinary houses. Some of the most prosaic aspects are also the most arresting: tracks on the roads where carts have worn down the stones, shop signs advertizing their wares, mosaics warning you to 'beware of the dog'. *T081 857 5347, www.pompeiisites.org. Apr-Oct 0830-1930, last entrance 1800, Nov-Mar 0830-1700, last entrance 1530. €11, 3-day ticket for Pompeii, Herculaneum, Oplontis and Stabia €20.*

Deep below the level of the surrounding contemporary city, **Herculaneum** (Ercolano) is extraordinarily unscathed; much more than Pompeii's mixture of ash and pumice, Herculaneum's mud solidified and sealed in the town below, preserving organic substance and the upper storeys of houses. *Corso Resina 6, Ercolano, T081 857 5347. Apr-Oct 0830-0730, last entry 1800, Nov-Mar 0830-1700, last entry 1530. €11.*

Sleeping

Costantinopoli 104 €€€
via S Maria di Costantinopoli 104, T081 557 1035, www.costantinopoli104.com.
Near piazza Bellini, this pristine and stylish place has a tranquil courtyard garden with a small pool. Don't miss one of its famously good breakfasts.

Caravaggio €€
piazza Riario Sforza 157, T081 211 0066, www.caravaggio hotel.it.
Modern rooms in a 17th-century building. Cosy feel and amiable staff.

Soggiorno Sansevero €€
piazza S Domenico Maggiore 9, T081 790 1000, www.albergosansevero.it.
In the heart of the Centro Storico, large rooms in a handsome old palazzo at a good price.

Albergo Bellini €
via San Paolo 44, T081 456 996.
This small, exceptionally welcoming and good-value hotel has an old-fashioned feel.

Donnalbina7 €
via Donnalbina 7, T081 1956 7817, www.donnalbina7.it.
Minimalistic, classy and chic but also welcoming and cosy, Donnalbina7 offers the best value in the city.

Eating

Pizzeria Brandi €€€
salita Sant'Anna di Palazzo 1-2, T081 416 928.
Daily 1230-1500, 1930-0100.
Inventors of the ubiquitous pizza Margherita. Also has a selection of traditional Neapolitan fare.

Caffè Letterario Intra Moenia €
piazza Bellini 70, T081 451 652.
Daily 1000-0200.
A literary café with a decent menu and a cultured atmosphere. Exhibitions, literary meetings, concerts and poetry evenings happen here and there's also internet access.

Da Michele €
via Sersale 1, T081 553 9204.
Mon-Sat 1000-2400.
The purists' pizzeria supreme. There are two choices, Margherita or Marinara, and service is lightning quick with no frills.

La Cantina di Via Sapienza €
via Sapienza 40/41, T081 459 078.
Mon-Sat 1200-1530.
Great home cooking in a popular lunch-only eatery. A delicious bowl of penne aum aum, with

tomato aubergine and mozzarella, is only €2.90.

La Vecchia Cantina €
vico San Nicola alla Carità 14, T081 552 0226.
Mon and Wed-Sat 1200-1600, 1900-2200; Sun 1200-1600.
Busy, traditional family place with lots of good fish dishes and exquisite torta caprese.

Osteria della Mattonella €
via G Nicotera 13, T081 416541.
Mon-Sat 1300-1500, 1930-2330.
Tucked away up the hill from the piazza del Plebiscito. You may need to knock on the door and wait to be let in. Fast, friendly and informal service combined with fairly simple but delicious Neapolitan fare.

Nightlife

Areas which buzz until late are: around piazza Bellini and via Benedetto Croce in the Centro Storico; Borgo Marinari (in summer), by the Castel dell'Ovo; Chiaia, mainly to the west of piazza dei Martiri; and Mergellina.

Bar Gambrinus, via Chiaia 1 (piazza Trento e Trieste), T081 417 582, 0800- 0130, is Naples' most refined bar and worth a visit for the luscious Liberty interior and the exceedingly good cakes.

Travel essentials

Getting there
Naples Airport, T081 789 6259, www.gesac.it, is 5 km from the centre. Alibus runs every 20 mins to piazza Garibaldi (central train and bus station) and piazza Municipio, by the port (€3). There's also an ordinary city bus, the C58, from the airport to Piazza Garibaldi (returning, it departs from Corso Navara, €1.10) Taxis to Centro Storico costs around €20. International trains, including sleeper services from Paris, arrive at **Napoli Centrale station**, piazza Garibaldi, northeast of the centre.

Getting around
The city is a fairly manageable size and, despite the crazy traffic, walking is the best way to get around the Centro Storico. There are also useful bus routes: R2 goes from piazza Garibaldi along corso Umberto I to piazza Trento e Trieste; R3 from piazza Carità to Mergellina past piazza Trento e Trieste and the Chiaia seafront; R4 north from the port to the Museo Archeologico. Linea 2 of the metro is useful for connecting piazza Garibaldi to Montesanto, Chiaia (piazza Amadeo) and Mergellina. For travel information on the city and local area, see www.unicocampania.it. Tickets, valid for 90 mins, cost €1.10 each but it's also possible to buy a day ticket (Giornaliero) for €3.10 (€2.60 at weekends). Four **funicular railways** go to Vomero, Centrale (via Toledo to piazza Fuga), Chiaia (via del Parco Margherita to via Cimarosa), Montesanto (piazza Montesanto to via Morghen) and Mergellina (via Mergellina to via Manzoni). The **Circumvesuviana**, T081 772 2444, runs from Naples' piazza Garibaldi around the bay to Sorrento every 30 mins, stopping at Torre Annunziata (for Oplontis), Pompeii (Pompei Scavi) and Herculaneum (Ercolano). A daily ticket costs €6.40.

Tourist information
Azienda autonoma di soggiorno, cura e turismo, piazza del Gesù, T081 552 3328, www.inaples.it. Mon-Sat 0900-2000, Sun 0900-1500. **Osservatorio Turistico-Culturale del Comune**, Portico di San Francesco di Paola, piazza Plebiscito, T081-247 1123. Mon-Fri 0900-1900, Sat 0900-1400. The useful bilingual monthly publication, *Qui Napoli*, is free and full of up-to-date information.

Ratings

Art and culture ☆☆☆☆☆
Eating ☆☆☆☆
Nightlife ☆☆
Romance ☆☆☆☆
Shopping ☆☆☆
Sightseeing ☆☆☆☆☆
Value-for-money ☆☆☆
Overall city rating ☆☆☆☆

Nice

Nice is justly described as the Queen of the Riviera. The city is blessed with 300 days of sun per year and boasts all the trappings derived thereof: rows of palm trees, pavement cafés on every corner and a medley of outdoor markets.

A clement climate has been the historical constant in this city of 350,000. In ancient times, Greeks and Romans came, saw and planted olives and vines. Medieval governorship under the Turin-based House of Savoy gifted the city its Italianate architecture, a ritzy cathedral, the Ligurian-style native cuisine and a hefty dose of *la dolce vita*. At the turn of the century Nice became the Côte d'Azur's tourism hub, as Europe's nobility followed Queen Victoria on her long winter vacations to the bourgeois suburb of Cimiez. Painters including Matisse and Chagall succeeded onto this exclusive stage, creating an art-filled legacy that runs at full force today.

The 4km-long Promenade des Anglais wraps Nice's southern flank and epitomises the city's liberal ethic. This seaside walkway is a daily procession of strollers and sightseers, 'bladers and bikers, joggers and snoggers. By night it's similarly *en fête*. A postprandial pageant of buskers, beer hawkers and wide-eyes visitors wander along the prom'. Down below, drums, guitars and impromptu singsongs chorus from the seashore, while games of beach volley are played into the early hours. Nice is alfresco, decadent, and a touch showy, and doesn't worry about getting up in the morning.

Port diving.

At a glance

Hemmed in by the Mediterranean to the south, the **Promenade des Anglais** runs right along this stretch of sea. Planes and private jets glide almost overhead and land at the airport at its western end, while sailboats, yachts and ferries to Corsica putter out from the **Nice Port** at its eastern extremity. But Nice's main action emanates out from **Old Town**, or Vieux Ville. A warren of pastel hues and lavender-blue shutters, it serves as a picturesque reminder of Nice's Italian connections.

Marking a loose border between the Old Town and the Promenade is the venerable **Cours Saleya**. This avenue of much-coveted mansions starts with the golden façade of Matisse's former home, passes westwards through lines of fruit and vegetable stalls, then stops at the daily flower market just before Nice's rococo opera house. At lunchtime, the market pitches give way to the outdoor tables of the surrounding restaurants, which in turn become aperitif spots in the evening, and dining terraces at night. The **Colline du Chateau** towers above, a vast public park with a children's funfair, *boules* runs and astounding views. This panorama takes in the suburb of **Cimiez** in northern Nice, where the museums of Chagall and Matisse are dotted around the Roman archaeological ruins of Nikaia, the original settlement from which Nice takes its name.

The recently renovated **Place Massena**, spliced by Nice's new tramline, lies at the city's geographical heart. Several public parks radiate out from it, as does the wide shopping boulevard of **Avenue Jean Médécin**. At the end of the road lies the Gare SNCF, where trains for Antibes, Monaco and Cannes – and even Paris, Milan and Brussels – wind their way past every half-hour or so.

Nice Old Town

It's not just stores selling Niçois-style home-made pasta and *pistou* pesto sauce that remind visitors of life across the Italian border. Those taking an evening *passeggiata* along these narrow lanes may notice other influences including local dialect Nissart, a Ligurian tongue, shouted from window to window as you wander beneath. The Old Town's crowning glory, the Italian-styled **Cathédrale Sainte-Réparate** on place Rossetti, is a baroque gem adorned with towering frescoes.

Decades ago guidebooks warned against visiting this area after dark, it being generally perceived as a warren of prostitutes, drug dealers and vice. These seedy elements have slowly been replaced by one-off boutiques and scores of galleries. The best of these art studios line **rue Droite**, which bisects the old city from north to south. Also along this pretty street is the **Palais Lascaris**, *15 rue Droite, Wed-Mon 1000-1800, free*, one of a dozen palatial dwellings that once belonged to local nobles, and the only one open to the public. Inside the restored mansion are heavy frescoes, statuary and 17th century *objets d'art.*

Bathed in the sunshine a block back from the beach is the **Cours Saleya**, the Old Town's most prestigious street. This café-strewn avenue is lined with plane trees and hosts a colourful organic fruit and vegetable market (Tue-Sun 0700-1230) and a great antiques fair (Mon 0900-1800) where linen, cutlery and ceramics filched from hotels and stately homes across Provence can be found. On the Cours Saleya's seaward side are the **Galerie de la Marine** and the **Galerie des Ponchettes** (59 & 77 quai des Etats Unis, Tue-Sun 1000-1800), two fine art galleries with cracking temporary exhibitions.

Musée Masséna

65 rue de France, T04 9391 1910.
Wed-Mon 1000-1800, free. Map A6/7.

Formerly a neoclassical palace, then a local museum, the Musée Masséna reopened in 2008 as an asset-rich historical study of Nice. The exhibits

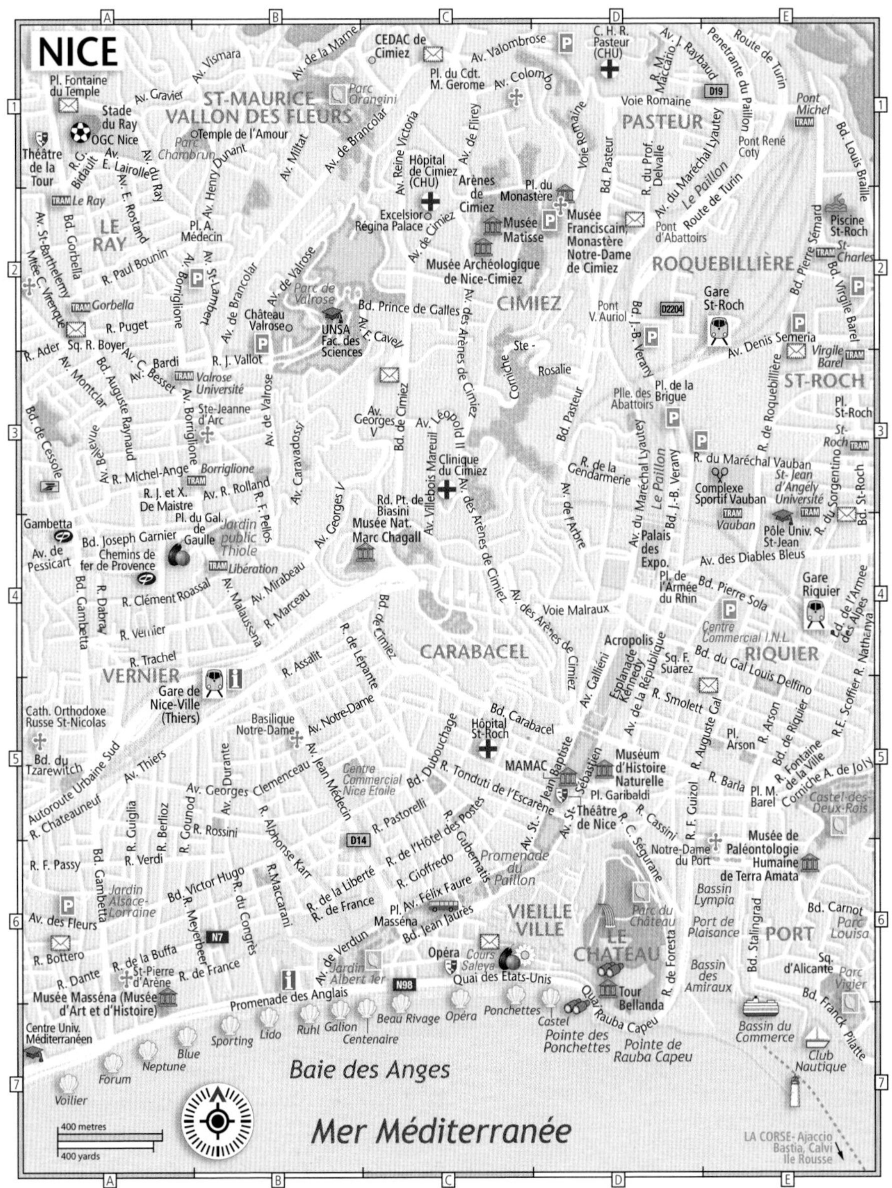
NICE
ST-MAURICE VALLON DES FLEURS
PASTEUR
LE RAY
CIMIEZ
ROQUEBILLIÈRE
ST-ROCH
CARABACEL
VERNIER
RIQUIER
VIEILLE VILLE
LE CHATEAU
PORT
Baie des Anges
Mer Méditerranée
400 metres
400 yards
LA CORSE- Ajaccio Bastia, Calvi Ile Rousse
Gare de Nice-Ville (Thiers)
Gare St-Roch
Gare Riquier
Musée Matisse
Musée Archéologique de Nice-Cimiez
Musée Franciscain, Monastère Notre-Dame de Cimiez
Musée Nat. Marc Chagall
MAMAC
Muséum d'Histoire Naturelle
Musée de Paléontologie Humaine de Terra Amata
Musée Masséna (Musée d'Art et d'Histoire)
Promenade des Anglais
Quai des Etats-Unis
Quai Rauba Capeu
Tour Bellanda
Opéra
Cours Saleya
Promenade du Paillon
Cath. Orthodoxe Russe St-Nicolas
Basilique Notre-Dame
Hôpital St-Roch
Hôpital de Cimiez (CHU)
C. H. R. Pasteur (CHU)
Clinique du Cimiez
Château Valrose
UNSA Fac. des Sciences
Pôle Univ. St-Jean
Centre Univ. Méditerranéen
Palais des Expo.
Acropolis
Théâtre de Nice
Théâtre de la Tour
Stade du Ray
OGC Nice
Complexe Sportif Vauban
Piscine St-Roch
Centre Commercial Nice Etoile
Centre Commercial I.N.L.
Bassin Lympia
Port de Plaisance
Bassin des Amiraux
Bassin du Commerce
Club Nautique
Pointe des Ponchettes
Pointe de Rauba Capeu
Voilier
Forum
Neptune
Blue
Sporting
Lido
Ruhl
Galion
Centenaire
Beau Rivage
Ponchettes
Castel
Jardin Albert 1er
Jardin Alsace-Lorraine
Jardin public Thiole
Parc du Château
Parc Chambrun
Parc Orangini
Parc de Valrose
Parc Vigier
Parc Louisa
Castel-des-Deux-Rois
Chemins de fer de Provence
Gambetta
Excelsior Régina Palace
Arènes de Cimiez
Temple de l'Amour
CEDAC de Cimiez
Av. Jean Médecin
Av. des Arènes de Cimiez
Bd. Victor Hugo
Av. Georges Clemenceau
Bd. Gambetta
Bd. Jean Jaurès
Pl. Masséna
Pl. Garibaldi
Av. de la République
Autoroute Urbaine Sud
Voie Romaine
Voie Malraux
Av. Thiers
Bd. Carnot
Bd. Franck Pilatte

Left: Cathédrale Sainte-Réparate.
Right: Russian Church.
Opposite page: Promenade des Anglais.

are bathed in glorious sunlight – the mansion overlooks the sea and Promenade – not to mention varied and fun. The 1920s era is covered by newspaper accounts of parties at the time, menus from dinner dances, and street plans of which buildings were owned by which particular Russian count or American millionaire. Paintings of Nice from a bygone age and artefacts from the city's famed Carnaval illuminate other periods.

Much is made on the ground floor of the Masséna family, regional aristocrats whose name still cuts ice in Nice (and secures dinner reservations in a jiffy). This empire-style villa was built in 1898 for Victor Masséna, variously a prince, and duke and a local noble. It was designed by Hans-Georg Tersling, who also had a hand designing – among other grand Riviera buildings – Monaco's Hotel Metropole and the Palais Carnoles in Menton.

Musée d'Art Moderne et d'Art Contemporain (MAMAC)

Promenade des Arts, T04 9713 4201, www.mamac-nice.org.
Tue-Sun 1000-1800, free. Map D5.

The MAMAC, as it's affectionately known, is a light-filled steel and glass edifice, surprisingly in harmony with the 300-year-old buildings of place Garibaldi and the Old Town immediately south. The permanent collection chronicles the history of Pop Art and French Modern Art. Andy Warhol is represented (not least in his amusing rejection letters from the New York Museum of Modern Art), as is Robert Indiana (LOVE imagery) and Roy Lichtenstein (of cartoon art fame).

The collections of the so-called Nice school of art include Yves Klein and Niki de Saint Phalle, each of whom have a dedicated room; the former includes a video installation of Klein shocking Paris society by daubing naked ladies with paint, while Saint Phalle's is filled with an army of mirror-covered humanoids. The museum is noted for its strong temporary exhibitions that take up the entire first floor: recent highlights have included Richard Long and Arman.

Russian Church

Av Nicolas II, T04 9396 8802, www.acor-nice.com.
Mon-Sat 0915-1200, 1430-1730, Sun 1430-1730, €3. Map A5.

During the late 19th and early 20th centuries, Russian visitors were as common on the Riviera as they are today. One of their legacies is this onion-topped cathedral, dazzlingly high from the outside, intoxicatingly beautiful – and hazy with incense – on the inside. No expense was spared during its construction during the last days of the tsars; the walls are covered with fine frescoes, tiles from Florence and icons from distant Moscow.

The leafy grounds hum with Russian voices, descendents of the White Russians who patronised the church after its construction in 1912. They mix uneasily with more recent arrivals, however. An ownership dispute puts the old guard, who have regarded the church as their own property since the early Soviet era, on crossed lines with the Russian state, who claim the property and want it back under the rule of the Moscow Patriarchate.

Musée Matisse

164 av des Arènes de Cimiez, T04 9381 0808, www.musee-matisse-nice.org.
Wed-Mon 1000-1800, bus No 15, free. Map C2.

Originally from the Calais region, Matisse had a long-term love affair with Nice. A quote on the wall of this Italianate villa, which serves as France's national Matisse museum, sums up his reason why: "When I opened my window and thought how I was going to have the light before my eyes every day, I couldn't believe my luck". The colourful displays cover his early Parisian period right up to his productive last years when he designed his masterpiece, the Chapelle du Rosaire in Vence, the workings of which form one of the key exhibits here.

In his later days Matisse lived in the fabulous Palais Regina building, a few minutes' walk west of the museum. Indeed, the surrounding *quartier* of Cimiez is decidedly sumptuous. The suburb's stock of art deco mansions lie juxtaposed with Nice's original Roman settlement dotted around the museum, the ruins of which include paved streets and an amphitheatre. The latter becomes a 2000-year-old stage at Nice's annual jazz festival.

Musée National Message Biblique Marc Chagall

Av Docteur Ménard, T04 9353 8731, www.musee-chagall.fr.
Wed-Mon, May-Oct 1000-1800, Nov-Apr 1000-1700, bus No 15, €9.50. Map B4.

Russian-born Marc Chagall was a creative and playful artist. In the words of Picasso: "When Matisse dies Chagall will be the only painter left who understands what colour really is." The museum's permanent collection is devoted to biblical themes, a subject the artist returned to frequently throughout his life. The museum is particularly unique as it was the first in France to be designed by a living artist: an artistic vessel created to display a specific set of artworks. The powerful, vibrant paintings are exhibited exactly as Chagall planned to have visitors view them.

Port and Colline du Chateau

Chateau Park: daily Apr-Aug 0800-2000, Sep 0800-1900, Oct-Mar 0800-1800, free. Map E6.

Nice's elegant Port is home to a historic fishing fleet and more than a few floating gin palaces. Ringed by great restaurants, it's a great place to stroll and generally just hang about on a sunny day. East past the Corsica Ferries terminal, a path descends from the road, leading to a score of sandy coves and grottos on the **Cap de Nice**. This is a locals-only swimming area, and makes a great snorkelling and picnicking spot. A coastal path now winds all the way to the ritzy resort of Villefranche, a blissful two-hour hike.

Also on the Port is the **Quartier des Antiquaires** (most shops open Tue-Sat), hemmed in by rue de Foresta to the west and rue Cassini to the north. Over 100 antique shops trade 1950s Milanese furniture, medieval daggers, vintage musical instruments and contemporary art. The tiny **Marché aux Puces** flea market (Tue-Sun) on place Robilante is less pricey.

Towering above, the **Colline du Chateau** separates the Port from the Old Town. Formerly the defensive bastion of Nice, a cannon still fires off from the top at midday – be aware, it's deafening if you're nearby. Now the Colline is where locals come to read books, jam on guitars and let their children run free in the state-of-the-art playground. The clutch of cafés at the top have cracking views and are a just reward for the climb up from either the Port or the three staircases dotted around the Old Town. Those with pushchairs might prefer to take the elevator next to the Hotel Suisse at the eastern end of the Promenade des Anglais. Of additional interest are the flamboyant graves in the **Christian and Jewish cemeteries**: only the rich and powerful made it up here. Note the preponderance of Italian names on the gravestones, a clue as to Nice's ethnological history.

Musée International d'Art Naïf Anatole Jakovsky

Château Sainte-Hélène, Av de Fabron, T04 9371 7833. Wed-Mon 1000-1800, bus No 8,11, 52, 59, 60, free. Off map.

Anatole Jakovsky was an art critic who put his money where his mouth was. His love of art naïf, or naive art – which essentially translates as vivid, playful and often cartoony images set on canvas or sculpted – inspired his collection of around 600 pieces from the last few centuries. And, very kindly, he gifted it all to the city of Nice, where it now resides in a pink art deco palace, the Château Sainte-Hélène.

Kids will love the bright colours inside, the giant sculptures in the garden and, perhaps best of all, the excellent minigolf course just up the road (Parc Carol de Roumaine, 23 av de Fabron, T04 9321 1338).

Best of the rest

Libération market
Map ??.

Nice's most colourful fruit and vegetable market. Find organic bites, fresh fish and cheese to take home on the plane. Surrounding restaurants are superb.

Théâtre de la Photographie
27 bl Dubouchage, T04-9713 4220, www.tpi-nice.org.
Mon-Sun 1000-1800. Map B2.

Collection of black and white prints of Nice from yesteryear, plus challenging photo exhibitions from the world over, exhibited inside an old movie theatre.

Parc Phoenix
405 Promenade des Anglais, T04 9229 7700.
Apr-Oct 0930-1930, Oct-Mar 0930-1800, €2.
Map (off map).

Tropical wildlife from parrots to butterflies and giant lizards. Find rainforest conditions under a huge glass hemisphere, plus outdoor gardens, streams and lakes. Kids adore it.

Musée Beaux Arts
33 avenue des Baumettes, T04 9215 2828, www.musee-beaux-arts-nice.org.
Tue-Sun 1000-1800, free. Map C6.

The city's fine arts museum is blessed with Rodin sculptures and Raoul Dufy paintings. A few prize exhibits were sadly stolen during an armed robbery in 2007.

Sleeping

Hotels fill up fast each summer, so an advance booking at one of these recommended places is essential. Out of season bargains abound when the crowds disappear. April to June, and September and October, are the optimum months for booking a sightseeing trip. For a week's stay, it's less expensive to book an apartment with a kitchen and balcony. Try Nice Pebbles (www.nicepebbles.com) for options.

Hi Hotel €€€
3 av des Fleurs, T04 9707 2626, www.hi-hotel.net.
Contemporary, industrial style with a rooftop pool and hammam. The nine room concepts – open bathrooms in some, movie projectors in others – are a soothing mix of leather, glass and colourful plastics. Boasts its own sushi bar and Franco-Japanese garden.

Hôtel Windsor €€€
11 rue Dalpozzo, T04 9388 5935, www.hotelwindsornice.com.
A tropical garden complete with parrot and a palm-dappled pool makes for perhaps the most memorable stay in Nice. The Windsor's offbeat elegance includes an Ottoman lounger in the foyer, one-off luxury bedrooms designed by local artists, and a low-key cocktail bar.

Hôtel Suisse €€
5 quai Rauba Capéu, T04 9217 3900, www.hotel-nice-suisse.com.

Panoramas from the Suisse's balconies – over the Baie des Anges, Nice Old Town and the Promenade – mimic the ranging perspectives portrayed in Raoul Dufy's paintings. A recent renovation has lent the guestrooms a comfy sophistication.

Hôtel Villa La Tour €€-€
4 rue de la Tour, T04 9380 0815, www.villa-la-tour.com.
A friendly, family-run guesthouse named for the landmark tower that marks the quietest and most authentic part of the Old Town. Rooms range from romantic to simple; many look out over red-tiled rooftops.

Villa Saint Exupéry €
22 av Gravier, T04 9384 4283, www.vsaint.com.
An award-winning hostel laying claim to every conceivable luxury. A host of complimentary facilities include Wi-Fi, parking, all-you-can-eat breakfast, towels and luggage storage. Comfy single, twin and triple rooms also available.

Eating

Nice is blessed with a fine indigenous cuisine. The surrounding hills are filled with olives, fruit and vegetables reared in a sub-tropical climate, while sea bass, urchins, red mullet, bream and rockfish are sourced from local waters. Thanks to several generations of immigration (it's not just artists, royalty and showbiz stars who have emigrated to the sun) visitors will find classic French cuisine alongside Japanese, Moroccan, Turkish, Russian and all manner of Italian. Dining (or indeed taking an alfresco breakfast) in the Old Town is utterly picturesque, although quality and value in this touristy zone are not the best unless you select one of the restaurants listed below. The Port makes for a pretty alternative as many restaurants have seats lined up by the bobbing boats. For more experimental cuisine try the streets just north of Nice's bus station including rue Gubernatis and place Wilson.

Breakfast

Le Pain à Table €
1 rue Saint-François-de-Paule, T04 9362 9432.
Tue-Sun 0800-2000.
Brunch-time favourite next to the flower market. Take lashings of marmalade, jam, pain au chocolate and café au lait on the outdoor terrace.

Lunch

Bar de la Bourse €
15 place St François, T04 9362 3839.
Mon-Sat 1200-1430.
An Old Town favourite, frequented almost exclusively by locals. The €11 four-course menu is a roller coaster of regional flavours: a kir aperitif to start, followed by grilled sardines, beef stew or grilled rabbit, topped off with a rich dessert. No nonsense *plat du jour* dishes around €8 each.

Brasserie Flo €€
2-4 rue Sacha Guitry, T04 9313 3838, www.flobrasseries.com.
Daily 1200-1430, 1900-2400.
A former theatre with service (silver salvers, bow ties) and OTT decor (red banquettes, chandeliers) that wouldn't look out of place on an Orient Express dining car. Great value *prix fixe* lunches, heavy on raw seafood from the on-site *fruits de mer* counter, plus classic bistro dishes.

Flaveur €€
25 rue Gubernatis, T04 9362 5395, www.flaveur.net.
Tue-Fri 1200-1400 & 2000-2230, Sat 2000-2230.
In 2009, three young chefs heralding from Nice's grander establishments set up this hip restaurant. The result: Provençal dishes modernised with a hint of Far Eastern flavour. *Prix fixe* lunches with wine are a steal at €15.

L'Univers de Christian Plumail €€€
54 bd Jean Jaurès, T04 9362 3222, www.christian-plumail.com.
Tue-Fri 1230-1430, Tue-Sun 1930-2130.
Upmarket, with a summer dining terrace on place Masséna. By night, the single Michelin-starred cuisine is extravagant: dishes based around foie gras, truffles and line-caught sea bass abound. Lunch is lighter and features the excellent value €20 two-course *menu de la semaine*.

Dinner

Chez Pipo €
13 rue Bavastro, T04 9355 8882.
Tue-Sun 1800-2230.
The sole three items on Chez Pipo's menu are all Niçois classics: socca (a chick-pea pancake) *pissaladière* (a local onion and olive pizza) and *anchoïade* (an anchovy laden dip). Tables are communal, house wines inexpensive and tasty.

Rossettisserie Restaurant €€
8 rue Mascoinet, T04 9376 1880.
Tue-Sat 1200-1430 & 1900-2300.
One can smell the roasting meats at this superb rotisserie specialist from nearby place Rossetti. Half chickens (€9), and joints of beef, lamb and pork (all €11), rotate straight from the oven and onto plates, with mashed potatoes, vegetables or frites to accompany. Owner-chef Jean-Michel will box up any main dish as a picnic box for €2 less than the menu price.

La Merenda €€
4 rue Raoul Bosio (no Tel).
Mon-Fri 1215-1400 & 1900-2200.
Award-winning chef Dominique Le Stanc left his Michelin stars at the venerable Negresco hotel to take over this hole-in-the-wall eatery. It's tiny, and there's no telephone for reservations or credit cards. Authentic local dishes, from salt cod to chickpea chips, make this a site of foodie pilgrimage.

Café de Turin €€€
5 place Garibaldi, T04 9362 2952.
Daily 0800-2200.
Le Turin is the literal first port of call for most visiting seafood fans. The plastic tables are served by a team of 20 or so waiters, oyster-shuckers, barmen and *fruits de mer* platter platers: the latter being giant *assiettes* of sea snails, urchins, crab, prawns and clams on ice. A Niçois institution for over a century.

La Voglia €€€
2 rue Saint Françoise de Paule, T04 9380 9916, www.lavoglia.com.
Daily 1200-1430 & 1900-2300.
There are no reservations at this cours Saleya favourite, so give your name to the young Maitre d' and stand by. It's well worth it. Serving bowls of spaghetti with clams, platters of antipasti and Italian desserts of mammoth proportions that simply blow diners away. Formal service in an atmosphere of noisy bustle.

Nightlife

Nice does a great job of being a party town for all people. Distractions vary from casinos to comedy and a healthy reggae scene. However, most visitors limit their nighttime activities to lingering over bottles of rosé, strolling along the Promenade and people-watching on the Cours Saleya, not that you can blame them.

In summer, the city dances all night long. The Tourist Office issues a monthly journal, *Les Plages*, which details every nocturnal event along the coast including firework displays, alfresco opera, open-air cinema screenings, jazz and blues festivals and classical recitals. In Nice, many of the festival-style events are held at the seaside Théâtre de Verdure (Espace Jacques Cotta, T04 9713 3770) and the Roman ruins of Les Arènes de Cimiez.

Cultural events occur year-round, with Nice's grand opera house, *4 rue Saint-François-de-Paule, T04 9217 4000, www.opera-nice.org*, leading the pack. For theatre, classical, ballet and yet more opera, the Acropolis, *Esplanade Kennedy, T04 9392 8300, www.nice-acropolis.com*, has a jam-packed calendar. For original language art house movies try Cinéma Mercury, *16 place Garibaldi, T04 9355 3781*, and the Cinémathèque Acropolis, *3 esplanade Kennedy, T04 9204 0666, www.cinematheque-nice.com*.

Bars are hopping in Nice year-round. For trendy try Bliss Bar, *12 rue de l'Abbaye, T04 9316 8238*, for trashy join the legions dancing on the tables at Wayne's, *15 rue de la Préfecture, T04 9313 4699, www.waynes.fr*.

Predominantly gay club Le Six, *6 rue Raoul Bosio, T04 9362 6664, www.le6.fr* is recommended for an early-hours extravaganza.

Travel essentials

Nice Cote d'Azur airport (T04 9321 3147, www.nice.aeroport.fr) is 5 km (3.5 miles) west of the town centre, along the Promenade des Anglais. According to its 10 million yearly passengers, it's a lesson on how to run a transport hub and a symbol of the easy brilliance of the French Riviera. Floor to ceiling windows flood the terminals with natural light, Wi-Fi is gratis, queues are unheard of, the coffee's great and a cycle track links it with the city centre.

The main players are easyJet, with flights to London, Paris, Berlin, Belfast, Bristol, Brussels, Edinburgh, Liverpool, Newcastle and Rome, and Air France, with links to London, Paris, Corsica and all over mainland France. Most of the world's flag carriers also operate flights to NCE, France's second busiest airport. These airlines include Aer Lingus to Dublin, Aeroflot to Moscow, Alitalia to Rome, BA to London, Delta to New York, Qatar Airways to Doha and Emirates to Dubai. Budget carriers including Flybe, Jet2 and BMIbaby connect some 15 British airports with the Cote d'Azur.

In 2016 the airport will be linked to Nice's newish tram system. Until then, the No 98 bus (0605-2350) run by Ligne d'Azur (T08 1006 1006, www.lignedazur.com) departs every 20 mins during business hours for Nice bus station, the No 99 (0755-2055) for Nice train station. Allow 25 mins for the trip. Tickets cost €4, and are valid for the entire day on the city's trams and buses.

Once downtown, the city is eminently walkable. It's also served by the Vélo Bleu (www.velobleu.org) bike-sharing scheme. One very useful bus route is the No 15, which runs from the bus station to the museums in Cimiez. Heading further afield, the No 100 bus runs from Nice's bus station every 15 mins during peak times to every coastal resort east of the city, including Monaco and Menton; No 200 runs every 30 mins at peak times (very slowly) down the coast in the other direction, passing through Cagnes-sur-Mer, Antibes and Cannes. The speedy coastal train service (T3635, www.voyage-sncf.com) stops at every Riviera hotspot from Grasse to the Italian border every half hour or so.

Tourist Information offices reside at Nice Cote d'Azur airport, Nice-Ville train station and by the beach at 5 Promenade des Anglais (all T08 9270 7407, www.nicetourisme.com).

Ratings

Art and culture ☆☆☆☆☆
Eating ☆☆☆☆☆
Nightlife ☆☆☆☆
Outdoors ☆
Romance ☆☆☆☆☆
Shopping ☆☆☆☆
Sightseeing ☆☆☆☆
Value-for-money ☆☆
Overall city rating ☆☆☆☆

Paris

Not a city for the faint-hearted, Paris engulfs the senses with its vibrant culture, architectural marvels, world-class galleries, stylish shopping, pavement cafés and simply fabulous food. With a list like this, it's hardly surprising that the city has a reputation for arrogance; something that could be called merely confidence in itself as both a historical showpiece and a fearless innovator. While it holds tight to its traditions, this modern city continues magically to evolve. Its essence is an effortless balance of old and new, of traditional elegance and creative thinking: it is Notre Dame through cherry blossom from the quai de la Tournelle and rollerblading to the Paris Plage along the banks of the Seine.

More than ever before, Paris of the 21st century is a feisty brew of peoples from around the world. Old-fashioned French flavours have not been lost, or even submerged – men in berets still play *boules* on the quai de la Seine and bourgeois madames still feed tasty titbits to their poodles from the restaurant table, but now there are more ingredients in the city mix, more viewpoints. (It is estimated that 20% of the two million people living in central Paris are immigrants.)

Twirling seductively to her own special tempo, with the rest of Europe gawping from the sidelines, Paris confidently expects to lead the way but is also not afraid to go against the prevailing wind.

Tour Eiffel.

At a glance

Central Paris is divided into 20 numbered districts (*arrondissements*) and is bisected by the River Seine. At its heart are two small islands – **Île de la Cité** (home to Notre Dame Cathedral) and **Île St Louis**: both are romantic, timeless and great for a stroll. On the **Left Bank** of the Seine (*Rive Gauche*), **St Germain** still has a high concentration of publishing houses and bookshops but tourist chatter has largely replaced debates on Existentialism and Surrealism. The **Latin Quarter**, to the east, is home to the Sorbonne, while the imposing seventh *arrondissement*, to the west, has a number of key landmarks, including the **Eiffel Tower**, **Les Invalides** and the **Musée d'Orsay**. Southwest is **Montparnasse**, once a place of wild entertainment. North of the Seine on the **Right Bank** (*Rive Droit*), the **Louvre** is a big pull for tourists who buzz around the place du Carrousel snapping the glittering **Pyramide** and the green expanse that is the **Jardin des Tuileries**. From here, the **Champs-Elysées**, long synonymous with wealth, sweeps up to the **Arc de Triomphe**. To the east of the Louvre are three adjoining *quartiers*: **Les Halles**, **Marais** and **Bastille**, while, to the north, **Montmartre** sits prettily on a hill, more like a village than anywhere else in the city and home to the fanciful **Sacré Coeur**. Thanks to some canny facelifts the working-class districts of **Belleville** and **Ménilmontant**, to the east, are now the hip places to be once the sun goes down.

24 hours in the city

Get up early and head to the Île de la Cité for **Notre Dame** and the **Sainte-Chapelle**. Linger at the flower market, grab a delicious sorbet from the renowned **Berthillon**, then cross the Pont Neuf to the Left Bank. After a caffeine and philosophy fix in *Café de Flore*, eye up the sculptures at the beautiful **Musée Rodin** or browse for books, antiques and fashion around **place St-Germain-des-Prés**. Treat yourself to lunch at *Ze Kitchen Gallerie* or *Le Hide*, in preparation for one of the great museums: the **Louvre** or the **Musée d'Orsay**, perhaps. In the late afternoon, head for the Marais for window shopping or **Montmartre** for the view. After dark, *Brasserie Flo* is great for dinner, followed by jazz at *Le Petit Journal*. Alternatively, succumb to the lure of the lit-up **Eiffel Tower**, or join the beautiful people drinking the night away at the bars along **rue Oberkampf**.

Île de la Cité and Notre Dame

6 pl du Parvis-de-Notre-Dame, 75001. Cathedral T01 4234 5610; www.notredamedeparis.fr. Mon-Fri 0800-1845, Sat-Sun 0800-1915; free. Tower T01 5310 0700; Apr-Sep daily 1000-1830 (summer weekends until 2300), Oct-Mar daily 1000-1730. €8. Metro Cité. Map E4.

On an island in the Seine, France's most famous place of worship, Notre Dame Cathedral, was built to replace and surpass a crumbling earlier church, on the site where a Roman temple to Jupiter once stood. Pope Alexander III laid the first stone in 1163 and the cathedral took more than 170 years to complete. The building has a spectacular Gothic façade, with a rose window at its western end and magnificent flying buttresses at its eastern end. The nave is at its best when the sun shines through the stained-glass windows, washing it with shafts of light in reds and blues. Place du Parvis de Notre Dame is an epicentre of tourist activity but the gardens at the rear and to the south are comparatively calm. Walk all the way round to appreciate the flying buttresses and the cherry blossoms in spring.

Île de la Cité was once the seat of royal power. Much survives from the original medieval palace complex on the western part of the island, namely the Conciergerie, the Palais de Justice (still the city's law courts) and the glittering jewel of **Sainte-Chapelle**, *4 blvd du Palais, 75001, T01 5373 7852, Mar-Oct daily 0930-1800, Nov-Feb daily 0900-1700, €8*, a chapel built by King Louis IX to house his precious religious relics. Since the early 19th century there has been a colourful and sweet-smelling **Marché aux Fleurs** at place Louis-Lépine, towards the centre of the island (on Sundays the market also sells caged birds and small pets). **Pont Neuf**, the best-loved of all the city's 36 bridges and the oldest (inaugurated in 1607), straddles the Seine at the western end of the island.

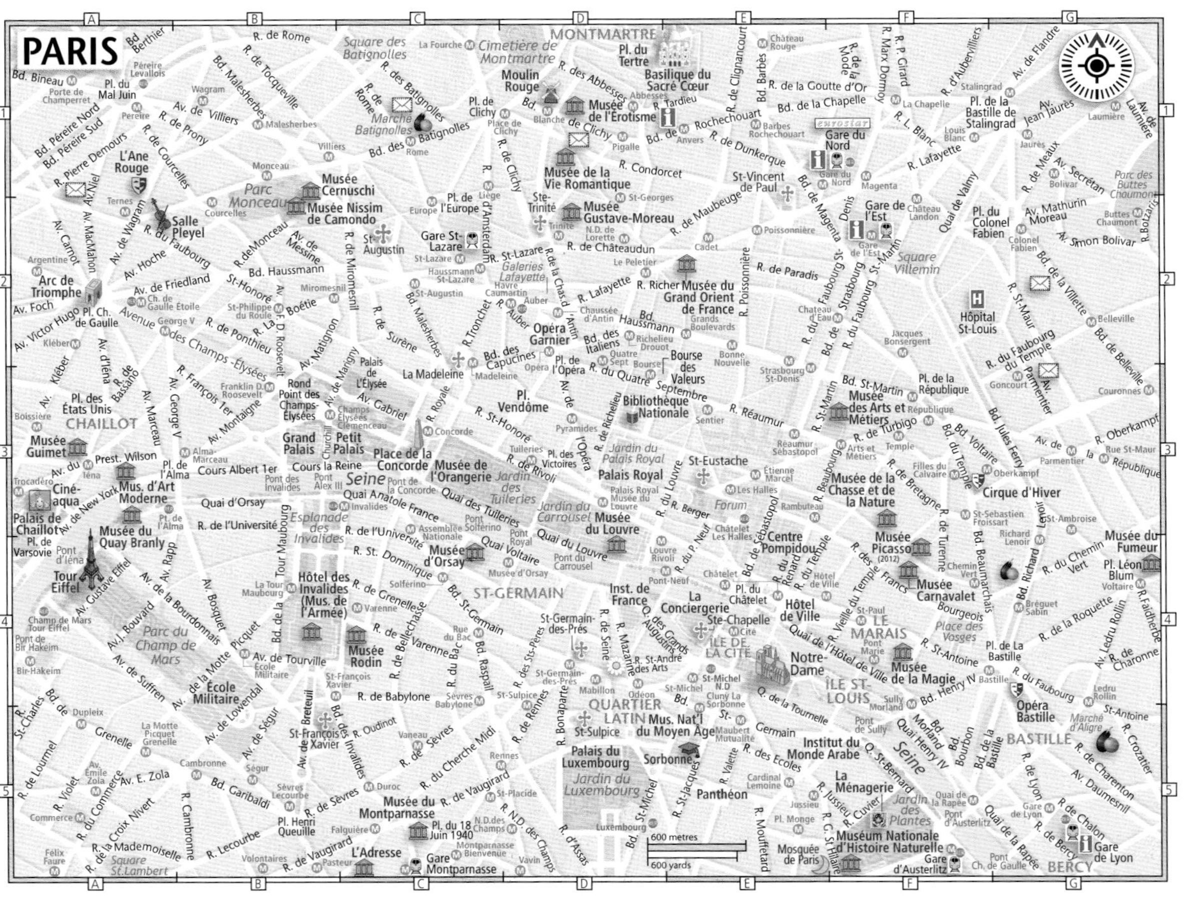
PARIS
MONTMARTRE
Cimetière de Montmartre
Moulin Rouge
Pl. du Tertre
Basilique du Sacré Cœur
Musée de l'Erotisme
Musée de la Vie Romantique
Musée Gustave-Moreau
Gare St-Lazare
Galeries Lafayette
Gare du Nord
Gare de l'Est
St-Vincent de Paul
Square Villemin
Hôpital St-Louis
Pl. de la Bastille de Stalingrad
Pl. du Colonel Fabien
Parc des Buttes Chaumont
Square des Batignolles
Marché Batignolles
Parc Monceau
Musée Cernuschi
Musée Nissim de Camondo
St-Augustin
Salle Pleyel
L'Ane Rouge
Arc de Triomphe
Pl. Ch. de Gaulle
Avenue des Champs-Élysées
Pl. des États Unis
CHAILLOT
Musée Guimet
Ciné-aqua
Palais de Chaillot
Mus. d'Art Moderne
Musée du Quay Branly
Tour Eiffel
Parc du Champ de Mars
École Militaire
Esplanade des Invalides
Hôtel des Invalides (Mus. de l'Armée)
Musée Rodin
Grand Palais
Petit Palais
Rond Point des Champs-Élysées
Palais de l'Élysée
Place de la Concorde
Musée de l'Orangerie
Jardin des Tuileries
Jardin du Carrousel
Seine
Musée d'Orsay
ST-GERMAIN
Musée du Louvre
Palais Royal
Jardin du Palais Royal
La Madeleine
Pl. Vendôme
Opéra Garnier
Bourse des Valeurs
Bibliothèque Nationale
Musée du Grand Orient de France
St-Eustache
Forum
Centre Pompidou
Musée de la Chasse et de la Nature
Musée des Arts et Métiers
Pl. de la République
Cirque d'Hiver
Musée Picasso (2012)
Musée Carnavalet
Place des Vosges
LE MARAIS
Musée de la Magie
Hôtel de Ville
La Conciergerie
Ste-Chapelle
ÎLE DE LA CITÉ
Notre-Dame
ÎLE ST-LOUIS
Inst. de France
St-Germain-des-Prés
St-Sulpice
QUARTIER LATIN
Mus. Nat'l du Moyen Âge
Sorbonne
Panthéon
Palais du Luxembourg
Jardin du Luxembourg
Institut du Monde Arabe
La Ménagerie
Jardin des Plantes
Muséum Nationale d'Histoire Naturelle
Mosquée de Paris
Musée du Fumeur
Pl. Léon Blum
Pl. de La Bastille
Opéra Bastille
BASTILLE
Marché d'Aligre
Gare de Lyon
BERCY
Gare d'Austerlitz
Musée du Montparnasse
Pl. du 18 Juin 1940
L'Adresse
Gare Montparnasse
Square St.Lambert
600 metres
600 yards

Tour Eiffel

Champ de Mars, 75007, T01 4411 2311, www.tour-eiffel.fr.
Mid Jun-Aug daily 0900-0045; Sep-mid Jun daily 0930-2345. Lift to Levels 1-2 €8.10, Level 3 €13.10; stairs to Levels 1-2, €4.50. Metro Bir Hakeim. Map A4.

Gustav Eiffel won a competition to design a 300 m tower for the Universal Exhibition of 1889. The result was originally reviled by Parisians and was only meant to stand for 20 years; now it's the city's most identifiable landmark. The highest viewing platform is at 274 m and, on a clear day, you can see for more than 65 km. Take the stairs to the first level, with a bistro and the cineiffel museum, which recounts the tower's history on film; on the second level, there are souvenir shops and Alain Ducasse's gourmet restaurant, Jules Verne. To avoid long queues (at least an hour), visit early in the morning or late at night, when the tower is lit up like a giant Christmas tree.

Les Invalides

Metro Invalides, Latour Maubourg. Map B4.

The seventh arrondissement breathes extravagance from every pore. Expect 19th-century elegance and grandeur rather than quaint backstreets and curiosities. The avenues, mansions and monuments proclaim their importance. Wander rues de Grenelle, St Dominique and Cler, east of the Champ-de-Mars, to see where high society shops and dines.

Sitting splendidly amid the broad avenues is **Hôtel des Invalides**, *129 rue de Grenelle, 75007, T08 1011 3399, www.invalides.org, daily 1000-1800 (till 1700 in winter), closed first Mon of month, €9, Metro Latour Maubourg, Varenne,* Louis XIV's hospice for war veterans. The vast Army Museum now charts French military history from prehistoric times to the present. The Église du Dôme is the final resting place of France's vertically challenged Emperor, Napoleon.

Around the corner, **Musée Rodin**, *77 rue de Varenne, 75007, T08 4418 6110, www.musee-rodin.fr, Tue-Sun 1000-1745, €6,* is housed in the light and airy 18th-century Hôtel Biron – the sculptor's last home. There are over 500 of Rodin's pieces here, as well as works by Camille Claudel (his model and lover) and Rodin's own collection of paintings, including work by Van Gogh. A wander through the sculpture-filled **gardens**, *€1,* is equally delightful.

Musée d'Orsay

1quai Anatole France, 75007, T01 4049 4814, www.musee-orsay.fr.
Tue, Wed, Fri, Sat, Sun 0930-1800, Thu 0930-2145 (last entry 45 mins before closing). €8, €10 for temporary exhibitions. Metro Solferino. Map C4.

This 1900 train station-turned-art gallery is worth visiting almost as much for the building as for the great Impressionist treasures it holds. The enormous space is enhanced and illuminated by a vaulted iron-and-glass roof. There are decorative arts and Rodin sculptures on the middle level, with the most popular works, by the likes of Monet, Cézanne, Degas and Signac, on the upper level. Visit during the week to avoid the crowds.

Jardin du Luxembourg

rue Guynemer and blvd St Michel, 75006, T01 4234 2000.
Summer daily 0730-1 hr before sunset; winter 0815-1 hr before sunset. Metro Notre Dame des Champs. RER Luxembourg. Map D5.

The lovely Luxembourg gardens cover more than 23 ha of the Left Bank. Their centrepiece, in front of the Luxembourg Palace, is the octagonal pool, surrounded by wide paths, formal flowerbeds and terraces. On the eastern side of the garden, accessed by boulevard St Michel, is the Médicis Fountain, an open-air café and ice cream sellers. From April to August there are free daytime musical concerts at the bandstand.

In the western section, towards rue Guynemer, there is an adventure playground and a puppet theatre. Photo exhibitions are often suspended along the garden's iron railings. Bartholdi's Statue of Liberty here is a smaller model of the one given to the United States in 1885.

Musée du Louvre

Palais du Louvre, 75001, T01 4020 5151, www.louvre.fr.
Fri-Mon 0900-1800, Wed, Fri 0900-2145. €9.50, €6 after 1800. Free 1st Sun of month. Ticket-holders can enter via Passage Richelieu. Metro Palais Royal. Map D4.

Paris's foremost art gallery is as vast as it is famous. It was constructed as a fortress in the 12th century, lived in as a palace by the late 14th century, rebuilt in the Renaissance style in the 16th century and finally converted into a museum by Napoleon. The wonderful glass pyramid entrance by I M Pei was added in 1989. Today the four floors of the three wings (Sully, Denon and Richelieu) hold some 350,000 paintings, drawings, sculptures and other items, dating from 7000 BC to the mid-19th century. Highlights include *Vénus de Milo* (2nd century BC), Rubens' *Life of Marie de Médici*, Italian sculpture in the Michelangelo Gallery and, of course, the crowd-pulling *Mona Lisa*.

Champs-Elysées and Arc de Triomphe

pl Charles de Gaulle, 75008, T01 5537 7377.
Apr-Sep daily 1000-2300; Oct-Mar daily 1000-2230. €9. Free first Sun of month. Metro Charles de Gaulle-Etoile. Map A2.

The Champs-Elysées has been an international byword for glamorous living since the 19th century. The eponymous avenue is Paris's 'triumphal way', leading from the vast **place de la Concorde** to the **place Charles de Gaulle**, site of the **Arc de Triomphe**. The arch has always been the focus of parades and celebrations: Napoleon's funeral procession was held here in 1840, as were the victory celebrations of 1919 and 1944, and it's the finishing point of the Tour de France cycle race. In recent times Parisians have been snooty about the surrounding tackiness but it seems that the area's fortunes are on the up. Culturally and commercially, the area is undergoing a mini-makeover, with an influx of new restaurants, designer shops and exhibition centres.

Les Halles

With its trendy boutiques, historic squares, hip hang-outs and aristocratic- mansions-turned-

museums, the Rive Droite is now fashionable and, in parts, smart. It has its low points too – the eyesore of Forum des Halles and brazenly drunken rue de Lappe in Bastille – but the good far outweighs the questionable. A highlight is the **Centre Pompidou**, *pl Beaubourg, 75004, T01 4478 1233, www.centrepompidou.fr, €12, Wed-Mon 1100-2100, €10 for exhibitions, permanent exhibitions free on the 1st Sun of the month, Metro Rambuteau*, an architectural masterpiece of the late 1970s that still brings a buzz to the surrounding area. The multi-coloured fun carries on with the funky fountains in the neighbouring place Igor Stravinsky, and there are plenty of galleries to choose from along rue Beaubourg and rue Quincampoix.

Marais

Metro Chemin Vert, St Sébastien Froissart. Map F4.

Sandwiched between Les Halles and Bastille is **Marais**, everybody's favourite place for aimless wandering, thanks to its winding medieval streets, charming tea rooms and ultra-fashionable shops.

The showpiece is **Place des Vosges**, *Metro St Paul*, a beautiful 17th-century square of arcaded buildings. Rue des Rosiers, a resolutely Jewish street, has bakeries, kosher restaurants and falafel takeaways, while the city's unabashedly gay centre is around rue Vieille-du-Temple and rue des Lombards.

Bastille

Metro Bastille. Map G5.

The winds of regeneration that the Pompidou Centre blew into Les Halles, brought the new **Opéra Bastille** to the Bastille just over a decade later. This gritty, working-class area has emerged as an after-dark hotspot and bastion of designer outlets but it still clings to its revolutionary credentials: raucous protests and demonstrations are a common sight on place de la Bastille. For a glimpse of the grittier side of life, away from trendy rue de la Roquette and rue du Fauboug St Antoine, head to the utterly authentic **Marché Aligre**, *place d'Aligre, 75012, Tue-Sat 0800-1300, 1600-1930, Sun 0800-1400, Metro Ledru Rollin*, and the surrounding streets, where old-style bars full of red-faced locals are still the norm.

Basilique du Sacré Coeur

Parvis du Sacré Coeur, 75018, T01 5341 8900. Daily 0600-2300 (dome and crypt 0900-1900, winter until 1800). Church free, dome €8. Metro Anvers, Lamarck-Caulaincourt, Abbesses plus funiculaire. Map E1.

It was the Romans who first erected a place of worship on top of this hill to the north of the city. They beheaded Denis, the first bishop of Paris, here in the third century AD. He was canonized as a result and the hill became the 'Mont des Martyrs' for early Christians. The current basilica – a glorious flurry of domes or a fanciful abomination, depending on your point of view – was designed by Paul Abadie and financed largely by national subscription. It took nearly 40 years to build, finally being consecrated in 1919, and now attracts some five million visitors each year. Inside, a golden Byzantine mosaic of Christ by Luc Olivier Merson hovers beatifically over the high altar. The spiral staircase to the dome is worth tackling, if you're partial to a long view, but you can enjoy a similar panorama from the steps of the basilica – along with the crush of tourists, hustlers and pigeons.

Best of the rest

Île St Louis
75001. Metro Pont Marie, Sully Morland.
This island on the Seine is like stepping into a film set for the 17th century.

104 Cent Quatre
104 rue d'Aubervilliers, 75019, T01 5335 5000, www.104.fr. Tue-Sat 1100-2100 (until 2000 Sun). €5. Metro Stalingrad, Riquet.
The city's latest contemporary art space housed in a vast old funeral parlour. Cutting edge instillations and new media art abound.

Canal St Martin
75010-75019, 4. Metro République for quai de Valmy, Stalingrad for quai de la Seine.
The canal was built in the 19th century as a shortcut on the Seine. Its most attractive sections have footbridges and barges.

Musée Jacquemart-André
158 blvd Haussmann, 75008, T01 4562 1159, www.musee-jacque mart-andre.com. Daily 1000-1800. €10. Metro Miromesnil.
In 1872 the portrait artist Nélie Jacquemart painted Edouard André. Nine years later they were married and living in this magnificent mansion on boulevard Haussmann.

Cimetière du Père Lachaise
16 rue Repos, 75020, T01 4370 7033, Nov-mid Mar, daily 0800-1730, mid Mar-Nov, daily 0800-1800. Free. Metro Père Lachaise, Gambetta.
The most celebrated cemetery in France and last resting place for the likes of Jim Morrison, Edith Piaf, Frédéric Chopin, Honoré de Balzac and Oscar Wilde, to name but a very few.

Sleeping

Hotels near the big sights are expensive, but there are popular, mid-priced options on rue Saint-Dominique, squeezed between the Eiffel Tower and Les Invalides. The bustling streets of Marais or St Germain also have some good hotels. There are romantic corners on Île St Louis and in Montmartre, while Bastille and Oberkampf are good for night owls.

Hôtel Bourg Tibourg €€€
19 rue du Bourg Tibourg, 75004, T01 4278 4739, www.hotelbourgtibourg.com.
Metro St Paul, Hôtel de Ville.
This wonderful Marais hotel is a Costes/Jacques Garcia masterpiece. The French designer has lived in the Marais for over 20 years. The rooms are exquisitely intimate and deluxe, seamlessly combining French and Oriental influences.

Villa Madame €€€
44 rue Madame, 75006, T01 4548 0281, www.hotelvillamadameparis.com.
Metro Saint-Sulpice.
Plush St Germain hideaway with board games, iPod docks and international magazines should Paris overwhelm.

The Seven Hotel €€€
20 rue Berthollet, 75005, T01 4331 4752, www.sevenhotelparis.com.
Metro Gobelins.
Wow-factor gadget-filled hotel with its own 007 suite (entire Bond DVD catalogue in the drawer). Less expensive rooms with floating baths plus light and sound shows. Awing guests since 2010.

Apostrophe Hotel €€€
3 rue de Chevreuse, 75006, T01 5654 3131, www.apostrophe-hotel.com.
Metro Vavin.
Urban chic concept hotel with 16 individually designed rooms: try the travel diary suite, the graffiti room or the paradise room for starters.

Hôtel Beaumarchais €€
3 rue Oberkampf, 75011, T01 5336 8686, www.hotelbeaumarchais.com.
Metro Filles du Calvaire, Oberkampf.
Primary colours and friendly staff the defining feature of this buzzing 33-room hotel.

Hôtel Danemark €€
21 rue Vavin, 75006, Montparnasse, T01 4326 9378, www.hoteldanemark.com.
Metro Vavin.
An elegant and welcoming hotel on a lively street, lined with little cafés and shops. Rooms are smart, cosy and excellent value.

Hôtel des Deux-Îles €€
59 rue St Louis en l'Île, 75004, T01 4326 1335, www.deuxiles-paris-hotel.com.
Metro Pont Marie.
Welcoming and comfortable on Paris's most idyllic island. Specify if you want a bath rather than a shower.

Hôtel Luxembourg €€
4 rue de Vaugirard 75006, T01 4325 3590, www.hotel-luxembourg.com.
Metro Odeón. 33 rooms.
Popular choice in Louis XIV building. Contemporary baroque interiors with far-out frescoes in rooms. Petite garden to rear. Great location right by the eponymous gardens and the Sorbonne.

Hôtel Jules €€
49-51 rue La Fayette, 75009, T01 4285 0544, www.hoteljules.com.
Metro Peletier.
This recent to the city's hip hotel scene is so '60s and so sexy, decked throughout with vintage furniture, Bakelite objet d'art and a trippy throwback foyer.

Grand Hôtel Lévêque €
29 rue Cler, 75007, T01 4705 4915, www.hotel-leveque.com.
Metro École Militaire, La Tour Maubourg.
Located in a market street, offering clean rooms, most with en suite bathroom. Singles and triples available.

Hôtel Esmeralda €
4 rue St-Julien- le-Pauvre, 75005, T01 4354 1920.
Metro St Michel.
A budget option with character.

Try to ignore the wonky bedside tables, the curling wallpaper and the tired breakfast room.

Eating

Breakfast

Le Comptoir du Commerce €€
1 rue des Petits Carreaux, 75002, T01 4236 3957, www.comptoirdu commerce.com.
Mon-Sat 0800-2400, Sun 1200-1900. Metro Sentier.
Pine walls and shutters and cushioned seating create a country kitchen ambience. Good range of breakfasts.

Café de Flore €
172 blvd St Germain, 75006, T01 4549 3129, www.cafe-de-flore.com.
Daily 0730-0100. Metro St-Germain-des Prés.
Renowned as an unofficial philosophical forum, the Café de Flore retains its intellectual air, although today's thinkers need deeper pockets than their forebears.

Lunch

Le Hide €€
10 rue de General Lanrezac, 75017, T01 4574 1581, www.lehide.fr.
Mon-Fri 1200-1500, 1930-2230, Sat 1930-2230. Metro Étoile.
Brilliant budget concept based on French bistro dishes (escargot, pot au feu) but with a Japanese twist, courtesy of chef-owner Hide Kobayashi.

Les Bouquinistes €€
53 quai des Grands Augustins, 75006, T01 4325 4594.
Mon-Fri 1200-1430, 1900-2300, Sat 1900-2300. Metro St Michel.
One of Guy Savoy's bistros, this place serves popular modern French cooking and overlooks Notre Dame. Healthy-sized portions of quality food, from delectable sea bass to melt-in-the-mouth scallops.

Ze Kitchen Gallerie €€
4 rue des Grands Augustins, 75006, T01 4432 0032.
Mon-Fri 1200-1500, 1900-2300, Sat 1900-2300. Metro St Michel.
Inspirational and inventive, with an emphasis on the nutritious as well as the delicious. The lunchtime menu (€35) can include beef cheeks, Alaskan crab and wasabi ice cream.

Pause Café €
41 rue de Charonne, 75011, T01 4806 8033.
Mon-Sat 0800-0200, Sun 0900-2000. Metro Bastille, Ledru-Rollin.
The relaxed atmosphere, large terrace and good, reasonably priced food have made this a very popular lunch spot.

Dinner

La Fermette Marbeuf €€€
5 rue Marbeuf, 75008, T01 5323 0800, www.fermettemarbeuf.com.
Daily 1200-1500, 1900-2330. Metro Franklin D Roosevelt.
An art nouveau extravaganza

The art of shopping

Shopping is an essential part of the Paris experience, even if it is only of the window variety. Inventive presentation is an art form here, especially among the city's specialist food retailers. **Place de la Madeleine** is renowned for its gourmet shops, including **Fauchon**, Nos 28-30, T01 4742 6011, Mon-Sat 0900-2100, a Parisian institution that sells wine, pastries, chocolates and more. There are also treats to be found on **Île St Louis**, such as the famous sorbets and ice cream at **Berthillon**, 31 rue St Louis-en-l'Île, Wed-Sun 1000-2000, and over 200 varieties of cheese at **La Ferme St-Aubin**, 76 rue St Louis-en-l'Île, Tue-Sun 1000-2000. Don't miss the impressive architecture of the city's department stores and of **Les Galeries**, the 19th-century covered shopping arcades between boulevard Montmartre and rue St Marc. The traditional hotspots for gold-card holders are **rue du Faubourg St Honoré**, rue de la paix, avenue Montaigne and place Vendôme. More recently, designer names have joined the books and antiques around place St-Germain-des-Prés. Smaller, cheaper boutiques are to be found in the **Marais**, the **Bastille** and **Abbesses**. Streets that combine morning food markets (Tue-Sun) and wonderful speciality shops include **rue Cler, rue de Buci**, **rue Lepic** and **Boulevard Raspail**.

with ceramic panels featuring animals and flowers. When booking your table, ask to be placed in the back room, under the glass roof with its delicate stained-glass panes.

Brasserie Flo €€
7 cour des Petites- Ecuries (enter 63 rue du Fg St Denis), 75010, T01 4770 1359.
Daily 1200-1500, 1900-0130.
Metro Château d'Eau.
Excellent food in a wonderful panelled art nouveau dining room. Classic Flo dishes include oysters in a champagne sauce and steak tartare.

L'Arpege €€€
84 rue de Varenne, 75007, T01-4705 0906, www.alain-passard.com.
Mon-Fri 1200-1400, 2000-2230.
Metro Varenne.
The multi-Michelin-starred offering of Paris's most innovative chef, Alain Passard, who sources ingredients from his own private garden. Brilliant.

Nightlife

For up-to-the-minute info on what's on check the listings magazines Pariscope or L'Officiel des Spectacles.

Bars and clubs

Paris has something to suit every taste, from authentic wine bars with red-faced old soaks propping up the zinc counter, to swish venues fit for glamorous celebrities. The **Bastille** is always a popular nightspot, although it can be overrun with tourists. **Oberkampf** is just as lively, but cheaper and more authentic. Nearby **rue St Maur** is getting hotter year by year. A lot of clubs double as live music venues some nights of the week. Many bars also serve food, albeit a limited menu, and there are a growing number of cross-over places. For cocktails hit any of the bar of any upscale hotel listed in this book or try the happy hour at **Fumoir**, 6 rue de l'Amiral Coligny, 75001, T01 4292 0024, www.lefumoir.com, Metro Louvre. More offbeat is the typically **Oberkampf Kitsch**, 10 rue Oberkampf, 75011, T01 4021 9441, Metro Oberkampf. For a Latin-infused blowout dance 'til dawn at **La Java**, 105 rue du Faubourg-du-Temple, T01 4202 2052, www.la-java.fr, Metro Bellville.

Dance and opera

National and international dance troupes regularly come to Paris to perform. **Opéra Garnier**, Palais Garnier, pl de l'Opéra, 75009, T08 9289 9090, www.operadeparis.fr, Metro Opéra, is the principal base of the Ballet de l'Opéra National de Paris, and the best place to see classical ballet and opera favourites. **Opéra Bastille**, pl de la Bastille, 75012, T08 9289 9090, www.operadeparis.fr, Metro Bastille, veers towards more contemporary choices, but for ground-breaking shows, with dazzling sets and musical effects, look no further than **Opéra Comique**, 5 rue Favart, 75002, T01 4244 4540, www.opera-comique.com, Metro Richelieu-Drouot.

Music

If you want a taste of good old-fashioned and newly fashionable chansons, head to **Au Lapin Agile**, 27 rue des Saules, 75018, T01 4606 8587, www.au-lapin-agile.com, Tue-Sun 2100, €24, including one drink, Metro Lamarck Caulaincourt. **L'Olympia**, 28 blvd des Capucines, 75009, T01 5527 1000, www.olympiahall.com, Metro Opéra, is the home of chanson, where Johnny Halliday and Edith Piaf once performed. It still pulls the crowds for a broad range of performers. Jazz lovers, meanwhile, will find blues, strings and brass at **Le Petit Journal Montparnasse**,13 rue du Commandant Mouchotte, 75014, T01 4321 5670, www.petitjournalmontparnasse.com, Metro Montparnasse. **L'Elysée Montmartre**, 72 blvd de Rochechouart, 75018, T01 5507 0600, www.elyseemontmartre.com, Metro Anvers, features acts from all musical backgrounds. Performances start late, so be prepared to sit on the floor and drink beer beforehand. **La Maroquinerie**, 23 rue Boyer,

75020, T01 4033 3505, www.lamaroquinerie.fr, Metro Gambetta, features world acts, from accordion players to flamenco troupes, indie bands to Middle Eastern oud ensembles. For classical music look out for concerts in auditoriums at the **Louvre**, T01 4020 8400, and the **Musée d'Orsay**, T01 4049 4817, as well as the concerts, mainly chamber music, held in churches, including **Sainte-Chapelle**. For a contemporary classical sound, **Cité de la Musique**, 221 av Jean-Jaurès, 75019, T01 4484 4484, www.cite-musique.fr, Metro Porte de Pantin, has a varied programme of jazz, ballet, world music and acoustic.

Travel essentials

Getting there

Eurostar (www.eurostar.com) runs up to 20 trains daily from London Waterloo to **Paris Gare du Nord**. (A few services stop in Calais and Lille en route.) **Charles de Gaulle Airport**, aka Roissy, www.aeroportsdeparis.fr, is 23 km northeast of Paris. The best way into the centre is by the RER B train to Châtelet-Les-Halles (45 mins/€8.40) from Terminal 2, with a free shuttle connection from Terminal 1. There is also the **Roissybus**, T08 3668 7714 (45 mins/€9.40) to rue Scribe, near the Opéra Garnier, or regular, albeit more expensive, **Air France** buses to Porte Maillot, the Arc de Triomphe, the Gare de Lyon and Gare Montparnasse. To reach the city from **Orly Airport**, 14 km south, the best bet is the **Air France** bus to Les Invalides and Montparnasse (40 mins/€11.50). The Orlyval shuttle train (8 mins/€7.40) runs to Antony RER station, from where train (25 mins/€6.10) run into central Paris. Or take the free bus to RER Pont de Rungis and catch the **Orlyrail** train to the city centre (50 mins/€6.60). The RATP **Orlybus** runs to Denfert-Rochereau (30 mins/€5.80). Ryanair flies to **Paris Beauvais Airport**, www.aeroportbeauvais.com, to the northwest of the city, from where there's a shuttle bus to Porte Maillot (1 hr 15 mins/€15). **Paris Airports Service**, T01 5598 1080, www.parisairportservice.com, will pick up from your hotel and charge €25 per person to either CDG or Orly airport (half the cost of a taxi), or less for small groups travelling together.

Getting around

Note that the last two digits of a Paris postcode indicate the *arrondissement*. Central Paris is walkable but you will almost certainly need to use the **metro** system at some point. There are 16 numbered lines, plus the small cable car (*funiculaire*) up to the Sacré Coeur. Trains run daily 0530-0120. Numbered buses ply the streets daily 0630-2030, with a select few operating a reduced service past midnight. There are fewer **buses** on Sun. Timetables and routes are posted at each bus stop. Always validate your ticket in the machine at the front of the bus when you board. **Tickets** for all of central Paris (Zones 1 and 2) are valid on buses, the metro and RER urban rail. A single costs €1.70; a carnet of 10 tickets is better value at €12. Tickets are sold at metro stations and some tobacconists. There are also a number of **passes** available: *Paris Visite* is valid for 1, 2, 3 or 5 days (€9, €14.70, €20 or €28.90) and can be used throughout Paris and its regions, including Disneyland Paris and Versailles. The pass comes with discount vouchers for certain sights.

Tourist information

Paris Convention and Visitors Bureau, 25 Rue des Pyramides, 75001, T08 9268 3000, www.parisinfo.com, daily 1000-1900. There are other tourist offices at the Gare de Lyon (Mon-Sat 0800-1800), Gare du Nord (daily 0800-1800), Notre Dame (daily 1000-1900) and the Champs-Elysées (daily 1000-1900).

Ratings

Art and culture ☆☆☆☆
Eating ☆☆
Nightlife ☆☆☆
Romance ☆☆☆☆☆
Shopping ☆☆
Sightseeing ☆☆☆☆
Value-for-money ☆☆☆
Overall city rating ☆☆☆

Prague

Visitors get rather poetic when they first clap eyes on Prague. The 'Golden City', the 'Belle of Bohemia' and the 'City of a Thousand Spires' certainly has a lot to live up to, but the reality matches the hype. Prague remained blessedly unharmed during the two World Wars, and the Velvet Revolution of 1989 came to pass without a single shot being fired. This translates into a beautiful city with a stunning showpiece centre: winding, medieval lanes flanked by elegant Gothic, baroque and art nouveau façades. As you wander through Europe's largest castle or over famous Charles Bridge, it's hard to imagine that Prague was off limits to western visitors as little as two decades ago. But time moves quickly in this part of the world: the Czech Republic has been a member of the EU since May 2004 and a new veneer of sophistication is spreading through the capital. Locals aren't surprised; Prague was, after all, at the vanguard of European culture for much of the 19th and early 20th centuries. Vestiges of this past are the main draws today; from the cobbled streets of Staré Město and the haunting atmosphere of the Jewish cemetery to the smoky cellar bars and the graceful concert halls that launched some of Europe's greatest composers. The essence of Prague, however, is something less tangible; getting lost in the medieval Old Town on a foggy evening, or watching the sun set over terracotta roofs and soaring church spires is, quite simply, poetry.

Charles Bridge.

At a glance

The Vltava River, running from south to north through the city centre, neatly splits up the area in which visitors spend most (if not all) of their time. On the right bank is **Staré Město** (Old Town), at the heart of which is **Staroměstské náměstí** (Old Town Square), famous for its astronomical clock. North of here is the old Jewish district of **Josefov**, edged by **Parízská** boulevard. The winding, narrow streets of the Old Town fan out south of Old Town Square, opening up in the southeast at **Václavské náměstí** (Wenceslas Square), site of the 1989 Velvet Revolution. This is the main hub of **Nové Město** (New Town), Prague's business and commercial district. To the north is the busy square, **Náměstí Republiky**, while, to the south, the wide streets hold many of the biggest hotels, restaurants and department stores. Further east is the residential area of **Vinohrady**, once the royal vineyards.

On the other side of the river is **Malá Strana** (Lesser Quarter). This area of 18th-century town houses and palaces is quieter and even more atmospheric than the Old Town, its streets rolling up towards Hradčany, the castle district. **Hradčany** is completely dominated by the magnificent castle complex, with the central road of **Nerodova** (always full of tour groups trudging to the castle) running back down into **Malá Strana**. To the south is the green expanse of **Petřín**, a tranquil, leafy hill topped by a little model of the Eiffel Tower.

24 hours in the city

Start early with a coffee in **Old Town Square** to beat the crowds – the astronomical clock begins its daily whirrings at 0900. Look into the brooding hulk of **Our Lady Before Týn** before striking north along Parízská and into the **Josefov** district. Take a look at the **Old-New Synagogue** and the exhibitions in the **Pinkasova Synagogue** before strolling through the eerily atmospheric **Jewish Cemetery**. For a snack or early lunch, stroll back along Parízská which is lined with cafés and restaurants. Veer west and you'll hit the river and picture-postcard **Charles Bridge**, with its buskers and views of the red-roofed houses of Malá Strana creeping up towards the castle. Once across the bridge, wander along the cobbled lanes centering on **Malostranské náměstí**, the area's busiest square. Lunch at trendy *Square*, before the stiff climb up to the castle. You'll need a good few hours to stroll around the complex, after which you'll have earned a Czech beer at one of the little, smoke-filled pubs in Malá Strana. Continue the traditional theme for dinner at *U Medvídkö*, back in the Old Town, before checking out the live jazz at AghaRTA, Zelezna 16, or catch the Prague Symphony Orchestra at the **X**.

Pražský hrad (Prague Castle)

T224 373 368, www.hrad.cz.

Castle grounds daily Apr-Oct 0500-0000; Nov-Mar 0600-2300. Buildings daily Apr-Oct 0900-1800; Nov-Mar 0900-1600. Combined ticket CZK350. Tram 12, 18, 20, 22 or 23, metro Malostranskă. Map, A/B1.

Prague Castle has dominated the city's skyline for over 1000 years and its sprawling complex merits at least half a day's exploration. The first evidence of a castle here dates back to AD 880 and, over the following millennium, the site became the monarchic and spiritual powerhouse of the country. Today it feels like a walled town and is

Prague Castle.

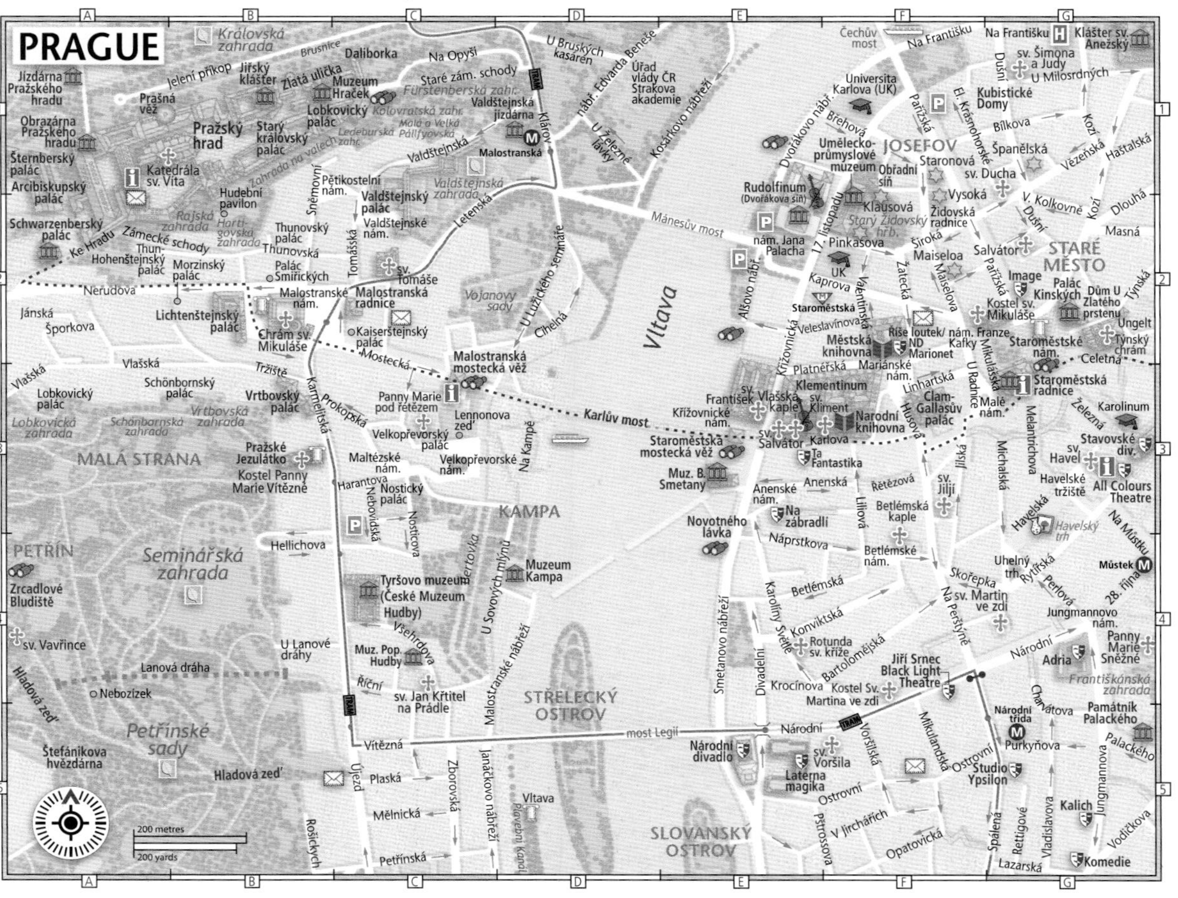
PRAGUE
Vltava
STARÉ MĚSTO
JOSEFOV
MALÁ STRANA
KAMPA
PETŘÍN
STŘELECKÝ OSTROV
SLOVANSKÝ OSTROV
Karlův most
Mánesův most
most Legií
Čechův most
Pražský hrad
Katedrála sv. Víta
Prašná věž
Jelení příkop
Královská zahrada
Jízdárna Pražského hradu
Obrazárna Pražského hradu
Šternberský palác
Arcibiskupský palác
Schwarzenberský palác
Zlatá ulička
Daliborka
Jiřský klášter
Starý královský palác
Lobkovický palác
Muzeum Hraček
Valdštejnský palác
Valdštejnská jízdárna
Valdštejnská zahrada
Malostranská
Klárov
Malostranské nám.
Chrám sv. Mikuláše
Malostranská radnice
Malostranská mostecká věž
Lennonova zeď
Vrtbovský palác
Pražské Jezulátko
Kostel Panny Marie Vítězné
Muzeum Kampa
Tyršovo muzeum (České Muzeum Hudby)
Seminářská zahrada
Petřínské sady
Lanová dráha
Hladová zeď
Štefánikova hvězdárna
Zrcadlové Bludiště
Národní divadlo
Národní třída
Rudolfinum (Dvořákova síň)
Klementinum
Staroměstská radnice
Staroměstské nám.
Týnský chrám
Stavovské div.
Karolinum
Můstek
Muz. B. Smetany
Betlémská kaple
Staroměstská mostecká věž
Novotného lávka
Smetanovo nábřeží
Laterna magika
Jiří Srnec Black Light Theatre
All Colours Theatre
Nerudova
Karmelitská
Újezd
Letenská
Národní
Celetná
Pařížská
Karlova
Husova
Jungmannovo nám.
200 metres
200 yards

reputedly the world's largest castle, its courtyards linking the palace, cathedral, several churches, museums, galleries and a monastery, all beautifully lit up an night.

Your first port of call should be St Vitus' Cathedral (Chrám sv Vita), the seat of the Archbishop of Prague. The interior of this magnificent Gothic structure is delicately lit by a series of mosaic-style stained-glass windows. Look out for **St Wenceslas's Chapel**, resplendent with over a thousand semi-precious stones.

The **Old Royal Palace** (Starý královský palác) is worth seeing for the soaring, empty expanse of Vladislav Hall. It once hosted coronation celebrations; today presidents of the Republic are sworn in here. Wander around the rest of the palace before exiting by **St George's Basilica** (sv Jiří), with its beautifully preserved Romanesque interior, where chamber music recitals are held. Next door is the old monastery, now a gallery.

Behind the monastery is **Golden Lane** (Zlatá Ulička), a cobbled street, lined with 16th-century cottages, today filled with craft shops. (The Prague-born writer, Franz Kafka, briefly stayed at No 22.) At the end of the lane is the **Toy Museum** (Muzeum hraček), *daily 0930-1730, CZK60*, filled with traditional wooden toys and, oddly, hundreds of Barbie dolls. Opposite is **Lobkovicz Palace** (Lobkovický palác), *Tue-Sun 0900-1700, CZK20, CZK40*, with its rambling historical collection. Also worth exploring are the castle gardens, particularly the peaceful **Royal Gardens**, which have beautiful views.

Malá Strana

Tram 12, 18, 20, 22 or 23, metro Malostranskă. Map A3.

This wedge of land between the castle and Vltava River, often bypassed by visitors, is a delightful, atmospheric area of cobbled lanes and crumbling baroque façades. At its heart is **Malostranské náměstí**, a busy square fringed with grand neoclassical houses and elegant colonnades. In the centre is the baroque **St Nicholas church** (Sv Mikuláš chrám), *Mon 1200-1600, Tue-Sat 1000-1600, Sun Mass 1030, 1200, 1500, free, apart from concerts*, built in the early 18th century. Its prominent green dome and tower quickly became a major Prague landmark. The inside is quite overwhelming, awash with hectic, multicoloured frescoes.

Petřín

Tram 6, 9, 12 or 20 to Újezd. Map A4.

A steep funicular railway, dating from the 1891 Jubilee Exhibition, climbs up green and leafy Petřín hill. At the top of the funicular, pause awhile to soak up the views, then follow the path along the old city wall, which passes a rose garden and observatory, to the **Petřín Observation Tower** (Petřínská rozhledna), *Nov-Mar Sat and Sun 1000-1700, Apr daily 1000-1900, May-Sep daily 1000-2200, Oct daily 1000-1800. CZK60.* This 60-m high structure is a small-scale version of the Eiffel Tower, also dating from the Exhibition, with a viewing platform offering fabulous views over rooftops, broken by the soaring silhouettes of dozens of spires. Next door is a small neo-Gothic castle with a mirror maze (same times and prices as tower).

Karlův most (Charles Bridge)

Prague's oldest bridge was founded in 1357 by Charles IV and, for many centuries, was the only link between the right and left banks. Today, it is best known for its dozens of statues, although most of these were added in the 18th century. The car-free bridge is thronged with tourists and buskers at all times of day but, at night, the bridge empties out and takes on a fairytale quality, never more so than in winter, with snowflakes drifting over the water.

Staroměstské náměstí (Old Town Square)

Tram 17 or 18, metro Staroměstská. Map G2.

All roads in Bohemia once led to Staroměstské náměstí, still Prague's most important and jaw-dropping square, a vast cobbled expanse flanked by brightly painted baroque houses. Centrepiece is the Town Hall, home to the extraordinary **Astronomical clock** (Orloj) in a tower to the right. Crowds gather on the hour (0900-2100) to watch the figures shuffle out from little doors. They portray various saints, as well as representations of death, vanity, history and greed – the latter is a dodgy depiction of a Jew clutching money bags, albeit minus his beard, which was removed at the end of the war.

Behind the Town Hall is the looming, blackened church of **Our Lady Before Týn** (Panna Marie pred Týnem), its Gothic hulk hiding a surprisingly pretty baroque interior. In winter, a **Christmas market** selling mulled wine, souvenirs and wooden toys is held on the square.

Above: Astronomical Clock.
Opposite page: St John of Nepomuk statue on Charles Bridge.

Josefov

Tram 17 or 18, metro Staroměstská. Map F1.

Prague's old Jewish ghetto is one of the most atmospheric quarters of the city. It's no longer the warren of old streets depicted by Kafka, but the main sights – four synagogues and the cemetery – remain. A good starting point is the **Old-New Synagogue** (Staranová synagoga), *Cervená 2, Jan-Mar Sun-Thu 0930-1630, Fri 0900-1400, Apr-Oct Sun-Fri 0930-1800, Nov-Dec Sun-Thu 0930-1700, Fri 0900-1400, CZK200*, a squat structure dating from 1275. It still functions as a

Jewish Prague

Before the Nazi occupation from 1939 to 1945, Prague's Jewish population was a thriving community, numbering some 50,000. Today, the number has dwindled to around 4,000. The focal point of the community remains the Josefov district, named after Emperor Josef II, whose 1781 reforms helped bestow civil rights to the Jewish community. The original ghetto actually dated back to the 13th century, although much of it was cleared in a huge late-19th century development project. This drove out the poorer sections of the community and transformed the winding old alleys into smart boulevards, lined with elegant mansions. With the arrival of the Nazis came forced removals, both to a new ghetto in Trezín, 60 km from the city, and, later, to concentration camps; a staggering two thirds of the population is thought to have died in camps before the end of the war. Ironically, what was left of the old ghetto was spared demolition by Nazi forces thanks to Adolph Hitler's chilling wish to preserve the area as an "exotic museum of an extinct race".

synagogue, making it the oldest still in use in Europe. The other sights in Josefov are visited as part of the **Jewish Museum** (Zidovské Muzeum), *T221 711511, www.jewishmuseum.cz, Sun-Fri Apr-Oct 0900-1800, Nov-Mar 0900-1630, CZK300*. The most striking is the **Old Jewish Cemetery** (Starý zidovský hrbitov). Used from 1439 to 1787, it is the oldest and largest Jewish cemetery in Europe. It is a poignant, mysterious place, with hundreds of ancient headstones bristling from the ground at haphazard angles. The adjoining **Pinkas Synagogue** (Pinkasova sinagoga) holds a moving Holocaust memorial, with chilling pictures drawn by children from the Trezín ghetto outside Prague, most of whom were later transported to concentration camps.

Náměstí Republiky (Republic Square)

Tram 3, 5, 14, 24 or 26, metro Náměstí Republiky. Off map.

This busy square, in the east of Nové Město, is worth visiting for the **Municipal House** (Obecní dům), *T222 002101, www.obecnidum.cz*, the city's finest art nouveau building. An exuberantly decorated cultural centre, it was opened in 1912 on the site of King's Court. A restaurant, opulent café and Smetana concert hall are on site. Next door is **Powder Tower** (Prasná brána), *Apr-Sep 1000-2200, Nov-Feb 1000-1800, Oct and Mar 1000-2000, CZK70*, one of a series of towers that once fortified the Old Town and were used to store gunpowder. The sharply pointed medieval tower is the starting point of the Royal Mile, along which Bohemian kings once marched towards their coronation. You can climb to the top for views over Staré Město.

Václavské náměstí (Wenceslas Square)

Tram 3, 9, 14 or 24, metro Muzeum or Můstek. Off map.

Site of the city's most important political protests for the last 150 years, this sloping space is more like a long, divided avenue than a square. Most famously, it was the backdrop to the Velvet Revolution of 1989, when half a million people protested against the government. At the southern end of the square is a statue of St Wenceslas, as well as the vast **National Museum** (see box below).

Statue in the Old Jewish Cemetery.

Best of the rest

National Museum (Národní muzeum)
T224 497111, www.nm.cz, daily 1000-1800, closed on first Tue of every month, CZK150.
This hulking, neo-Renaissance building houses a huge collection of almost 14 million items of natural history, art and music.

Puppet Museum (Marionette Muzeum)
Karlova 12, T222 220 913, www.puppetart.com, daily 1200-2000.
Impressive collection of wooden puppets and a marionette theatre with regular performances (phone for times and tickets). This is also the headquarters of the international puppetry organization, UNIMA.

Church of Our Lady Victorious (Chrám Panny Marie Vítezné)
www.pragjesu.info, Mon-Sat 0930-1730, Sun 1300-1800.
Home of the Infant Jesus of Prague, a 14th-century wax statue measuring 28 cm that was presented to the Carmelites in 1628 and is revered in Catholic countries around the world. Its spangly outfits are changed regularly by the nuns.

Sleeping

Prague is crammed with characterful guesthouses and hotels; those in Staré Město tend to be more expensive, while those in Malá Strana are quieter.

Hotel Aria €€€
Triziste 9, T225 334 111, www.ariahotel.net.
As implied by the name, this is one for music lovers. It's a baroque hotel with a contemporary interior and composer-themed rooms, a comprehensive CD library, a musical director on hand to advise on concert venues in Prague, a music salon and a rooftop café.

Hotel Josef €€€
Rybná 20, Josefov, T221 700 111, www.hoteljosef.com.
Prague's most stylish hotel is a minimalist haven of glass, calm white lighting and the odd splash of colour. Rooms have groovy touches like DVD players and Sony Playstations. Models and rock stars make this their first port of call.

Alchymist Grand Hotel & Spa €€€
Trziste 19, T257 286 011, www.alchymisthotel.com
This magnificent building, dating back to 16th century, stands proudly at the base of Prague Castle. The rooms are both traditional and charming and the restaurant serves some of the city's finest food. A great central location, yet manages to remain quiet.

The Icon €€
V Jame 6, T221 634 100, www.iconhotel.eu
Urban chic in the heart of the city. A top notch team of designers have created an ultra modern, slick and stylish environment within a 19th century building. The hotel's Zen Asian Wellness centre offers up a range of massage treatments to soothe those aching limbs after a busy day of sightseeing.

U Karlova Mostu €€
Na Kampe 15, T257 531 430, www.archibald.cz.
Atmospheric, old-fashioned house just 50 m from Charles Bridge. Cosy rooms with wooden floors and stencilled walls; the room in the attic has a lovely beamed ceiling.

U Zlatého Jelena €€
Celetná 11/Štuparská 6, T222 317 237, www.uzlateho-jelena-prague.com.
Simple, airy rooms with parquet flooring, brass beds and tall windows, just a few steps from Old Town Square. Ask for a room overlooking the quiet courtyard. The staff are friendly and the breakfasts (included in the price) are substantial.

Sir Toby's Hostel €
Delnicka 24, T246 032 610, www.sirtobys.com.
Although not based in the city centre, Sir Tobys is worth the 10-minute tram ride. In return you get a gem of a hostel with friendly staff, a cellar bar and regular events including live music, quizzes, beer tasting and organised tours. Great value and good fun.

Eating

The restaurant scene in Prague has improved immeasurably in recent years; for one thing, pork is no longer the key ingredient in all dishes. Although a traditional meal in a *pivnice* (pub) remains an essential part of a visit to Prague, there are now also a number of top-notch restaurants serving international cuisine.

Breakfast

Au Gourmand €
Dlouhá 10, T222 329 060, www.augourmand.cz.
Upmarket French boulangerie in the Old Town serving a delicious selection of pastries, cakes, snacks and Italian coffees in a cool, tiled interior.

Café Imperial €
Na Poříčí 15, T222 316 012, www.cafeimperial.cz.
Gorgeous high-ceilinged Hapsburg-era café, with tiled walls, rickety furniture and excellent coffee, which is served with free doughnuts in the morning. Breakfast is a big plate of eggs and sausages, and there are more substantial meals throughout the day.

Lunch

Nebozízek €€
Petrínské sady 411, T257 315 329, www.nebozizek.cz.
Brilliant views from this traditional restaurant half-way up the funicular to Petřín, with a bright glass-covered terrace. Good salads and Bohemian onion soup, plus fresh fish and hearty game dishes.

Plzenska Beer Hall Restaurant €€
Republic Square 5, T222 002 770, www.plzenskarestaurace.cz.
Located inside one of Europe's most impressive Art Nouveau buildings, Municipal House. The restaurant is in an old-fashioned beer hall with plenty of atmosphere. The menu offers a wide choice of traditional local fare, washed down with a large glass of frothy Czech beer.

Dinner

Kampa Park €€€
Na Kampě 8b, T296 826 102, www.kampagroup.com.
This is Prague's most sophisticated restaurant, with a heated terrace looking over the river. It has a contemporary menu, complemented by a 150-strong wine list. The cooking is sublime: expect dishes like langoustine ravioli and baby chicken with chanterelles and chorizo.

Cervena tabulka €€
Lodecka 118/4, T224 810 401, www.cervenatabulka.cz.
One of Prague's hidden gems. A cosy little restaurant with two open fires that provide a warm welcome in the winter months. In the summer there is a beautiful little courtyard for dining. The contemporary Czech food is fabulous and the atmosphere is very relaxed.

U Medvídků €
a Perštý§ 7, T224 211 916, www.umedvidku.cz.
This wood-panelled and smoke-filled genuinely old-fashioned beer hall attracts a mix of local regulars and tourists. The food is traditional Czech stodge – pork, dumplings and sauerkraut – perfect for soaking up a few jars of the delicious on-tap Budvar.

Nightlife

The English-language *Welcome to Prague* publication, produced by the tourist office, has basic seasonal information on up-to-date events. Tickets for the majority of venues can be bought online at www.ticketpro.cz or www.ticketportal.cz.

Bars and clubs

Traditional Prague nightlife revolves around top-notch beer and smoky pubs (pivnice), such as **Baráčnická rhychta** (Tržiště 23) in Malá Strana or **Kozicka** (Kozi 1) in Staré Město. The local beer is the main draw, thanks to famous names such as *Pilsner Urquell*, *Staropramen* and *Budvar*. One drawback of these good-value brews is that they attract a profusion of stag parties from the UK. Many bars and pubs now ban such groups from their premises.

Beer aside, many bars offer nightly live music; the jazz scene is thriving and it suits the vaulted, smoky cellars of the Old Town particularly well. The **Prague Jazz Festival** is held every autumn at **AghaRTA**, Zelezna 16, www.agharta.cz.

A number of stylish cocktail bars have sprung up around the city in recent years, not to mention some dodgy Irish-themed pubs, mostly aimed at tourists. To find some of the best of the former, head to the streets around the north of Old Town Square.

Most of the city's nightclubs are yet to undergo a 21st-century style makeover but they continue to pull in the punters until the wee small hours.

Live music

The jazz scene is thriving and it suits the vaulted, smoky cellars of the Old Town particularly well. Music lovers flock to Prague every May for **Prague Spring**, T257 312547, www.festival.cz, one of the world's leading classical music festivals. It has been running since 1946 and attracts scores of symphony, philharmonic and chamber orchestras. It begins every year on 12th May with a performance of Smetana's *Má vlast* (My Country) and closes three weeks later with Beethoven's *9th Symphony*.

High-quality concerts can be enjoyed at other times of year, too. Prague's classical music venues are among the most beautiful buildings in the city. The Prague Symphony Orchestra plays at the **Municipal House**, on Námestí Republiky (see page 172), while the illustrious Czech Philharmonic performs at the splendid **Rudolfinum**, Alsovo nabr 12, T227 059 352, www.ceskafilharmonie.cz.

Performances of opera and ballet are held amid the neo-Renaissance magnificence of the **National Theatre** (Národní divadlo), Národní trída, T224 901448, www.narodni-divadlo.cz; at the opulent **State Opera** (Státní opera), Legerova 75, T296 117111, www.opera.cz, and at the **Estates Theater** (Stavovské divadlo), Ovocný trh, T224 215 001, www.stavovskedivadlo.cz. The latter, a beautiful cream and pistachio building, is Prague's oldest theatre and hosted the premieres of Mozart's *Don Giovanni* and *La Clemenza de Tito* in the 18th century. *Don Giovanni* remains one of the most popular operas performed here to this day.

Travel essentials

Getting there

Ruzyně Airport, www.prg.aero, is 20 km northwest of the centre. Buses run every 20 mins to the city centre, taking 20 mins. Take No 119 to Dejvicka metro station, No 100 to Zlicin metro, and No 179 or No 225 to Nove Butovice metro. CZK26 gets you 75 min on all means of public transport. **CEDAZ**, T220 114 296, www.cedaz.cz, runs a minibus shuttle to Náměstí Republiky (CZK90 per person) every 30 mins daily 0600-2130. Private CEDAZ buses can be booked for up to 4 people and cost CZK480. Taxis from outside the airport terminal should cost from CZK500 to the centre. International trains arrive at Hlavní nádraží, the city's main railway station. Call T840 112 113, or see www.vlak-bus.cz.

Getting around

The Old Town is easy to walk around, as is Malá Strana, although there's a fairly steep climb to the castle. **Dopravní Podnik** (DP), T296 191 817, www.dp-praha.cz, runs Prague's limited **metro** system, extensive **tram** and **bus** network, as well as a funicular train to the top of Petřín hill. The metro system has 3 lines: A (green), B (yellow) and C (red), running daily 0500-2400. Trams operate daily 0430-2400; buses run at similar times. Tram Nos 51-59 and bus Nos 502-514 and 601-603 run at night. The funicular runs daily Apr-Oct 0900-23.30 and Nov-Mar 0900-23.20. Tickets need to be bought before boarding and are available from DP Information offices, some metro stations, tourist information centres and news-stands. The single ticket system is complicated, so visitors are better off buying a 1-,3-, or 5-day pass (CZK100, CZK330, CZK500 respectively). Tickets must be validated in the machines at stops and in metro stations before travel.

Tourist information

Prague Information Office, T124 44, www.praguewelcome.cz, has several outlets. A new office has opened at Rytírská 31 (daily Apr-Oct 0900-1900, Nov-Mar 0900-1830). There is also an office in the Old Town Hall (Apr-Oct Mon-Fri 0900-1900, Sat-Sun 0900-1800; Nov-Mar daily 0900-1900) and in the summer a temporary office operates at the Lesser Town Bridge Tower (Apr-Oct 1000-1800). The **Prague City Card** is available as a 2, 3 or 4 day option (with or without transport). It gives free access to over 50 monuments and museums and can be purchased with an online discount at www.praguecitycard.com; 4 days with transport costs CZK1600; 2 days without CZK790.

Exchange rate Czech Koruna (CZK). £1 = CZK29.3. €1 = CZK24.8.

Ratings

Art and culture ☆☆☆
Eating ☆☆
Nightlife ☆☆☆☆
Outdoors ☆☆☆☆☆
Romance ☆
Shopping ☆
Sightseeing ☆☆
Value-for-money ☆
Overall city rating ☆☆☆

Reykjavík

Reykjavik is the coolest of cities. And that's not just because it's the most northerly capital in the world. Set in an expanse of lava fields, close to both the largest desert and biggest glacier in Europe, this remote outpost is so far off the European map it has virtually been granted a licence to be quirky, unconventional and ground-breaking in its music, architecture, sculpture and even lifestyle. With a population of only around 113,000, it is hardly a teeming metropolis but, what it lacks in size, Reykjavik more than makes up for in the brio and creativity of its youthful population. This restless energy is reflected in powerful, subterranean forces of nature which, with typical ingenuity, have been harnessed to make life more bearable in this harsh, unforgiving environment.

Hallgrimskirkja Church.

Austurvöllur Square

Although Lækjatorg Square is the actual centre, Austurvöllur is the real heart of the city. The grassy space was originally six times bigger than it is today and thought to be the site of Ingólfur Arnarson's farm – Reykjavik's first settler. Today it's a popular meeting place, surrounded by cafés and bars. The small church (1787) is actually the modest **city cathedral**; next to it is the Alþing (Parliament House), overlooked by a stern-looking statue of **Jón Sigurdsson**, who led Iceland to independence from Denmark in 1944. In the corner of the square is **Hotel Borg**, a graceful art deco hotel, frequented by the rich and famous. Surprisingly, the Icelandic rock revolution of the 1980s began here and the hotel became a magnet for the city's young punks.

At a glance

The bohemian old town of Reykjavik, known as **101**, is situated between two water features: the harbour and the pond. In between you'll find the heart of the city, **Austurvöllur Square**, with the historic Alþing parliament building and cathedral. Follow the main street, **Austurstraeti**, and you reach Lækjatorg Square, from where the buses leave and the roads radiate. Across the road and up the hill is **Laugavegur**, Reykjavik's busiest street, buzzing with shops, bars and cafés. Down by the harbour, you'll find the flea market at weekends, where you can try specialities such as dried cod or putrefied shark meat (only for those with strong stomachs). Towering above the city is the soaring steeple of **Hallgrímskirkja**, always useful for getting your bearings. The other dominant feature on Reykjavik's skyline is **Perlan** (the Pearl), which sits above the city's hot water tanks. To the east of 101 is **Laugardalur Valley**, where you'll find the city's largest thermal swimming pool, the botanical gardens, zoo and one of the best sculpture museums. Just beyond Reykjavik itself is the vast emptiness of Iceland's weird and wonderful volcanic countryside. Even if you only have a few days, it's worth making the effort to get out of the city.

Aðalstræti

This is the oldest street in Reykjavik. Archaeological excavations under the Hotel Centrum have revealed the remains of what is thought to be one of the very first settler houses, dating from AD 874 to AD 930. The city's oldest surviving house, dating from 1752, is also on Aðalstræti at No 10; it's now a bar-bistro called Viðalín.

Tjörnin and around

The town pond, Tjörnin, is popular with people out for a stroll or feeding the ducks and greylag geese. It was created at the end of the last Ice Age as a sand and gravel bar, built up by the pounding waves of Faxaflói Bay. The futuristic building that seems to rise right out of the pond is the **City Hall**, *Mon-Fri 0800-1900, Sat and Sun 1200-1800, free.* Inside is a large relief map of Iceland, a café and a small information desk. On the east side of the pond is the **Icelandic National Gallery**, *Fríkirkjuvegur 7, T515 9600, www.listasafn.is, Tue-Sun 1100-1700, ISK500, free on Wed*, which has exhibitions from around the world and a small sculpture garden. On the opposite side is **Tjarnargata** street with its colourful early 20th-century timber houses.

National Museum of Iceland

Suðurgata 41, T530 2200, www.natmus.is.
1 May-15 Sep daily 1000-1700; 16 Sep-30 Apr Tue-Sun 1100- 1700; guided tours daily 1100. ISK 1000; Wed free. Off map.

South of the pond, the National Museum is the best place to get a sense of 1200 years of Icelandic

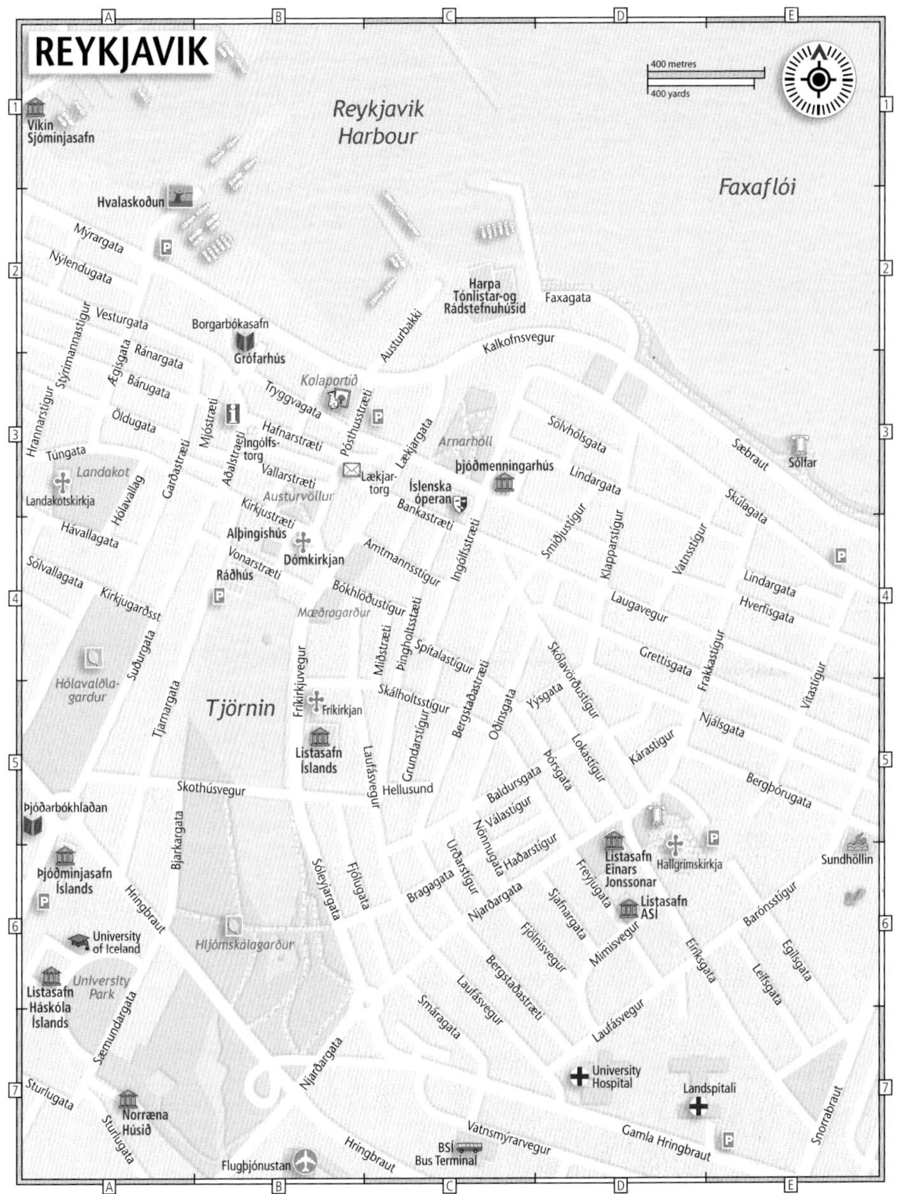

REYKJAVIK
400 metres
400 yards
A
B
C
D
E
1
2
3
4
5
6
7
Reykjavik Harbour
Faxaflói
Víkin Sjóminjasafn
Hvalaskoðun
Mýrargata
Nýlendugata
Harpa Tónlistar-og Ráðstefnuhúsid
Faxagata
Austurbakki
Vesturgata
Borgarbókasafn
Grófarhús
Kalkofnsvegur
Ránargata
Ægisgata
Stýrimannastígur
Hrannarstígur
Bárugata
Kolaportið
Tryggvagata
Pósthusstræti
Öldugata
Mjóstræti
Hafnarstræti
Lækjargata
Arnarhóll
Sölvhólsgata
Sæbraut
Sólfar
Túngata
Landakot
Landakotskirkja
Garðastræti
Aðalstræti
Ingólfs-torg
Vallarstræti
Lækjar-torg
Þjóðmenningarhús
Lindargata
Íslenska óperan
Hólavallag
Austurvöllur
Kirkjustræti
Bankastræti
Skúlagata
Hávallagata
Alþingishús
Dómkirkjan
Amtmannsstígur
Smiðjustígur
Klapparstígur
Vatnsstígur
Ingólfsstræti
Sólvallagata
Vonarstræti
Ráðhús
Lindargata
Kirkjugarðsst
Bókhlöðustígur
Laugavegur
Hverfisgata
Mæðragarður
Suðurgata
Hólavallagardur
Miðstræti
Þingholtsstræti
Spítalastígur
Skólavörðustígur
Grettisgata
Frakkastígur
Vitastígur
Fríkirkjuvegur
Fríkirkjan
Tjörnin
Tjarnargata
Skálholtsstígur
Bergstaðastræti
Óðinsgata
Ýysgata
Njálsgata
Listasafn Íslands
Laufásvegur
Grundarstígur
Lokastígur
Kárastígur
Þórsgata
Baldursgata
Skothúsvegur
Hellusund
Bergþórugata
Þjóðarbókhlaðan
Válastígur
Nönnugata
Bjarkargata
Þjóðminjasafn Íslands
Hringbraut
Sóleyjargata
Fjólugata
Urðarstígur
Bragagata
Haðarstígur
Listasafn Einars Jonssonar
Hallgrímskirkja
Sundhöllin
Freyjugata
Njarðargata
Sjafnargata
Listasafn ASÍ
Barónsstígur
University of Iceland
Hljómskálagarður
Fjölnisvegur
Mímisvegur
Egilsgata
Leifsgata
Eiríksgata
University Park
Listasafn Háskóla Íslands
Sæmundargata
Bergstaðastræti
Laufásvegur
Smáragata
Laufásvegur
Njarðargata
University Hospital
Landspitali
Sturlugata
Norræna Húsið
Sturlugata
Vatnsmýrarvegur
Gamla Hringbraut
Snorrabraut
Hringbraut
BSÍ Bus Terminal
Flugþjónustan

history. Tangible exhibitions and multimedia displays provide a fascinating insight into the Icelandic culture and how the nation has developed from the times of the earliest settlers to the present. The museum covers diverse aspects of the country's history, including mythology, the construction of early Viking buildings, the adoption of Christianity, the Reformation and the Census of 1703. It is well worth a visit.

Old Harbour

Although commercial fishing is now focused around Sundahöfn to the east, the old harbour area to the north of Austurvöllur Square has a certain charm (if you don't mind the lingering smell of fish) and remains busy with an influx of small fishing boats every now and then. The **Kolaportið flea market**, *Geirsgata, T562 5030, Sat and Sun 1100-1700*, is held in the old customs building by the quay. Locals flock to browse through piles of bric-a-brac and second-hand clothes, and it's a good place to taste some Icelandic delicacies, such as dried cod.

Just behind the customs building, the **Harbour House Museum**, *Tryggvagata 17, T511 5155, www.listasafnreykjavikur.is, Fri-Wed 1000-1700, Thu 1000-2200, free*, houses diverse exhibitions by Icelandic and foreign artists. The focus is modern and experimental, with a permanent exhibition by contemporary Icelandic artist, Erró.

Hallgrímskirkja

Skólavörðustígur, T510 1000, www.hallgrimskirkja.is. **Daily 0900-1700. Suggested donation ISK50, tower view ISK500 adults. Map D6.**

Dominating Reykjavik's skyline is this controversial 74 m-high church, reminiscent of a volcanic eruption. It was designed as part of a competition and took 49 years to build. (It was completed in 1986.) While the interior is quite bare, the views from the top out over the city are wonderful. In front of the church is a statue of **Leifur Eríksson**, the Viking who is believed to have discovered America around AD 1000.

Perlan and the Saga Museum

Öskjuhlíð Hill, T562 0200, www.perlan.is. **Observatory daily 1000-2330. Free. Bus 13 from Lækjatorg Sq. Off map.**

Sitting on top of Öskjuhlíð Hill, the Pearl is the nearest thing the city has to the Eiffel Tower, with viewpoints out over the city, a café and revolving gourmet restaurant inside. The iconic circular glass building sits atop the city's hot-water storage tanks and holds regular art exhibitions, expos and concerts. It also houses one of the city's best museums, the **Saga Museum**, *T511 1517, www.saga museum.is, daily 1000-1800, winter 1200-1700, ISK1500*, which charts the early history of the country through the medieval stories of the sagas.

Down at the foot of the hill you'll find **Nauthólsvík Beach**, a quirky man-made beach with imported yellow sand and geothermal pools. A dip here is a must, come rain or shine.

Laugardalur Valley

Bus 14 from Lækjatorg Sq.

The name Reykjavik literally translates as 'smoky bay', the first settlers having mistaken the steam from the hot springs in the Laugardalur Valley for smoke. The springs are now used to feed **Laugardalslaug Thermal Pool**, *Sundlaugavegur 30a, T553 4039, Mon-Fri 0630-2230, Sat and Sun*

0800-2200, Winter Sat and Sun 0800-2000, ISK300, the city's biggest swimming pool.

Across from the Laugardalslaug pool complex is the white-domed **Ásmunder Sveinsson Sculpture Museum**, *Sigtún, T553 2155, www.listasafnreykjavikur.is, May-Sep daily 1000-1600, Oct-Apr 1300-1600, ISK500.* Ásmunder Sveinsson was one of the pioneers of Icelandic sculpture and many of his abstract pieces draw on Icelandic literature, fairytales and nature.

Blue Lagoon

240 Grindavík, Reykjanes Peninsula, T420 8800, www.bluelagoon.is.
Sep-May daily 1000-2000, Jun-Aug daily 0900-2100. ISK4,200. Buses Jun-Sep from BSÍ terminal and Keflavík airport.

One of Iceland's most popular tourist attractions, the Blue Lagoon is best visited en route to the airport and is the perfect way to relax at the end of your trip. The lagoon is a steaming pool of milky turquoise water that leaches minerals from the lava bed, filling it with healing properties. Lie back, put on a mud pack and try not to let that whiff of sulphur put you off.

Above: Blue Lagoon.
Opposite page: Modern art installation.

Outdoors

Being so close to nature is a major appeal when visiting Reykjavik and it's easy to get out of the city for a half or full day. One of the most popular day trips is the Golden Circle, which takes in three of Iceland's finest natural and historic features within a day's journey of Reykjavik. It is a good way to get a taste of the country's bizarre scenery. **Þingvellir National Park**, 49 km northwest of the city, www.thingvellir.is, was the site of the ancient Viking parliament. In the centre of the park you can see a dramatic rift in the earth where the Eurasian and American continental plates are pulling part by 2 cm a year. To the northeast, **Geysir**, www.geysircenter.is, is the site of the original spouting hot spring that gave its name to all such natural features. Although it's no longer very active, another hot spring, **Strokkur**, spurts up to around 30 m, every four minutes. Ten kms further on, **Gulfoss** is a huge two-step waterfall that partially freezes in winter. It's best to hire a car to reach these sights, but there are plenty of tours available. **Iceland Excursions**, www.icelandexcursions.is, and the **Activity Group**, www.activity.is, offer tours and a variety of activities, including dog sledding, horse riding across lava fields, white-water rafting and snowmobiling – an exhilarating way to see the ice fields and glaciers. Whale-watching trips provide the chance to see minke, humpback and orca whales, as well as dolphins and seals.

Sleeping

Reykjavik has a great range of accommodation from extravagant hotels to quality guesthouses. Many hotels shut down Oct-May.

Hotel 101 €€€
Hverfisgata 10, T580 0101, www.101hotel.is.
An ultra-fashionable boutique outfit with sculptures, murals, Icelandic art and an airy bar and restaurant. It's all very minimalist chic and the spa and gym downstairs will help you keep as glam as the surroundings. A futuristic, luxury experience in the heart of the city.

Hotel Borg €€€
Pósthússtræti 11, T551 1440, www.hotelborg.is.
Reykjavik's finest, an art deco hotel in Austurvöllur Sq with lovingly preserved rooms and modern art. It's a movie-star haunt: Catherine Deneuve shacked up here when she came to visit Björk and Marlene Dietrich stayed in 1944.

4th Floor Hotel €€
Laugavegur 101, T511 3030, www.4thfloorhotel.is.
A sleek, modern and intimate hotel in a prime spot for exploring the city's museums and art galleries. Laugavegur is also the city's main shopping street and home to some of Reykjavik's best nightlife. Location, location, location.

Guesthouse 101 €€
Laugavegur 101, T562 6101, www.iceland101.com.
Modern and spacious guesthouse in a large concrete building just off the main street. Moderate-sized rooms. Ideal location in the centre of the city for shopping, drinking and dining .

Reykjavik Backpackers €
Laugavegur 28, T578 3700, www.reykjavikbackpackers.com.
A fun and lively option for those on a budget. The hostel is clean and bright and the staff are warm and welcoming. A great location on the main shopping drag on Laugavegur makes it a popular choice. An excellent tour booking service on site.

Eating

There is plenty of Icelandic and international cuisine. Standards are high – and so are the prices.

3 Frakkar €€€
Baldursgata 14, T552 3939, www.3frakkar.com.
Mon-Fri 1130-1430 and 1800-2200, Sat and Sun 1800-2300.
Meaning the 'three Frenchmen', this seafood restaurant specializes in Icelandic classics such as puffin and whale meat. Small and traditional. Free wine if you have to wait for a table.

Fiskfelagid (Fish Company) €€€
Vesturgotu 2a, T552 5300, www.fiskfelagid.is
The name suggests fish, but there are plenty of other options on offer however. Groups may like to choose the 'Round the World' menu or the 'Round Iceland' menu for some tantalising taste sensations. One of the city's more expensive dining options, but worth splashing out on.

Tveir Fiskar €€€
Geirsgata 9, T511 3473, www.restaurant.is.
Daily 1700-late.
Refined Icelandic fish restaurant overlooking the harbour. Specialities include oyster soup, smoked puffin with pear marmalade and caviar. A high-quality gourmet affair with a feng-shui inspired interior.

Sægreifinn €
Verbúð 8, T553 1500, www.saegreifinn.is.
Daily 0800-1800.
Run by three local fishermen including the 'sea baron' himself, this is actually a fish shop with a couple of wooden benches outside. The charming harbour setting and truly rustic feel make it a good, cheap spot for lunch. Try the delicious lobster soup or a barbecued fish kebab.

Nightlife

Baejarins Beztu €
corner of Tryggvagata and Pósthússtræti.
Reykjavik's original hot dog kiosk has become something of an institution. The hot dogs (pylsur) come with mustard, ketchup and raw or fried onions and are very tasty.

Check the 'what's on' section of www.icelandreview.com for details of current entertainment listings.

Bars and clubs

For many people, Reykjavik's nightlife is the main reason for coming to this cold and windswept spot. It's different to clubbing in other European destination, partly due to the size of the city, but just as the country is geologically young and dynamic, so is its nightlife. The long summer days and yawning winter nights give a whole new twist to the concept of partying till dawn. Fri and Sat are the wildest nights, with clubbing till 0800. Bars and clubs don't really fill up until 2400 as the high alcohol prices – ISK700 for a pint of beer – force many locals to drink at home before heading into town. There are plenty of bars around Laugavegur such as bohemian Kaffibarinn, Bergstadastræti 1, funky **Sirkus**, Klapparstígur 30, cool **Astro**, Austurstraeti, and lively **Vegamót**, Vegamótastígur 4. Later on, music fans often head to **NASA**, Thorvaldsenstraeti 2, and its three floors of live music, disco and house. A smaller version is the popular **Café Solon**, Bankastraeti 7A, that turns from a daytime bistro into a night time club with guest DJs. **Austurvollur Sq** seems to be the in place for clubbers to congregate after closing time.

Live music

It's possible to find live music being performed on every night of the week. Try **Gaukur á Stong**, Tryggvagata 22, and **Nelly's Café**, Þingholtstræti 2, for anything from jazz to rock.

Travel essentials

Getting around
Keflavík International Airport, T425 6000, www.kefairport.is, is 48 km from Reykjavik. The reliable **Flybus** (www.re.is/flybus) meets all incoming flights and drops you at your hotel or guesthouse, ISK1950, 45 mins. If you're determined not to fly, it is also possible to get to Iceland by boat with **Smyril Line**, T+298 345 900, www.smyril-line.com, from Denmark and Norway via the Shetland and Faroe Islands. (**NorthLink Ferries**, T+44 (0)845 600 0449, www.northlinkferries.co.uk, link Lerwick in Shetland with Aberdeen.) The ferry lands at Seyðisfjörður on the east coast, 682 km from Reykjavik.

Getting around
101 Reykjavik is small enough to walk around on foot. A stroll around town takes 20 mins; to walk to Laugavegur Valley or Öskjuhlíð Hill takes 30 mins. The yellow **Straeto** city buses operate Mon-Fri 0700-2400, Sat and Sun 1000-2400. They are reliable and efficient, running every 20 mins, less frequently at weekends. A single fare is ISK280. Lækjatorg Sq is the main bus terminal for local travel, where you can pick up route maps and timetables. Reykjavik is well suited to cycling as it is mainly flat. Bike rental is available from guesthouses and other places for around ISK1700 a day. To get out of the city, it's best to hire a car (**ALP Car Rental**, T562 6060, www.alp.is) or take a tour. Otherwise, buses run from the BSÍ terminal, Vatnsmyrarvegur, T552 2300.

Tourist information
The main tourist office is **The Centre**, Aðalstræti 2, T590 1500, www.visitreykjavik.is, Jun- Aug daily 0830-1900, Sep-May Mon-Fri 0900-1800, Sat and Sun 0900-1400. It provides all the information you could possibly need and can arrange tours, car hire and concert tickets. There's a bureau de change, internet access and tax refund centre here. Also useful is **This is Iceland**, Laugavegur 20, T561 6010, www.icetourist.is, which offers free internet and a tour booking service. A **Reykjavik Card** (ISK1500 for 24 hrs, ISK2000 for 48 hrs and ISK2500 for 72 hrs) is available from the tourist office and offers free entry to the major museums and swimming pools as well as being a free bus pass.

Exchange rate Icelandic Kronur (ISK). £1 = ISK183. €1 = ISK152.

Ratings

Art and culture ☆☆☆☆☆
Eating ☆☆☆☆
Nightlife ☆☆☆☆
Outdoors ☆
Romance ☆☆☆☆
Shopping ☆☆☆☆
Sightseeing ☆☆☆☆☆
Value-for-money ☆☆☆
Overall city rating ☆☆☆☆

Rome

All roads lead here, it wasn't built in a day and while in the city you should do as the locals do, which might at first glance appear to be a lot of suicidal driving, sitting in piazzas drinking *aperitivi* and shopping in expensive boutiques. The Eternal City is so layered with history, sights and legend that it's unwise to aim to do much more than scratch the surface. Much of Italy's best ancient Roman remains and Renaissance art and architecture is here, sometimes alongside (or even underneath) pared-down Futurist minimalism. The city's baroque fountains, despite being continually draped in camera-toting tourists, are spectacularly grand. And you should leave time for markets and museums, designer shops and *pizzerie* serving the thinnest, crispest pizzas. The Vatican – the world's smallest sovereign state, beloved of quizmasters everywhere – has more of interest than many large countries, from the gasp-inducing Sistine Chapel and Raphael masterpieces to the cathedral of St Peter's. Massively cleaned up and restored for the millennium, Rome has regained some of its patina but still has more monuments and churches open than was the case in the past. Its economy is bigger than New Zealand's and as the capital of a major European country and the centre of a world religion, it has a sense of being an intensely relevant, living city – a quality sometimes lacking in other Italian cities. Surrounded by over 2000 years of history, contemporary Rome continues to blithely go about its business.

Fiat 500 in Aventino.

At a glance

Trains, and most of Rome's many visitors, arrive at **Termini** station, to the east of the city centre. Beyond the chaos in front of the station, via Nazionale heads from **piazza della Repubblica** southwest towards **piazza Venezia** and the main area of sights. The grandiose ugliness of the white marble **il Vittoriano** (Victor Emmanuel II monument), sits to the south of piazza Venezia, with the hill of the **Campidoglio** (one of Rome's famous seven hills, complete with great museums and a beautiful piazza) behind it. The biggest area of ancient ruins stretches east and south from the Campidoglio: the vast **Colosseo** (Colosseum) is beyond the **Foro Romano** (Forum) and the hill of the **Palatino**, effectively a single archaeological zone of temples, arches, political and civic remains. The river **Tevere** (Tiber) winds through the city, with the central areas enclosed in the eastern side of a large bend. **Piazza Navona**, with grand fountains and buildings, is usually considered to be the central point of the city though the more earthy market piazza of **campo de' Fiori** just to the south has more reason to be thought of as Rome's heart. Also here are many of Rome's main sights – the **Pantheon** is the city's most complete Roman building and there are also many good shopping streets. On the northeastern edge of this central area, **via del Corso** is a long straight road lined with many of the city's smartest shops, leading north to **piazza del Popolo** and the green hill of **Pincio**. On the eastern side of via del Corso are two of the prime stopping points on tour guides' itineraries: the **Fontana di Trevi** (Trevi Fountain) and the **Scalinata Trinità dei Monti** (Spanish Steps). On the other side of the river, **Trastevere** is boho and arty and has laid-back streets filled with bars and restaurants, though there's less in the way of conventional sights. To the north, also on the western side of the river, the **Castel Sant' Angelo** stands guard over a statue-lined bridge. From here, Mussolini's grand via della Conciliazione is the best approach to San Pietro (St Peter's) and the **Vatican**.

24 hours in the city

Get up early to wander around **piazza Navona** and the fruit and vegetable market in **campo de' Fiori**. Dedicate the rest of the morning to the **Forum** and the **Palatine**, ending up in the **Colosseum**. Then head northwest through the atmospheric streets near the river for lunch. In the afternoon hit **St Peter's**, leaving enough time to queue and to climb up into the dome and onto the roof for spectacular views. (Even longer queues mean that trying to see the Sistine Chapel and the rest of the Vatican in one day is probably an inefficient use of your time. If you must see them, get here as early as possible and be prepared to wait.) In the evening return to the campo de' Fiori, by this time transformed into a chic aperitivi spot. After a prosecco here, head across the river for food in **Trastevere**, and, if you want to party, head further south to the increasingly fashionable area of **Testaccio**.

Musei Capitolini

piazza del Campidoglio, T06 6710 2475, www.museicapitolini.org.
Tue-Sun 0930-2000. €9. Map E4.

Designed in the 16th century by Michelangelo, the piazza del Campidoglio and museums on the Capitoline hill are a brilliantly conceived ensemble.

Michelangelo's regal Cordonata staircase leads up to the piazza from the via del Teatro di Marcello, just south of piazza Venezia. In placing the stairs on the western side of the piazza, Michelangelo changed its orientation: instead of facing the Forum it faces contemporary Rome.

The museums themselves are in the Palazzo dei Conservatori and Palazzo Nuovo: two

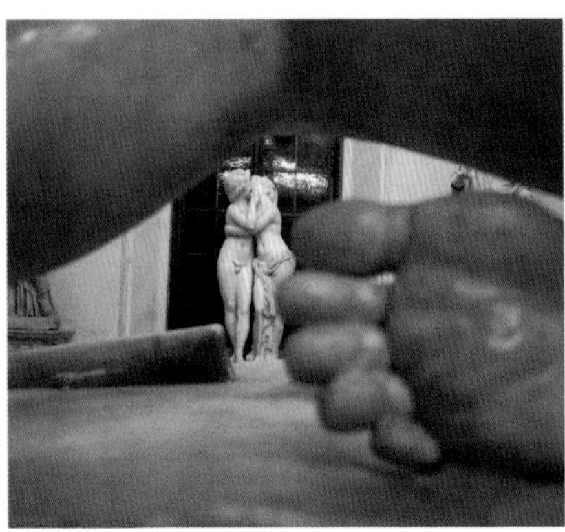

Musei Capitolini.

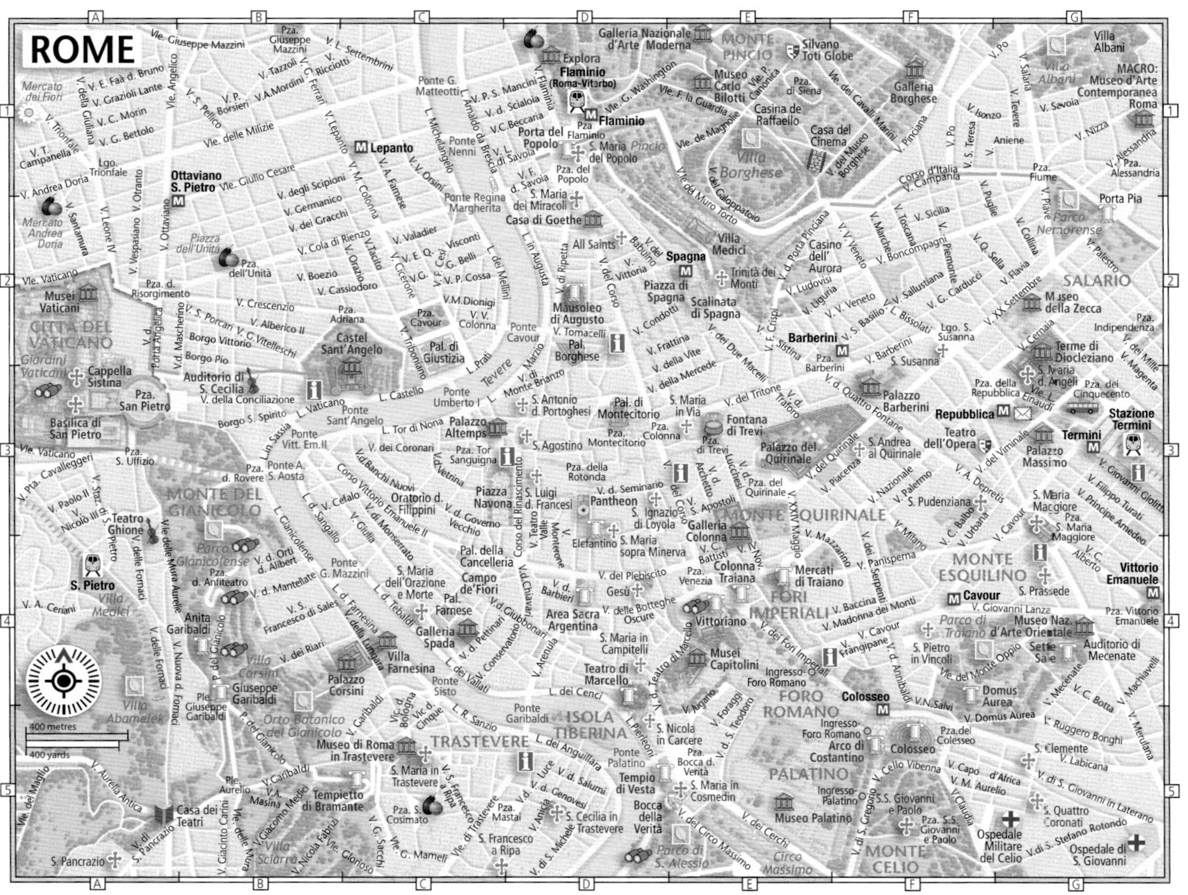
ROME
Galleria Nazionale d'Arte Moderna
MONTE PINCIO
Silvano Toti Globe
Villa Albani
MACRO: Museo d'Arte Contemporanea Roma
Explora
Flaminio (Roma-Viterbo)
Flaminio
Museo Carlo Bilotti
Casina de Raffaello
Galleria Borghese
Casa del Cinema
Villa Borghese
Porta del Popolo
S. Maria del Popolo
Lepanto
Ottaviano S. Pietro
Porta Pia
Villa Medici
Spagna
Piazza di Spagna
Scalinata di Spagna
Trinità dei Monti
SALARIO
Museo della Zecca
Musei Vaticani
CITTÀ DEL VATICANO
Casa di Goethe
Mausoleo di Augusto
Castel Sant'Angelo
Pal. di Giustizia
Barberini
Terme di Diocleziano
Cappella Sistina
Pza. San Pietro
Basilica di San Pietro
Auditorio di S. Cecilia
Palazzo Barberini
Repubblica
Stazione Termini
Termini
Fontana di Trevi
Palazzo del Quirinale
Teatro dell'Opera
Palazzo Altemps
Piazza Navona
Pantheon
MONTE DEL GIANICOLO
MONTE QUIRINALE
Galleria Colonna
MONTE ESQUILINO
Vittorio Emanuele
Cavour
Campo de' Fiori
Area Sacra Argentina
Mercati di Traiano
FORI IMPERIALI
Vittoriano
Musei Capitolini
Galleria Spada
Villa Farnesina
Palazzo Corsini
Teatro di Marcello
FORO ROMANO
Colosseo
Domus Aurea
ISOLA TIBERINA
TRASTEVERE
Museo di Roma in Trastevere
Arco di Costantino
PALATINO
Museo Palatino
Tempietto di Bramante
Tempio di Vesta
Bocca della Verità
MONTE CELIO
Casa dei Teatri
400 metres
400 yards

buildings facing the piazza and connected by the **Galleria Congiunzione**, an underground passage opened as a part of the Millennium celebrations and also allowing access to the Roman **Tabularium**, the archive of ancient Rome. There are good views from here over the Roman Forum.

The **Capitoline Museum** in the Palazzo dei Conservatori contains statues, bronzes and other artefacts. In its courtyard are the remnants of the enormous statue of Constantine that once stood in the Forum, including his gigantic foot. The rest of the statue was made of wood and has not survived. The second floor has works of art including a Caravaggio and a Titian.

The **Palazzo Nuovo** contains an impressive collection of ancient marble statuary.

Foro Romano and Palatine

via de Fori Imperiali, T06 3996 7700.
Daily 0830-1 hr before sunset. €12, combined with the Colosseum and valid for two days. Map E5.

Rome was almost certainly first settled on the Palatine hill, overlooking a crossing of the river Tiber. According to legend, it was here that Romulus and Remus, the founders of the city, were brought up by a she-wolf. Roman emperors built their palaces on the hill, at the bottom of which – in the Forum – commerce, worship and justice took place.

Visitors are largely free to wander among the broken columns and it's not hard to imagine the centre of the Roman Empire as it would have been 2000 years ago. There's little or no information, however, and a map of the ruins is useful in order to make out what is what. Highlights include the **Temple of Castor and Pollux**, the **Arch of Septimus Severus** and the **Arch of Titus**. The **Casa delle Vestali** was home to the Vestal Virgins for a minimum of 30 years of chastity.

The Palatine hill has remains of grand palaces including recently opened rooms in the Casa di Augusto, as well as the 16th-century **Hortus Farnese**, Europe's oldest botanical gardens.

Romulus and Remus

In Roman mythology, Romulus and Remus were twins who founded the city of Rome. Their mother, Rhea Silvia, despite being a Vestal Virgin, was raped by Mars, the god of war and conceived the twins. Their uncle, Amulius, ordered a servant to kill the twins but instead they were cast adrift in a boat on the river Tiber. They were found by Tiberinus, the river god, and suckled by a she-wolf on the Palatine Hill, before being discovered by a shepherd who raised the children as his own. Once they became adults, Romulus and Remus returned home, killed their uncle and then built a settlement on the Palatine Hill, according to tradition in 753 BC. Remus killed Romulus but then, feeling remorse, named the city after his brother.

The extent to which Romulus and Remus were historical figures is unclear, and it seems that there was a settlement on the Palatine Hill which predates the traditional date of the founding of the city. However, such apparent facts haven't stopped the she-wolf becoming a symbol of the city – a bronze of her suckling the twins can be seen in the Capitoline Museums. A similar image was used on Second World War propaganda posters.

Colosseo

piazza del Colosseo, T06 3996 7700.
Daily 0830-1 hr before sunset. €12 including Forum and Palatine, valid for two days. To avoid the queues, it's quicker to buy the joint ticket at the Forum. Map F5.

Rome's most iconic building, sold in plaster miniature by souvenir sellers all over the city, the Colosseum is an impressive structure. Built from AD 72 to 80, the city's ancient amphitheatre once seated as many as 70,000 people. Used for gladiatorial combat, 9000 animals are reported to have been killed during its 100-day opening celebrations.

Built by Emperor Vespasian and his son Titus, it sits on the site of one of Nero's palaces, the Domus Aurea. A floor has been constructed at the level where the original would have been but you can still see into the underground section where animals and combatants were kept.

The remaining marble with which it was once clad was removed during the Renaissance and baroque periods and used to build houses, and to construct St Peter's. A new museum has interesting exhibitions.

Musei Vaticani

viale Vaticano 100, T06 6988 4947, www.vatican.va. Mon-Sat 0900-1800, €15; last Sun of month 0900-1400, free. Map A2.

The Vatican Museums have an extraordinary wealth of art, including the masterpieces of Michelangelo in the **Capella Sistina** (Sistine Chapel), and those of Raphael in the **Stanze di Raffaello**. Michelangelo famously lay on his back for four years, between 1508 and 1512, to create his astonishing *Creation* on the ceiling. (Goethe said of it: "Without having seen the Sistine Chapel one can form no appreciable idea of what one man is capable of achieving.") He returned 23 years later to spend another six years painting the darker *Last Judgement* on the end wall above the altar. There is a self-portrait in it – Michelangelo paints himself as a flayed skin in the hand of St Bartholomew. Both paintings were subject to a controversial restoration in the 1980s and 1990s which some claim now makes the frescoes too colourful.

The **Raphael Rooms** are only slightly less astounding: four rooms are frescoed with themes of truth and beauty as well as the achievements of popes. The most famous image includes depictions of Leonardo as Plato, Michelangelo as Heraclitus and Raphael as himself.

Start early and, especially in high season, be prepared for a long wait to get in. Once inside, colour-coded routes help find a way through the Papal treasure troves. Most head straight for the Sistine Chapel but there is plenty more to see.

Below: Colosseo.
Opposite page: Foro Romano.

Basilica di San Pietro

piazza San Pietro, T06 6988 1662.
Apr-Oct daily 0700-1900; Nov-Mar daily 0700-1800. Free. Cupola, Apr-Oct 0800-1800; Nov-Mar 0800-1700. €5. Bare shoulders and knees not allowed in the basilica. Map A3.

The biggest church in Christendom, **St Peter's** can hold 60,000 people. The basilica's current incarnation was started in 1506. The original plans were drawn up by Bramante but then changed by Raphael, who took over after the original architect's death. Michelangelo then took charge and changed the plans again and it was largely his Greek cross design and his enormous dome that was finally consecrated in 1626.

Inside, the enormity of the Vatican's church is emphasized by a line in the floor displaying the lengths of other big churches around the world. Of the many highlights Michelangelo's Pieta (a depiction of Mary holding the dead body of Jesus on her lap), sculpted from marble when he was only 24 years old, is the most affecting. Regrettably now behind glass, the sculpture loses some, but not all, of its disarmingly human qualities. Another highlight not to be missed is the climb up into the dome and out onto the terrace. From here there are great views down into the Vatican gardens in one direction and, in the other, over the 140 statues of saints on the colonnade to the piazza below. Note that there are 320 steps to climb even if you opt to take the lift up the first stage.

Basilica di San Pietro.

If you're here on a Wednesday morning, you can get a glimpse of a distant Pope addressing enthusiastic crowds in piazza San Pietro.

Il Vittoriano

piazza Venezia.
Monument and museum daily 0930-1730 in summer; 0930-1630 in winter. Free. Map E4.

The Monumento a Vittorio Emanuele II, more often called simply il Vittoriano, or, with less deference, the wedding cake or the typewriter, is one of Rome's most memorable monuments, if not its most beautiful. Always controversial, its construction involved the demolition of an old part of the city and many Romans consider it out of proportion and out of style with its surroundings.

Built at the turn of the 20th century in honour of King Victor Emmanuel, it now serves various purposes – the tomb of the unknown soldier is here, with an eternal flame, as are various exhibition spaces and the Museo del Risorgimento, with information about the unification of Italy. The upper levels are a good point from which to look across at the Mercati di Traiano (Trajan's Markets). A new lift ascends right to the top for an expensive but impressive view over the city.

Fontana di Trevi

piazza di Trevi. Map E3.

Made especially famous by Anita Ekberg, who took the plunge in *La Dolce Vita*, the Trevi Fountain sits at the end of the Aqua Virgo, one of the aqueducts that supplied ancient Rome with crucial pure water from outside the city. Rome's grandest, the baroque Trevi Fountain follows a Roman tradition of building fountains at the ends of aqueducts. Designed by Nicola Salvi in 1730 using elements of an earlier design by Bernini, the fountain is these days purified with chlorine and semi-permanently surrounded by a sea of coin-throwing tourists and security guards to stop anyone wading in.

Scalinata di Spagna

In some ways an unlikely candidate for tourist must-see status, the 18th-century **Spanish Steps** consist of 138 stairs originally built into the hill to connect the Spanish embassy with the Holy See. At the top of the monumental stairs is the church of **Trinità dei Monti** from where the views across the city's rooftops are spectacular. Shoppers gather for a rest in the piazza di Spagna at the bottom. **John Keats** lived in a house at the bottom of the steps and died there in 1821. There is now a museum dedicated to the poet.

Pantheon

piazza della Rotunda, T06 6830 0230.
Mon-Sat 0900-1830, Sun 0830-1300. Free. Map D3.

Built in AD 125 by Emperor Hadrian to replace an earlier building that had been destroyed by fire, the Pantheon is ancient Rome's most complete monument. A perfectly circular rotunda, the building is 43 m wide and 43 m high. A central oculus in the dome is open to the sky and lets through striking shafts of sunlight into the shadows. The dome was the largest in Western Europe until Brunelleschi's dome in Florence's Duomo was built in 1436.

The building was consecrated in AD 609 as a Christian church. Partly for this reason the Pantheon was spared the damage inflicted on other Roman structures. The reason for the dome's survival may also have something to do with the composition of Roman concrete.

Since the Renaissance the building has been used as a tomb for the famous. Those buried here include Raphael and two Italian kings.

Top: Pantheon.
Above: Piazza Navona.

Piazza Navona

Map C3.

The central piazza of Rome, piazza Navona was built on top of the first-century Stadium of Domitian, which explains its rectangular shape. Surrounded by baroque architecture, the main points of interest in the piazza are its fountains, notably Bernini's central

Fontana dei Quattro Fiume (Fountain of the Four Rivers), representing the Danube, the Ganges, the Nile and the Río de la Plata. The **Fontana Nettuno** (Fountain of Neptune), to the northern end of the piazza, is by Giacomo della Porta.

Campo de' Fiori

Map C4.

A more proletarian counterpoint to piazza Navona's aristocracy, the campo de' Fiori (commonly referred to simply as Il Campo) has a lively and high-quality fruit and vegetable market and plenty of equally lively bars and restaurants. In recent years Il Campo has been increasingly gentrified but it retains some of its down-to-earth feel. It really comes into its own in the evenings, once the stalls are cleared away and locals descend to drink *aperitivi* at the outdoor tables and watch the world go by. The central statue is of Giordano Bruno, a philosopher burned at the stake here in 1600 for suggesting that philosophy was superior to religion. Julius Caesar also died nearby.

The Ghetto

Museo Ebraico di Roma, Lungotevere de' Cenci, T06 6840 0661, www.museoebraico.roma.it. Jun-Sep Sun-Thu 1000-1900; Oct-May Sun-Thu 1000-1700. €7.50. Map D4.

Jews have lived in Rome for over 2000 years, meaning that the Roman Jewish community is the oldest in Europe. The relative security of Roman Jews through the ages came at the cost of a tax imposed by the Catholic church from the 14th century onwards.

Shops offer kosher pizza and there is an attractive synagogue in which the **Jewish Museum** details centuries of maltreatment by the Vatican as well as the rounding up of 2000 Jews in 1943.

Trastevere

Map C5.

The name Trastevere (the stress is on the first 'e') comes from the Latin trans *Tiberim*, meaning over the Tiber, and the area retains some of its centuries-old otherness and a somewhat bohemian identity.

The area of Trastevere is at its best in the evenings, when many Romans come and visit its lively bars and relatively cheap restaurants. It is also worth a wander during the day, however.

The church of **Santa Maria in Trastevere**, *piazza Santa Maria in Trastevere, T06 581 4802, daily 0730-2100*, is the area's most obvious sight and has some glitteringly spectacular 13th-century mosaics. It is one of the oldest churches in Rome and is set in a cobbled piazza.

To the north is a green area of parks around the Gianicolo hill, including the **Orto Botanico** (Botanical Gardens), *largo Cristina de Svezia 24*. Originally established in 1833, it hosts over 3500 species and includes a section of a 'scent and touch' garden.

Best of the rest

Ara Pacis
Lungotevere in Augusta, www.arapacis.it, Tue-Sun 0900-1900, €8.
Richard Meier's boldly contemporary space holds Emperor Augustus's altar, one of the great works of Ancient Rome.

Museo e Galleria Borghese
Piazzale del Museo Borghese 5, T06 841 3979, www.galleriaborghese.it, Tue-Sun 0830-1930, €8.50.
Some of the city's best Renaissance art and statuary in Rome's elegant park. Includes masterpieces by Bernini and Titian.

Castel Sant'Angelo
Lungotevere Castello 50, T06 681 9111. Tue-Sun 0900-1930. €5.
Hadrian's final resting place was built in AD 135 and has great views as well as a chapel designed by Michelangelo. Over the centuries it has served as both a refuge and a prison for popes and it was the setting for Puccini's opera Tosca.

San Luigi dei Francesi
piazza San Luigi dei Francesi, T06 688 271. Fri-Wed 0830-1230, 1530-1900; Thu 0830-1230.
Rome's French church has three Caravaggio paintings in its Contarelli Chapel.

Sleeping

Many of Rome's cheaper sleeping options are near the station, though few can be wholeheartedly recommended. The southern part of the centro storico offers many of the best mid-range options, while further north, around the Spanish Steps, prices and standards of service rise still further. In general the city's hotels are expensive compared to the rest of Mediterranean Europe.

Hotel Art by the Spanish Steps €€€
via Margutta 56, T06 328711, www.hotelart.it.
Sleekly modern and self-consciously hip, Hotel Art sometimes tries too hard, but generally its efforts pay off. It has micro-lighting, wooden floors and colour schemes in place of floor numbers.

Hotel Eden €€€
via Ludovisi 49, T06 478121, www.hotel-eden.it.
This hotel has refined old-fashioned elegance, a stylish bar and restaurant and great views from the terrace garden. If money is no object you may want to consider booking the penthouse – a snip at €3600 a night.

Donna Camilla Savelli €€€-€€
via Garibaldi 27, T06 588 861, www.hotelsavelli.com.
Recently converted, this ex-convent in Trastevere has plush rooms arranged around an attractive garden courtyard. There are excellent views of the city from the imperial suite.

Astoria Garden €€€-€€
via Bachelet 8, T06 446 9908, www.hotelastoria garden.it.
One of the best options near the station, the Astoria Garden has smart if rather generic rooms and, as the name suggests, a garden. Good value out of season.

Campo de Fiori €€€-€€
via del Biscione 6, T06 6880 6865, www.hotelcampodefiori.com.
Ivy-clad and antique-filled, with great views from the roof terrace; the hotel also has apartments for rent nearby.

Casa Howard €€€-€€
via di Capo Le Case 18 and via Sistina 149, T06 6992 4555, www.casahoward.com.
The name is the Italian title of EM Forster's novel, Howard's End, from which you might imagine a staid attempt at Englishness – you'd be wrong. This excellent-value designer B&B has two houses where the design is bright and colourful and the attention to detail commendable, from the slippers and the fresh breakfasts to the carefully sourced soap.

Hotel Santa Maria €€€-€€
vicolo del Piede 2, T06 589 4626, www.htlsantamaria.com.
A friendly place in the middle of Trastevere, Santa Maria has an attractive central courtyard with orange trees, where a good breakfast is served. Nearby, a newer residenza, run by the same people, has stylish family rooms.

Hotel Navona €€
via dei Sediari 8, T06 686 4203, www.hotelnavona.com.
Very central and good value, Navona has some antique style and you'd be hard pushed to find anything else as reasonable within a stone's throw of piazza Navona itself. The same owners also run the more upmarket Residenza Zanardelli.

Guesthouse Arco dei Tolomei €€
T06 5832 0819, via Arco dell'Arco dei Tolomei 27, www.bbarcodeitolomei.com
A homely little Trastevere B&B with lots of faded floral wallpaper, books and plenty of antique charm.

Eating

Many of the best restaurants in the centre are in the area around campo de' Fiori or across the river in Trastevere, where eating out is traditionally a little cheaper. Spaghetti carbonara is the archetypal traditional Roman dish, which you'll find nearly everywhere.

Lunch

Òbikà €€
via dei Prefetti 26a, T06 683 2630.
A restaurant based entirely around one ingredient: mozzarella. The real buffalo milk stuff arrives fresh daily from Naples, Salerno and Caserta. The design mixes steely minimalism with ancient Roman touches.

Il Forno di Campo de' Fiori €
campo de' Fiori 22, T06 6880 6662.
Simple but notoriously delicious white or red pizza by the slice attracts lots of local workers at lunchtimes. Closes for the afternoon at 1430, so don't leave it too late.

Da Lucia €
vicolo del Mattonato 2, T06 580 3601.
Popular and steadfastly old-fashioned, this Trastevere back-street eatery is one of the best places to get a simple bowl of spaghetti.

Il Bocconcino €
via Ostilia 23, T06 7707 9175.
A traditional osteria popular with locals despite being close to the Colosseum. Tasty dishes made with fresh local ingredients.

Dinner

Al Bric €€€
via del Pellegrino 51-52, T06 687 9533.
A well-informed wine list is the centrepiece of this enoteca (wine bar), which also serves imaginative food, combining the traditional and the modern. Dishes include swordfish stroganoff and duck pappardelle.

Da Felice €€
via Mastro Giorgio 29, T06 574 6800.
In the increasingly fashionable district of Testaccio, a smart place offering contemporary tweaks on Roman classics.

Dar Poeta €
vicolo del Bologna 46, T06 588 0516.
One of Rome's most popular pizzerias, Dar Poeta also packs in customers after its chocolate calzone.

Filetti di Baccalà €
largo Librai 88, T06 686 4018.
Closed Sun.
A Roman institution, this battered cod joint has changed very little in a very long time. The menu consists of not much other than its trademark Roman dish but what it does it does very well.

Trattoria da Augusto €
piazza de' Renzi 15, T06 580 3798.

On communal tables outside in a less smart piazza than the nearby Santa Maria, Trattoria da Augusto can be chaotic but is never less than good-natured. The food is excellent and traditional fare. You'll do better with some Italian – menus are mostly of the spoken variety. Be prepared to hang around in the piazza for a table.

Cafés and gelaterias

Il Gelato di San Crispino
via della Panetteria 42, T06 679 3924.
Some have suggested that the exceedingly good ice cream served here from under stainless steel lids might be the best in the world. Try the trademark gelato di San Crispino, flavoured with honey, and you may never be able to eat a Cornetto again.

Nightlife

Bars and clubs

Trastevere and the area around campo de' Fiori are often considered the liveliest for nocturnal Roman activities but Testaccio, a previously working class area to the south, has the best nightclubs. Wine bars are becoming trendier but in general are places to eat as much as to drink. **Campo de' Fiori** is an especially good location for an early evening *aperitivo*.

Many of the city's nightclubs are smart and pricey and the live music scene is limited, though the number of alternative venues is increasing. Interesting events often happen at the city's *centri sociali*. During the summer months some clubs move out to the coast. Nights start (and finish) late – don't expect much action before midnight. Listings magazines like *Roma C'è* give up-to-date details of what's on.

Live music

Classical music and opera tends to fare better than other music, especially in summer, when festivals mean that events sometimes take place in great outdoor settings, from Testaccio's ex-slaughterhouse to the Baths of Caracalla and the Botanical Gardens. The Renzo Piano-designed **Auditorium Parco della Musica**, via P de Coubertin 15, www.auditorium.com, has injected new life into Rome's music scene.

Shopping

Rome still has plenty of small shops run by local families rather than big chains – **Trastevere** and in the streets around **campo de' Fiori** are great areas for discovering bookshops, delicatessens, and shops selling antiques and crafts.

Rome's most famous products are shoes and other fashion accessories, such as bags and gloves. For fashion, **via del Corso** and the roads that run off it make up Rome's main shopping area and you'll find the headquarters of brands such as Gucci and Bulgari here.

Via Frattina, via Condotti and via del Babuino are especially good for burning holes in wallets.

Travel essentials

Getting there

Fiumicino Airport, T06 6595 3640, www.adr.it, 25 km southwest of the city centre, is the city's main airport. The **Leonardo Express** rail service connects the airport to Rome's main train station every half an hour from around 0630-2330. It's a 35-min journey and costs €14. A taxi to or from the centre of the city costs €45. **Ciampino Airport**, T06 794 941, www.adr.it, 15 km southeast of the centre, is the smaller airport and serves budget airlines. There are various ways of getting to Ciampino, some of which are not quite as simple or cheap as they should be. A Terravision bus service runs to coincide with Ryanair and easyJet flights, €4 single.
A taxi costs €35. Alternatively you can catch a bus (every 20 mins) to make the short hop to Ciampino station from where trains connect to Roma Termini every 10 mins. International trains, including the Palatino sleeper service from Paris, arrive at the Termini station, www.trenitalia.com.

Getting around

The same ticket system covers bus, metro and tram systems. Standard tickets cost €1 and are valid for 75 mins from the time of being stamped on all forms of transport. Confusingly, however, they can only be used once on trains and metros. For €4 you can buy a *giornaliero* ticket which lasts all day. The bus system is relatively efficient, though routes from the station to the Vatican have a reputation for pick-pockets. The metro is also efficient, but less useful to visitors since it mostly links the suburbs to the city centre. Licensed taxis are white and have meters. Don't use anything else purporting to be a taxi.

Tourist information

Azienda per il Turismo Roma, via Parigi 5, T06 3600 4399, en.turismoroma.it, near the train station. There are equally useful *Punti Informativi Turistici* around the city centre at locations such as at piazza delle Cinque Lune, T06 6880 9240, near piazza Navona.

Ratings

Art and culture ☆☆
Eating ☆☆☆☆
Nightlife ☆☆☆
Outdoors ☆☆
Romance ☆☆☆☆
Shopping ☆☆
Sightseeing ☆☆☆☆
Value-for-money ☆☆☆☆
Overall city rating ☆☆☆☆☆

Seville

Even within Spain the name of this one-time mercantile powerhouse is spoken like a mantra, a word laden with sensuality and promise. Delving beyond the famous icons; the horse carriages, the oranges, the flamenco, the haunting Semana Santa celebrations, you find a place where being seen is nothing unless you're seen to be having fun, a place where the ghosts of Spain walk the streets, be they fictional, like Don Juan or Carmen, or historical, like Cervantes or Columbus.

Seville has an astonishing architectural heritage within its enormous old town, still girt by sections of what was once Europe's longest city wall; you could spend weeks here and not get to see all the sights. But don't bank on overdoing the sightseeing, for the supreme joy of the city is its tapas. They claim to have invented them here; many of your most pleasurable moments in this hot, hedonistic city will come with glass and fork in hand.

Cistern in the Real Alcázar.

At a glance

The historic hub of Seville is dominated by two awesome symbols of power and wealth, the **Real Alcázar palace**, and the **cathedral** with its emblematic **Giralda** – a sublime tower in beautiful brick. Nearby, Seville's Moorish and Jewish heritage is still elusively alive among the narrow streets of **Barrio Santa Cruz**, just east of the cathedral, and home to some fine tapas bars. South of the cathedral, the optimistic buildings erected for the 1929 Exhibition have been put to fine use; students bustle about and city folk stroll in the blessed shade of the **Parque María Luisa**, with its improbably-grand **Plaza de España** and two museums. **El Arenal**, west of the cathedral and once the sandy, seedy, flood plain of the Guadalquivir river, was built up around Seville's bullring and is now a riverside area with a theatre, good tapas and the fine art of the Hospital de la Caridad. To the south, **Triana**'s trendified riverbank is a mass of bars and restaurants; its backstreets full of tradition and beautiful tiles. A cluster of plazas and shopping streets fill Seville's old town (**Centro**), with baroque churches tucked away in its side streets. Nearby, quiet **San Vicente** offers the fine Museo de Bellas Artes. **La Macarena**, to the north, has friendly local bars, lively markets and quiet lanes brimming with Gothic- Mudéjar convents and churches. The river island of **Isla de la Cartuja** was the site of World Expo 1992.

Below: Cathedral.
Bottom: Tiles in the Real Alcázar.

Cathedral and La Giralda

Pl del Triunfo s/n, T954 563 150, www.catedraldesevilla.es.
Sep-Jun Mon-Sat 1100-1730, Sun 1430-1830; Jul-Aug Mon-Sat 0930-1630, Sun 1430-1830. Last entry half an hour before. Admission €8 (every day). Map D3.

At the beginning of the 15th century, 150 years after the fall of Seville to the Christians, a cathedral was erected over the site of a mosque. Santa María de la Sede is the result: a Gothic edifice of staggering proportions and crammed full of artistic treasures in nearly 50 chapels and its massive five-naved central structure. The mosque's minaret, the superb Giralda tower (and the city's symbol), was retained as the bell tower, and can be climbed via a series of ramps, while pretty Patio de los Naranjos, the Moorish ablutions area, has also survived. The exterior is spectacularly ornate, while the immense, solemn interior is crammed full of artistic treasures.

Real Alcázar

Pl del Triunfo s/n, T954 502 323, www.patronato-alcazarsevilla.es.
Oct-Mar 0930-1700 (daily), Apr-Sep 0930-1900, last entry 1 hr earlier, €7.50. Map D4.

The present Alcázar owes its Islamic look (horseshoe arches, stucco, Arabic calligraphy and coffered ceilings) not to the Moorish rulers (little remains from that period) but to the Castillian kings Alfonso X and his son Pedro I. As well as being a sumptuous palace and a popular residence for visiting Spanish royalty, the Alcázar was once a considerable fortress, as you can see when you pass through the chunky walls of the red **Puerta del León**. From here you emerge into a large courtyard where the king's hunt once assembled. It's dominated by the impressive façade of the main palace of the Castillian kings (inscriptions about the glory of Allah – Pedro I was a pretty enlightened man – adjoin more conventional Latin ones proclaiming royal greatness). To the left is the **Patio del Yeso**, one of the few remaining Moorish structures. Across the courtyard are chambers built by Fernando and Isabel to control New World affairs. Magellan planned his trip here and there's an important *retablo* from this period of the Virgen de los Navegantes. There's also the vast, fantastic garden to stroll in; take a peaceful break from the sometimes frenetic centre.

Museo de Bellas Artes

Plaza del Museo 9, T954 786 500.
Tue-Sat 0900-2030, Sun 0900-1430. Free for EU citizens. €1.50 for others. Map B2.

Seville's major art gallery is a must-see, housed in a picturesque 17th-18th century convent. Thoughtfully laid out and thankfully uncluttered, it's a treasure trove of Spanish art from the 15th-20th centuries including El Greco, Velásquez, Murillo, Zurbarán – and a late portrait by Goya.

Barrio Santa Cruz

Once home to much of Seville's Jewish population, atmospheric Santa Cruz is the most charming of the city's barrios: a web of narrow, pedestrian lanes linking attractive small plazas with orange trees and shady terraces aplenty. There is a fairly

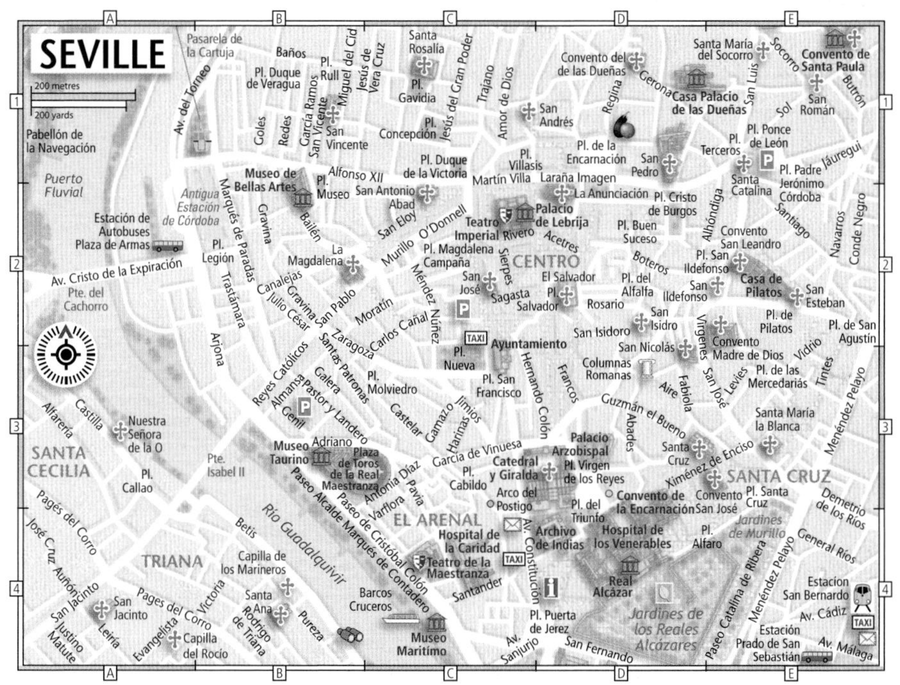

Semana Santa and Feria de Abril

Seville's Holy Week processions are an unforgettable sight. Mesmeric candlelit lines of hooded figures and cross-carrying penitents make their way through the streets accompanied by the mournful notes of a brass band and two large *pasos* (floats), one with a scene from the Passion, one with a statue of Mary. This isn't unique to Seville but what makes it so special is the Sevillians' extraordinary respect for, and interest in, the event. Members of nearly 60 *cofradías* (brotherhoods) practise intensively for the big moment, when they leave their home church and walk many hours through the streets to the cathedral and then home again. Some of the brotherhoods have well over a thousand in the parade; these consist of *nazarenos*, who wear pointed hoods (adopted by the KKK, but designed to hide the face of a man repentant before God), *penitentes*, who carry crosses, and *costaleros*, who carry the *pasos*. The first brotherhoods walk on Palm Sunday and the processions continue up until Easter Sunday, when a single *cofradía* celebrates the Resurrection.

Feria de Abril (usually in April, depending on Easter), originally a livestock market but now a major event in the Seville calendar, provides a lively antidote to the solemnity of Semana Santa. Line upon line of colourful marquees (*casetas*) reverberate to the slurping of manzanilla and the gyrations of pairs dancing *sevillanas*.

standard tourist beat but you can easily get away from it. It's also a good place for hotels, restaurants and shopping. While there are a few sights of interest, such as the excellent baroque church of **Santa María la Blanca** and the **Hospital de los Venerables**, *T954 562 696, www.focus.abengoa.es, daily 1000-1400, 1600-2000, €4.75*, the main enjoyment to be had is wandering around and trying to guess where you'll end up.

South of the cathedral

Much of the area south of the cathedral is taken up with the large green space of **Parque María Luisa**. It was used as the site for the grandiose 1929 Ibero-American Exhibition that the Primo de Rivera dictatorship hoped would return Seville and Spain to the world spotlight. The legacy is a public park and a beautiful series of buildings. The **Plaza de España** is an impressive colonnaded space and the **Hotel Alfonso XIII** to the northwest is one of the most sumptuous in Spain. Next door, the **Antigua Fábrica de Tabacos**, *C San Fernando 4, T954 551 000, Mon-Fri 0800-2030, free*, is the cigarette factory made famous in the late 19th century by Carmen; it's now used by the university. In the park beyond, two of the pavilions have been converted into outstanding museums: the colourful **Museo de Artes y Costumbres Populares de Sevilla**, *Pl de América 3, T954 712 391, Tue-Sat 0900-2030, Sun 0900-1430, free to EU residents, €1.50 for others*; and the rich **Museo Arqueológico**, *Pabellón de Bellas Artes, Pl de América s/n, T954 786 474, same opening details*. A walk through this part of town provides a fascinating view of an architectural ensemble built just years before the Civil War that plunged the city and country into decades of poverty and monoculturalism.

El Arenal

Built up in the 19th century, El Arenal has some of Seville's major landmarks. The **Torre del Oro**, *Paseo de Colón s/n, T954 222 419, Tue-Fri 0930-1330, Sat-Sun 1030-1330, €2*, is a beautiful Moorish tower. The exhibition is mediocre but worth seeing for the prints of Seville in the late 16th century. La Maestranza, *Paseo de Colón 12, T954 224 577, www.realmaestranza.com, daily 0930-1900 winter, to 2000 summer except fight days when it's open 0930-1500, €6*, is one of Spain's most important temples to bullfighting.

The Hospital de la Caridad, *C Temprado 3, T954 223 232, Mon-Sat 0900-1930, Sun 0900-1230, €5*, is a nursing home with a remarkable collection of 17th-century Sevillan art including haunting masterpieces by Juan de Valdés Leal. The Río Guadalquivir itself is also a major attraction here; although there are no longer galleons bound for the Spanish Main, there are several outdoor bars, river cruises, and a place to hire canoes.

Best of the rest

Archivo de las Indias

Pl del Triunfo s/n, T954 500 528, www.mcu.es. Mon-Sat 0930-1700, Sun 1000-1400. Free.

In the 18th century this square and sober Renaissance building was converted into the state archive. It's a fascinating record of the discovery and administration of empire; from the excited jottings of Columbus to mundane book- keeping of remote jungle outposts.

Casa de Pilatos

Plaza de Pilatos s/n, T954 225 298. Nov-Mar 0900-1800, to 1900 Apr-Oct, €6 lower floor, €8 both, free Tue from 1300.

A stunning 15th-century blend of Renaissance classicism and Mudéjar styles.

Triana

Triana is many people's favourite part of Seville. It has a picturesque riverfront lined with bars and restaurants, and was for a long time the gypsy barrio and home of flamenco in Seville (its backstreet bars are still the best place to catch impromptu performances). Triana is also famous for ceramics; most of the *azulejo* tiles that so beautifully decorate Seville's houses come from here, and there are still many workshops in the area. It's got a different feel to the rest of the city, and *trianeros* are still a tight-knit social group. Many residents once lived in *corrales de vecinos*, houses centred around a common courtyard and there are still a few around to see. While the riverfront and surrounds are fairly trendy these days, venture into some of the smaller backstreets and you'll find that Triana preserves more of its history and associations than any other part of Seville.

Right: Giralda tower, Cathedral.
Opposite page: Real Alcázar.

Sleeping

With dozens of hotels in renovated old Seville mansions, there's a wealth of attractive, intimate lodgings to choose from.

Corral del Rey €€€
Corral del Rey 12, T954 227 116, www.corraldelrey.com.
This boutique hotel is a faultlessly realized restoration of an historic palacio, with an irresistible romantic ambience.

Las Casas de la Judería €€
Cjón Dos Hermanas 7, T954 415 150, www.casasypalacios.com.
Spread across several old palacios, this hotel has sparkling patios, pretty nooks and hanging foliage.

Las Casas del Rey de Baeza €€
Pl Jesús de la Redención 2, off C Santiago, T954 561 496, www.hospes.es.
An enchanting old corral de vecinos near Casa Pilatos, superbly restored. Rooftop pool and terrace as well as a beautifully decorated library and lounges.

Hotel Alminar €€
C Álvarez Quintero 52, T954 293 913, www.hotelalminar.com
This solid three-star hotel trades in warm personal service; with only a dozen rooms, it feels like they've got time for all their guests.

Hotel Amadeus €€-€
C Farnesio 6, T954 501 443, www.hotelamadeussevilla.com.
A lovely small hotel with a classical music theme. Some rooms are fabulous, some merely excellent. Roof terrace with views of the centre and the Giralda. Highly recommended.

El Roy Moro €
C Lope de Rueda 14, T954 563 468, www.elreymoro.com
Sitting between two central Santa Cruz streets, this excellent hotel is built around a large three-storey patio with wooden columns.

YH Giralda €
C Abades 30, T954 228 324, www.yh-hoteles.com.
This is a minimalist marble-decorated hotel in a great but quiet location. Good service and elegant, comfortable rooms are value at any time but real bargains off-season.

Eating

Your best moments in Seville are likely to be spent eating. Tapas was invented here and it's one of the places in Spain where it's done best. There's little distinction between tapas bars and restaurants, so we've listed them all together. A standard tapa will cost €1.50-3. The menú del día, a filling, set price three-course lunch (1330-1530 roughly) normally costs €8-14.

Egaña Oriza €€€
C San Fernando 41, south of Alcázar, T954 227 254, www.restauranteoriza.com.
Mon-Fri 1330-1530, 2030-2330, Sat 2030-2330.
A smart restaurant mixing Andalucían and Basque cuisine. Try the *salmorejo*, stewed wood pigeon, sole with saffron sauce and a great ceviche of monkfish and grouper.

Kiosco de las Flores €€€
C Betis s/n, T954 274 576, www.kioscodelasflores.com.
Dining on the riverfront in Triana is a classic Sevilla experience. This is one of the best places to do it, with an enormous range of seafood and a lovely outlook.

Taberna del Alabardero €€
C Zaragoza 20, T954 502 721.
Hospitality school and one of the city's best restaurants, with a delicious seasonal menu. House specials include *corvina* (sea bass). Downstairs is an atrium bar serving snacks and raciones.

Bar Pepe Hillo €
C Adriano 24, T954 215 390.
1200-0100.
A legend in its own tapas time, especially for stews and croquettes. High-ceilinged and buzzing.

Bodega Santa Cruz €
C Rodrigo Caro 2, T954 213 246.
1200-2400.
A busy and cheerful bar serving

some of Seville's choicest tapas and *montaditos* (delicious little toasted sandwiches).

Casa Morales €
C García Vinuesa 11, T954 221 242.
Great old traditional place with big sherry jars, *montaditos* served on wooden trays, and the tab chalked up on the bar in front of you.

La Goleta €
C Mateos Gago, Barrio Santa Cruz, T954 218 966.
Tue-Sun 0900-1500, 2000-2300.
Tiny bar with loads of character. Limited but excellent tapas, particularly the 'candid' tortilla.

Nightlife

Seville's nightlife can't compete with Barcelona or Madrid but around Plaza Alfalfa and Calle Betis in Triana it's usually lively into the wee small hours. While much of the flamenco is geared to tourists, the quality of these performances is usually high, even if the atmosphere's a bit sterile. It's also possible to track down a more authentic experience; many bars have dedicated flamenco nights. The quality varies but the cost is minimal and occasionally you'll see something very special.

Shopping

Seville's main shopping area is the Centro around **Calles Sierpes**, **Tetuán**, **Velásquez**, **Cuna** and **Plaza del Duque**. This busy area is the place to come for clothes, be it modern Spanish or essential Seville Feria fashion: shawls, flamenco dresses, mantillas, ornamental combs, fans and castanets. Head to the **Alameda de Hércules** area for more offbeat stuff. If it's ceramics you're after, **Triana** is the place to go; there are dozens of attractively decorated shops. Most can arrange reasonably priced secure international delivery.

Travel essentials

Getting there

Seville Airport, T954 449 000, is 10 km northeast of the centre. A bus runs to and from the airport to central Seville (Puerta de Jerez) via the train and bus stations every 30 mins weekdays (less frequently at weekends) and coincides with international flights. It takes 30 mins to Puerta de Jerez (€2.30). The last bus leaves the airport at 2330. A taxi to the city is around €21, slightly more at night or on public holidays. Sevilla's modern train station, Santa Justa, is a 15-min walk from the centre on Av Kansas City. For train information contact RENFE, T902 240 202, or see their excellent website, www.renfe.es. A handy central RENFE office is on C Zaragoza 29.

Getting around

Although Seville's old town with the main sights is a large area, walking is by far the best way to get around. A stroll from the cathedral to the Museo de Bellas Artes takes 15-20 mins, from the Plaza de España to the Alameda de Hércules about 30 mins. The city's new Metro so far has only one line; it's not terribly useful for visitors except to get to Isla de la Cartuja. Handier is the associated tram, **Metrocentro**, which zips between Plaza Nueva and Prado de San Sebastián bus station, via the cathedral and Puerta de Jerez. The most useful **TUSSAM bus** services are the circular routes: C1 and C2 run via the train station and Expo site (C1 clockwise, C2 anti-clockwise), while C3 (clockwise) and C4 (anti-clockwise) follow the perimeter of the old walls, except for C3's brief detour into Triana. Single fares are cheap, and there are multi-day tickets.

Tourist information

Junta de Andalucía, Av de la Constitución 21, T954 787 578, otsevilla@andalucia.org, Mon-Fri 0900-1930, Sat-Sun 0930-1500. Near the cathedral, this is the handiest tourist office, but it is usually busy. Other tourist offices are at Plaza San Francisco 19, T954 595 288, www.turismo.sevilla.org, the airport and Santa Justa train station.

Ratings

Art and culture ☆☆☆
Eating ☆☆☆
Nightlife ☆☆☆
Outdoors ☆☆☆☆☆
Romance ☆☆☆
Shopping ☆☆☆
Sightseeing ☆☆
Value-for-money ☆☆
Overall city rating ☆☆☆

Stockholm

Elegantly built over several small islands, Stockholm can lay a fair claim to having one of the world's most beautiful city locations. In recent years it has shed its reputation as a provincial backwater and transformed itself into a far more cosmopolitan and dynamic place. No longer blond or bland, the city now pulsates with a creative energy that has helped form an urban culture with its sights firmly set on the world stage. Synonymous with both high design and hi-tech, it remains an eminently manageable and civilized place whose laid-back charm is reflected in its friendly, confident inhabitants, around a quarter of whom were born outside Sweden. Predominately young, these "new Swedes" are changing the way Stockholm thinks about itself.

Stockholm City Hall.

Gamla Stan

Metro Gamla Stan. Map C5.

This island is the site of the majority of Stockholm's historic buildings and has been the stage on which much of Swedish history has been played out. Gamla Stan combines a residential area with a selection of government and royal buildings, not to mention plenty of cafés in its narrow streets with gabled roofs.

Just behind the main square, **Stortorget**, is Stockholm's impressive Cathedral and Royal Church, **Storkyrkan**, *Trångsund 1, daily 0900-1800, guided tours Thu 1100, free*. It is ornately decorated and has a number of important Baroque artworks including the outstanding *St George and the Dragon* (Berndt Notke) from 1489.

At a glance

The most important of Stockholm's 14 islands are those on which the city centre is built, only a few metres from the mainland. Stadsholmen, better known as **Gamla Stan**, is a mixture of narrow lanes and grand buildings, while adjacent **Riddarholmen** is also rich in historical associations. **Skeppsholmen**, to the east, has the ultra-cool modern art museum, while **Kungsholmen** to the west, houses the iconic City Hall. To the south, **Södermalm** is the biggest island and one of the city's main entertainment districts. Here, around the central **Medborgarplatsen**, you'll find bars and restaurants that reflect the cosmopolitan, design-led influences of 'new' Sweden. This is also the centre of Stockholm's relaxed gay scene.

The modernist-inspired **city centre** is on the mainland to the north, 10 minutes from **Södermalm**. The streets around **Stureplan** offer exclusive clubbing and shopping and **Vasastaden** is a busy commercial hub centred around T-Centralen train station.

Heading east from the city centre along the waterfront to the island of **Djurgården** is one of the most beautiful walks in any European city. Boasting three of Sweden's biggest attractions (Gröna Lund amusement park, Skansen and the Vasa museums), Djurgården is also a great place to relax in rural tranquillity.

Royal Palace (Kungliga Slott)

www.royalcourt.se.
Times vary; some sections closed during state visits. SEK100. Metro Gamla Stan. Map C4.

The massive bulk of Nicodemus Tessin's building dominates central Stockholm and is a powerful statement of the ambitions of the Swedish monarchy in the 18th century. Replacing an earlier palace which burnt down, it was completed in several stages and finally occupied in 1754. The austere façade is guarded by several stone lions. Its sumptuous interior is undeniably impressive and about as far as you can get from modern Swedish minimalism.

During state visits the Royal Apartments are closed but the three museums within the palace stay open and contain some interesting collections associated with the monarchy. The changing of the guard, which takes place at 1215 every day (1315 on Sunday), is a well-drilled reminder that the Swedish monarchy is still solidly in place.

Vasa Museum (Vasamuseet)

Galärvarvsvägen 14, Djurgården, T08 5195 4800, www.vasamuseet.se.
Thu-Tue 1000-1700, Wed 1000-2000. SEK110. Bus 47 or 69 from Central Station. Map E3.

In 1628, at the height of Sweden's military power, the warship Vasa, which was to be the flagship of the Swedish navy, made its maiden voyage.

It sank barely one mile out to sea. The story of the building of the Vasa, its demise and rescue from the seabed is well told in this purpose-built museum. There is plenty of historical background and multimedia displays but the main draw is the ship itself. It is huge and its stern has an impressive number of warlike figures and martial symbols.

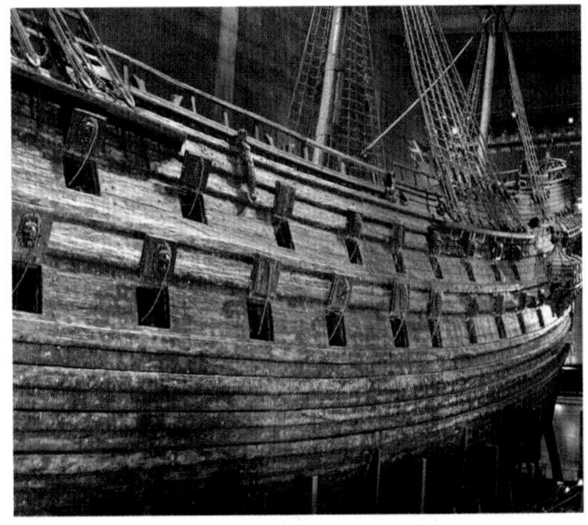

Above: Vasa Museum.
Opposite page: Royal Palace.

Skansen

Djurgården, T08 442 8000, www.skansen.se.
May daily 1000-2000; Jun-Aug daily 1000-2200; Sep daily 1000-1700; Oct-Apr daily 1000-1500. SEK70. Bus 47 from Central Station or 44. Off map.

The prototype of all open-air museums, Skansen holds a sentimental place in every Swede's heart.

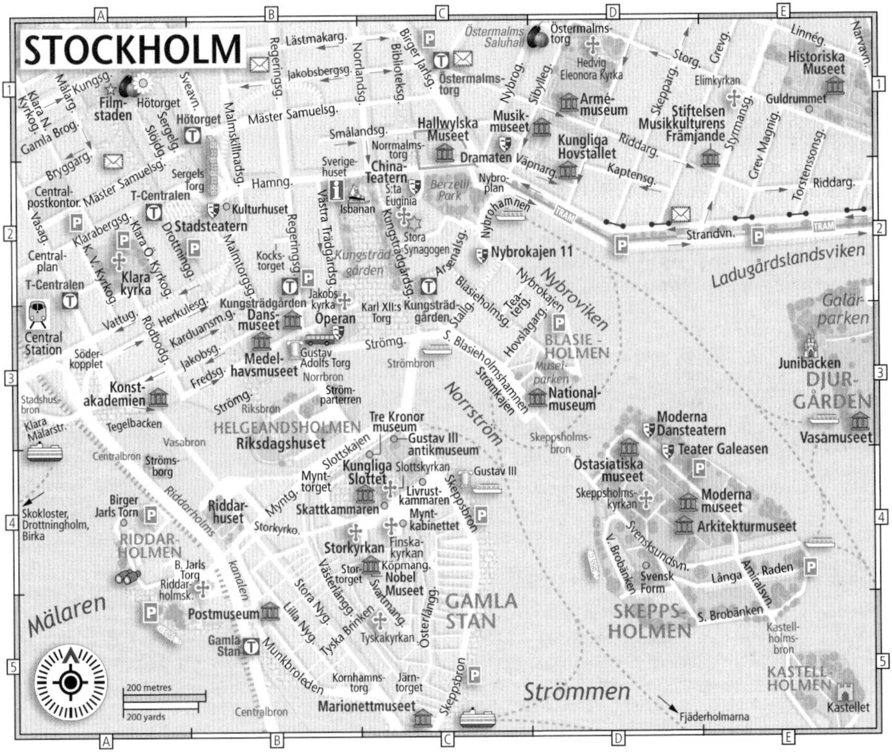
STOCKHOLM
A
B
C
D
E
1
2
3
4
5
Lästmakarg.
Regeringsg.
Jakobsbergsg.
Norrlandsg.
Birger Jarlsg.
Biblioteksg.
Östermalms Saluhall
Östermalms-torg
Hedvig Eleonora Kyrka
Linnég.
Narvavn.
Historiska Museet
Storg.
Grevg.
Elimkyrkan
Guldrummet
Kungsg.
Mälarg.
Klara N. Kyrkog.
Film-staden
Hötorget
Sveavn.
Östermalms-torg
Nybrog.
Sibylleg.
Armé-museum
Skeppparg.
Stiftelsen Musikkulturens Främjande
Styrmansg.
Grev Magnig.
Torstenssonsg.
Gamla Brog.
Hötorget
Sergelg.
Slöjdg.
Malmskillnadsg.
Mäster Samuelsg.
Smålandsg.
Hallwylska Museet
Musik-museet
Kungliga Hovstallet
Riddarg.
Bryggarg.
Normalms-torg
Dramaten
Väpnarg.
Kaptensg.
Sverige-huset
China-Teatern
Hamng.
Sergels Torg
Central-postkontor.
Mäster Samuelsg.
T-Centralen
Berzelii Park
Nybro-plan
S:ta Euginia
Isbanan
Västra Trädgårdsg.
Kungsträdgårdsg.
Nybrohamnen
Riddarg.
Vasag.
Kulturhuset
Stadsteatern
Klarabergsg.
Klara Ö. Kyrkog.
Drottningg.
Stora Synagogen
Strandvn.
TRAM
Ladugårdslandsviken
Central-plan
K. V. Kyrkog.
Malmtorgsg.
Kocks-torget
Kungsträdgården
Arsenalsg.
Nybrokajen 11
T-Centralen
Klara kyrka
Regeringsg.
Jakobs kyrka
Blasieholmsg.
Nybrokajen
Nybroviken
Teaterg.
Galär-parken
Herkulesg.
Vattug.
Karduansm.g.
Kungsträdgården
Dans-museet
Operan
Karl XII:s Torg
Kungsträd-gården
Stallg.
Hovslagarg.
Central Station
Rödbodg.
Söder-kopplet
Jakobsg.
Medel-havsmuseet
Gustav Adolfs Torg
Strömg.
S. Blasieholmsg.
BLASIE-HOLMEN
Strömbron
Musei-parken
Junibacken
Fredsg.
Norrbron
Blasieholmshamnen
Strömkajen
DJUR-GÅRDEN
Stadshus-bron
Konst-akademien
Strömg.
Riksbron
Ström-parterren
National-museum
Norrström
Klara Mälarstr.
Tegelbacken
HELGEANDSHOLMEN
Riksdagshuset
Tre Kronor museum
Gustav III antikmuseum
Moderna Dansteatern
Vasamuseet
Vasabron
Skeppsholms-bron
Teater Galeasen
Centralbron
Ströms-borg
Slottskajen
Kungliga Slottet
Slottskyrkan
Gustav III
Östasiatiska museet
Mynt-torget
Skeppsholms-kyrkan
Moderna museet
Birger Jarls Torn
Riddarholms
Livrust-kammaren
Skeppsbron
Skokloster, Drottningholm, Birka
Riddar-huset
Myntg.
Skattkammaren
Mynt-kabinettet
Arkitekturmuseet
Storkyrko.
RIDDAR-HOLMEN
Storkyrkan
Finska-kyrkan
Svensksundsvn.
V. Brobänken
B. Jarls Torg
Riddar-holmsk.
Stor-torget
Köpmang.
Nobel Museet
Svensk Form
Långa
Amiralsvn.
Raden
Mälaren
kanalen
Västerlångg.
Svartmang.
Österlångg.
GAMLA STAN
SKEPPS-HOLMEN
S. Brobänken
Postmuseum
Stora Nyg.
Lilla Nyg.
Tyska Brinken
Tyskakyrkan
Kastell-holms-bron
Gamla Stan
Munkbroleden
Kornhamns-torg
Järn-torget
Skeppsbron
KASTELL-HOLMEN
Strömmen
200 metres
200 yards
Centralbron
Marionettmuseet
Fjäderholmarna
Kastellet

Below: Skansen Park.
Bottom: Stockholm panorama.

Best of the rest

Stadshuset (City Hall
Hantverkargartan 1, T08 5082 9058, www.stockholm.se/cityhall. SEK80 with tours every 30 mins in summer (between 0930 and 1600) and every hour in winter (between 1030 and 1500). Metro T-Centralen.
The Blue Room, modelled on an Italian Piazza, and the Byzantine-inspired mosaics are the highlights of this iconic building which hosts the Nobel Prize dinner; you can try the menu in the Stadshuskälleren cellar restaurant.

National Historical Museum
Narvavägen 13-17, T08 5195 5600, www.historiska.se. Oct-Apr Tue-Sun 1100-1700, Thu 1100-2000; May-Sep daily 1000-1700. SEK70.
Ancient gold, art from the Romanesque and Gothic periods plus the world's oldest carpet and a unique Viking collection out in Östermalm.

Hallwylska Museum
Hamngatan 4, T08 519555, www.hallwylskamuseet.se. Tue, Thu-Sun 1145-1600, Wed 1145-1900. SEK50.
A remarkably opulent house standing as a monument to the various collections built up over a lifetime by its magpie-like owners.

A kind of Noah's Ark for Swedish rural buildings and industry, it first opened its doors in 1892. All the buildings were moved here from other parts of Sweden in an attempt to preserve a rural heritage that was rapidly disappearing with industrialization. There are displays of traditional crafts and a collection of Scandinavian animals including bears and elks. The summer-only open-air theatre hosts sing-a-long concerts which are an unmissable celebration of all things Swedish.

Nationalmuseum

Södra Blasieholmshamnen, T08 5195 4300, www.nationalmuseum.se.
Sep-May Tue and Thu 1100-2000, Wed, Fri and Sun 1100-1700; Jun-Aug Tue 1100-2000, Wed-Sun 1100-1700. SEK 120. Metro Kungsträdgården. Map D3.

The paintings housed in this elegant building reflect all periods of art history. Highlights include Lucas Cranach's portrait of Martin Luther from 1526 and some fine Rembrandts. Swedish painters such as Larsson and Zorn are also well represented. The other permanent collection focuses on Swedish design and is a must-see for anyone who has ever bought IKEA furniture or marvelled at a cleverly-designed household appliance.

Museum of Modern Art and Swedish Museum of Architecture

Exercisplan, Skeppsholmen, T08 5195 5200, www.arkitekturmuseet.se, www.modernamuseet.se. Wed-Sun 1000-1800, Tue 1000-2000. SEK50. Metro Kungsträdgården. Off map.

Located on the city centre island of Skeppsholmen and housed in the same converted military building, these museums are rapidly becoming Swedish design icons. The Modern Art museum's permanent collection include Magritte's *The Red Model* and paintings by Picasso, Dali and Matisse. The outstanding Museum of Architecture has a permanent display illustrating the history of Swedish urbanism as well as temporary exhibitions. There is an excellent restaurant and café.

Östermalms Saluhall

Östermalmstorg, www.saluhallen.com. Mon-Thu 0930-1800, Fri 0930-1830, Sat 0930-1600. Metro Östermalmstorg (take the Östermalmstorg/Nybrogatan exit).

This superb indoor market, in a late 19th-century characterful building, is the place to visit for good food, either in the form of ingredients or handmade meals, including takeaways that are perfect for a picnic. Choose anything from sushi to Swedish specialities at over 20 stalls, delis, cafés and restaurants.

Travel essentials

Getting there
Stockholm is served by four international airports. The main one, **Arlanda**, T08 797 600, www.arlanda.se, is 45 km from the city. **Arlanda Express** trains, www.arlandaexpress.com, depart from underneath the terminal to T-Centralen (20 mins; SEK460 return). Buses run by **Flygbussarna**, www.flygbussarna.se, leave every 15 mins for the 40-min journey to the centre and cost SEK99 single, SEK198 return. A taxi will cost SEK480 and takes around 45 mins. Stockholm Taxi, T08 150 000, www.taxistockholm.se.

Skavsta airport, T01 552 804, www.skavsta.se, is 100 km from the city and is the base for budget airlines. Buses to and from Stockholm take 80 mins and cost SEK238 return, SEK119 single. A taxi will cost around SEK1400. Contact **Nyköping Taxi**, T01 5521 7500.

Västerås airport, T021 805 600, www.vasterasflygplats.se, is 85 km from the city. Flyggbussarna take 75 mins and charge SEK238 return. A taxi will cost about SEK1600 and take an hour. **Västerås Taxi**, T021 185 000.

From **Bromma Airport**, T08 797 6874, www.lfv.se, the 20-min journey with **Flyggbussarna** costs SEK150 return. A taxi (**Stockholm Taxi**, T08 150 000) will take 15 mins and cost about SEK300.

Mainline **train services** all run from T-Centralen and are operated by either Swedish Rail (www.sj.se) or Connex (www.connex.se). The high-speed X2000 tilting train links Stockholm with Copenhagen in around 5½ hrs.

Getting around
Central Stockholm is compact and easily walkable. **Stockholm Transport**, www.sl.se, operates the efficient metro system as well as local buses and commuter trains. Tickets valid for 24 or 72 hrs (SEK100 or SEK200) allow unlimited access to the whole network. Ferries to the archipelago (see box on page 221) are run by Waxholmsbolaget, T08 679 5830, www.waxholmsbolaget.se, and Strömma Kanalbolaget, T08 587 140, www.stromma.se, and depart from Nybroplan on the mainland. Rentabike, T08 660 7959, www.rentabike.se, is well established and reliable. Canoe hire from Djurgårdsbrons Sjöcafé, T08 660 5757.

Tourist information
The main tourist office, **Sverigehuset**, Hamngatan 27, T08 5082 8508, www.stockholmtown.com, Mon-Fri 0900-1900, Sat 1000-1700, Sun 1000-1600, will deal with all enquiries. They also have a hotel booking service in T-Centralen T08 5082 8508.

Exchange rate
Swedish Krona (SEK). £1 = SEK11. €1 = SEK9.10.

Sleeping

Finding reasonably-priced accommodation in Stockholm can be a challenge and you are advised at all times to book well in advance. Most places to stay in the centre have discounted weekend rates or other special offers. Try the tourist office website, www.stockholmtown.com, for bed and breakfast accommodation.

Grand Hotel €€€
Södra Blasieholmshamnen, T08 679 3500, www.grandhotel.se.
Metro Kungsträdgården.
Stockholm's most famous hotel has an unrivalled position on the waterfront and is unsurpassed for class and service. Its exquisite bar is a good place to spot a famous face.

Rival Hotel €€€
Mariatorget 3, T08 5457 8900, www.rival.se.
Metro Mariatorget.
Stylish and classy hotel in central Södermalm with individually designed rooms. The hotel is owned by Benny (from Abba) and if one of his musicals is in town there are good-value packages on offer.

Hotel Stureplan €€
Birger Jarlsgatan 24, T08 440 6600, www.hotelstureplan.se.
Beautiful boutique hotel, blending modern and traditional seamlessly when it comes to design. It offers a fantastic base for exploring the city, located in the best neighbourhood. The mammoth buffet breakfast allows you to fuel up for the day ahead.

City Backpackers Hostel €
Upplandsgatan 2, T08 206 920, www.citybackpackers.org.
An ideal location for the budget conscious traveller. The hostel is only 500 m from the main travel hubs including Central Station. The rooms are clean with a funky edge and there are lots of freebies on offer including Wi-Fi, hot showers, pasta (24/7!) and use of the sauna between 1700-1900.

STF Hostel af Chapman €
Flagmansvägen 8, Skeppsholmen, T08 463 2266, www.svenskaturistforeningen.se.
Metro Kungsträdgården.
Deservedly famous central hostel. Most of the rooms are land-based but some are aboard an old clipper moored to Skeppsholmen. Book well in advance if you want one of these. There is also a bar.

Eating

Swedish food has undergone something of a revolution in the past few years with the opening of a wave of international restaurants. Södermalm is the best place to find these, while Gamla Stan has traditional Swedish food of a high quality and price.

Den Gyldene Freden €€€
Österlånggatan 51, T08 249 760, www.gyldenefreden.se.
Mon-Fri 1130-1430, 1700-2300, Sat 1300-2300.
Metro Gamla Stan.
Sweden's oldest restaurant has been around for over 200 years. The fish-heavy menu always has some Nordic influences. Romantic and classy.

Gondolen på Södermalm €€€
Katarinahissen, Stadsgården 6, T08 641 7090.
Mon-Fri 1130-0100, Sat 1600-0100. Metro Slussen.
Sitting on top of the KF Huset at Slussen (take the lift from the waterfront), this is one of Stockholm's best restaurants. The modern menu competes with the decor for sophistication and the view from the restaurant is spectacular.

Restaurang Prinsen €€
Master Samuelsgatan 4, T08 611 1331, www.restaurangprinsen.com. Having first opened its doors over a century ago, Prinsen is well and truly established as the city's top bohemian eatery. Artists and writers rub shoulders with tourists, all there to soak up the special atmosphere and enjoy the excellent Swedish and Continental dishes on offer.

Vapiano €
Munkbrogatan 8, T08 222 940, www.vapiano.de. Having arrived on the restaurant scene in 2009, Vapiano has fast become known as a great budget option for those who enjoy fresh food and tasty dishes. Part of the dining experience is the open kitchen so you can watch your dish being prepared. Pizzas and pastas are a speciality.

€ Ortagarden
Nybrogatan 31, T08 662 1728, www.ortagarden-gastrogate.com. This is the city's oldest vegetarian restaurant. It offers a never-ending buffet, crammed full of fresh vegetarian dishes. The interior has an old-fashioned feel with its high ceilings and stylish décor, making it a relaxing place to pull up a chair and while away an afternoon.

Nightlife

Going out in central Stockholm is an expensive, flashy affair with a lot of queuing involved. The pubs around Medborgarplatsen and Frihemsplan are more relaxed. The best option is to pick a place with live music and spend the evening there. Note that all Swedish bars are non-smoking.

For clubs, **Berns**, *Berzelii Park, T08 5663 2222, Metro Östermalmstorget*, is an impressive complex tucked away at the back of Berzelii Park with a relaxed atmosphere and a young crowd. Book in advance to get to the **Absolut Ice Bar**, *Nordic Sea Hotel, T08 5056 3520.* SEK150 entrance including drink. You're only likely to go here once but it's an unforgettable experience. After donning your silver parka you will be served a drink in a bar where everything is made of ice. **The White Room**, *Jakobsbergsgatan 29, T08 5450 7600, www.whiteroom.se*, is an incredibly trendy club that attracts the city's über-cool. For live music, check out one of Debaser's two venues, Karl Johans **Torg 1** or **Medborgarplatsen 8**, *www.debaser.se.* Both host Swedish and International bands.

Stockholm's islands

With picturesque red houses, perfect beaches and beautiful scenery, the thousands of islands which make up Stockholm's archipelago make an excellent place for an excursion from the city. No matter how short your time in Stockholm a day trip should be a priority. Stockholmers are very proud of having the islands on their doorstep and the lucky ones try to commute by boat during the summer.

The islands vary in size and character. Some, like **Vaxholm**, are lived on all the time, while others have no permanent population. Geographically they are divided into the Northern, Middle or Southern archipelago depending on their position in the Baltic. The closest are the **Fjärderholmarna islets**, about 25 minutes by boat. Vaxholm is a year-round option and a good introduction to the archipelago.

Some of the islands can be reached by ferry throughout the year from Nybroplan on the mainland. The main companies operating ferries to the archipelago have detailed information on their websites. Waxholmsbolaget and Strömma Kanalbolaget are the biggest operators (see Travel essentials box). The tourist office website, www.stockholmtown.com, has details of individual islands and accommodation options. For longer stays in wooden cottages, Dess, T08 5424 8100, **www.dess.se**, has an online booking service.

Ratings

Art and culture ☆☆☆
Eating ☆☆☆
Nightlife ☆☆☆☆
Outdoors ☆☆☆
Romance ☆☆
Shopping ☆☆
Sightseeing ☆☆☆
Value-for-money ☆☆☆
Overall city rating ☆☆☆

Valencia

Valencia once languished in the shadow of flashy Madrid and trendy Barcelona but its days as a wallflower are long over. The word is out: Valencia, with its vibrant medieval core, its fantastic nightlife, shopping and restaurants, its sandy beaches and some of the most spectacular new architecture in Europe, is the hottest destination on the Mediterranean. Appointed the 2011 European Capital of Sport, the city has twice hosted the America's Cup, and the Formula 1 Grand Prix takes place every June. The new marina and entertainment zone, an extended metro and a slew of slick new amenities have cemented the city's position as one of the most forward-looking destinations in Spain. But its traditional charms – the palm-lined boulevards, baroque belltowers, Modernista markets and golden beaches – still assert their pull. It's a city in which old and new, shabby and sleek, co-exist peacefully.

Fresh produce on display.

At a glance

Valencia divides neatly into three general areas, each with a distinctive atmosphere. The **Old City**, 4 km inland, is still the heart of Valencia, home to most of the sights and the best selection of nightlife and shopping. It's the perfect neighbourhood for a wander – you won't need public transport. Spreading out from the Old City eastwards to the sea is the **New City**, a largely anonymous area of bland offices and apartments, but also the site of the glittering **Ciutat de les Arts i les Ciències** (City of Arts and Sciences). It's quite a walk (around 3 km) from the Old City, but a pleasant stroll along the gardens which line the former riverbed of the Riu Túria. The New City links the Old City with Valencia's vast working **port** (El Grau), its glossy new marina and the main city beach of **Malvarrosa**. This long, golden stretch is lined with a modern promenade, behind which are the scruffy, cheerful neighbourhoods of Malvarrosa and Cabanyal which once belonged to the dock workers and fishermen.

La Seu and El Micalet (Catedral and El Miguelete)

Pl de la Reina 1, T963 918 127, www.archivalencia.org. Cathedral: summer: daily 1000-1830; winter Mon- Sat 1000-1800, Sun 1400-1730; €4/€3. Museu de La Seu: Mon-Sat 1000-1300,1630-1900; €1.20/ 0.80. Micalet 1000-1300, 1630-1900, Sun 1000-1300, 1700-1930; €2/€1. Bus 6, 16, 28. Map B2.

Plaça de la Reina, a long, elegant space surrounded by cafés and palm trees, is one of the city's most important squares. (It's also the most touristy: you can't miss the horse-drawn carriages clattering around the narrow streets for a fat fee.) It's dominated by Valencia's vast and imposing **cathedral**, topped with the city's much-loved symbol, the octagonal bell tower known as the Micalet. It was largely completed by the end of the 15th century but, in the late 1700s, baroque craftsmen added the florid façade, with its thickly encrusted sculptural decoration and swooping lines.

The cathedral's greatest treasure is kept in the **Capilla del Santo Cáliz**, where a jewel-encrusted chalice carved from agate is set into a pale alabaster altarpiece that fills an entire wall. (Drop a euro in the machine to light up the altarpiece for full operatic effect.) The chapel sits next to the Sala Capitular, which houses the cathedral **museum** with a fascinating collection of religious art, statuary and sculpture.

A separate entrance leads to the **Micalet**, the slim bell tower with lacy Gothic tracery. Huff and puff up the 207 steps for staggering views across the blue-tiled cupolas, baroque towers and higgledy-piggledy maze of the Old City.

Mercat Central (Mercado Central)

Pl del Mercat, T963 829 100, www.mercadocentralvalencia.es. Mon-Sat 0730-1500. No fish market on Mon. Bus 26, 27. Map A2.

Southwest of the cathedral in the other main square of the old city, Valencia's central market is one of the most beautiful in the country; a vast, Modernista concoction of wrought iron and stained glass surmounted with cupolas and whimsical weathervanes. The Comunitat Valenciana isn't known as 'Spain's orchard' for nothing and inside you'll find a breathtaking array of colourful, fresh produce with almost 1000 stalls to choose from. The market is always busy, but get there early to catch it in full swing – breakfast at one of the dozens of stalls inside the market or tucked around the edges is an institution.

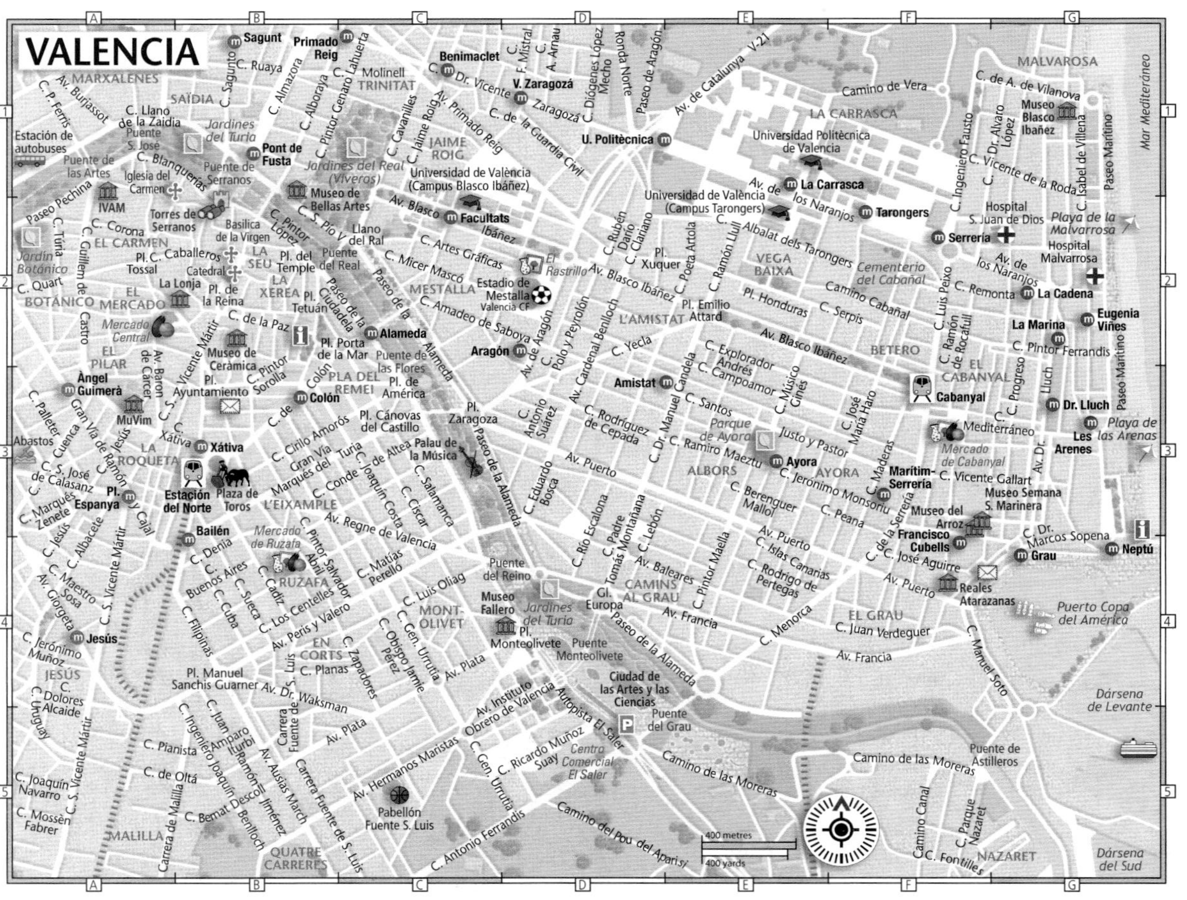

VALENCIA
Mar Mediterráneo
Paseo Marítimo
Playa de la Malvarrosa
Playa de las Arenas
MALVAROSA
Museo Blasco Ibañez
Hospital Malvarrosa
Hospital S. Juan de Dios
Eugenia Viñes
La Cadena
La Marina
Dr. Lluch
Les Arenes
Neptú
Grau
Serrería
Cabanyal
EL CABANYAL
Mercado de Cabanyal
Museo Semana S. Marinera
Museo del Arroz
Francisco Cubells
Marítim-Serrería
Reales Atarazanas
Puerto Copa del América
Dársena de Levante
Dársena del Sud
NAZARET
EL GRAU
Tarongers
La Carrasca
LA CARRASCA
Universidad Politècnica de Valencia
Universidad de València (Campus Tarongers)
Cementerio del Cabañal
BETERO
VEGA BAIXA
AYORA
Ayora
Parque de Ayora
ALBORS
Amistat
L'AMISTAT
CAMINS AL GRAU
Ciudad de las Artes y las Ciencias
Puente del Grau
Puente de Astilleros
Centro Comercial El Saler
U. Politècnica
V. Zaragozá
Benimaclet
Facultats
Universidad de València (Campus Blasco Ibáñez)
Estadio de Mestalla Valencia CF
El Rastrillo
Aragón
MESTALLA
JAIME ROIG
TRINITAT
Primado Reig
Pont de Fusta
Sagunt
Alameda
Jardines del Real (Viveros)
Museo de Bellas Artes
Jardines del Turia
Torres de Serranos
Basílica de la Virgen
Catedral
LA SEU
LA XEREA
Colón
PLA DEL REMEI
Palau de la Música
Museo Fallero
MONT-OLIVET
Puente Monteolivete
Puente del Reino
Pabellón Fuente S. Luis
Museo de Cerámica
Xàtiva
Estación del Norte
Plaza de Toros
L'EIXAMPLE
RUZAFA
Mercado de Ruzafa
Bailén
EN CORTS
QUATRE CARRERES
MALILLA
La Lonja
Mercado Central
EL MERCADO
EL CARMEN
Iglesia del Carmen
IVAM
MuVim
Àngel Guimerà
Pl. Espanya
Jesús
JESÚS
EL PILAR
BOTÁNICO
Jardín Botánico
Estación de autobuses
MARXALENES
SAÏDIA
LA ROQUETA
Abastos
Av. Blasco Ibáñez
Paseo de la Alameda
Gran Vía de Ramón y Cajal
Av. Francia
Av. Puerto
Av. de Catalunya V-21
Autopista El Saler
Camino de las Moreras
C. S. Vicente Mártir
400 metres
400 yards

La Llotja (La Lonja)

Pl del Mercat, T963 525 478.
Tue-Sat 1000-1400, 1630-2030, Sun 1000-1500. €2/€1. Bus 26, 27.

The silk exchange is quite simply the most beautiful building in Valencia. Sitting squarely opposite the main entrance to the central market, it is one of the finest examples of civic Gothic architecture in Europe and was declared a World Heritage Monument by UNESCO in 1996. Construction began in 1483 under the direction of the brilliant Pere Compte, a master stonemason, engineer and architect. The project was completed in just 15 years. The splendid main hall, the Sala de Contratación, is vast, with a lofty, vaulted ceiling which reaches almost 18 m at its highest point. To feel an echo of the buzz that would have animated the Llotja 500 years ago, visit it on a Sunday morning when a popular stamp and coin market is held in the Sala de Contratación.

Bioparc

Avda Pío Barjoa 3, 46015 Valencia, T902 250 340, www.bioparcvalencia.com.
Bus 7, 17, 29, 61, 81 and 95. Metro to Nou d'Octubre, then 10-min walk. Open daily: hours change regularly, so check the website. €21.50, children 4–12 €16, under 4s free. Off map.

Take a stroll through the gardens which line the former Turó riverbed to find the city's newest blockbuster attraction: the Bioparc. This 'new-

generation' zoo employs clever landscaping to recreate the natural habitats of its animal residents, and has hidden the enclosure fences so that visitors feel as though they are strolling with wildebeest or hanging out with the lions. Unsurprisingly, it's a huge hit with kids.

Ciudad de las Artes y las Ciències (Ciudad de las Artes y las Ciencias)

Av Autopista al Saler 1-7, T902 100 031, www.cac.es.
Museu de les Ciències: mid Sep-Jul daily 1000-1900; Aug daily 1000-2200; €7.50/€5.80. L'Hemisfèric: daily 1000-2100; €7.50/€5.80. L'Oceanogràfic: Jan-mid Jun and mid Sep-Dec Sun-Fri 1000-1800, Sat and hols 1000-2000; mid Jun-Jul and early Sep daily 1000-2000; Aug 1000-2400; €23.90 /€18. Combined tickets also available from €31.60. Bus 35, 95. Map D4.

Having seen how new architecture revitalized the fortunes of Barcelona up the coast, Valencia commissioned the glossy La Ciutat de les Arts i les Ciències in order to raise its international profile. The futuristic complex designed by local celebrity architect Santiago Calatrava has been an overwhelming success and you may need to book in advance to get into some of its attractions in the high season. There are five main sections: **Museu de les Ciències** (a science museum that looks more like a 23rd-century airport), **l'Hemisfèric** (laser shows, IMAX and planetarium), **L'Umbracle** (a palm-lined walkway), **L'Oceanogràfic** (an aquarium

Travel essentials

Getting there

Valencia's International Airport, T961 598 500, www.aena.es, is in Manises, 8 km west of the centre of town. The Aerobus runs into the centre every 20 mins daily 0600-2200 (€2.50) and is more direct than the local bus. Taxis from outside the departures hall cost €15-18 to the city centre. Trains, including the high-speed Euromed service from Barcelona, arrive into the Modernista Estació del Nord, near the Old City, T902 240 202, wwww.renfe.es.

Getting around

The Old City is best explored on foot; most of the main sights are within walking distance of each other. An excellent **bus** network will take you to places further afield like La Ciudad de las Artes y las Ciències , the port and beaches, and the Llac Albufera. The N1 night bus connects the seaside neighbourhoods with the centre. A single ticket (available on the bus) costs €1.10. Bus Turístic runs a hop-on/hop-off city tour; tickets are €12 and valid for 24 hrs. The **metro** system is largely aimed at commuters, but Line 4 (a tram-line above ground) is handy for the beach at Malvarrosa. Single metro or tram tickets (€1.10) are available from machines in stations. Useful **travel passes** include: BonoBus (10 single rides for €5.20) and T1/2/3 (1-, 2- or 3-day tickets valid for unlimited transport on bus, tram and metro for €3.10, €5.50 and €8 each). The **Valencia Card** is valid for 1, 2 or 3 days (€6/€10 /€15) and offers unlimited public transport, plus discounts in museums, shops and restaurants. It is available from tourist offices, metro stations, some tobacconists and hotels.

Tourist information

Offices at: Pl de la Reina, T963 153 931, Mon-Sat 0900-1900, Sun and hols 0900-1400; Pl de l'Ajuntament, T963 510 417, Mon-Fri 0830-1415 and 1630-1815, Sat 0915-1245; C de la Paz 48, T963 986 422, Mon-Fri 1000-1830, Sat 1000-1400; and Estació del Nord, C Jàtiva 24, T963 528 573, Mon-Fri 0900-1830, www.turisvalencia.es, www.valencia.es.

in a series of beautifully sculpted pale pavilions, the biggest in Europe), and the **Palau de les Arts** (a venue for the performing arts). The buildings – although that seems too tame a term for these bold, graphic shapes – seem to emerge from the cool, blue pools which surround them.

Platjas (Beaches)

North: bus 1, 2, 19, 31 and summer- only services 20, 21, 22. South: to El Palmar with Autocares Herca approximately every hour in winter, every half hour in summer. Buses are yellow; takes buses 'El Perellò or El Palmar, fares from €1.20, approx. 30 mins.

Heading north of the port is a long sandy beach which runs for several miles. Valencianos usually just call the whole stretch Platja de Malvarrosa, but in fact it is divided into sections: nearest the port is **Platja de Levante** or **Platja Las Arenas**, with a string of restaurants, hotels and bars squeezed next to each other on the Passeig Neptuno. It quickly becomes the **Platja de Cabanyal**, before turning into the **Platja de Malvarrosa**, and finally the **Platja de Alboraia**. The water is a tad murky, owing to the proximity of the port (the beaches south of the city are cleaner), but it is still fine for swimming. There are rows of stripy beach huts, loungers for rent, snack bars and showers, and the whole length of the beach is backed by a modern promenade lined with palms and an outdoor market in summer. The further north you trek, the fewer people you'll find, but this is still a city beach and you won't find a quiet corner in the height of summer.

The beaches south of the port are quieter, cleaner and wilder than the main city beach of Malvarrosa. They are also harder to get to, unless you have your own transport, and have fewer amenities, so bring a packed lunch and lots of bottled water. The beach of **El Saler** becomes the beach of **La Devesa**, with a small nudist section at its most southerly end. These beaches are backed by beautiful sand dunes and a dense, gnarled pine forest. There are walks through the forest and opportunities to see the birds which make their home around Llac Albufera.

Sleeping

Las Arenas €€€
C/Eugenia Viñes 22–24, T963 120 600, www.h-santos.es.
A long neglected 19th-century spa hotel on the beachfront has been magnificently transformed into the city's grandest five-star resort hotel. It features contemporary rooms, most with sea views, a spa and beauty centre, and an outdoor pool set amid extensive gardens. The service is outstanding.

Ad Hoc €€
C Boix 4, T963 919 140, www.adhochoteles.com.
A chic little hotel in a converted 19th-century mansion. Service can be frosty. The restaurant (expensive) has become a very fashionable haunt.

Parador El Saler €€
Platja del Saler, T961 611 186, www.parador.es.
Yellow metrobus services 190a, 190b, 191, 290 to El Perelló. Ask to be dropped off at the parador.
A modern hotel overlooking sand dunes and surrounded by pine forest. There's an 18-hole golf course, swimming pool and good restaurant and the beaches are empty (well, sometimes) and golden. It often has special deals, so check the website before you go.

La Casa Azul €€-€
C/Palafox 7, T963 511 100, www.lacasaazulvinosandrooms.com.
An unusual B&B set above a wine shop opposite the Mercat Central, this has just three ornately decorated rooms each with a different theme. Expect antiques, four-poster beds, and plenty of quirky charm, but bring ear plugs against the din of the market traders setting up in the morning.

Antigua Morellana €
C/En Bou 2, T963 915 773, www.hostalam.com.
Excellent hostal in an 18th-century mansion just a step from the Llotja and the Mercat Central, with charming owners and clean, well-equipped rooms, all with bathrooms.

Eating

Restaurants

Arrop Ricard Camarena (ARC) €€€
In the Hotel Palacio Marqués de Caro, C/Almirante 14, T963 925 566.
Open Tue–Sat 1345–1530 and 1945-2300.
A favourite with Valenciano gourmets, this elegant hotel restaurant is run by rising young star Ricard Camarena, who is celebrated for his adventurous Mediterranean cuisine and has been awarded a Michelin star. Carefully sourced produce is key to creations such as his signature dish pescadilla en salazón con jugo al amontillado (whiting with sherry). Book in advance.

Ca Sento €€€
CMéndez Núñez 17, T963 301 775.
Tue-Sat 1330-1530, 2100-2330, Sun and Mon 2100-2330. Closed Aug.
One of the most talked- about restaurants in the city. Tuck into classic, regional recipes given a creative new twist

Casa Mario €€
C Roters 3, T963 924 452.
Mon-Sat 1200-1600, 2000-0100.
An elegant, relaxed restaurant and tapas bar tucked behind the cathedral, specializing in fresh and tasty seafood. The revueltos (scrambled egg dishes) are also good.

La Pitanza €€
C/Quart 5, T963 910 927, www.lapitanza.com.
Open daily 1330–1600 and 2030–2400.
Perfectly located in the fashionable Carme district,

this stylish but relaxed spot offers delicious local fare, including rice dishes and seafood, prepared with a modern twist. The food is accompanied by a good selection of local wines – choose from the set menus or go a la carte.

Corretgeria 33 €€
C Corretgeria 33, T963 924 161.
Tue-Fri and Sun 1330-1700 and 2100-2400; Sat 2100-2400.
A stylish and cosy choice in the Barri del Carme serving innovative Mediterranean specialities.They do a good set lunch menu for €12.50 (Mon-Fri).

Tapas bars and cafés

Bar Pilar
C Moro Zeit 13, T963 910 497.
Daily 1200-2400.
A timeless old bar just off the Plaça del Tossal, where people order up a portion of mussels and toss the shells in the orange buckets underneath the bar. Give your name to the waiter if you want to get a seat.

Bodega Casa Montaña
CJosep Benlliure 69, T963 672 314.
Mon–Fri 1300–1530 and 2000–2330, Sat 1230–1530 and 2000–2330, Sun and public hols 1230–1530.
Traditional, buzzy tavern still going strong thanks to its excellent wines and tapas.

Café Lisboa
Pl Dr Collado 9, T963 919 484.
Daily 0900-0230.
A favourite, this arty café looks out over a pretty square with an ancient olive tree and serves great sandwiches and salads as well as cocktails in the evenings.

Café Sant Jaume
C Cavallers 51, T963 912 401.
Daily 1200-0200.
Beautiful little café set in a former pharmacy, with swirling Modernista woodwork. In the centre of the city's main nightlife street so it's perfect for people watching.

Bodeguilla del Gato
C/Catalans, T963 918 235.
Open daily 2000–0200.
Charming and old-fashioned tavern, serving a wide range of classic tapas at reasonable prices. It's always full, so get there early, especially if you want a seat on the terrace.

Nightlife

Valencia's nightlife is concentrated in different areas, but the best place to start is the hip **Barri del Carme** in the Old City, where stylish restaurants, clubs, and bars are nudged up against each other. The heart of the gay scene is here on C Quart. There are also bars and clubs near the **university** in the new part of town: check out the streets around the Pl Honduras, near Avinguda Blasco Ibáñez and look out for the following favourites: **Radio City** (Old City), **La Indiana**, **The Music Box** (live music), **Akuarela** (by the beach), **Jimmy Glass** (for jazz), **Roxy Club** (New City club). In summer, everyone heads to big outdoor clubs (terrazas) in the suburbs. There's plenty going on around the port and along the bar-lined seafront promenade.

Infernal affairs

Les Falles is one of the most important fiestas in Spain. It dates back to the Middle Ages, when carpenters used to light a bonfire in honour of Sant Josep, their patron saint. Gradually, effigies were thrown into the fire, often depicting rival organizations. Now, the vast creations take all year to build and are paraded through the streets from 13-19 March. They can be of anything – cartoon characters, politicians, buxom ladies, animals – and each neighbourhood vies to create the best. They are accompanied by mini-versions (Ninots), the winning Ninot being the only one to escape the flames. Each day, firecrackers blast out over Plaça de l'Ajuntament, bullfights are held and the evenings culminate with a massive firework display. The fiesta finishes with a bang on 19 March when the Falles are thrown into an enormous pyre, the Cremá. You can find out more about the event at **Museu Faller (Museo Fallero)**, *Pl Monteolivete 4, T963-525478, Tue-Sat 1030-1500, Sun and holidays 1000-1500. €2/€1, free on Sat, Sun and holidays.*

Ratings

Art and culture ☆☆☆☆☆
Eating ☆☆☆
Nightlife ☆
Outdoors ☆☆
Romance ☆☆☆☆☆
Shopping ☆☆☆
Sightseeing ☆☆☆☆☆
Value-for-money ☆☆
Overall city rating ☆☆☆☆

Venice

Peerlessly photogenic, Venice can seem like a beautiful relic – a vulnerable novelty without much of a contemporary purpose. A one-time global sea power, the city may or may not actually be sinking but its precarious hold on dry land is increasingly at risk from rising sea levels – high tides in winter regularly flood its piazzas and streets. Precarious and extraordinary, it is a gorgeously unlikely city, built on shifting sands, filled with great art, churches and palaces and a wonderfully peaceful absence of road traffic. And if you can get away from the massed tourists in piazza San Marco to one of the city's less popular corners, you'll find that, despite the *acque alte*, there is life in Venice, and no small amount of pride.

San Marco.

At a glance

Most visitors to Venice arrive in the city's far west, from where, once you leave the train or car, all transport is by water or on foot. From here, the **Canal Grande** snakes in a reverse 'S' through the city, crossed only by the **Ponte degli Scalzi** (by the station), the arcaded **Ponte Rialto** and the **Ponte Accademia**. The sweeping new **Ponte di Calatrava**, designed by Santiago Calatrava, opened in 2008 between the station and the road terminus at piazza Roma. To the north of the canal are the generally quieter districts of **Cannaregio** in the west and **Castello** to the east. In the second bend of the canal is the busy central area of **San Marco** and many of the city's main sights. On the southern side, **Santa Croce** and **San Polo** are nestled into the first bend of the Grand Canal, with another, more residential area, the **Dorsoduro**, on Venice's southern edge. Orientation in the narrow winding streets is famously hard, though you can get an excellent overview of the city from the top of the Campanile in **piazza San Marco**. Many visitors converge here, having followed a series of signposts that mark out a circuitous route to and from the station, via the Rialto. Around the Venetian lagoon, a ferry ride away, are islands of **Giudecca**, **Murano**, with its glass-blowing industry, colourful **Burano** and the packed but fashionable beaches of **Lido**.

24 hours in the city

Venice is at its best early in the morning, so get up with the sun, when only locals and workers will be around. Have a *caffé* and *cornetti* in a café (the touristy ones won't open until the trains start arriving a bit later) and check out the fruit and vegetable markets and, especially, the *pescaria* (fish market) in the **Rialto.** Starting early will also enable you to get to **San Marco** before the tour groups and hordes of pigeon feeders. Have a look in the basilica and, perhaps, the **Palazzo Ducale** and then climb to the top of the **Campanile** before the crowds get too big. For lunch, pick one of the cafés and restaurants on or around the busy **campo Santa Margherita** in the Dorsoduro, such as Il Caffe. From here you are well placed for a wander along the waterside **Zattere** and to take in some art at either the **L'Accademia** or the **Peggy Guggenheim Collection.** Next, head slowly across the city to reach atmospheric **Cannaregio** by supper time, perhaps looking in on a church, such as **Santa Maria dei Frari** in San Polo, and having an ice cream or an *aperitivo* along the way. A boat ride is probably best left until the evening; avoid the twee temptation of a gondola and opt instead for a *vaporetto* up the **Grand Canal.**

San Marco

www.basilicasanmarco.it.
Apr-Sep Mon-Sat 0945-1700, Sun 1400-1700; Oct-Mar Mon-Sat 0945-1700, Sun 1400-1600. Museum €4, Treasury €3, Pala d'Oro €2. Map F4.

Originally built in the ninth century to house the body of St Mark (stolen from Alexandria), the ornate and spectacular basilica of San Marco is the city's cathedral and its piazza is a magnetic gathering point for Venice's pigeons and tourists. John Ruskin called San Marco a 'treasure-heap' and it is indeed a bewildering collection of styles and ornamentation, from the Gothic spires of its façade and 19th-century mosaics, to a group of porphyry figures (the Tetrarchs), probably from fourth-century Egypt.

The centrepiece of the city, it has a large dome surrounded by four marginally smaller ones. Despite having been rebuilt and redecorated over

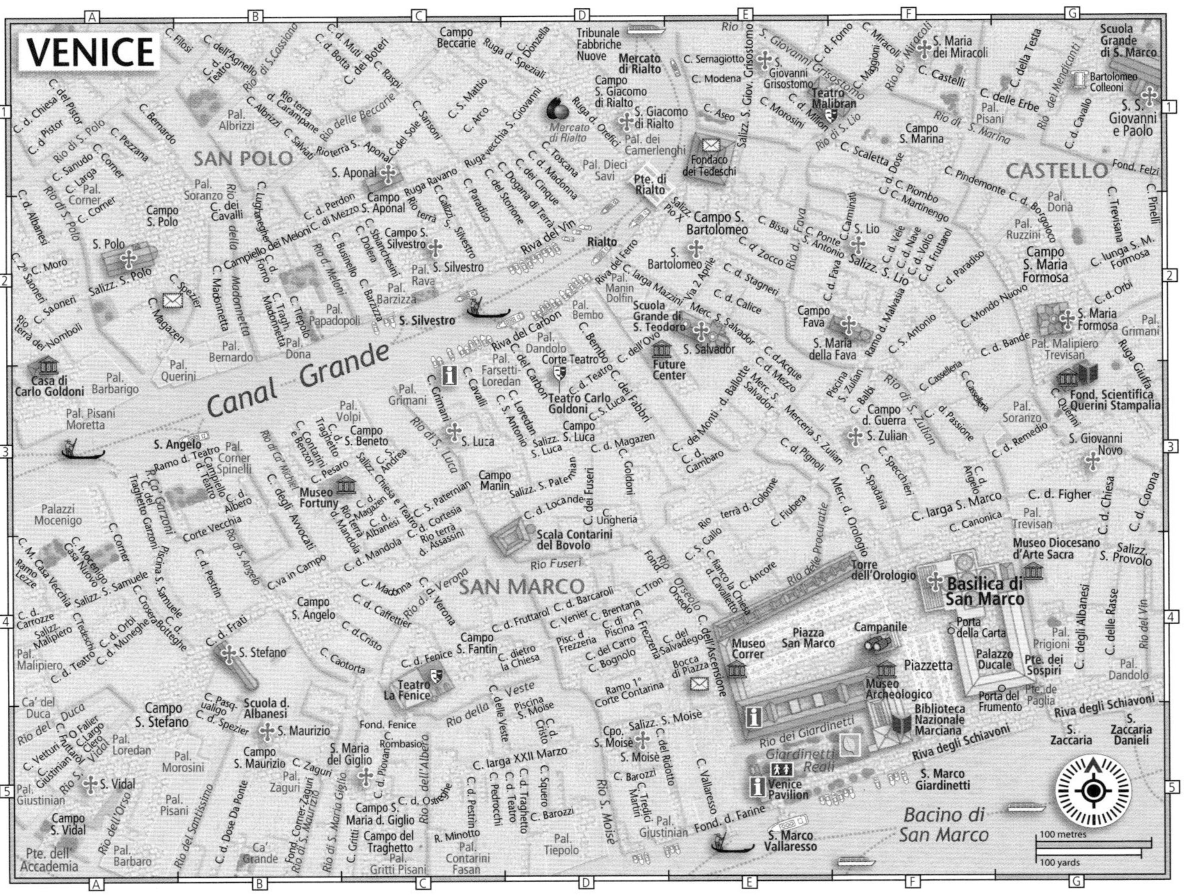
VENICE
SAN POLO
CASTELLO
SAN MARCO
Canal Grande
Bacino di San Marco
Basilica di San Marco
Palazzo Ducale
Piazza San Marco
Piazzetta
Campanile
Museo Correr
Museo Archeologico
Biblioteca Nazionale Marciana
Torre dell'Orologio
Porta della Carta
Pte. dei Sospiri
Museo Diocesano d'Arte Sacra
Pte. di Rialto
Rialto
Mercato di Rialto
Fondaco dei Tedeschi
Teatro La Fenice
Scala Contarini del Bovolo
Museo Fortuny
Casa di Carlo Goldoni
Teatro Malibran
Teatro Carlo Goldoni
Future Center
Campo S. Stefano
Campo S. Polo
Campo S. Maria Formosa
Fond. Scientifica Querini Stampalia
S. S. Giovanni e Paolo
Scuola Grande di S. Marco
Riva degli Schiavoni
Giardinetti Reali
Venice Pavilion
S. Marco Vallaresso
S. Zaccaria
Pte. dell' Accademia
100 metres
100 yards

Painting by numbers

Exactly why the houses in Burano are painted such bright colours may be lost in myth – the story most often told is that it was so that fishermen could recognize their houses from the sea. What is clear is that the island's colour scheme is now its biggest selling point and permission to paint one's house is closely controlled. But there are attractions other than the colourful houses: the ferry journey across the northern lagoon gives a good perspective to Venice's seafaring roots and its lagoon position. The island's lace industry, which began in the 16th century, means there is a school, a museum and lace shops, though genuine hand-woven Burano lace is hard to find. The Church of San Martino has a tall campanile, a Tiepolo painting of the crucifixion and, overall, a slow, quiet charm. Neighbouring Mazzorbo is connected by a wooden bridge and has orchards and a 14th-century church with its original 1318 bell. Vaporetto No 12 from Fondamente Nuove, 40-50 mins, sometimes via Torcello.

the years, its form has changed little, though much of it dates from the 11th century.

The **Pala d'Oro** – the extravagantly rich golden altarpiece – is the highlight. The **Loggia**, complete with life-size horses (the original bronzes, probably second-century Roman, are in the Museo), is well worth the climb for the view over the piazza below.

Palazzo Ducale

T041 271 5911.
Apr-Oct 0830-1830, Nov-Mar 0830-1730. Musei di Piazza San Marco ticket (€12) also allows entrance to other museums around the city: Museo Correr, Museo Archeologico and the Sale Monumentali della Biblioteca Marciana. Map G4.

Adjacent to the basilica, the Doge's Palace – largely a result of 14th- and 15th-century construction – combines Verona pink marble with ornate Gothic porticos to great effect. Doges were crowned at the top of the so-called Giants' Staircase. Inside, Domenico and Jacopo Tintoretto's *Paradiso* covers the end wall of the Great Council Hall.

The **Ponte dei Sospiri** (Bridge of Sighs) is an enclosed passageway through which prisoners once walked between their cells and the interrogation rooms in the palace. The best view of it is from Ponte della Paglia, at the palace's southeastern corner.

Campanile di San Marco

T041 522 4064, www.basilicasanmarco.it.
Apr-Jun 0930-1700, Jul-Sep 0945-2000, Oct-Mar 0945-1600. €6. Map F4.

The smaller **Torre dell'Orologio**, *T041 522 4951*, may be more ornate, but the 99 m-high Campanile is easily Venice's top tower. Originally ninth-century, the present incarnation of San Marco's bell tower dates from 1514. Views from its summit are fantastic – big vistas are rare in the city and here is nearly the whole island laid out in one broad sweep. The Campanile collapsed in 1902 and was subsequently rebuilt.

L'Accademia

Dorsoduro 1050, T041 522 2247, www.gallerieaccademia.org.
Mon 0815-1400, Tue-Sun 0815-1915. €6.50. Off map.

Across the wooden Ponte dell' Accademia, Venice's art school occupies an ex-convent on the south side of Canal Grande and houses one of Italy's great art collections, including works by Titian, Canaletto, Giovanni Bellini, Tintoretto, Andrea Mantegna and Paolo Veronese.

Canal Grande

Venice's most famous canal is its biggest: a watery highway cutting the city in two. Currently crossed only by three bridges, a trip on the canal is a must. Apart from being the quickest way to travel, it's also the best way to see some of Venice's greatest buildings: baroque **Ca' Rezzonico**, decorative **Ca d'Oro**, Michele Sanmicheli's frescoed **Palazzo Grimani**, Gothic **Ca' Foscari**, and **Palazzo Barbarigo** with its Murano glass mosaics. Also on the canal is the **Peggy Guggenheim Collection**, *Palazzo Venier dei Leoni, 701 Dorsoduro, www.guggenheim-venice.it, Mon and Wed-Sun, 1000-1800, €13.50.* Once the collector's home, there's now Picasso, Kandinsky, Pollock and a notoriously erect horse rider on view.

Pescaria

For a glimpse of Venice as it might be without tourists, head to the fish market near the Ponte Rialto early in the morning. Next door in the **Erberia** market the abundant fruit and vegetables of the Veneto are sold with equal panache. Venice's market moved here to the Rialto area in 1097.

Ponte Rialto

The city's oldest bridge, originally made of wood, collapsed in 1444 and again in 1524. Antonio da Ponte's stone design was completed in 1591 and has stood ever since, becoming one of Venice's icons. The jewellery shops which line the arcades of the bridge are expensive and best avoided.

That sinking feeling?

That Venice is sinking is a fact that has been repeated so often as to be accepted by almost all visitors to the city. However, most recent studies have suggested that the subsidence of the city from 1920 to 1970 has all but stopped. Venice is probably sinking by only 0.5 mm a year – roughly in line with the rest of the Adriatic coast.

That may not be much consolation to local residents as they wade through their city or move their valuables upstairs. The *acque alte* (high waters) are an increasingly frequent problem in winter – high tides combined with wind from the wrong direction brings the sea sweeping across Venice's *campos* and streets and into its buildings. Sirens and a network of raised walkways mean that life goes on but it's far from a happy situation in which to live.

In part the flooding can be blamed on rising sea levels. The loss of 10 cm of height during the 20th century also contributed. (Most now accept that this was due to the industrial extraction of water from rocks below the surface – a practice that was outlawed in the 1960s.) There is much less agreement about the solution, however. In 2003 the Italian government under Silvio Berlusconi gave their approval to MOSE (nominally the Modulo Sperimentale Elettromeccanico, but with a biblical nod to the holding back of the Red Sea), a grand plan to block the high water with a series of pontoons at the entrances to the lagoon. Costing around €3 billion and due to be completed around 2012, environmentalists think the pontoons will destroy the important ecosystem of the Venetian lagoon. Others point out that a project originally designed in the 1980s may be ineffective to cope with sea levels that are now predicted to rise with global warming.

Museo Diocesano di Arte Sacra

Castello 4312, T041 296 0630, www.veneziaupt.org. Daily 1000-1700, €4. Map G4.

The beautiful Romanesque Chiostro di Sant' Apollonia, inside the Museum of Sacred Art, is one of Venice's less well-known architectural beauties and dates from the early 14th century. The museum itself is less impressive, but it does contain some remnants of an earlier version of the Basilica of San Marco which are nearly 1000 years old.

Cannaregio

With fewer sights than most other Venetian sestieri, Cannaregio is perhaps the least touristy of the city's quarters, except along its southern edge. Long parallel canals retain some of their working class feel and it can be one of the most rewarding parts of the city in which to wander. It also has some of the best restaurants. The **Canale di Cannaregio** was once the main way into the city and has some suitably grand buildings. East of here, three parallel canals have less ostentatious charms. Just south off the Rio di San Girolamo, the **Ghetto Nuovo** was the original Jewish ghetto and the origin of the name. The **Museo Ebraico**, *www.museoebraico.it, Jun-Sep Sun-Fri 1000-1900, Oct-May Sun-Fri 1000-1800 €3,* tells the story of Venetian Jews. In the far east of the district, **Santa Maria dei Miracoli** is an exquisite early Renaissance church built in the 1480s.

Le Zattere and the Dorsoduro

The Zattere, the 2 km of quayside at Venice's southern extremity, is one of the city's best spots for the evening *passegiata*, with great views across to Giudecca island. North of here, the Dorsoduro is Venice's youngest, hippest quarter, centring on buzzing **Campo di Santa Margherita**, which has some great bars and is especially lively in the evenings. The **Ponte di Pugni** (Bridge of the Boxers) still has engraved footprints where those taking part in east (*castellani*) versus west (*nicolotti*) punch-ups were supposed to stand.

Best of the rest

Lido
vaporetti from San Zaccaria.
Venice's famously fashionable beach sits on the far side of an island dedicated almost entirely to it. Just about every grain of sand is occupied in summer and you have to pay (or be staying at smart hotels) for access to many parts.

Frari
campo dei Frari, T041 275 0462, €3.
An enormous church filled with art by Titian, Giovani Bellini and others, Santa Maria Gloriosa dei Frari is almost always referred to by its shorter name.

Ca' Rezzonico
Fondamenta Rezzonico 3136, T041 241 0100, €6.50.
Perhaps the best chance to experience the interior of one of Venice's baroque palaces. Giorgio Massari's enormously grand ballroom and paintings by Canaletto and Tiepolo are some of the highlights.

Murano
vaporetti from Fondamente Nuove.
On this island, a near neighbour of Venice, there is a museum dedicated to Venetian glass and you can visit glass-blowing factories. There are also some interesting churches.

Sleeping

Venice's accommodation is, by reputation, expensive and over- booked. It's certainly worth reserving ahead at busy times, and during the Biennale or the Film Festival rooms may be hard to find but at other times a little ringing around should suffice. Most of Venice's visitors are day trippers and the advantages of being able to wander around the relatively unfrequented city in the evenings or early mornings far outweigh the price of a room.

Al Ponte Antico €€€
Calle dell'Aseo, Cannaregio 5768, T04 2411 944, www.alponteantico.com.
Abundant Venetian palatial style overlooking the Grand Canal comes at a price.

Ca' Pisani €€€
Dorsoduro 979/a, T041 240 1411, www.capisanihotel.it.
A Venetian rarity, Ca' Pisani is a chic modern hotel in a 16th-century building. Sharp lines and hip colour schemes contrast effectively with the Dorsoduro surroundings.

Hotel Flora €€€-€€
San Marco 2283/a, T041 520 5844, www.hotelflora.it.
Venetian opulence abounds – lots of antiques and a vine-covered courtyard in a building where Titian may have painted.

Locanda ai Santi Apostoli €€€-€€
Cannaregio 4391/a, campo Santi Apostoli, T041 521 2612, www.locandasantiapostoli.com.
Some of the city's most reasonably priced views over the Grand Canal, from wooden-beamed rooms.

Ca' delle Acque €€
San Marco 4991, T041 241 1277, www.locandadelleacque.it.
About as central as you can get, halfway between piazza San Marco and the Rialto, Ca' delle Acque is a pretty place with apartments sleeping up to eight as well as rooms.

Pensione Seguso €€-€
Zattere 779, T041 528 6858, www.pensionesegusovenice.com.
On the corner of a canal and the Zattere waterfront in the Dorsoduro, the smart Seguso has an English colonial air, very proper service and some excellent views.

Villa Rosa €€-€
C della Misericordia 389, T041 716569, www.villarosahotel.com.
Very convenient for the station yet far enough back from the tourist traps of Rio Terrá Lista di Spagna to be quiet, the flower-clad Villa Rosa is an attractive option on the edge of Cannaregio.

Eating

Venice's culinary arts are not the city's strong point but find a table outside in a piazza on a warm summer's evening or beside a canal watching the boats go by and the food will almost certainly taste good. It's worth bearing in mind that most places close much earlier in the evening (around 2100) than in the rest of Italy. Eating out is also expensive here. The Dorsoduro and the northwest parts of Cannaregio are the best places to get away from the trilingual menus and experience something cheaper and nearer Venetian tradition. Risotto is a Venice staple, as is seafood, but there are plenty of restaurants specializing in other Italian delights.

Harry's Bar €€€
San Marco 1323, T041 528 5777.
Closed Mon.
Famous (and wealthy) enough to threaten legal action against places around the world who copy the name, Harry's is a Venetian institution on the Canal Grande. Frequented by film and opera stars, those who can afford the high prices for both food and drink, and those who come just to gawp.

All'Arco €€
San Polo 436, T041 520 5666.
Closed evenings and Sun.
One of Venice's *ombre* (dialect for a glass of wine) places which also serve cicheti (snacks and light

dishes). Near the Rialto, you could accompany your Prosecco with crostini, ham and gorgonzola.

Aqua Pazza €€
campo Sant'Angelo, San Marco 3808/10, T041 277 0688.
Open late, Aqua Pazza serves truly excellent southern Italian pizzas out in the campo for extortionate prices and with an authentic air of slightly surly chaos. There are also other good southern Italian options such as deep fried vegetables and a mixed fish grill which make putting up with the poor service worthwhile.

Osteria Alla Zucca €€
Santa Croce 1762, Ponte del Megio, T041 524 1570.
Near San Giacomo dell'Orio, this friendly little trattoria is good for vegetarians. The four or five tables outside on the street fill up quickly.

Osteria Anice Stellato €€
Fondamenta de la Sensa, Cannaregio 3272, T041 720744.
Closed Mon.
A reminder of Venice's one-time status as an important port linking east and west, Anice Stellato uses more spices than are usual in Italian cooking, combining them with Venetian cuisine to good effect. Out of the way on one of Cannaregio's long, quiet canals, this colourful little place usually has more locals than visitors. If it's full, Ai 40 Ladroni, *T041 715736*, next door is also a good option.

Osteria Bea Vita €€
3082 Fondamenta degli Ormesini.
A rarity in that you can sit outside beside a canal and be as likely to share tables with locals as with tourists. The good value €10.50 lunch menu is pasta- and risotto-based.

Osteria Vecio Forner €€
Dorsoduro 671/B, campo San Vio, T041 528 0424.
Closed Sun.
A fashionably smart little bar on the corner of a campo near the Guggenheim museum with good food options, especially for a light lunch. Dishes of the day €8-15.

Osteria da Toni €
Fondamenta di San Basilio 1642, T041 528 6899.
Closed Mon.
A long hike from San Marco, da Toni is a traditional no-nonsense trattoria of a kind rarely found in Venice. Popular with students and locals it's an excellent place for Venetian seafood and simple pasta and wine lunches. Not far from the western end of the Zattere, there are a few tables outside beside the canal.

Taverna da Baffo €
San Polo 2346, Campo Sant'Agostin, T041 520 8862.
Closed Sun.
A popular café which opens early and stays open until 0200 with good coffee early, live music late and decent food in between. Free buffet on Tue evenings.

Nightlife

Bars

Venice's nightlife is infamously somnolent – wander around the city at an hour when most Mediterranean cities would be sparking into life and you will probably find dark empty streets. The **Dorsoduro** is the area which bucks this trend somewhat; campo Santa Margherita is the best for a *giro de ombre*. When performed by Venetians these bar crawls of local nightspots usually involve the over-consumption of glasses of spritz, a misleadingly cheap and quaffable combination of wine, soda water and a bitter, usually Campari, Aperol or Cynar.

Live music

Nightclubs are practically non-existent though some bars have live music (**Il Caffe**, campo Santa Margherita) and the jazz scene is perhaps the least moribund of the Venetian performing arts. **Paradiso Perduto**, Fondamenta della Misericordia in Cannaregio, has jazz and blues. **La Fenice**, *www.teatrolafenice.it*, is one of the country's top opera venues.

Travel essentials

Getting there

Venice Marco Polo, T041 260 9240, www.veniceairport.it, is the city's main airport, 19 km by road and 8 km by sea from the city, to the north of the lagoon. It is connected by boat to San Marco and the Zattere every hour (www.alilaguna.it, 1 hr, €13). Water taxis are much more expensive (up to €100 for 4 people) but will take you right to your hotel. Or travel by bus to piazzale Roma, every 30 mins (40 mins, €1).

About 32 km from the city, **Venice Treviso**, T042 231 5131, www.trevisoairport.it, is a small airport used by Ryanair. Buses run to and from piazzale Roma to coincide with flights (45 mins; €5 single, €9 return). Alternatively, bus 6 (10-15 mins; €1) runs from to Treviso train station every 30 mins for frequent train connections to Venice.

Special day and night rail services connect **Venice Santa Lucia** train station with Paris, Nice, Vienna and Salzburg (www.trenitalia.it). The **Venice Simplon-Orient Express** (www.orient-express.com) luxury train service runs from London or Paris.

Getting around

Despite the canals, the best way to get around is on foot. *Vaporetti* are fairly large passenger boats which ply several routes around and through the city, primarily up and down the Canal Grande and the Canale di Cannaregio and to other islands. Traghetti are gondolas without the silly hats, which cross the Canal Grande at places where there are no bridges. Vaporetti tickets cost €6.50 single, €18 for 24 hrs or €33 for 72 hrs and are available from booths at the stops. Traghetti cost €0.50 per crossing – pay the boatman and stay standing, if you can. Gondolas cost €80 for 40 mins, maximum 6 people per gondola. The price rises to €100 after 1900.

Tourist information

Azienda di Promozione Turistica, www.turismovenezia.it, has 2 central offices: in piazza San Marco, S Marco 71/f, T041 529 8711, daily 0900-1530, and in the Ex Giardini Reali, T041 529 8711, daily 1000-1800.

Venice Discovery Tours, http://venice.city-discovery.com, combine a walking tour in the morning with a boat tour (limited to 8 people) in the afternoon, €60 per person. You can also hire a private boat and a driver to take you around the canals or out into the lagoon, although this is significantly more expensive.

Festivals

Venice comes into its own during festivals. There's the profusion of contemporary art in the **Biennale**, *www.labiennale.org*, the cinematic buffs of the **Film Festival** (late Aug, early Sep) or the masks and thicker-than-ever throngs of tourists during **Carnevale** (Feb). Look out too for lesser known festivals such as **Festa di Liberazione**, the Communist Party's annual knees-up in late summer.

Ratings

Art and culture ☆☆☆
Eating ☆☆☆☆
Nightlife ☆☆
Outdoors ☆☆
Romance ☆☆☆
Shopping ☆☆
Sightseeing ☆☆☆
Value-for-money ☆☆☆
Overall city rating ☆☆☆

Verona

Red-roofed and pastel-shaded, on the edge of the mountains and the cusp of the plain, Verona likes to think of itself as both the beginning and the distillation of the real Italy. At the crossroads of the north-south route from the Brenner Pass to Rome, and the east-west Milan-Venice road, the city has long been of strategic importance. Apart from Rome itself, Verona is Italy's best-preserved Roman city (with a Roman amphitheatre, a bridge, gates and theatre) and also has richly decorated Romanesque, Gothic and Renaissance aspects, with spectacular frescoed churches and houses. All this antiquity is given an opulent sheen by a well-dressed 21st-century population who have, in the main, done very well out of wine, opera, European integration and a select brand of tourism.

Statues in the Piazza dei Signori.

Centro storico

Bordered on three sides by the River Adige, the streets of Verona's ancient centre follow the Roman layout. The city's main shopping streets, including the shiny **via Mazzini**, and most of the well-known sights are here, between **Ponte Pietra**, the bridge which predates the city, in the north, along narrow winding streets to the original Roman gates of **Porta Leoni** in the south and **Porta Borsari** in the west. The site of the old Roman forum is now the expansive **piazza Erbe**, the heart of the city and filled with Renaissance and Gothic buildings dating from the 14th to the 18th centuries. On the eastern side of the piazza, **Casa Mazzanti** has a cycle of allegorical frescoes by Cavalli from around 1530, which face onto the square. The portico, filled with cafés selling ice-cream concoctions, was built in 1480. In the cellars, 3.5 m below the present-day surface, the original paving of the Roman forum has been found. **Fontana Madonna Verona** in the piazza's centre and one of the beloved symbols of the city, is a mishmash of local Roman remains: the basin was taken from the thermal baths of Sant'Anastasia, the statue from the Capitol. Originally erected in the fourth century in honour of the emperor's lifting of the city's debts, the fountain was added by Cansignorio della Scala in 1368.

Piazza dei Signori, leading off piazza Erbe, is more refined; a celebration not of commerce and the market, but of power and of poets, and in particular of the Scaligeri family, rulers of the city in the 13th and 14th centuries. While the foundations are also Roman, much of what sits on top is Gothic, Romanesque and Renaissance, and narrow streets of ancient palazzi, many still frescoed, stretch up to the Adige. The piazza's most attractive building, and the best place to sit and watch the daily comings and goings, is the Renaissance **Loggia del Consiglio** (built between 1476 and 1492 by Fra' Giocondo).

The **Duomo**, *piazza Duomo, T045 592813, Nov-Feb, Mon-Sat 1000-1300, Sun 1330-1700; Mar-Oct Mon-Sat 1000-1730, Sun 1330-1730, €2.50, €5 for combined ticket for 4 main churches*, is just one of many spectacular churches in Verona. It has a beautiful façade, a stunning Titian (Assumption in the Cappella Cartolari-Nichesola, the first on the left), a Sanmicheli-designed bell tower, griffins, and plenty of historical interest. The stamp of the medieval rulers, the della Scala family, is visible most ostentatiously in their elaborate Gothic tombs.

The **Scavi Scaligeri**, the collection of ancient excavated remains under piazza Viviani and the cortile del Tribunale in the very centre of old Verona is the spectacular, if slightly damp, setting for excellent large-scale photography exhibitions at the **Centro Internazionale di Fotografia**, *T045 800 7490, Tue-Sun 1000-1900 during exhibitions. €5*. Recent exhibitions have included John Phillips and Luciano Perbellini.

Also within the walls of the old city is **Casa di Giulietta (Juliet's House)**, *23 via Cappello, T045 803 4303, Mon 1330-1930, Tue-Sun 0830-1930, entrance to the house €6, courtyard free*, an extraordinary indictment of modern tourism but also strangely magnetic. A heaving mass of day trippers throng in and out of the courtyard to take photos of the famous fictional balcony (added to the building in the 1930s).

Duomo.

Arena

piazza Bra, T045 800 3204, www.arena.it.
Mon 1345-1930, Tue-Sun 0830-1930, 0900-1530 during opera season. €6, €1 first Sun of month. Map D4.

At the other end of via Mazzini from the enormous spread of piazza Erbe, **piazza Bra** forms an alternative centrepiece to the city, with the giant

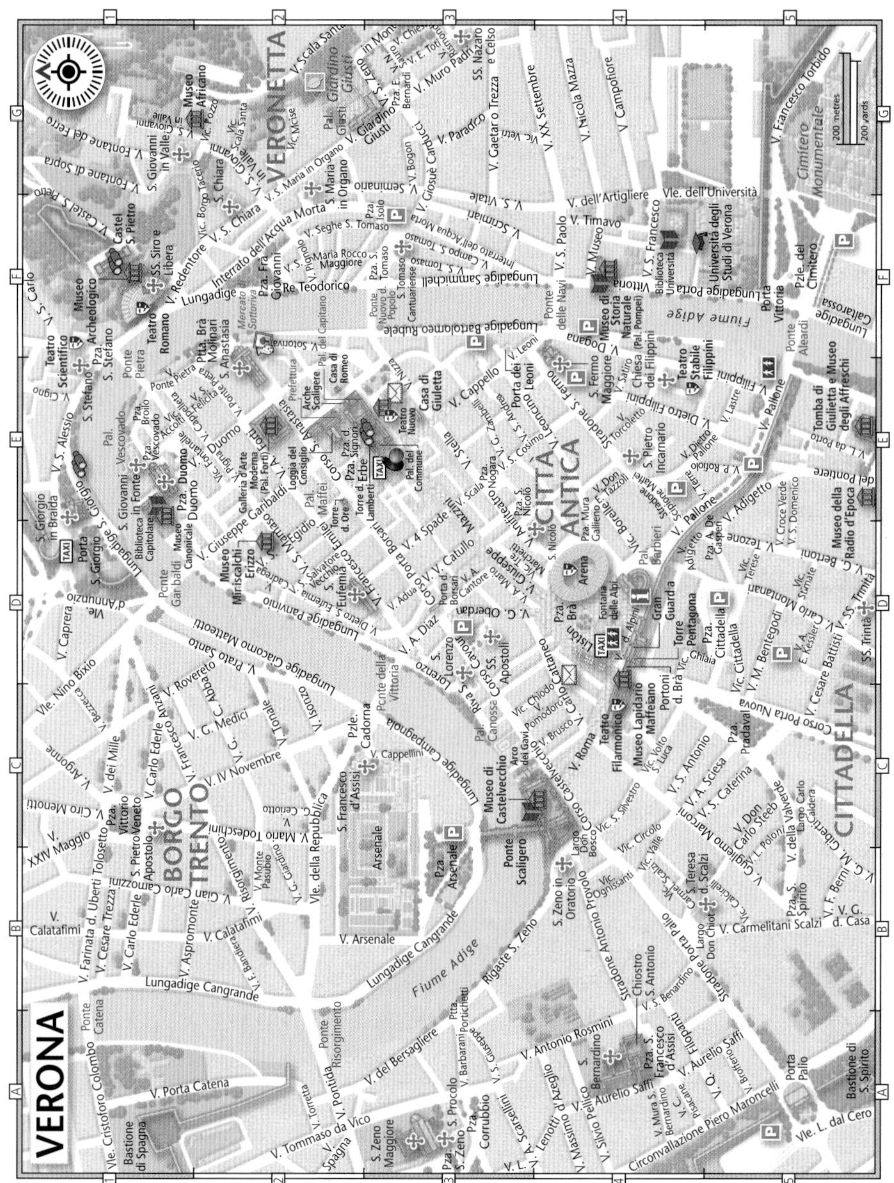
VERONA
VERONETTA
CITTÀ ANTICA
BORGO TRENTO
CITTADELLA
Fiume Adige
Arena
Pza. Brà
Pza. Erbe
Pza. Signori
Casa di Giuletta
Castel S. Pietro
Teatro Romano
Museo Archeologico
Pza. Duomo
S. Anastasia
Arche Scaligere
Museo di Castelvecchio
Ponte Scaligero
Arsenale
S. Zeno Maggiore
Giardino Giusti
Università degli Studi di Verona
Museo di Storia Naturale
Tomba di Giulietta e Museo degli Affreschi
Cimitero Monumentale
Porta Nuova
Gran Guardia
Museo Lapidario Maffeiano
Teatro Filarmonico
Ponte Pietra
Ponte Garibaldi
Ponte Risorgimento
Ponte della Vittoria
Ponte Navi
Ponte Aleardi
Bastione di Spagna
Bastione di S. Spirito
Porta Palio
Porta Vittoria
Corso Porta Nuova
Corso Porta Borsari
Corso Cavour
V. Roma
V. Mazzini
Lungadige Cangrande
200 metres
200 yards

Arena carvings.

elliptical Roman Arena dominating it. Verona's most famous sight is the third largest Roman amphitheatre still in existence after the Colosseum and the little-visited amphitheatre in Capua. Still dominating much of the city, it is used as a 20,000-seater stadium and a theatre for the summer opera season. To the west, **Castelvecchio**, *corso Castelvecchio 2, T045 592985, www.comune.verona.it/castelvecchio/cvsito, Mon 1345-1930, Tue-Sun 0830-1930, ticket office closes 1845, €6, free first Sun of the month*, has all the attributes you'd wish for in a castle, plus a great bridge, and is now the Civic Museum of Art. Further west, the ornate 12th-century **Basilica San Zeno**, *piazza San Zeno, T045 800 6120, Q, Apr-Oct Mon-Sat 0830-1800, Sun 1300-1800, Nov-Mar Tue-Sat 1000-1300 and 1330-1600, Sun 1300-1700, €2.50, €5 combined ticket for 4 churches*, is justifiably the city's favourite church.

North and east of the Adige

The steep hill of San Pietro was the original site of settlement in the city. At its base, looking out across the river, sits the **Teatro Romano** and the **Museo Archeologico**, *Rigaste Redentore 2, T045 800 0360,4, Mon 1345-1930, Tue-Sun 0830-1930, ticket office closes 1845, €4, free first Sun of the month, information on summer events T045 807 7201*. From its top are fantastic panoramic views over the city. To either side of the hill are residential areas of the old city. There are atmospheric little districts of winding streets, especially in Veronetta to the south, with many of the city's best bars and restaurants. Beyond rise hills of olive trees and vineyards, with the first signs of the Alps to the north.

Travel essentials

Getting there

Verona Villafranca Airport (Valerio Catullo), T045 809 5666, www.aeroportoverona.it, is served by APTV bus every 20 mins to and from the train station, 0635-2335. (Journey time is around 15 mins, €5 each way). Taxis cost around €20 to the centre. Tiny **Brescia Montichiari Airport** (Gabriele D'Annunzio) T030 965 6599, www.aeroportobrescia.it, used by Ryanair, is about an hour away from Verona by bus. Ryanair runs a service between the airport and Verona train station to coincide with their flights and costs €11 single. Tickets are available from an office inside the arrivals/departures hall (or, on the return journey from Verona, on the bus). International trains, including services from Paris and Munich, arrive at Porto Nuovo station, www.trenitalia.com.

Getting around

The size of Verona's compact centre means that walking is by far the best way to get around and see the sights. Orange **AMT**, T045 887 1111, buses serve the city. All services centre on the sprawling bus station, opposite the train station, south of piazza Bra. Tickets must be bought (either from tobacconists, marked with a large 'T' outside or from AMT machines at the station) before boarding and stamped on board, after which they are valid on any bus for 1 hr. An ordinary ticket costs €1.10. A 10-journey ticket (una tessera) is also available for €10, and a day ticket (giornaliero) for €3.50. The most useful city services are likely to be 11, 12, 13, and 14 between the station (from beside the AMT booth) and piazza Bra, continuing over the river. At weekends and on holidays these are replaced by services 91, 92 and 98.

Tourist information

The main office is at via degli Alpini 9 (just behind the Arena), T045 807 7774 , Mon-Sat 0900-1900, Sun 0900-1500, iatbra@tiscalinet.it. There's an 'office' at the railway station, Porta Nuova FS, T045 800 0861, iatfs@tiscalinet.it, Mon-Sat 0900-1800, Sun 0900-1500, which is no more than a man at a desk, but can nevertheless be useful for those arriving at the station. The **Verona Card** is probably a worthwhile investment, giving access to all the major sites and museums, as well as free bus travel. €5 for 1 day, €10 for 3 days.

Sleeping

Sogno di Giulietta €€€
Via Cappello 23 -Cortile di Giulietta, T045 800 9932, www.sognodigiulietta.it.
Facing Juliet's balcony, the Sogno di Giulietta has plush and suitably romantic rooms done in medieval style.

Aurora €€
piazza Erbe, T045 594 717, www.hotelaurora.biz.
Overlooking piazza Erbe, the friendly Hotel Aurora has a great sunny terrace and unfussy air-conditioned rooms.

Torcolo €€
vicolo Listone 3, T045 800 7512, www.hoteltorcolo.it.
On a quiet road behind piazza Bra, Torcolo has charm and style. Attic rooms on the 3rd floor, with sloping ceilings, are particularly attractive.

Armando €
via Dietro Pallone 1, T045 800 0206.
In an attractive, quiet area between piazza Bra and Ponte Aleardi, Hotel Armando has been renovated in a contemporary style but remains good value.

Eating

The line between bars and restaurants is a fine one in Verona. Osterie serve food of varying complexity and trattorie often have good, and enormously long, wine lists. There is little tradition of drinking without eating but, having said that, Verona's student population adds a lively edge and some of the city's drinking spots stay open well into the early hours. (Via Sottoriva, around San Zeno and Veronetta are the best areas.) Wine predominates, though most places also have beer on tap.

Al Bersagliere €€
via Dietro Pallone 1, T045 800 4824.
Mon-Sat 1200-1430, 1930-2200, also open as a bar from 0800.
Traditional Veronese and Lessinian food, plenty of polenta-based dishes as well as smoked goose breast, trout with Soave wine and lots of wine and home-made desserts.

Hostaria la Vecchia Fontanina €€
piazetta Chiavica 5, T045 591 159.
Mon-Sat 1200-1430, 1930-2230.
An attractive little restaurant serving a mixed crowd of mainly Italians. A varied and interesting menu includes pasta with nettles and even the bread and house wine are a cut above the rest.

Carro Armato €
vicolo Gatto 2a, T045 803 0175.
Mon, Tue, Thu-Sat 1100-0200, Sun 1100-0000.
Generally considered a nightspot, Carro Armato buzzes in the evenings, has an excellent wine list and extremely good local dishes.

Corte Farina €
Via Corte Farina 4, T045 800 0440, www.cortefarina.com
Mon-Sat 1100-1500, 1800-0000, kitchen 1200-1430, 1930-2230.
Verona's best pizzas are made here using organic flour and Argentinian meat.

Zeno Gelato Cioccolato
Piazza San Zeno 12a, www.zenoverona.it
Exquisite organic ice-cream made using the best local ingredients.

Ratings

Art and culture ☆☆☆☆
Eating ☆☆☆☆
Nightlife ☆☆☆
Outdoors ☆☆
Romance ☆☆☆☆☆
Shopping ☆☆☆
Sightseeing ☆☆☆
Value-for-money ☆☆
Overall city rating ☆☆☆

Vienna

For centuries the most powerful city in continental Europe, Vienna oozes with the memories, traditions, riches and ambitions of Europe's most calculatingly expansionist dynasty: the Habsburgs. Imposing yet florid palatial architecture defines the city, whether lining grand boulevards or set among landscaped parks. The opera house, myriad concert halls and art collections bear testimony to a taste for high culture in a city that harboured Beethoven, Mozart, Brahms, Klimt and Schiele. Traditionally straight-laced and uptight, this one-time outpost of the Cold War now finds itself again at the heart of an expanded Europe that it once would have ruled. Blowing off its cobwebs and newly alive with the influences of its position at a cultural crossroads, it is impossible not to have a good night in Vienna.

Vienna Opera House.

At a glance

The cultural core of Vienna lies within the city's old town (Altstadt), defined by the **Ringstrasse**, formerly the medieval walls. A tram ride will cast you back to fin de siècle Habsburg times and past the famous **Opera** that echoes with Mozart, Brahms and Beethoven. The **Museums Quarter** (MQ) lies in the southwest of the Ring and consists of the Imperial Palace (now the Kunsthistoriches Museum – one of the most important fine arts museums in the world), the former Imperial Stables with their unique balletic Lippizaner white stallions, and also the MUMOK and Leopold museums of contemporary and modern art. Between your Brueghels and Klimts, you'll be able to enjoy a host of atmospheric, relaxed and even hip bars, restaurants and shops in the ultimate meeting of high art and high life. For film aficionados (and kids) the **Prater funfair** and Ferris wheel of *Third Man* fame lie to the northeast across the Danube. If you'd rather just recline and be Austrian for the weekend, the elegant, tightly packed streets of the Altstadt are the home of Vienna's unsurpassable cafés. By day you can follow in the footsteps of Trotsky and Freud with some cake and a whipped-cream coffee, and by night enjoy the studied melange of new-imperial and ultra-modern. Vienna is a long way from the waltzes of Johann Strauss and that famous 1980s pop video by Ultravox.

Der Wiener Ring

In 1857 the Habsburgs razed the city's medieval wall to create a monument to their vanity. This took the form of a grand boulevard circling the centre, lined with extravagant and imposing royal buildings, private residences, vast squares and parks, puffed up monuments and elegant cafés. One hundred and 50 years on it acts as a walk-by window on the Habsburg dynasty and is best viewed by hopping on either the No 1 or No 2 tram. In doing so you will be able to take in, at least from the outside, Otto Wagner's Post Office building, the Vienna Opera House, the Imperial Palace, Museum of Fine Arts, the Burgtheater and the University.

St Stephen's Cathedral

T01 515 52 3526, www.stephanskirche.at.
Mon-Sat 0600-2200, Sun 0700-220. €1.
U-bahn Stephansplatz, bus 1A, 2A, 3A. Map E2.

Austria's most important Gothic building, Vienna's cathedral was begun in the 12th century although the oldest remaining parts are the Romanesque Great Gate and the Towers of the Heathens, dating from the 13th century. If you have a head for heights, climb the 343 steps to the top of the 137 m-high South Tower (*Steffl* to locals). Gothic was out of vogue by 1579 when the North Tower was capped by a cobbled-together Renaissance spire. Inside are a number of treasures, notably the red marble sepulchre of Emperor Frederick III, sculpted from 1467 to 1513 by Niclas Gerhaert van Leyden.

Imperial Palace and Museums Quarter (MQ)

MQ, T01 523 5881 1730, www.mqw.at.
Daily 1000-1900, individual museum times vary.
U-bahn Museums Quartier, Volkstheater. Bus 2A, 48A, tram 49. Map A4/A5.

Until the end of the First World War, the Imperial Palace was the centre of the Austro-Hungarian empire. Since then it has been transformed into a veritable empire of the arts. The Museums Quarter ranks as one of the 10 largest cultural complexes in the world, complete with bars and restaurants in which to digest it all. The following are just some of the highlights the area encompasses.

Imperial Palace.

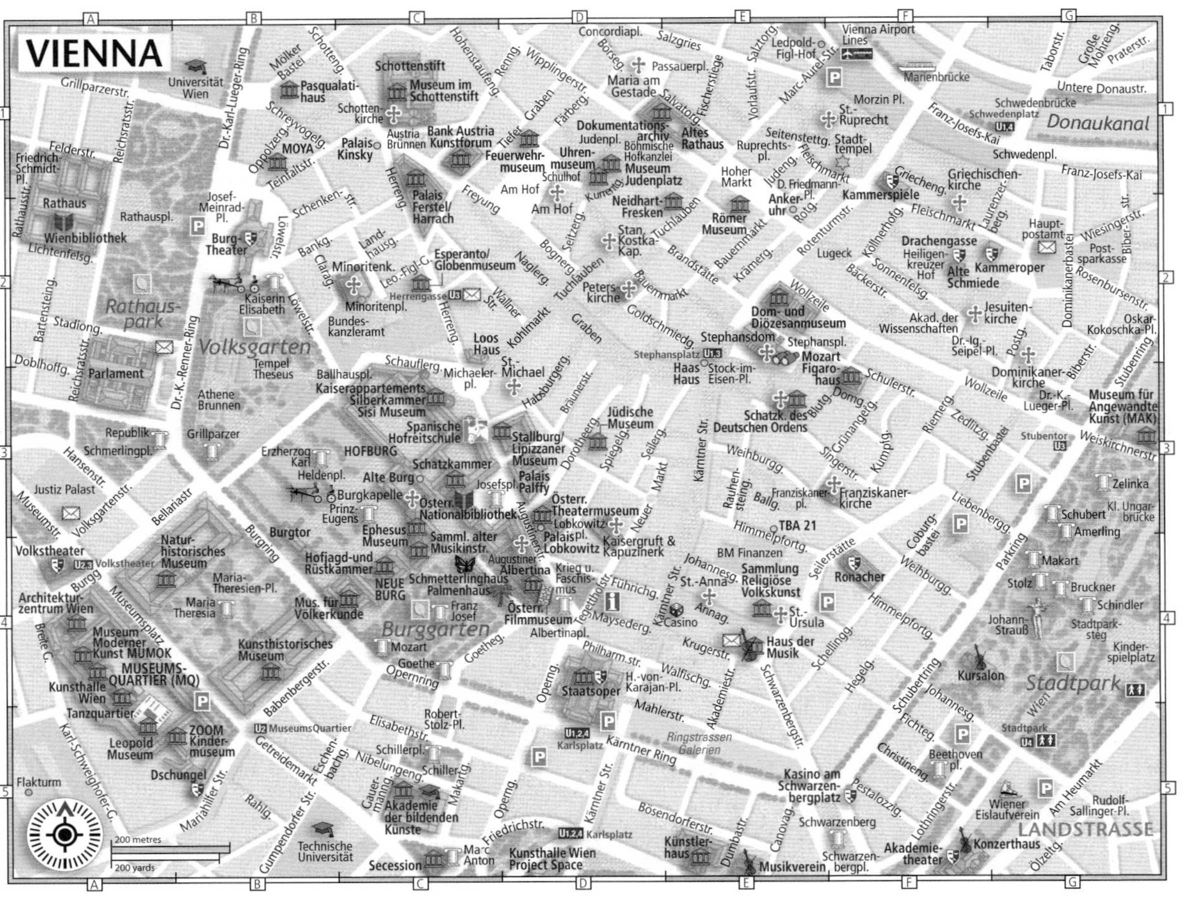

VIENNA
Donaukanal
Volksgarten
Rathauspark
Burggarten
Stadtpark
LANDSTRASSE
Rathaus
Wienbibliothek
Parlament
Universität Wien
Burg-Theater
Schottenstift
Museum im Schottenstift
Schottenkirche
Palais Kinsky
Pasqualatihaus
MOYA
Palais Ferstel/Harrach
Bank Austria Kunstforum
Feuerwehrmuseum
Uhrenmuseum
Am Hof
Dokumentationsarchiv
Museum Judenplatz
Maria am Gestade
Altes Rathaus
Römer Museum
Neidhart-Fresken
Ankeruhr
St.-Ruprecht
Stadttempel
Kammerspiele
Griechischenkirche
Drachengasse
Heiligenkreuzer Hof
Alte Schmiede
Kammeroper
Jesuitenkirche
Dominikanerkirche
Akad. der Wissenschaften
Hauptpostamt
Postsparkasse
Museum für Angewandte Kunst (MAK)
Dom- und Diözesanmuseum
Stephansdom
Stephansplatz
Haas Haus
Mozart Figarohaus
Schatzk. des Deutschen Ordens
Franziskanerkirche
Ronacher
Sammlung Religiöse Volkskunst
Haus der Musik
St.-Ursula
Kursalon
Konzerthaus
Wiener Eislaufverein
Akademietheater
Kasino am Schwarzenbergplatz
Musikverein
Künstlerhaus
Kunsthalle Wien Project Space
Karlsplatz
Staatsoper
Albertina
Österr. Filmmuseum
Kaisergruft & Kapuzinerk
Jüdisches Museum
Palais Lobkowitz
Österr. Theatermuseum
Palais Pálffy
Stallburg/Lipizzaner Museum
St.-Michael
Loos Haus
Esperanto/Globenmuseum
Minoritenk.
Bundeskanzleramt
Kaiserappartements Silberkammer Sisi Museum
Spanische Hofreitschule
Schatzkammer
HOFBURG
Alte Burg
Burgkapelle
Österr. Nationalbibliothek
Schmetterlinghaus
Palmenhaus
Ephesus Museum
Samml. alter Musikinstr.
NEUE BURG
Hofjagd-und Rüstkammer
Mus. für Völkerkunde
Burgtor
Heldenpl.
Prinz Eugens
Erzherzog Karl
Kaiserin Elisabeth
Tempel Theseus
Athene Brunnen
Grillparzer
Mozart
Goethe
Schiller
Kunsthistorisches Museum
Naturhistorisches Museum
Maria-Theresien-Pl.
Maria Theresia
MUSEUMSQUARTIER (MQ)
Museum Moderner Kunst MUMOK
Leopold Museum
Kunsthalle Wien
Tanzquartier
ZOOM Kindermuseum
Dschungel
Architekturzentrum Wien
Volkstheater
Justiz Palast
Secession
Akademie der bildenden Künste
Technische Universität
Flakturm
Ringstrassen Galerien
Casino
TBA 21
Schubert
Johann-Strauß
Kärntner Str.
Graben
Wollzeile
Rotenturmstr.
Herreng.
Dr.-Karl-Lueger-Ring
Dr.-K.-Renner-Ring
Burgring
Opernring
Kärntner Ring
Schubertring
Parkring
Stubenring
Franz-Josefs-Kai
Schwedenplatz
Stubentor
200 metres
200 yards

Spanish Riding School (Spanische Hofreitschule)

1 Michaelerplatz, T01 533 9031, www.srs.at. Dec-Aug Tue-Sun 0900-1600, Sep-Nov daily 0900-1600, on Fri performance days 0900-1900. Free, 15-min guided tours Tue-Sat 1230-1700. U-bahn Herrengasse, bus 2A. Map C3.

Even if you are not of an equine inclination it is impossible not to be moved by the beauty of the famous Yugoslavian Lippizaner white stallions on display. The art of classical riding taught by the school dates back to the Renaissance. (The stables are some of the few Renaissance buildings in Vienna.) Here you can live the history of these horses and admire gala balletic exhibitions of incredible precision. The impressive riding hall was furnished in baroque style by Joseph Emanuel Fischer von Erlach between 1729-1735 and was supposed to provide children of the aristocracy with the chance to take riding instruction. You can watch the morning training sessions and visit the stables.

Travel essentials

Getting there

Schwechat Airport, T01 70 070, www.viennaairport.com, is 19 km southeast of the city centre. The **City Airport Train** (CAT), www.cityairporttrain.com, takes you non-stop to the City Air Terminal at Wien-Mitte junction near Vienna Hilton and St Stephen's Cathedral. Journey time is around 15 mins, daily 0538-2335 (€9, €16 return). On the way back you can check in at the City Air Terminal. **Vienna Airport Lines** buses link the city to the airport from Schwedenplatz, Suedtiroler Platz, the City Air Terminal at Hotel Hilton and Westbahnhof (€6, €11 return). Journey time is around 20 mins, daily 0500-2400. The S-bahn is the cheapest option. Take line S7 (every 30 mins; journey time 35 mins). Get an Aussenzonen (outer zone) ticket for €4.40 (€2.20 if you have a Vienna Card, see below) and have it punched before entering the train. A taxi costs around €15. Bratislava's **MR Štefánika Airport** in Slovakia is only 60 km east of Vienna and close enough to be an alternative to Schwechat. There are various options for shuttling to and from the airport as well as car rental desks.

As Central Europe's main rail hub, Vienna has good connections to most other major European destinations. **Eurostar**'s London-Vienna service via Paris takes around 14 hrs. Vienna has several train stations; check whether you're arriving at Westbahnhof, Südbahnhof or Franz Josefs Bahnhof.

Getting around

Vienna is very pleasant for exploring on foot. The city's network of efficient and picturesque trams (especially Nos 1 and 2 which go clockwise and anti-clockwise around the famous Ring), buses or the art nouveau underground system, is easy to use. A single trip costs €1.80, a 24-hr card costs €5.70 and a 72-hr card costs €13.60.

Tourist information

Over 200 discounts are available in the city with the **Vienna Card** (€18.50), available at hotel and the Tourist Information Centre, 1 Albertinaplatz, T01 2111 4222, www.info.wien.at, daily 0900-1900. The card is also available at all sales offices or information booths of the Vienna transport system. It allows unlimited travel by underground, bus and tram, discounts on airport transfer services, reductions (see prices in brackets in Sights section) at museums, theatres, concerts, shops, restaurants, cafés and bars. There's another tourist office in the Arrivals hall at the airport, 0700-2200. **Wien-Hotels & Info**, T01 24555, 0900- 1900, has a hotel booking service.

Kunsthistorisches Museum

1 Maria-Theresien-Platz, T01 525 240, www.khm.at.
Daily 1000-1800, Thu 1000-2100. Closed Mon. €12 (€11). U-bahn Volkstheater, MuseumsQuartier, bus 2A, 57A. Map B4.

Vienna's Museum of Fine Arts was built in 1891 next to the Imperial Palace in order to house the extensive collections of the Habsburgs. During their reign they managed to amass the largest collection of Brueghel paintings in the world, including his *Farm Wedding*. Also among their collection are Raphael's *Madonna in the Meadow*, Vermeer's *Allegory of Painting*, Velazquez's Infanta paintings and masterpieces by Rubens, Rembrandt, Duerer, van Dyk, Holbein, Titian and Tintoretto. As such, it must surely rank among the most important fine art museums in the world.

Leopold Museum

7 Museums platz, T01 52570, www.leopoldmuseum.org.
Wed, Fri-Mon 1000-1800, Thu until 2100. €11 (€9.90). U-bahn Museums Quartier. Map A5.

The passionate art lover Dr Rudolf Leopold amassed hundreds of masterpieces and has his own museum to showcase, among other things, the world's largest collection of works by Egon Schiele. Other major artists featured here are Gustav Klimt and Oskar Kokoschka, and furniture and other pieces by Otto Wagner. Combined, they give an insight into early 19th-century Vienna.

MUMOK

T01 52500, www.mumok.at.
Daily 1000-1800, until 2100 on Thu. €9 (€7.20). U-bahn Volkstheater. Map A4.

The Museum of Modern Art traces the path of Vienna's avant garde through Pop Art, Nouveau Réalisme and Vienna Actionism. Warhol, Jasper Johns, Marcel Duchamp, George Brecht and Otto Muehl are all here. MUMOK also presents art history from classic modern works up to the present, ranging from Kupka to Kandinsky.

Schloss Schönbrunn

Schönbrunnner Schlossstrasse 13, T01 8111 3239, www.schoenbrunn.at.
Apr-Jun and Sep-Oct daily 0830-1700; Jul-Aug until 1800; Nov-Mar 0830-1630. €12.90 (€11.40). U-bahn Schönbrunn, bus 10A, trams 10, 58.

This mouthwatering baroque palace was built around 1700 and is now a UNESCO World Heritage Site. It includes 2000 rooms of wall-to-wall imperial splendour (only 40 can be visited), all set in a symmetrical classically landscaped garden complete with maze and the world's oldest zoo. Emperor Franz Joseph (1848-1916) was born here in 1830, later marrying the Empress Sisi and keeping her in unsustainable style, and spending the last two years of his reign here.

Sigmund Freud Museum

Berggasse 19, T01 319 1596, www.freud-museum.at.
Jul-Sep daily 0900-1800; Oct-Jun daily 0900-1700. €7 (€5.50). U-bahn Schwarzspanierstrasse, or bus 40A, tram D or trams 37, 38, 40, 41, 42. Off map.

Psychology students or anyone who rails against the therapy culture should visit the apartments where it arguably all started. Freud lived and worked here from 1891 to 1938 and all his furniture, possessions, letters, documents, photographs and even an oedipal home movie by his daughter are here.

Left: Ice skating in front of the Vienna town Hall.
Opposite page: Spanish Riding School.

Sleeping

Vienna is rich in stylish, sometimes overblown, hotels recalling its imperial past, as well as a new breed of design hotels more conscious of the city's contribution to modernism. However, there is not as much choice at the bottom end.

The Third Man

In his 1949 story of drug racketeering in war-torn Vienna, film director Carol Reed masterfully turned the city into as towering and brooding a character as the film's central figure – Orson Welles' Harry Lime. With his sense of Impressionism coupled with stark chiaroscuro he produced some of the most iconic and memorable scenes in world cinema, the locations of which are easily visited to this day. Harry Lime first appears, or rather a white cat appears at his shiny feet, in the doorway of **No 8 Schreyvogelgasse** before the two set off in a nocturnal chase around the city. The famous Ferris wheel scene, which closes with Lime's immortal (but factually inaccurate) put-down about the Swiss and cuckoo clocks, takes places on the 19th-century **Riesenrad** (Prater 90, T01 729 5430, www.wienerriesenrad.com, May-Sep 0900-2345, Oct, Mar and Apr 1000-2145, Nov-Feb 1000-1945, €8.50/7.20). The 65 m Ferris wheel with its wood cabins sits within the city's Prater funfair park where there are still many original and traditional carousel rides. The windblown cemetery where Lime is twice buried (alongside Beethoven and Brahms) is the **Zentral Friedhof** on Simmerigen Hauptstrasse. Joseph Cotton stays at the Sacher Hotel, famous for its eponymous cake. If you can stomach it, parts of the sewers, where the film reaches its climax, can be visited by joining a guided **Third Man tour of the city**, www.viennawalks.tix.at.

Grand Hotel Wien €€€
Karntner Ring 9, T01 515 800, www.grandhotelwien.com.
Located just a few steps from the Vienna State Opera, this Viennese institution (est 1870) is right in the heart of the city. five-star luxury accommodation, matched by the international gourmet cuisine on offer at the hotel's four restaurants.

Hotel Sacher €€€
Philharmonikerstrasse 4, T01 514 560, www.sacher.com.
Deliberately and eccentrically old fashioned, this family- run hotel likes to live in a 19th-century time warp. Romantic, at times camp, but never dull, this is the best address for a taste of Habsburg decadence.

Style Hotel €€€
Herrengasse 12, T01 22780, www.stylehotel.at.
Housed in an art nouveau building opposite the city's famous Café Central, the interiors are more art deco. The 78 well-appointed rooms offer every luxury while delicious Italian cuisine is served in the Sapor restaurant and the bar is increasingly attracting a stylish post-prandial clientele.

Hotel Das Triest €€
Wiedner Hauptstrasse 12, T01 589 180, www.dastriest.at.
Not for those wanting a slice of Old Vienna but bright, clean and comfortably modern; 17th-century on the outside but Conran on the inside.

Alstadt Vienna Hotel €€
Kirchengasse 41, T01 522 6666, www.altstadt.at.
Old-world pretentions at half the price. A historic patrician's house in the centre of the old city comfortably furnished with Italian furniture and a striking decor. Family-run, 25 rooms,

some with lovely views and plenty of atmosphere.

Meininger City Hotel €
Columbusgasse 16, www.meininger-hotels.com.
Much better than your average hostel, here you'll find clean, modern, cheap and cheerful accommodation with friendly staff and a great central location. A great inexpensive choice.

Eating and nightlife

The line between food and fun has been blurred in Vienna, as in many European cities. There are classic Viennese restaurants but as an alternative, or even after your *Wienerschnitzel*, the main focus is on a wide variety of hybrid bar-restaurants and restaurant- clubs. A visit to at least one of Vienna's famous cafés should not be missed.

Steirereck im Stadtpark €€€
Am Heumarkt 2A, Landstrasse,1030, T01 713 3168, www.steirereck.at.
Mon-Fri 1130-1500 and 1830-2300.
An old gourmet favourite of Vienna foodies. Choose your room for a formal or relaxed ambience. Always grand but refreshingly laid-back.

Café Central €€
Herrengasse 14.
Daily 0900-2300.
With its gaudy Gothic vaulted ceiling, this was a favourite of Trotsky and also allegedly where Hitler thought up *Mein Kampf.* A piece of the city's heritage as much as any museum.

Immervoll €€
Weihburggasse 17, T01 513 5288.
Daily 1200-0000.
The restaurant's name means "always full" and as it always is, it's best to book! This is affordable and authentic Austrian food at its very best. Simple fare, popular with locals and tourists alike, rumoured to serve Vienna's best Schnitzel.

Lutz/A1 lounge €€
6-7, Mariahilfer Strasse, T01 585 3646, www.lutz-bar.at.
1000-0400 (Lutz), Mon-Wed 0930-2200; Thu-Fri 0930-2400 (A1).
Two bar-restaurants in one. Lutz is elegant and classic, themed with wood panelling and a great cocktail and wine list. A1 is futuristic with glass, metal and dry ice, and packed with technical gimmicks.

Palmenhaus €€
Burggarten, T01 533 1033, www.palmenhaus.at.
Mar-Oct daily 1000-0200, Nov-Dec Mon-Thu 1130-0000, Fri and Sat 1000-0200, Sun 1000-0000, Jan and Feb Wed and Thu 11.30-0000, Fri and Sat 1000-0200, Sun 1000-0000.
A beautifully renovated palmhouse in the heart of the museum district. Summer seating outside and good quality nibbles year round. On Fri night, the sophisticated air is replaced by a groovy club scene.

Café Alt Wien €
Bäckerstrasse 9, T01 512 5222.
Daily 1000-0200.
A studenty vibe ensures that the intellectual traditions of this café continue over illuminating drinks and a renowned goulash.

Point of Sale €
Corner Schleifmühl-gasse 12, Operngasse, T01 966 9891.
Sun-Thu 1000-0100, Fri-Sat 1000-0200.
Late breakfast is the principal attraction here, served into the afternoon as you watch life go by on the lively Schleifmuehlgasse.

Porgy & Bess
Riemengasse 11, T01 512 8811, www.porgy.at.
Gigs usually play from 2030-late. Originally a porn cinema, a complete refurbishment now sees this building play home to one of Vienna's best jazz clubs. An eclectic mix of music from around the globe sits alongside traditional jazz. A great place to while away an evening.

Credits

Footprint credits

Project editor: Alan Murphy
Text editor: Damian Hall
Design: Angus Dawson
Picture editor: Angus Dawson
Maps: Gail Townsley
Cover design: Pepi Bluck
Managing Director: Andy Riddle
Commercial Director: Patrick Dawson
Publisher: Alan Murphy
Publishing Managers: Felicity Laughton, Nicola Gibbs
Digital Editor: Jo Williams
Marketing and PR: Liz Harper
Sales: Diane McEntee
Advertising: Renu Sibal
Finance and administration: Elizabeth Taylor

Contributors

Ally Thomson: Amsterdam, Berlin, Brussels, Budapest, Copenhagen, Dublin, Lisbon, Munich, Prague, Reykjavík, Stockholm, Vienna.
Julius Honnor: Florence, London, Milan, Naples, Rome, Venice, Verona.
Mary-Ann Gallagher: Barcelona, Bruges, Madrid, Valencia.
Andy Symington: Bilbao, Seville.
Tristan Rutherford: Istanbul, Nice, Paris.
Alan Murphy: Edinburgh.
Jane Foster: Athens.

Print

Manufactured in India by Replika Press pvt Ltd.
Pulp from sustainable forests

Footprint Feedback

We try as hard as we can to make each Footprint guide as up to date as possible but, of course, things always change. If you want to let us know about your experiences – good, bad or ugly – then don't delay, go to footprintbooks.com and send in your comments.

Publishing information

Footprint European City Breaks
© Footprint Handbooks Ltd
April 2011

ISBN 978-1-907263-37-8
CIP DATA: A catalogue record for this book is available from the British Library

Published by Footprint
6 Riverside Court
Lower Bristol Road
Bath BA2 3DZ, UK
T +44 (0)1225 469141
F +44 (0)1225 469461
www.footprinttravelguides.com

Distributed in North America by
Globe Pequot Press, Guilford, Connecticut

The colour maps are not intended to have any political significance.